ANARCHY & CULTURE

A volume in the series
Critical Perspectives on Modern Culture

Edited by David Gross and William M. Johnston

DAVID WEIR

ANARCHY &
CULTURE

The Aesthetic Politics of Modernism

University of Massachusetts Press
Amherst

LC 96-50314
ISBN 1-55849-083-3 (cloth); 084-1 (pbk.)

Designed by Dennis Anderson
Set in New Baskerville
Printed and bound by Braun-Brumfield, Inc.

Library of Congress Cataloging-in-Publication Data

Weir, David, 1947 Apr. 20–
   Anarchy and culture : the aesthetic politics of modernism / David Weir.
p.   cm.—(Critical perspectives on modern culture)
Includes bibliographical references and index.
   ISBN 1-55849-083-3 (cloth : alk. paper).—ISBN 1-55849-084-1 (pbk. : alk. paper)
   1. Politics and literature.   2. Literature, Modern—19th century—History and
criticism.   3. Modernism (Literature)   4. Anarchism.   5. Literature and society.
I. Title.   II. Series.
PN51.W345   1997
809′.933358—dc21   96-50314
                                                                                CIP

British Library Cataloguing in Publication data are available.

Alles funktioniert, nur der Mensch selber nicht mehr.

—Hugo Ball, *Die Flucht aus der Zeit*

In memory of David Geoffrey Weir (1973–1991)

CONTENTS

ACKNOWLEDGMENTS   ix

INTRODUCTION   1

1 **DEFINITIONS**
   The Ideologies of Anarchism   11

2 **REACTIONS**
   Anarchism as Cultural Threat   42

3 **RESPONSES**
   Culture in the Anarchist Camp   87

4 **AFFINITIES**
   Anarchism and Cultural Promotion   116

5 **AESTHETICS**
   From Politics to Culture   158

6 **ARTISTS**
   Anarchism and Cultural Production   201

AFTERWORD   259

NOTES   269

INDEX   297

ACKNOWLEDGMENTS

This book is mainly the product of my own autonomous impulses. Had I subjected those impulses more to the mutualist considerations of my academic comrades a better book might have been the result. Those comrades and colleagues who have tried to direct my egoistic endeavors toward more meaningful social and scholarly contexts include Dore Ashton, Peter Buckley, James Rubin, Maren Stange, and Brian Swann at the Cooper Union for the Advancement of Science and Art. I must also thank my students, whose ability to somehow extract a portion of their integral education out of me is truly remarkable. To Sven Zbinden, Brian Booth, Goon Koch, and Elizabeth Murray I say: "You've had the course, now read the book." If they do, they should be grateful, as I am, for the labor of Liselot Van der Heijden, Fernanda Perrone, Betty Waterhouse, and Pam Wilkinson, who assured that my own ideas and those suggested by the Colorado *Kopfarbeiter* David Gross would take material form. The final synthesis of material and intellectual culture was overseen by Clark Dougan (better known as the Dialectical Anarchist of Amherst), to whom I am most grateful. Finally, I would like to thank Camille Norvell, who has caused me to question Benjamin Tucker's and Friedrich Engel's critique of the institution of marriage.

Permission to quote from material in the Benjamin Tucker Papers, Rare Books and Manuscripts Division, The New York Public Library, Astor, Lenox and Tilden Foundations, is gratefully acknowledged.

ACKNOWLEDGMENTS

ANARCHY & CULTURE

INTRODUCTION

The surrealist poet André Breton was also a socialist. A surrealist, *also* a socialist: Breton himself never ceased to grapple with the problems this formulation posed for his poetry and for art in general.[1] The alchemy of the adverb *also* led to any number of proclamations and positions, manifestoes and clarifications, appeals and denials. In the long lecture titled "Political Position of Today's Art," the poet's most extensive treatment of the problem, Breton forces himself to accept what is, for him, an unfortunate but poignant paradox: that innovative, progressive art is no guarantee of social progress. The artist who rebels against aesthetic tradition may nonetheless be politically conservative. By the same token, the most reactionary political figures may *also* be the most receptive to avant-garde art. The adjective "revolutionary" carries with it "a most regrettable ambiguity": it refers at once to the nonconformist innovator who breaks with artistic tradition and to the activist ideologue who "tends to define a systematic action aiming at the transformation of the world."[2] All too often, the revolutionary artist is not revolutionary in the second sense of the word; nonconformity, in fact, implies a paradoxical acceptance of social conditions and abrogates the need to transform them. The bohemian artist, for example, may separate from society without so much as commenting on the condition of alienation caused by the very society from which he separates.

Breton cites a number of examples to strengthen the point that revolutionary art and reactionary politics do not exclude one another. Paul Claudel's technical innovations in poetry do not make him any less of a militarist. The royalist Léon Daudet edits the rightist journal *L'Action française* but praises the avant-garde Picasso as the

1

greatest painter alive. Breton also repeats the corollary "common-place" that "leftist political circles appreciate in art only time-honored, or even outworn forms": one specialty of the progressive journal *L'Humanité* is the rendering of Mayakovsky's poems into dog-gerel (214–15). This problem of overtly political art and lifeless technique has its greatest exemplar in the neoclassicist painter David: an active observer of the French Revolution who recorded some of its most powerful scenes, but did so in the stiff, academic style of Poussin. Strangely, David was an artist who was simultaneously a thoroughly contemporary witness to history and "very much be-hind his own times." The contrary case is illustrated by Gustave Courbet: like David, he witnessed a great social upheaval; unlike David, he was aesthetically innovative. But Courbet, a hero of the Paris Commune, nonetheless chose not to register that political ex-perience in his art. Breton describes himself leafing through an album of Courbet's paintings—"here are forests, here are women, here is the sea"—but failing to discover in them any "clear trace . . . of his social preoccupations" (218). Even in Breton's model and precursor Rimbaud, another witness to the Commune, "social preoc-cupations" are secondary in the extreme to artistic innovations. Such is the case even with those poems that grew directly out of Rimbaud's Commune experience. Breton concludes that "Chant de guerre par-isienne," for instance, is "no less hermetic" than Rimbaud's later "verbal experiments" (220). Again and again, Breton wonders how it might be possible for avant-garde, leftist artists to give "our work the meaning we would like our acts to have" (218). At one point he imagines a wall dividing the revolutionary spirit in half: one group on one side of the wall is engaged in the destruction of the old social order, while on the other side another group is involved in the creative work of organizing life anew; neither group is in communi-cation with the other (224). A quotation from Malraux seems to sum up the dilemma: "Marxism is the consciousness of the social; culture is the consciousness of the psychological" (229).

Breton's remarks were made in 1935, in Prague, at a meeting of an organization known as the Leftist Front. It is striking how difficult it was for Breton to formulate a concept of ideologically motivated art at a time when ideology was everything. Breton was speaking at a great historical moment when it truly meant something to be a Marx-ist in Central Europe, a Republican in Spain, a Communist in

France, and so on. In stark contrast to our own age, when Democrats and Republicans shift allegiances and change parties at will, unswerving dedication to a particular political position was de rigueur during the 1930s.[3] Then, a fascist was a threat and not an epithet, and political correctness was a matter of life or death, not simply tenure or dismissal.[4] The contrast between the way Breton agonized over politics and culture in 1935 and the ease with which culture is imagined to have political ramifications today is indeed remarkable. One suspects that Breton's difficulties reflect a more deeply committed attachment to both art and politics than our own facile elision of the two into "political art" allows. The temptation is to say that ideological rhetoric runs highest when the political stakes are lowest. Since the collapse of the Soviet empire in 1989, an event universally proclaimed the death agony of Marxism, the Marxist critic Fredric Jameson has published several considerable books, and his disciples have published many more, including a recent study of Jameson himself, subtitled *The Aesthetics of Marxist Theory*.[5] This title goes to the heart of the problem Breton faced, as he struggled to reconcile individualist aesthetics with collectivist theory. The contemporary critical strategy of aestheticizing politics is one way to make this type of problem go away. Terry Eagleton's and Jameson's elegant books, for example, make the case for an aesthetics of ideology even as they argue for the ideology of the aesthetic. This solution to Breton's problem—adapting aesthetics to politics—would never have occurred to Breton because he was coming at the problem from the perspective of a poet, not a theoretician or an ideologue. The ideologue may have something to gain by making his discourse aesthetic in some sense, but the poet has everything to lose by writing ideological poetry (see Breton's remarks on the doggerel potential of Mayakovsky). There is, however, another solution to the problem of ideology and art that the practicing poet might pursue: adapt the politics to the aesthetics. Unfortunately for Breton, the lone ideology that might have made politics possible for poetry—and Breton's poetry in particular—was being eclipsed from history in 1935. I refer to anarchism, the one ideology that might have allowed Breton to reconcile art and action, since anarchism as a form of individualist politics is perfectly suited to the type of individualist poetics Breton practiced. Indeed, several important dadaists, the precursors of the surrealists, had clear affinities with anarchism; because of this they never found themselves in the kind of position Breton did in 1935. Breton himself, rather belatedly, tried to include anarchism in his aesthetic formulations only three years after his Prague speech, when, realizing that Stalin's regime in Russia was not collectivist but totalitarian, he and Trotsky published their joint manifesto, "Towards a Free Revolutionary Art": "If, for the better development of the forces of material production, the revolution must build a *socialist* regime with centralized control, to develop intellectual creation an *anarchist* regime of individual liberty should from the first be established."[6] Even here, however, the wall remains between development and creation, progress and poetry. The only way the socialist artist can reconcile the collectivist idea with the individualist ideal, it seems, is to establish two separate "regimes." The anarchist artist, on the other hand, has no trouble saying, as Breton wanted to, that the art has the same meaning as the act. Individualist aesthetics is perfectly compatible with individualist politics. The problem of reconciling politics and culture goes away if anarchism is the ideology that informs both.

But the problem did not go away; anarchism did. There is no question that the ideology of anarchism failed to survive in political form. With the isolated and important example of Spain, no European nation was capable of nurturing anarchism after World War I, as other ideological allegiances made themselves felt. In Russia, the anarchists were overcome by the Bolsheviks; in Europe, they disappeared into the divide that separated the fascists from the communists; in America, they merged back into the libertarian tradition that had produced them in the first place. Anarchism was, quite simply, an outmoded ideology in the period between the world wars, too antiquated to be of use to anyone. The historical destiny of anarchism tells us a great deal about the ideology itself, which had always seemed out of touch with the times. The anarchists evoked models of society that allowed them either to idealize some remote political past or imagine a grand utopian future. Indeed, there was always something vaguely mythic about anarchist thought that connected it more to culture than to politics. Whether practicing anarchists realized this themselves in every case is not clear, but there is no question that a great many anarchists, faced with their obvious isolation from politics at large, were driven toward culture as the only available means of disseminating their ideology. In the long run, the desired effect was not achieved: the cultural sphere was ultimately no substitute for the political arena, and anarchism ceased to exist as a mass movement.

The death of anarchism, however, should not be exaggerated. The ideology has enjoyed periodic revivals, and its occasional recrudescence may be observed emerging from either the Left or the Right. During an earlier period of conservative politics (c. 1957), Irving Howe made this observation: "Conservatism is the anarchism of the fortunate, anarchism the conservatism of the deprived. Against the omnivorous state, conservatism and anarchism equally urge resistance by the individual."[7] Thus, the 1960s saw a revival of leftist anarchism in America and elsewhere, while the 1990s is witness to the rightist variety of individualist ideology. In this book, however, I am less concerned with the periodic revivals of anarchism that take political form, and more interested in the abiding presence of anarchism in culture itself. My main argument, in fact, is that anarchism succeeded culturally where it failed politically.

The success of anarchism in the sense I intend has to be measured by the structural resemblance of much of twentieth-century culture to the political model anarchism provides. Anarchism proposes a type of politics that allows individuals an unprecedented degree of social autonomy. They may, if they choose, form associations with other autonomous individuals, so long as no hierarchies are created within the associations, and, most important, no government controls the activities of either the individuals or the associations they form. In theory, anarchist society is endlessly and actively fragmenting, as individuals break from some associations to join or form others—or none at all. A single person can be as valid a political entity as a group of people. I hold that this political model has had widespread cultural effect. Modernist culture, for example, is characterized by nothing so much as a tendency toward fragmentation and autonomy, a dual formula that holds regardless of whether the topic is the behavior of individual artists and writers or the works they produced. The anarchist strain in modernist culture is no less manifest today, for nothing could be further from contemporary conceptions of culture than homogeneity. Whereas in the past culture was viewed as a shared sensibility that bound society together and integrated its diverse elements, today culture is identified with diversity itself, and cultural sensibilities follow from the fact of social diversity. Today, no single culture has the power to integrate the various cultures of the late twentieth century. Society is pluralistic, and culture is pluralized, but somehow the term *pluralism* is no longer adequate to describe the current cultural condition. Indeed, the term belongs to an older social grammar that inflects individualism and makes it part of a common culture. Diversity differs from pluralism on precisely this point, namely, that the various cultural languages spoken today are not inflected by a universal grammar. The new social syntax lends itself, then, to an anarchic variety of cultural styles.

The argument for anarchism as the unstable base for the proliferating, fragmented cultures of the twentieth century requires an exposition of anarchism itself. I provide such an exposition in Chapter 1, which details in summary form the main arguments of the principal anarchist theoreticians: Godwin, Proudhon, Bakunin, and Kropotkin. Chapter 2 presents the brief against anarchy urged by the defenders of an integrated culture. Whether this brief takes polemical form, as in Matthew Arnold's *Culture and Anarchy,* or fictional form, as in Dostoyevsky's *The Possessed,* anarchism nonetheless asserts its appeal as a cultural sensibility even as the anti-anarchists build their bulwarks against it. Chapter 3 takes stock of the positive response to libertarian politics in novels by William Godwin, the Rossetti sisters, and Frank Harris. These novels of anarchism are not anarchistic novels, however, as the radical politics in them is still expressed in conventional cultural form. Chapter 4 details the affinities between anarchists and artists at the fin de siècle and beyond, as the appeal of anarchism is frankly recognized and widely promoted. This chapter examines the diverse history behind the modulation of anarchism into culture, and considers the broad impact of anarchistic novels, journals, theaters, and schools. Chapter 5 complements the documentary history of the drift of anarchism toward culture with a theoretical account of the transformation of anarchist politics into modernist aesthetics. Finally, Chapter 6 analyzes the anarchistic elements in twentieth-century culture through an examination of representative figures, some of whom are already well known for their relationship to anarchism (such as Ibsen), while others (such as Joyce and Buñuel) are generally not understood as anarchistic artists. I close with a brief Afterword that connects certain strains of contemporary culture and politics to the antiquated but evidently durable ideology of anarchism, posing anew the abiding problem of reconciling aesthetic modernism and social modernity.

I must emphasize at the outset that my approach to the problems of politics and culture is limited to the rather eccentric confines of anarchist ideology. The reader who wants a broad theoretical explanation of the ways in which politics affects culture had best read some other book besides this one. Fredric Jameson's *The Political Unconscious* (1981) and the more recent *Postmodernism; or, The Cultural Logic of Late Capitalism* (1991) are both models of theoretical analysis that manage to maintain a strong historicist perspective on politics and culture within the context of Marxist criticism. One looks in vain for "anarchist criticism" at the same high level of theoretical analysis found in Jameson's books, finding instead a number of cultural histories that include anarchism as one among several ideologies which have had an impact on art and literature, or, alternatively, that focus on a particular period of anarchist activity or even on a specific cultural figure with ties to anarchism. The broadest view is provided by Donald D. Egbert in *Social Radicalism and the Arts* (1970), subtitled *A Cultural History from the French Revolution to 1968*. In this book anarchism plays a small but significant role in the development of aesthetic modernism, as such chapter titles as "The Neo-Impressionists, the Symbolists, and Anarchism" or "Futurism and Anarcho-Syndicalism" show. Renee Winegarten's *Writers and Revolution* (1974) covers the same period of politics and culture as Egbert's book, but narrows the focus to literature alone. The treatment of anarchism in this book is largely insular, limited to the figure of Percy Shelley and the phenomenon of decadence; also, the impact of anarchism on modernist culture is gauged only in negative terms as a "phase of aesthetic nihilism." The critical attitude is more neutral and much narrower in an earlier book by Eugenia W. Herbert, *The Artist and Social Reform: France and Belgium, 1885–1898* (1961), which contains a general exposition, entitled "French Anarchism and Art," that establishes *l'esprit anarchisant* as both a political and an aesthetic attitude. Even more focused is Richard D. Sonn's *Anarchism and Cultural Politics in Fin de Siècle France* (1989), easily the most detailed and coherent exploration of political and aesthetic ideology in the context of anarchism. The scope is further narrowed with Joan Halperin's *Félix Fénéon: Aesthete and Anarchist in Fin-de-Siècle Paris* (1988), a study of an important critic of postimpressionist art with clear anarchist connections.[8] My own study falls somewhere between the broadly theoretical approach of ideological criticism and the narrower concerns of cultural history. Such positioning seems appropriate to the paradoxical thesis I advance: that anarchist ideology and modernist culture have something in common that keeps them apart. Despite such common values as heterogeneity and autonomy, the anarchist realization of these values in social form is one thing, their modernist expression in aesthetic form another. Because of this important distinction, radical politics and radical art usually proceed along different lines in the modernist period, a certain shared sensibility notwithstanding. The historical divergence of practicing anarchists from practicing artists coincides with the conceptual convergence of anarchist politics and modernist aesthetics. Not surprisingly, the historical divergence occurs in the context of collectivist anarchism, while the conceptual convergence takes place mainly within the individualist tradition of anarchist ideology. For this reason, a minor individualist anarchist like Benjamin Tucker becomes more important to my argument than such major collectivists as Bakunin and Kropotkin.

My purpose, then, is not to provide a broad explanation of the relationship of politics and art, but, rather, to examine one strain of a particular ideology in the context of the culture specific to modernism, mainly literature. I must add, however, that I hesitate to claim authority over any of those big words that make us so unhappy: ideology, politics, culture.[9] These terms have become so highly charged and vague that anyone who uses them had better provide a glossary. Such a glossary, however, can only obscure the meanings it intends to clarify. The term *culture* itself is a case in point: any attempt to seize on a single meaning, such as *civilization,* or *fine arts,* or *intellectual growth,* risks the loss of larger (and largely inexpressible) meanings. As Raymond Williams says, what is significant about the word *culture* is its "range and overlap of meanings."[10] To me, *culture* only makes sense if it is understood as the dynamic center of a series of semantic exchanges that include, on the one hand, the totalizing processes of civilization at large, and, on the other, individualist efforts either to reduplicate or to resist those totalizing tendencies. *Kultur* is a powerful force that urges individuals to create culture, some of whom cooperate with it while others struggle against it. To some extent the terms *ideology* and *politics* are analogous to the contrary dynamics of culture. Ideology, like *Kultur,* seeks to provide a larger rationale or set of ideas, in all their abstract purity, while politics concerns itself with the messy business of putting ideas into action. It is precisely in the area of politics that anarchism falters; in fact, most political theorists would hesitate to use the term *politics* at all in the context of anarchism. Still, the anarchists always posited something like a *polis* (in the broad sense of a community of some kind or other), even though they were never too clear about how it would function: anarchists were clearer about ideological theory than political practice. If the relationship of ideology to politics is that of theory to practice, then we may be witness now to a certain separation of ideology *from* politics, a phenomenon that requires some commentary, since a similar dissociation occurred in the history of anarchism. Generally speaking, ideology and politics are regarded as mutually reinforcing; for example, Marx provided the ideology that made Leninist politics possible. Ideology takes material form in the actual political practice of governing the *polis.* There should be a relationship, in other words, between the party platform and the party's program of action. Lately, however, ideology and politics, the platform and the program, appear to be drifting apart. The end of Marxism as actual political practice has not yet resulted in the end of Marxist ideology. In fact, Marxism today finds itself in the position anarchism was in a century ago: a true political vacuum. The situation whereby ideology attempts to operate outside of politics has already pointed Marxism toward postmodernist culture, just as anarchism moved into the culture of modernism when it ceased to have political validity.[11]

A curious corollary of this phenomenon could be observed in American politics following the Republican ascendancy of 1994. The political efforts of Newt Gingrich and other rightist members of the Republican Party were directed toward the dismantling of the so-called welfare state, the return of political power to local communities, the financial empowerment of individuals through a reduction of the federal income tax, and so on. In many ways, this group of Republican neofederalists tried to restructure society in ways that resembled the anarchist model. But did this quasi-anarchism also draw cultural inspiration from the original anarchists of the last century? Not at all. Republican politics circa 1994–96 encouraged a proliferation of power not unlike anarchism, even though Republican ideology dictated homogeneity of culture and common values. Paradoxically, Mr. Gingrich promoted a totalizing form of American culture even as he sought to break political structures down into ever-smaller units. Today, Republicans and Marxists mirror each other precisely: one has separated politics from ideology; the other has separated ideology from politics. One imagines American culture as something uniform and shared by all; the other is drawn to the diverse cultures of postmodernism where separate identities proliferate. Politics and culture? The anarchists tried to have it both ways, also: in their case, the alchemy of the adverb transformed one into the other. Anarchism was *also* culture because the politics was impossible to realize.

1

DEFINITIONS
The Ideologies of Anarchism

> Anarchy does not mean simply opposed to the *archos,* or political
> leader. It means opposed to *archē.* Now, *archē,* in the first instance,
> means beginning, origin. From this it comes to mean *a first principle,
> an element;* then *first place, supreme power, sovereignty, dominion, command,
> authority;* and finally *a sovereignty, an empire, a realm, a magistracy, a
> governmental office.* Etymologically, then, the word anarchy may have
> several meanings. But the word Anarchy as a philosophical term and
> the word Anarchist as the name of a philosophical sect were first appro-
> priated in the sense of opposition to dominion, to authority, and are
> so held by right of occupancy, which fact makes any other philosophi-
> cal use of them improper and confusing.[1]

This definition of anarchy "as a philosophical term" comes from
Benjamin Tucker, the turn-of-the-century American anarchist based
in Boston and, later, New York City. The definition tells us more
about anarchism than Tucker may have realized. On the one hand,
anarchy is opposed to origins and any authority based on the appropriation of origins; on the other, the term itself has that meaning
based on the very process it opposes. In Tucker's definition, anarchism resists any authority conferred by origins, but it does so "by
right of occupancy" because that is the meaning that has been "first
appropriated": some kind of originary authority informs anarchism's
disavowal of authoritative origins. The paradox that emerges from
this simple deconstructive maneuver on Tucker's definition of anarchism has a number of implications. Indeed, the uncertainty that
the maneuver generates is borne out by the contradictions and ambi-
guities that arise whenever political theorists attempt to clarify the
term: "Some hold anarchism to be complete absence of political

authority; others see it as compatible with a minimal form of government. For still others anarchism is essentially a moral attitude, an emotional climate, or even a mood, rather than a prescription for specific social, economic, or political arrangements. . . . [O]thers . . . conceive of anarchism as consisting of many species, extending from the strictly individualist to the expressivist communitarian."[2] Tucker's definition at least avoids the pitfall of making anarchism seem like all things to all people, but when he makes the contradictory claim of opposing origins by appropriating them the inconsistency between his politics and his rhetoric is obvious.

The contradiction at work here goes much deeper than the simple difference between "what" Tucker says and "how" he says it. The inconsistent rhetoric of anarchism is important precisely because anarchism can hardly be said to have existed *apart* from rhetoric—with two significant exceptions: the terrorist activity known as "propaganda by the deed" and the labor movement known as "anarcho-syndicalism." Both of these developments are of considerable historical importance, but their importance as history does not imply the success of anarchism as politics. The ambiguous attitude toward origins that Tucker's rhetoric involves raises the question of whether the anarchists really had a consistent political model in mind for the type of society their rhetoric proposed. If they did not, or if the political model was at best secondary to the rhetoric used to articulate it, then the rhetoric really is original; that is, the language originates the politics. Anarchism, then, gives special meaning to the "politics of style": anarchism is as much a cultural as a political phenomenon—more rhetoric than reality, less a movement than a myth. And it is a troubled myth because anarchists try to tell the story of origins by obliterating them.

1

Anarchism is fraught with a number of internal contradictions that create the need for endless clarifications by its proponents and, at the same time, justify its dismissal by detractors. Conventionally regarded as the odd man out in a set of political ideologies that have developed out of the Enlightenment in the wake of the French Revolution—liberalism, conservatism, socialism, and utilitarianism—anarchism clearly lacks the support and respect the other ideologies enjoy. Today, one might claim to be a liberal, a conservative, a socialist, or even a utilitarian, but the person who embraces anarchism is likely to be regarded as a crank at best or a terrorist at worst. This marginal status is inevitable because anarchism appears to make many of the same claims as the more successful ideologies. Raymond Williams makes the point that at various times anarchists have been characterized in a way that is "very close to *democrats* and *republicans* in their older senses"; he also says that an 1862 assessment of "the anarchist" as one who "denies the right of any government to . . . trench upon his individual freedom" is "now often the terms of a certain modern liberalism or indeed of a radical conservatism." [3] Like the liberal, the anarchist supports the rights and freedoms of the individual against all types of oppression. At the same time, most anarchists are highly moralistic, even to the point of treating political issues as matters of morality, an attitude that chimes with conservatism. But the anarchist turns against both liberals and conservatives regarding the economic organization of society, and, like the socialist, takes the side of the worker against the capitalist. However, the anarchist parts company with the socialist on the issue of the state, whose vast administrative power the socialist requires in order to organize society for the benefit of all, whereas the anarchist dispenses with the state altogether. The anarchist is utilitarian on the issue of social organization, but diverges from utilitarianism proper because the practice of providing the greatest good to the greatest number is not in line with anarchistic individualism, and so the anarchist turns again to liberalism. Certainly this cyclical scheme linking anarchism to other, better-known ideologies must not be taken literally; clearly, not all anarchists are as conservative as the moralistic Proudhon or as liberal as the libertarian Tucker. The larger point is simply that anarchism collects elements of other ideologies into itself, and this phenomenon may account for the inherent contradictions so many critics observe. Nonetheless, anarchism can hardly be called a synthesis of liberalism, conservatism, socialism, and utilitarianism; rather, anarchism is an aggregate ideology that selects points from all of them. This aggregate quality is undoubtedly the source of both the abiding appeal of anarchism and its perennial failure.

Another conventional way of placing anarchism is to situate the development in relation to Enlightenment thought in more general terms, rather than in terms of specific ideologies. Most anarchists participate in the Enlightenment belief in the ultimate perfectibility of society, although not all accept the premise that the grand goal of a stateless society can be achieved by reason alone. The classical anarchists are divided on this point, as some put their faith in the gradual improvements that reason brings, while others insist on the more expeditious method of revolution. Richard Sonn makes the point that the "[a]narchists were *revolutionaries* in the original sense of the term; rather than believing in the limitless progress proclaimed by liberals or the deterministic dialectic of history envisioned by Marxists, they wished to 'revolve' back to a more harmonious society. The anarchist rejection of contemporary society was nearly total; their proposed alternative fused elements of a remembered past with a vision of a utopian future."[4] Thus, the anarchist idea of liberal progress includes a component of romantic regress. In this sense, the internal contradictions of anarchism can be reduced to a conflict of Enlightenment reason and romantic reaction. Indeed, political and cultural historians sometimes try to clarify anarchism by grouping its adherents into Enlightenment and romantic camps. The rationalistic Godwin and the "Darwinian" Kropotkin thus emerge as Enlightenment figures, while the egoistic Stirner and the revolutionary Bakunin appear as romantic types. The characterization of anarchism as fundamentally romantic is certainly defensible. Any number of romantic figures can be seen as providing some model for the anarchists. William Blake's observation in the *Marriage of Heaven and Hell* that "Prisons are built with stones of law, / Brothels with bricks of religion" strikes a rather strident anarchist chord. In a quieter way Chateaubriand provided a fictional model of anarchist society in his idealized vision of "primitive" life among Native Americans in *Atala* and *René*.

Anarchism has been treated as a species of romanticism almost since its beginnings. In the middle of the nineteenth century, Friedrich Engels located the source of anarchism in "the depths of antediluvian German philosophy," and described his preparations to analyze the origins of anarchist thought by invoking these lines from Wieland's poem *Oberon:* "O Muses, saddle Pegasus for me once more / To ride forth to the ancient land of romance."[5] Later, Marx and Engels together sustained the notion of "antediluvian" politics when they described anarchism as a primitive phase in the development of the proletarian movement, "just as astrology and alchemy

are the infancy of science." [6] Even though Marx and Engels have an
ideological ax to grind, their negative valuation of anarchism as
a primitive, anterior form of socialism is an important linking of
anarchism to romanticism. Ironically, from the perspective of the
late twentieth century Marx has joined the anarchists in the ranks of
romanticism, at least according to Charles Taylor: "[T]hose thinkers
who stand in a romantic or expressivist tradition of whatever kind,
disciples of Rousseau, or of de Tocqueville, or Marx, whether they
be socialists, anarchists, [or] partisans of 'participatory democracy'
. . . are all estranged from modern Western society. And those who
feel fully at home in it are the heirs of the Enlightenment mainstream." [7] One problem with this statement, aside from the way the
historical rivalry of anarchism and socialism is elided and combined
into equally estranged varieties of romanticism, is the definition of
romanticism itself as simply expressivist. There is no question that
anarchists were expressivist in their advocacy of individualism, but
that very individualism was expressed or expressible in Enlightenment terms. In this sense, romanticism and Enlightenment are not
opposed; rather, a romantic vision of society becomes the goal toward which Enlightenment thought tends. The gradualist, rationalist
process of Enlightenment has as its end the free, expressivist goal of
romantic individualism. Anarchism, therefore, involves a constant
interplay of both Enlightenment idea and romantic vision.

2

The ambiguity that attaches to the idea of anarchism derives in
large part from late Enlightenment responses to Rousseau. These
responses are, in turn, based on fundamental contradictions in Rousseau's political philosophy. To the extent that Rousseau is an Enlightenment philosophe, he is every anarchist's common enemy, a
proponent of government and obedience to the general will, rather
than an advocate of free association and individual liberty. To the
extent that Rousseau is a romantic revolutionary, he is the anarchist's
greatest ally, the defender of natural law and absolute equality
against the encroachments of artificial, outside authority. Given this
division, the *Social Contract* would appear to be the one document
that all anarchists love to hate, whereas the *Discourse on the Origin of
Inequality* (also known as the *Second Discourse*) should be a constant
source of inspiration. As we shall see, the matter is not quite so

clear-cut. But what is clear is that both documents provided anarchist thinkers with arguments that could be variously refuted or extended, or otherwise manipulated.

The opening chapter of the fourth book of the *Social Contract* begins with a sentence that first appears to be completely opposed to anarchistic principles: "So long as a number of men in combination are considered as a single body, they have but one will, which relates to the common preservation and to the general well-being."[8] From the anarchist point of view, the problem here lies with the passive verb: surely it makes a difference *who* or *what* is considering a group of people not as a collection of individuals but as "a single body." The success of this model depends on the assent of the people to remain anonymous units in a larger collective. Given such assent, the social contract is maintained on both sides and, as Rousseau says, "[a] State thus governed needs very few laws" (*Contract,* 109). The paucity of laws has some appeal to the anarchist, but the state still governs, and the laws, though few, nonetheless exist. Worse, the more individuality is exercised, the greater the need for new laws: "But when the social bond begins to be relaxed and the State weakened, when private interests begin to make themselves felt and small associations to exercise influence on the State, the common interest is injuriously affected and finds adversaries; unanimity no longer reigns in the voting; the general will is no longer the will of all" (*Contract,* 110). From the anarchist point of view, the problem Rousseau describes disappears if the state does: private interests and small associations are the very stuff of anarchism. Indeed, one of the curious things about Rousseau is how close he comes to the expression of ideas that can later be called anarchistic, even when he writes as an advocate of government. For example, Rousseau describes the weakening of the state "when the general will becomes dumb" as the reason for the introduction of new laws: "all, under the guidance of secret motives, no more express their opinions as citizens than if the State had never existed; and, under the name of laws, they deceitfully pass unjust decrees which have only private interest as their end" (*Contract,* 110). Precisely: the anarchist agrees that laws serve the interests of some individuals at the expense of others; in other words, in his advocacy of the state Rousseau inadvertently constructs an anarchist argument against legislation.

Elsewhere in the *Social Contract,* Rousseau provides some grist for the anarchist mill in his description of the formation of the state through association, and the subsequent definition of the state itself as a *passive* political unit. Here, Rousseau explains how the individual will is subordinated to the general will by an "act of association" that "produces a moral and collective body, which is composed of as many members as the assembly has voices, and which receives from this same act its unity, its common self *(moi)*, its life and its will. This public person, which is thus formed by the union of all the individual members, formerly took the name of *city,* and now takes that of *republic* or *body politic,* which is called by its members *State* when it is passive, *sovereign* when it is active, *power* when it is compared to similar bodies" (*Contract,* 19). Anarchists would agree with two points in this key passage, given certain qualifications: first, they would agree with the principle of association, provided the associations formed did not encroach upon individual freedoms or upon the rights of other associations; second, they would affirm, or at least allow, the possibility of a state so long as the state remained passive. Rousseau seems to use the term *l'état* almost in a scientific sense, that is, as a description of an existing condition. As George Crowder points out, classical anarchism argues against government, not against the state itself, provided the state is simply a passive means of performing purely administrative functions.[9] It is only when the state begins to *govern,* regulate, or direct individuals in some way that the anarchist ideal of a "stateless society" has meaning. In other words, the moment the state becomes active, it ceases to be a state and becomes a government, and government is always intrusive. But so long as the state is passive, the anarchist can live with it.

Additional examples from the *Social Contract* might be cited in support of this general point: that Rousseau's arguments in favor of the subordination of the individual to the general will assume the presence of a passive and virtually lawless state. The anarchist rejects the idea of the general will, and sees a different solution to the problem Rousseau sets down: if the exercise of individuality creates the need for an active state, a government of laws, then the obvious anarchistic resolution of the matter is the elimination of the state altogether. The *Social Contract* thus provides a base for anarchist arguments in that different conclusions can be drawn from Rousseau's premises, just as other inferences may be drawn from certain of his conclusions. The *Second Discourse,* however, provides a more direct means of imagining an anarchistic society in its description of humanity living in a harmonious state of nature before the political fall into repressive government. Indeed, the purpose of the *Second Discourse* is to show the process whereby "nature became subject to law" and the weak came to govern the strong (*Contract,* 176). In Rousseau's vision of primitive society, people in a state of nature need no laws because their innate virtue or "natural sentiment" leads them to sympathize with their fellows and live in harmony with their neighbors: "It is therefore certain that pity is a natural sentiment, which, by moderating in every individual the activity of self-love, contributes to the mutual preservation of the whole species. It is this pity which hurries us without restriction to the assistance of those we see in distress; it is this pity which, in a state of nature, takes the place of laws" (*Discourse,* 204). Given the sentimental goodness of humanity in the state of nature, Rousseau asks if the evils of present society "did not spring up with the laws themselves; for . . . even if the laws were capable of repressing these evils, it is the least that might be expected of them, that they should check a mischief which would not exist without them" (*Discourse,* 205). In the second part of the *Discourse,* as Rousseau begins his investigation proper into the origins of inequality, he provides a model for anarchistic society in his description of primitive social organization. Rousseau imagines the moment when nomadic tribes "gradually flock[ed] together, . . . united in character and manners, not by laws or regulations" (*Discourse,* 217). Such passages, absent any reference to the general will, suggest later anarchist constructions that allow for the free association of like-minded individuals. In other passages Rousseau is almost doctrinaire in making the point that in the just society government is irrelevant: "And as laws . . . are in general less strong than the passions, and restrain men without changing them, it would be no hard matter to prove that every government . . . was set up unnecessarily; and that a country, where no one either eluded the laws, or made an ill use of magistracy, required neither laws nor magistrates" (*Discourse,* 239).

3

Despite the apparent alignment of Rousseau's ideas in the *Second Discourse* with anarchistic principles, the fit is far from precise. And the relationship of Rousseau to his first anarchist successor, William

Godwin, is problematic. Although he is generally sympathetic with the Rousseau of the *Second Discourse,* in Godwin's *Enquiry Concerning Political Justice* Rousseau's belief in natural virtue comes up for criticism. The criticism is based on moral criteria, which, for Godwin, are the equivalent of political criteria since both morality and politics are grounded in strict rationality. Godwin may be thinking of Rousseau when he observes that "[n]o well informed man can seriously doubt of the advantages with respect to happiness of a capacious and improved intellect over the limited conceptions of a brute. Virtuous sentiments are another source of personal pleasure, and that of a more exquisite kind than intellectual improvements. But virtue itself depends for its value upon the energies of the intellect." [10] As Crowder puts it, for Godwin "[t]he morally right course is not to be known by any immediate 'feeling' of inner certainty, but is arrived at by dispassionate calculation." [11] In Godwin, the equation of virtue with rationality would seem, at first, to preclude the presence of Rousseau, since the moral principles he encourages are strictly based in reason, not feeling: "To be truly rational, for Godwin, is necessarily to be virtuous." [12] A description of the reserved nature of Godwin's anarchism (a word Godwin never used to describe his politics) helps to show how unlike Godwin seems from Rousseau: "[P]erhaps of all the anarchist thinkers, he deserves most to be called a utopian for the perfect rationality of his conception of humanity and society. When all people were educated and rational, he believed, all would be virtuous and all forms of external constraint superfluous." [13] But as Alan Ritter points out, "Godwin's hostility to emotions is not absolute. Without 'the genuine emotions of the heart' we are mere shadows of men . . . destitute of substance and soul. An emotionless person, though logically able to be an individual, will not become one. Feelings which encourage independent thinking are thus valued aids to individuality. Godwin wants to direct emotions, not expunge them." [14] There is reason to believe that this emotional tempering of rationality derives from Godwin's reading of Rousseau, which was quite extensive and coincided with the writing of *Political Justice.* Godwin's diary indicates that his reading of Rousseau came hard upon the composition of the political treatise: "[S]hortly before [Godwin] began writing the book he consulted the *Considerations on Poland* and the *Social Contract.* Just the day before he started writing he was reading the *Second Discourse,* to which he returned a week later." [15] Godwin's treatise shows evidence of this reading. The *Second Discourse* lies behind Godwin's claim that a "fundamental distinction" exists between society and government and the observation that "[m]an associated at first for the sake of mutual assistance" (*Enquiry*, 167). He differs from Rousseau, however, in his endorsement of Thomas Paine's explanation of the origins of society and government: "Society and government . . . are different in themselves, and have different origins. Society is produced by our wants, and government by our wickedness" (*Enquiry*, 168). By contrast, Rousseau argues that government creates the "wickedness" it seeks to regulate.

Elsewhere, Godwin reverses the causal relationship of government and wickedness and echoes Rousseau, arguing that "political government" is a "brute engine" that "has been the only perennial cause of the vices of mankind" (*Enquiry*, 554). Rousseau also sounds through Godwin's observation that fewer and fewer laws are needed the smaller the political unit becomes: "A large city, impelled by the principles of commercial jealousy, is not slow to digest the volume of its by-laws and exclusive privileges. But the inhabitants of a small parish, living with some degree of that simplicity which best corresponds to the real nature and wants of a human being, would soon be led to suspect that general laws were unnecessary, and would adjudge the causes that came before them, not according to certain axioms previously written, but according to the circumstances and demands of each particular cause" (*Enquiry*, 611). Here, the suggestion is clear that the closer one gets to nature the fewer laws are needed; however, native simplicity must be supplemented with rationality in order to arrive at Godwin's ideal of moral self-direction. In general, Godwin is in fundamental agreement with the model of society imagined in Rousseau's *Second Discourse*, even though Rousseau omits discussion of the rationalistic means whereby such a society might become a reality. Godwin argues, in fact, that Rousseau "has been subjected to continual ridicule for the extravagance of the proposition with which he began his literary career; that the savage state was the genuine and proper condition of man. It was however by a very slight mistake that he missed the opposite opinion which it is the business of the present enquiry to establish. He only substituted, as the topic of his eulogium, the period that preceded government and laws, instead of the period that may possibly follow upon their abolition" (*Enquiry*, 496–97). The passage makes the double

relationship of Godwin's anarchism to Rousseau's thought quite
clear: the ideal society has no government or laws, but such a society
is inconceivable in the state of nature because the "genuine and
proper condition of man" is not one of savagery but enlightenment.
The rationalist and the romantic both agree on the desirability of a
world without government and laws, but they are in sharp disagreement over the conditions that make such a world possible.

4

Godwin's utopian rationalism and Rousseau's nostalgic sentimentalism can hardly be reconciled, but both attitudes are present
in the writings of the prolific and inconsistent Proudhon, who was
evidently the first political thinker to ameliorate the term *anarchiste*
and apply it to himself.[16] Like Godwin, Proudhon believed in the
perfectibility of humanity through reason; like Rousseau, his notion
of the just society involves rejection of present politics and a selective
effort to recuperate the past. But the past that Proudhon sought to
revive was much more immediate than Rousseau's primitive and
benign state of nature. Proudhon thought of the industrial revolution as a threat to the world of small shops and independent artisans
that he knew as the son of a brewer and innkeeper. Proudhon himself was trained as a printer, a profession consistent with the anarchistic idea that the worker should be involved in every phase of
production. Still, the idea that Proudhon and Rousseau have something in common because of a shared dissatisfaction with urban,
industrial life, however valid, misrepresents the relationship between
the two. No name comes up more often in Proudhon's voluminous
writings than Rousseau's, but a consistent attitude toward the citizen
of Geneva is not apparent. Crowder observes that Proudhon more
often than not takes "the negative view, at times exhibiting a near-
hysterical hatred of Rousseau." Indeed, Proudhon rails against Rousseau's "intellectual pride, aridity of soul, baseness of tastes, depravity
of habits," and so on. Despite such censure, Proudhon also sees
Rousseau as a "great innovator" and "the apostle of liberty and
equality." [17]

While the relationship of Proudhon to Rousseau is too complicated to explore fully here, a few key points need to be made. The
first concerns Proudhon's critique of the *Social Contract;* the second,
Proudhon's model of a mutualist society that resembles Rousseau's

description in the *Second Discourse* of a mythic society before the introduction of government.

In his *Idée générale de la Révolution au XIXe siècle,* Proudhon argues that Rousseau had misunderstood the idea of the social contract as it had developed since the sixteenth century. Proudhon urges the view that this earlier "revolutionary tradition . . . gave us the idea of the Social Contract as an *antithesis* to the idea of Government." [18] Basically, Proudhon thought that a social contract which granted freedom to individuals in exchange for obedience to the state was one-sided: "The state . . . gives me nothing in exchange: it simply practices extortion upon me. . . . Citizen of Geneva, you talk well. But . . . tell me first what is my share of the bargain." [19] At the same time, nothing is more important to Proudhon's anarchist philosophy than the idea of the contract: "That I may remain free, that I may be subjected to no law but my own, and that I may govern myself, the edifice of society must be rebuilt upon the idea of Contract" (*Anarchism,* 71). However, Proudhon's contract differs from Rousseau's in a number of significant respects. The social contract as Proudhon understood it is a concrete agreement between and among individual members of society, not an abstract pact between citizens and state:

> Proudhon's basic difference with Rousseau on this point is that he did not think of the contract as a single act or as particularly political in character. Instead he thought in terms of many contracts, indeed of an all but endless multiplication of contracts among specific individuals for specific ends and purposes that would cover the entire spectrum of human desires and aspirations. "The idea of contract," Proudhon wrote in 1851, is "the only moral bond which free and equal beings can accept," and it was the social contract which Proudhon relied upon "to bind together all the members of a nation into one and the same interest." [20]

In addition, because the contract is a concrete agreement, it involves true reciprocity, or justice. Justice, for Proudhon, is a principle of balance fundamental to the idea of the contract, for contracts must be kept if they are to be effective; that is, the parties to the contract must do what they have agreed to do to maintain the balance or justice of the agreement.

Indeed, the concept of justice as balance or reciprocity underlies virtually every phase of Proudhon's thinking. As a moral principle, "Justice is respect, spontaneously felt and mutually guaranteed, for human dignity, in whatever person and under whatever circumstances we find it compromised, and to whatever risk its defence may expose us" (*Anarchism*, 67). As an economic principle, justice motivates Proudhon's critique of both capitalism and communism, especially on the subject of property: "[I]n defining property, what I am wanting . . . is not a destruction: I have said it until I am tired. That would have been to fall with Rousseau, Plato, Louis Blanc himself, and all the adversaries of property, into *Communism*, against which I protest with all my might; what I ask for property is a balance, [that is,] justice" (*Anarchism*, 83). Even Proudhon's famous dictum that "property is theft" is meaningful only in terms of justice: "What I demand with respect to property is balance. It is not for nothing that the genius of nations has equipped Justice with the instrument of precision. Justice applied to economy is in fact nothing but a perpetual balance" (*Anarchism*, 84–85). The social contract as Proudhon understood it prohibits "theft" in the following sense: "Do you promise to respect the honor, the liberty, the goods, of your brothers? Do you promise never to appropriate to yourself, neither by violence, by fraud, by usury, nor by speculation, another's product or possession?" (*Anarchism*, 71–72). Thus, Proudhon does not prohibit individual ownership of property so long as that property has been produced by the individual and is possessed by right of production. In fact, Proudhon draws an important line of distinction between "property" and "possession," the latter referring to the ownership of those things necessary for day-to-day life, including land, place of dwelling, and whatever tools or implements the individual's trade requires.[21] Property is theft only when the contractual principle of justice is violated and one person comes to possess what has not been produced by his own labor: "[A]nd so the famous aphorism 'property is theft' turns out to be less paradoxical and somewhat less radical in its implications than it appears at first sight. But Proudhon's position is radical enough. The ownership he opposes is basically that which is unearned—he sometimes uses the word *aubaine*, or windfall—including such things as interest on loans and income from rents."[22] Proudhon himself refers to the economist Jérôme-Adolphe Blanqui's observation "that property is abused in many harmful ways" and then adds: "I call *property* the sum of these abuses exclusively." Simply stated, property is any type of revenue obtained without labor.[23]

Although Proudhon frequently criticizes Rousseau for neglecting economic issues in favor of political solutions to the problems of society, Rousseau provided the starting point for Proudhon's social theory by his investigation into the origins of inequality in the *Second Discourse*. In particular, Proudhon owes a debt to the opening of the second part of Rousseau's treatise, in which the philosopher traces all the ills of civil society back to the moment when "[t]he first man, who after enclosing a piece of ground, took it into his head to say, *this is mine*" (*Discourse*, 211). Rousseau here raises an issue of natural law that harmonizes with Proudhon's ideas: "For Proudhon as for Rousseau, social and economic inequality is a violation of the natural, and therefore moral, order."[24] In the *Second Discourse* Rousseau had posited the existence of a society of interconnected family groups whose organization anticipates Proudhon's important concept of mutualism: "Living permanently near each other could not fail eventually to create some connection between different families. The transient commerce required by nature soon produced, among the youth of both sexes living in neighboring huts, another kind of commerce, which besides being not less agreeable is rendered more durable by mutual association" (*Discourse*, 218). Although Rousseau is describing a stage in the progressive corruption of the state of nature that eventually led to the introduction of laws (the "other kind of commerce" is public interaction that leads to a point where "public esteem acquired a value," which is fatal to equality [*Discourse*, 218]), he provides a model for the just society in the suggestion that certain types of social organization are somehow "natural," and people form themselves into "natural groups," which Proudhon defines as follows:

> Whenever men together with their wives and children assemble in some one place, link up their dwellings and holdings, develop in their midst diverse industries, create among themselves neighborly feelings and relations, and for better or worse impose upon themselves the conditions of solidarity, they form what I call a natural group. This group then takes on the form of a community or some other political organism, affirming in its unity its independence, a life of movement that is appropriate to itself, and affirms its autonomy.[25]

For Proudhon, always the concrete thinker, the "natural group" has "effective sovereignty" over itself because of the contracts its members have entered into with each other, a different arrangement altogether from the "artificial" or "abstract" sovereignty Rousseau promoted through the development of political institutions. Because the sovereignty of each citizen is based on the balanced principle of reciprocity and justice implicit in each contract, society itself may be said to be composed as much of contracts as citizens; each citizen is, in a way, a personification of the total number of contracts he has entered into. Proudhon's term for the contractual society he imagined is "mutualism," as when he calls such a society a "régime de mutualité."[26] The theory of mutuality or the *mutuum* makes it possible for Proudhon's model of the "natural group" to be extended to include larger groupings of society, up to and including the nation itself, so long as the "bottom-up" principle of organization is maintained: "That a nation may manifest itself in its unity, it must be centralized in its religion, centralized in its justice, centralized in its army, centralized in its agriculture, industry, and commerce, centralized in its finances,—in a word, centralized in all its functions and faculties; the centralization must work from the bottom to the top, from the circumference to the center; all the functions must be independent and severally self-governing" (*Anarchism*, 79). This passage makes the point that the kind of anarchism Proudhon had in mind has much in common with socialism, albeit a socialism without the kind of top-down state apparatus advocated by Marx. Proudhon therefore represents one strain of the socialist tradition, and he may be termed an anarcho-socialist.[27] In his vision of society at large he stands out from the later anarchists who took their inspiration from him: for all the emphasis on individual relations, he is ultimately more interested in organizing those relations into some workable, collective whole; he therefore appears more a collectivist than an individualist anarchist. Later, we shall have to consider the impact of such collectivism on culture.

In his practical approach to social issues, Proudhon is an undeniably progressive proponent of reform. But he is also as reactionary as Rousseau in his criticism of contemporary morals, an attitude manifested in his reverence for marriage and family life. Also, Proudhon appears to be genuinely out of touch with the industrial revolution, preferring the shop to the factory. And even though he was one of the first social theorists to recognize the relationship of economic inequality to class struggle, his understanding of the complexities of industrial economy is limited, to say the least. While Proudhon's idea of a people's bank as a means of distributing interest-free capital will have later adherents, none of the later anarchists are quite so single-minded as Proudhon in insisting that economic value is to be measured strictly in terms of the labor required to produce goods and services, rather than the market forces that drive supply and demand. Thus, there is something unquestionably conservative about Proudhon's progressivism, a reactionary element in his ideas for social reform. Sonn's point that anarchism "fused elements of a remembered past with a vision of utopian future" seems especially relevant to Proudhon. Similarly, what Crowder says of Godwin is true of Proudhon as well and of anarchism in general: "Rousseau's narrative locates a happy, virtuous, and free anarchy in the primitive past and presents it as irrevocably displaced by the misery and servitude of the modern regime of property secured by government. Godwin would accept relevantly similar categories but place them in reversed chronology." [28] Anarchism, then, does not reject origins so much as it seeks to reconstruct them, provided the crucial point is upheld that the *archon* is everyman.

5

The attitude of Godwin and Proudhon to Rousseau combines elements of reaction and reform: an impulse to "progress" toward an anterior anarchic condition. While it is oversimple to say that this double sensibility simply combines elements of romanticism and Enlightenment, such an assessment of anarchism is borne out by an analysis of other anarchist thinkers. In many ways, it makes a great deal of sense to think of anarchism as having some dual affiliation with those two great movements in European thought that are often imagined in conflict with one another. One possible objection to the idea that anarchist thought is simultaneously enlightened and romantic is the notion that the Enlightenment and romanticism occupy two separate spheres of cultural life, with the philosophers belonging to intellectual history and the poets to literary history. After all, one rarely speaks of "Enlightenment art" or "romantic philosophy." But it is easy to argue that the relegation of reason and feeling to separate cultural tracks is a false dichotomy. Goethe, for one, clearly belongs to the history of both the Enlightenment and romanticism, as does his contemporary William Godwin. Likewise, one need look only as far as Kant's treatise on the sublime to find the romantic element in the Enlightenment philosopher. Thus, there is no reason why romantic sentiment and enlightened intellect should not combine in the history of social thought, yet this is hardly the way anarchism is understood. Largely because of the Marxist critique, the negative image of anarchism is a romantic one, with the anarchist himself depicted either as a dangerous rebel or a moody dreamer. On the other hand, the positive image of anarchism promoted by its followers clearly derives from the Enlightenment and is presented as a progressive, scientific solution to the ills of society. Thus, conventional criticism of Mikhail Bakunin casts him as a romantic rebel, while the typical, progressive portrait of Peter Kropotkin shows us an enlightened scientist. But a truer picture of these two anarchists— and of anarchism itself—would allow us to see the tension between the romantic and the scientist, the idealist and the materialist.

Mikhail Bakunin's romantic temper was first forged in the late 1830s at the university in Moscow, steeped at the time in German idealism. Bakunin's first major influence was the romantic writing of Fichte, whose musings on the interpenetrations of the *Ich* and the *Geist* led Bakunin to proclaim that "one must totally annihilate one's personal ego, annihilate everything that forms its life, its hopes and its personal beliefs. One must live and breathe only for the absolute through the absolute." [29] Bakunin moved to Berlin in 1840 to study idealism at its source, but there his interests shifted. Like other young men of the time, Bakunin had studied Hegel for several years and had counted on deepening his understanding in the German capital and eventually becoming a professor of philosophy himself. Once in Berlin, however, Bakunin found himself caught up in the excitement created by Feuerbach and other Young or Left Hegelians. Of particular importance was Feuerbach's *Essence of Christianity*, with its materialist thesis that God Himself is merely a sublimation of man's finer qualities: "Theology must be replaced by anthropology," Feuerbach argued, "if man, overcoming the sense that he is sinful and flawed, is to stop projecting all of his own positive attributes onto God and instead make himself godlike." [30] Bakunin, like Marx, was decisively affected by Left Hegelianism and the crucial shift away from the belief that reason is immanent in reality. The "practical" effect of this philosophy was the idealistic historicism that made it possible for Hegel to imagine Prussian absolutism as the highest ethical attainment to date. After two years among the Young Hegelians, Bakunin in 1842 published his pivotal essay, "The Reaction in Germany: From the Notebooks of a Frenchman" (so titled because of its pseudonymous authorship, Bakunin adopting the name "Jules Elysard"). This essay contains the famous conclusion that shows just how far Bakunin had come from the romantic Fichte; the spirit of annihilation, earlier turned inward toward the individual ego, is no longer directed at the self: "Let us therefore trust the eternal Spirit which destroys and annihilates only because it is the unfathomable and eternal source of all life. The passion for destruction is a creative passion, too!"[31] The destructive passion, in other words, is the will of nature. Even though this is still a Hegelian formulation, Bakunin is clearly beginning to modify his idealism as he adapts the Hegelian principle of logical negation to serve the political end of revolution. A few months later, in Zurich, Bakunin met the revolutionary socialist Wilhelm Weitling, whose *Guarantees of Harmony and Freedom* (1842) pointed Bakunin toward anarchism, as this passage, which Bakunin quoted to a friend, suggests: "The perfect society had no government, but only an administration, no laws, but only obligations, no punishments, but only means of correction" (Morris, *Bakunin*, 11).

This sketch of Bakunin's early career makes his gradual abandonment of German romantic idealism clear. After the 1848 revolutions had confirmed, for Bakunin, the destructive doctrine laid out in his 1842 essay, overt advocacy of idealism was no longer possible. From 1848 on, Bakunin's support of the contrary doctrine of materialism is quite doctrinaire: "Who are right, the idealists or the materialists? The question once stated in this way, hesitation becomes impossible. Undoubtedly the idealists are wrong and the materialists are right. Yes, facts are before ideas; yes, the ideal, as Proudhon said, is but a flower, whose root lies in the material conditions of existence. Yes, the whole history of humanity, intellectual and moral, political and social, is but a reflection of its economic history" (Morris, *Bakunin*, 78). The shift to materialistic explanations of reality seems quite complete, and Bakunin sometimes sounds like Kropotkin in his appropriation of evolutionary theory to express the melioration of society from "lower" forms to "higher": "One can clearly conceive the gradual development of the material world, as well as of organic

life and of the historically progressive intelligence of man, individually and socially. It is an altogether natural movement, from the
simple to the complex, from the lower to the higher, from the inferior to the superior" (Morris, *Bakunin,* 78). This representation of
social evolution, however, is less scientific than it seems, because
Bakunin's model of nature is still Hegel's, not Darwin's. The socially
progressive element is part of what Bakunin calls "Universal Nature":
"It seems to me quite evident . . . that no revolt is possible on the part
of man against what I call universal causality, or Universal Nature; the
latter envelops and pervades man; it is within and outside of him,
and it constitutes his whole being" (Morris, *Bakunin,* 79). Given such
determinism or "universal causality," the place of individual liberty
in Bakunin's thought would seem to be problematic, a serious matter
for any anarchist. But what Bakunin means is that freedom itself is
the ultimate goal toward which nature progresses, so that the destiny
of mankind is liberty—no revolt against revolution is possible. At
such points it is difficult to separate Bakunin's evolutionary scientism
from his Hegelian idealism, which only makes the point again that
the anarchist often weaves strains of the Enlightenment and romanticism together. The mix also helps to explain Bakunin's lifelong advocacy of violent revolution, of the need to wipe the slate clean. Violent
revolutionary activity is necessary because nature embodies it: not
reason, but revolution is immanent in nature; or rather, revolution
is the higher reason, based on the logic of negation, that leads to
the perfection of society through the destruction of certain parts
of it. The negative capability of revolution ties Bakunin to the romantic tradition, even as it maintains the positive telos of the
Enlightenment.

6

Just as Bakunin's later materialism is, in part, the product of his
earlier idealism, Kropotkin's scientism often betrays a fundamentally
romantic bias toward the problem of reconciling humanity and history. A generation younger than his predecessors Proudhon and
Bakunin, Kropotkin was much more positivistic than they were, con-
tending that "anarchism was a science firmly rooted in natural law
and in the modern world." [32] Kropotkin's best-known expression of
scientific anarchism appears in the essays written between 1890 and
1896 in response to T. H. Huxley's 1888 article, "The Struggle for

Existence." In these articles, later collected as *Mutual Aid: A Factor of Evolution* (1902), Kropotkin attempted to revise Huxley's doctrine of Social Darwinism by asserting that the natural mechanism that made survival of certain species possible was cooperation, not competition. The survival of social animals (e.g., ants and bees) in particular pointed to the survival of the altruistic, not the fittest. Kropotkin "claimed that the principle of voluntary cooperation was . . . basic to human society, and saw the recent trend toward competitive individualism as an aberration." [33] According to Kropotkin, "the philosophy of evolution" reveals "the admirable adaptability of organisms . . . to the needs of free cooperation":

> [T]hroughout organic nature the capacities for life in common grow in proportion as the integration of organisms into compound aggregates becomes more and more complete; and it has enforced thus the opinion already expressed by social moralists as to the perfectibility of human nature. It has shown us that, in the long run of the struggle for existence, "the fittest" will prove to be those who combine intellectual knowledge with the knowledge necessary for the production of wealth, and not those who are now the richest because they, or their ancestors, have been momentarily the strongest. [34]

The smartest, not the strongest, survive, and they survive by cooperating with fellow members of society rather than by overcoming them.

One way Kropotkin supports his assertions is by arguing that cooperative or communist anarchism is consistent with other aspects of the natural world as science at present understands it. Astronomy, for example, which formerly held the earth and then the sun to be the center of the universe, now finds the order of the universe sustained and governed not by large central bodies like the earth or sun, but by "infinitely small bodies" working together: "[T]he power . . . which govern[s] the system is itself but the result of the collision among those infinitely tiny clusters of matter," and "the harmony of stellar systems is harmony only because it is an adaptation, a resultant of all these numberless movements uniting, completing, equilibrating one another" (*Fugitive Writings*, 101). What Kropotkin describes here we would now call a paradigm shift, a change in the overriding conception of reality that may be applied to different areas of human knowledge. Indeed, Kropotkin shows that the cosmological model involving "clusters" and "agglomeration" is relevant to other fields.

The physicist, for example, no longer sees an undifferentiated mass of matter, but "the vibrations of infinitely small atoms which dash in all directions, vibrate, move, live, and by their vibrations, their shocks, their life, produce the phenomena of heat, light, magnetism or electricity." Likewise, the physiologist who "speaks now of the life of a plant or an animal" sees "an agglomeration, a colony of millions of separate individuals, rather than a personality, one and indivisible." Following this model, the physiology of human beings is such that the individual organs are independent, "each living its own life," yet connected to each other: "Each organ, each part of an organ in its turn is composed of independent cellules which associate to struggle against conditions unfavorable to their existence. The individual is quite a world of federations, a whole universe in himself" (*Fugitive Writings*, 101–2). This formulation is immediately recognizable as an evolutionary variation on the Great Chain of Being, only now the relationship between the physical body and the body politic, and the similitude that links microcosm to macrocosm, involves agglomerative rather than hierarchical organization.

Although Kropotkin sometimes implies that the workings of anarchistic agglomeration is a law of nature, his particular brand of scientism seems to preclude "natural law," and in this he differs from Bakunin. Kropotkin is careful to say that whatever harmony or order science discovers in nature is not immanent in it:

> [T]he modern man of science no longer tries to explain [nature] by the action of laws conceived according to a certain plan pre-established by an intelligent will.
> What used to be called "natural law" is nothing but a certain relationship among phenomena which we dimly see, and each "law" takes a temporary character of causality; that is to say: *If* such a phenomena is produced under such conditions, such another phenomena will follow. No law placed outside the phenomena: each phenomena governs that which follows it—not law.   (*Fugitive Writings*, 103).

Obviously, it is important for an anarchist who bases his theories on analogies with nature to make this point, and to cut off the possibility of inferring that laws in nature justify laws in society. In this regard, Kropotkin's anarchism is philosophically opposed to the deterministic theories of the naturalist writers who were his contemporaries. The novels of Zola and other naturalists offer a Darwinian image of society where human beings are subject to deterministic "laws" of heredity and environment that are inexorable in their workings, whereas Kropotkin's causality is quite flexible, governed only by the "independent" nature of individual phenomena.

Even though Kropotkin denies the operation of natural law in any immanent sense, natural science and "moral science" follow the same logic. Kropotkin argues, again, that "the struggle for existence" should be understood not "in its restricted sense of struggle between individuals for the means of subsistence but in its wider sense of adaptation of all individuals of the species to the best conditions for the survival of the species." Understood in this way, the philosophy of evolution "has permitted us to deduce the laws of moral science from the social needs and habits of mankind. It has shown us the infinitesimal part played by positive law in moral evolution, and the immense part played by the natural growth of altruistic feelings, which develop as soon as conditions of life favor their growth" (*Fugitive Writings*, 78). Kropotkin thus uses evolutionary theory to posit a future condition not unlike the positive anarchy of Rousseau's state of nature. In the *Second Discourse,* Rousseau had argued that the "natural sentiment" of pity had "contribute[d] to the mutual preservation of the whole species" by "moderating in every individual the activity of self-love" (*Discourse,* 204). Although Kropotkin may never have read Rousseau,[35] there is little difference between the altruism Kropotkin saw at the end of social evolution and the sentiment or pity that Rousseau imagined before society developed at all. Kropotkin, however, is no avatar of Rousseau: his faith in technology to provide a modernist utopia is completely within an Enlightenment tradition that cannot include Rousseau.

Bakunin and Kropotkin both illustrate the contradictory tensions involved in anarchistic thought in their paradoxical appropriations of Hegel and Darwin, respectively, to their own political philosophy. Just as Bakunin injected an element of revolutionary materialism into Hegel's staid idealism, Kropotkin uses evolutionary science to posit a new age of romantic sentiment and cooperation. This is not to say that Bakunin turned Hegel into a materialist (as Marx did), or that Kropotkin transformed Darwin into a romantic figure, but the pattern of interference that is set up by the contradictory claims of romantic idealism and scientific materialism says a great deal about the anarchistic tradition.

7

The exposition of anarchism presented thus far has emphasized its contradictory nature while at the same time arguing for a certain cultural coherence: that is, the contradictions are consistent with the weave of Western thought since Rousseau. Anarchism is rationalistic and sentimental by turns, alternately progressive and reactionary, sometimes materialist, often idealist; in some cases, the anarchist manages to maintain opposing ideas and attitudes simultaneously. The contradictory, aggregate quality of anarchism has many implications, including the possibility of some cultural alignment with modernism. Indeed, if anarchism has affinities with both the romantic and the Enlightenment traditions, then it is already analogous to the culture of modernism, which often combines the expressivist aesthetic of romanticism with the objectivist tendencies of the Enlightenment. But a consideration of anarchism in cultural terms soon shows that the culture of anarchism cannot be explained simply as the heritage of romantic art and Enlightenment philosophy. This double heritage is most important in the cultural relationships described by the northern European countries, mainly Great Britain, France, and Germany. This cultural triad, in turn, contrasts with another set of traditions formed by Spanish, Italian, and Slavic culture. Political history shows that the socialists had their greatest success in northern Europe, while the anarchists found greater sympathy among the less industrial peoples of the south and east. Indeed, the proletarian socialists dismissed the serf and peasant classes so dear to the anarchists as mere *Lumpenproletariat*. Engels, for example, singled out the southern slavs—the Czechs, Slovaks, Serbs, and Croats—as little more than "residual fragments of peoples" who were effectively outside of history and would "never be able to achieve any kind of independence" (Morris, *Bakunin*, 17). Later commentators, however, point out that Marx and Engels were simply wrong to ignore the revolutionary potential of the *Lumpenproletariat* class: "The peasantry and the unskilled workers, groups for whom Marx expressed disdain, have become the mass base of twentieth-century social upheavals which, though often labelled 'Marxist' are more accurately described as 'Bakuninist.' "[36]

This split between northern and southern Europe has many implications for the study of anarchy and culture. It is even possible to argue that the relative success of anarchism in Latin Europe is not due solely to economic factors but to some broader cultural condition. In a sense, northern Europe did not really "need" anarchism because of an earlier tradition of religious dissent largely absent from the south, whereas in those deeply Catholic Mediterranean countries anarchism is, to some extent, a surrogate form of Protestantism. One way of making this case about the south is to point north to Catholic Ireland, where forms of political dissent and political organization were often anarchistic in principle if not in name (although the English were quick to link the Fenians with anarchism), but where obedience to the church remained unquestioned. Certainly the relationship of anarchism to Catholic culture and to Protestant culture is a large topic, and one beyond the scope of this study. But the idea of two European cultures—one Protestant, industrial, and sympathetic to socialism; the other, Catholic, agricultural, and amenable to anarchism—is at least as important to questions of anarchy and culture as the interference of Enlightenment and romantic values already discussed.

Finally, the simplest way to address the cultural questions posed by anarchism is to examine the kind of culture the anarchists themselves promoted or produced. If we turn our attention now to the question of anarchism and aesthetics, focusing on the attitudes toward artistic practice that the anarchists themselves took, we can observe in the aesthetic realm many of the same types of conflicts and contradictions between romantic and Enlightenment perspectives that inform the anarchists' social theory. In the case of William Godwin, the rationalistic approach that forms the basis for self-governing human conduct in the *Enquiry Concerning Political Justice* gives way to romantic sentiment in *Caleb Williams,* Godwin's novel (see Chapter 3). Proudhon, on the other hand, is more dialectical than dualistic in his assigning of politics and art to separate but interrelated realms. Bakunin did not devote his attentions to aesthetic theory and at times is genuinely hostile to art, as when he states flatly that the arts do not ennoble but enslave. Still, even Bakunin refers to the progressive value of romantic literature, as when he cites the poet Heine's revolutionary potential.[37] Kropotkin likewise thought of culture mainly in terms of its usefulness to progressive politics. Of these writers, Godwin seems especially concerned that culture not usurp the place of politics, and so he separates the art of culture from the science of politics, while Proudhon is more ambivalent about their relationship. An examination of the place of aesthetics in the political schemes of these two writers will, therefore, be helpful in understanding some of the subsequent attempts to combine anarchy and culture into a single social ideal.

In a section of his *Enquiry Concerning Political Justice* titled "Of Good and Evil," William Godwin seeks to undermine the arguments of those who claim that social injustice can only exist when those who suffer under its constraints are aware of their sufferings. Advocates of the slave trade, for example, say that "[t]he slaves in the West Indies . . . are contented with their situation [because] they are not conscious of the evils against which you exclaim; why then should you endeavor to alter their conditions?" (*Enquiry*, 392). Godwin answers by devising a "scale of happiness" (the subtitle of his treatise is *Its* [political justice's] *Influence on Modern Morals and Happiness*) and then ranks men on this scale, which attempts to calibrate the spectrum of social consciousness from the lowest level of awareness to the highest. As we shall see, culture occupies an important place in Godwin's hierarchy of consciousness. The slaves of the West Indies, unconscious of the injustice under which they labor, are at the lower end of this scale. Slightly higher are "the laboring inhabitants of the civilized states of Europe," peasants whose limited happiness is conditioned by a kind of imposed stoicism: because his days are occupied with labor, "the general train of [the peasant's] sensations comes as near as the nature of human existence will admit to the region of his indifference." The working-class stoic is contrasted with the next type in this hierarchy of happiness, the man of "rank, fortune and dissipation," whose days are taken up with aristocratic amusements (393). This man is happier than the peasant, but, like the peasant, his happiness is circumscribed by the limitations of consciousness imposed by his class: "He never reads, and knows nothing beyond the topic of the day. He can scarcely conceive the meaning of the sublime or pathetic; and he rarely thinks of anything beyond himself." This type of man, in short, lacks culture, which is necessary to a fuller form of human happiness. Indeed, "the man of taste and liberal accomplishments" occupies a much higher place on Godwin's scale. The man of taste possesses a developed and ex-

panded consciousness that allows him to appreciate the sublime and
the picturesque in nature; he is also capable of moments of romantic
self-reflection: "The beauties of nature are all his own. He admires
the overhanging cliff, the wide-extended prospect, the vast expanse
of the ocean, the foliage of the woods, the sloping lawn and the
waving grass. He knows the pleasures of solitude, when man holds
commerce alone with the tranquil solemnity of nature." The man of
taste is highly cultured, gifted with both aesthetic capacities and
creative abilities: "He enters, with a true relish, into the sublime and
pathetic. He partakes in all the grandeur and enthusiasm of poetry.
He is perhaps himself a poet" (394).

But culture comes up short in the larger scheme of political
justice and individual happiness: "The sublime and pathetic are bar-
ren unless it be the sublime of true virtue, and the pathos of true
sympathy." The "man of benevolence" is happiest of all, because his
consciousness takes in all of mankind. Paradoxically, this type of
happiness includes the painful awareness of the unhappiness of others. If the slave and the laborer are not unhappy because of their
constrained knowledge of what happiness is, then the man of benevolence will be unhappy on their behalf. This man's happiness is
informed not only by the elements designated to the other classes
(namely, labor, amusement, and culture) but also by "the cultivation
and improvement of the sciences" (395). Elsewhere in the *Enquiry*
Godwin makes it clear that "[p]olitics is a science," and, like all
sciences, it is by nature "progressive in its advances" (273). When
Godwin writes that the happiness of humanity will be achieved by
the "improvement of the sciences," in a sense what he means is that
politics is a science of social improvement. The main reason culture
is inadequate to this task of improvement is its tendency to cultivate
solitary individuals, alone and isolated from others. Social improvement cannot occur in the context of culture for this reason alone.
The man of benevolence is happiest because he cultivates the science
of politics, which requires a specific social consciousness in order to
bring about the improvement of mankind: "No man so truly promotes his own interest as he that forgets it. No man reaps so copious
a harvest of pleasure as he who thinks only of the pleasures of other
men" (395). While there is an abundance of romantic thought in
Godwin's treatise, the aesthetic sensibility and artistic tastes that ac-

company it are clearly separate from and subordinate to Enlightenment ideology.

Of the principal anarchists Proudhon seems most typical of the transfer of the romantic-Enlightenment mixture of ideas from social to aesthetic theory. Proudhon's aesthetic ideas are especially contradictory, although such an assessment does not do justice to the anarchist's complicated dialectical approach to the relation of art and society. An important passage from the *Système des contradiction économique ou Philosophie de la misère* of 1846 extends the idea of art to include any type of "human practice" ("la pratique humaine") that contributes to "the progress of civilization":

> Art, that is to say, the search for the beautiful, for the perfection of the true, in one's person, in one's wife and children, in one's ideas, discourse, actions, and products: such is the final stage in the evolution of the worker, the phase that is destined gloriously to close the circle of nature. *Aesthetics*, and above aesthetics, *Morality*, these are the keystones of the economic edifice.
>
> The whole of human practice, the progress of civilization, the tendencies of society all bear witness to this law. All that man does, all that he loves and hates, all that affects and interests him becomes the subject of art.[38]

A key to this passage is Proudhon's conception of the worker as a specialized craftsman who devotes to his craft all the care and attention of the artist in the root sense of the word (from Latin *ars*, "skill"). Art in this simultaneously contracted and expanded sense forms an aesthetic that is, as Proudhon says, intertwined with morality and economics; this is so because austere, ascetic devotion to work provides the basis for the new social order paradoxically known as anarchy (elsewhere Proudhon observes that "[j]ust as man seeks equality in justice, society seeks order in anarchy")(Rubin, *Realism*, 16). As James Rubin explains, "Since Proudhon saw the highest form of social evolution as that which would take its inherent structure from man's natural inclinations (and hence must be based on the rational observation of them), it could be concluded that a society in which all workers had become artists would eventually replace political forms of organization" (Rubin, *Realism*, 51). Among the paradoxes involved in Proudhon's aesthetic is the assumption that a romantic, not to say medieval, conception of labor can do the work of Enlightenment progress. Also, the idea of a society populated by worker-artists raises the question of the place of the artist proper, a question that may be addressed by a brief sketch of Proudhon's influence on Gustave Courbet.

In his study of Proudhon and Courbet, Rubin details how as a result of the anarchist's influence the painter shifted his conception of the artist from bohemian to worker, a shift reflected in Courbet's use of the term *atelier* or "workshop" to refer to his studio, a word that denoted a place of manual labor. Similarly, Courbet preferred to call himself a *peintre* or *maître-peintre,* that is, a master craftsman in the tradition of the medieval or Renaissance guild, rather than an *artiste,* a word that had acquired "spiritual" connotations over the earlier romantic period (Rubin, *Realism,* 7, 19). Proudhon's influence is also evident in a letter that Courbet wrote in 1853 to his patron Bruyas in which he details his rejection of an official invitation to exhibit in the Universal Exposition of 1855 extended by the government arts commissioner Alfred-Emilien de Nieuwerkerke: "I immediately answered that I understood absolutely nothing of all that he had just told me, mainly because he claimed to represent a Government and I felt myself in no way included in this Government, that I was a Government, too, and I challenged his to find something it might do for mine that I might find acceptable." Ironically, the letter goes on to announce an aspect of Courbet's aesthetic that Proudhon eventually found objectionable. The painter adds that he alone, "of all my contemporaries among French artists, had the ability to express and translate in an original manner both my personality and my social environment" (Rubin, *Realism,* 15). What Proudhon looked for in art was a synthesis of personal and social concerns, and he ultimately came to judge Courbet's stress on individual personality to be too strong. In the posthumously published *Du principe de l'art et de su destination sociale* (1865), Proudhon offers a less dialectical explanation of art than he did in 1846, but one that continues to emphasize the importance of work in social organization: "To paint men in the sincerity of their natures and their habits, in their work, in their civic and domestic functions, with their present day appearance, above all without pose; to surprise them, so to speak, in the dishabille of their consciousness, not simply for the pleasure of jeering, but as the aim of general education and by way of aesthetic information: such would seem to me to be the true point of departure for modern art."[39] Courbet's painting is said to have succeeded only partially in using aesthetic information for the purpose of general education; Proudhon grants that the painter has helped to "announc[e] the end of capitalism and the sovereignty of the producers," but he also claims that Courbet's vanity and egoism have compromised his career as a painter (53). In the end, Proudhon saw Courbet once again as an *artiste,* someone separate from the collective social conditions that gave meaning to the individual expression of those conditions: "Being himself part of a larger collective, the genius expresses 'a collective thought expanded by time,' and his role is to represent it as an actor acts out the character he portrays. Like the actor . . . the painter must never let his own personality overshadow that of his characters" (Rubin, *Realism,* 97).

The subordination of aesthetic to social concerns is also evident in Bakunin's attitude toward art, even though it is difficult to detect a consistent attitude toward culture in Bakunin's political philosophy. Just as Godwin did earlier, Bakunin imagined that "art and science" occupied a particular position on a scale of human happiness that was well below politics and revolution. The first degree of happiness on Bakunin's scale is "to die fighting for liberty," the second, "love and friendship." "Art and science" follow in the third position, just ahead of the four remaining degrees of happiness on the scale, which are, in descending order of importance, smoking, drinking, eating, and sleeping.[40] Whether such positioning means that "Bakunin gave art considerable importance in his system," as one commentator has it,[41] seems questionable. Bakunin did love the music of Beethoven, and, like other Left Hegelians, may have heard in it the inexorable dialectics of revolution. Indeed, it was not long after hearing his friend Richard Wagner conduct the Ninth Symphony at the Dresden opera house that the two of them participated in the Saxon insurrection of 1849.[42] In general, however, Bakunin makes culture secondary to politics; in fact, he is capable of outright antagonism to art. He sometimes suggests that art is nothing more than an instrument of oppression that the coming revolution will be obligated to destroy. Bakunin's essay "All-Round Education" poses the question, "Don't artistic creations ennoble everyone's life?" To which the answer is "No, not at all," precisely because the influence of the arts extends only "over a very small portion of society, to the exclusion of the vast majority and hence also to their detriment."[43]

The characteristic elisions in Bakunin's overheated logic show that here, at least, he has precious little use for high culture. The extent of Bakunin's hostility toward certain types of art is hard to gauge, but the historical reality may be less important to the topic than the legend. A case in point is the evidently apocryphal story that during the Dresden uprising Bakunin devised a strategy to repel the Prussian troops and keep them from retaking the city: "Bakunin proposed, unsuccessfully, that the insurgents take the paintings out of the museums, and put them on a barricade at the entrance to the city, to see if this might inhibit the firing of the attacking troops." [44] The quote is taken from a pamphlet by Guy Debord, the leading voice of the Situationists who took their inspiration from the anarchists during the May 1968 insurrection in Paris. Bakunin's biographer E. H. Carr states that "[t]he story that Bakunin proposed to hang the Sistine Madonna on the barricades, on the ground that the Prussians were 'too cultural to fire on Raphael,' belongs to the world of picturesque legend." [45] Nonetheless, the survival of the legend and Debord's use of it, where it seems to be cited as fact, shows how extensive the anticultural anarchist tradition is.

The idea that art might literally be sacrificed for the revolution makes the place of culture in Bakunin's politics problematic, but the willingness to make this type of sacrifice is not limited to the Bakunin legend. As we shall see in a later chapter, Bakunin's anti-art stance will have many adherents among artists themselves. If his creative-destructive ideology of anarchism is converted into an aesthetic, it accommodates completely the work of Lautréamont and, later, the dadaists as well. In fact, Bakunin's nihilist anarchism is much easier to reconcile with modernist aesthetics than Kropotkin's communist anarchism. Kropotkin's "Appeal to the Young" means to inspire young artists to use their creative abilities "at the service of the revolution," but in making this appeal the great anarchist does not elevate art in any way over other potentially revolutionary occupations, such as engineering and medicine. [46] The artist is simply one among many anonymous soldiers in the pacifist army of anarchists; as such Kropotkin's brand of anarchism cannot inspire an aesthetic response that is in any way distinctive. Curiously, Bakunin's apocryphal call for sacrifice may have greater cultural implications than Kropotkin's historical call for service.

It remains to be seen whether Kropotkin's faith in modernity and his dislike of modernism pose a cultural problem; whether Emma Goldman's devotion to Ibsen and her promotion of anarchism are deeply related; whether the Ferrer Schools that sprang up in America and Europe in tribute to the assassinated anarchist Francisco Ferrer really espoused a cultural curriculum different from other leftist establishments; whether Benjamin Tucker's Unique Book-shop and Press in New York City was truly a cultural center or simply a propaganda factory, and so on. These matters will be addressed in time. But of equal importance is the cultural treatment accorded to anarchism by those who never had political ties to the movement, or whose political attitude was ambiguous. Matthew Arnold, for example, targeted anarchy as the negation of culture, and while he was not attacking anarchism as a political movement per se, his conceptions of anarchy and culture have political undertones that need to be examined. In like manner, the politics of the unpolitical emerges in Henry James's *The Princess Casamassima*, Dostoyevsky's *The Possessed*, Conrad's *The Secret Agent*, and other novels that satirize or subvert anarchism without positing a clear political basis for the critiques that are offered. In such works, it seems that anarchism is as much a source of fear as an object of ridicule, but this is often the case when authority is confronted by a competing culture it does not understand.

2

REACTIONS
Anarchism as Cultural Threat

After 1848, as the transformations of society set in motion by the French Revolution finally begin to make themselves felt, a parallel movement also begins in the cultural sphere. As European society is remade using new political models, and the modern nation-states start to emerge, so do national cultures. At the same time, however, a countermovement develops: surely culture is what it has always been, not a plurality but a totality—something that by definition is not divisible. Continents may be partitioned, but not culture. Men of culture must have something in common. Politics may divide nations into peoples, but culture brings them together as humanity. Given this logic, politics is intrinsically anarchic because of its potential to separate and divide populations along ideological lines. Democratic politics is the most divisive force of all because of the tendency to produce "individuals" whose primary allegiance is to themselves. The end result of democratic politics is hardly distinguishable from anarchy, as society loses its cohesion altogether. But culture can compensate for the social disintegration wrought by politics: culture can weave disparate individuals together again, integrating them on the basis of a common sensibility. This is, ultimately, Matthew Arnold's argument in *Culture and Anarchy*, but in the course of making this type of argument Arnold and other writers end up affirming anarchism even as they deny anarchy. The perceived threat of social disorder is countered by culture all right, but culture itself is no longer the universalizing force outside of history the man of culture believes it to be.

1

In *Culture and Anarchy*, Matthew Arnold presents the paired terms of his title as antinomies: anarchy is the negation of culture; culture exists only when anarchy is absent. In Arnold's vocabulary, the word *anarchy* has the traditional meaning of "disorder," so the logic of the title seems to dictate that "order" is a primary meaning of the word *culture*. Again and again, Arnold emphasizes how much "a society like ours" requires "a profound sense of settled order and security" so that it may "live and grow." [1] What threatens this settled, ordered society and the culture that lives and grows within it does not come from without but within. The tendency toward anarchy is caused by "this exclusive attention of ours to liberty, and of the relaxed habits of government which it has engendered" (79). The drift toward "anarchy and social disintegration" (82) is attributable mainly to "doing as one likes" (to give the title of Arnold's second chapter). Significantly, the anarchy Arnold cautions against is not lawless; in fact, he is careful to distinguish the type of insidious, gradual anarchy he has in mind from the more overt brands of lawlessness, such as, say, Fenianism. Outright lawlessness does not pose so great a threat as the quieter forms of disorder because "our conscience is free enough to let us act resolutely" against the "fierce and turbulent dangers" of outright anarchy. The disorder of anarchy that Arnold describes is not only lawful, but institutionalized, in, for example, Puritan Nonconformist religion and Liberal political policies: Arnold objects to the antiestablishment practices of Puritan dissenters and to a host of Liberal programs, including free trade. Against this liberal, lawful "anarchy" comes Arnold, proposing a program of cultural reform and encouraging the growth of a society sufficiently stable and ordered to allow culture to flourish. But what is culture?

At first, the meaning of culture seems completely unambiguous: "it is *a study of perfection*" (45); moreover, "culture places human perfection in an *internal* condition, in the growth and predominance of our humanity proper, as distinguished from our animality" (47). Since culture is "an inward condition of mind and spirit," it is "at variance with the mechanical and material civilisation in esteem with us." And since that civilization is characterized mainly by "doing as one likes," culture is also "at variance with our strong individualism"

(49). Arnold's idea of culture derives in part from Goethe and the German tradition of *Bildung,* variously translated as "growth" or "education." But the German idea is involved too much with *self-cultivation*, and this notion of egoistic culture forms part of the mid-nineteenth-century critique of Goethe as too "aesthetic." In 1844, Jane Sinnett, described as "one of the most able readers of German literature in the period," expressed skepticism about Goethe's "career of self-cultivation" and his egoism—"that complete living for himself which caused so many expressions of dislike."[2] While Arnold was a great admirer of Goethe, he gradually became aware of the need to describe culture as something public and even national: "To put the matter schematically, the unblinkable *facts* of the unsolved nineteenth-century social problem were already forcing Arnold to put aside, however reluctantly, his early dreams of a detached and elevated mode of consciousness and creativity—the Goethean paradigm of the self-culture of the artist."[3] Arnold attempted to transfer the notion of *Bildung* from an individual to a social context, so that culture would appear as the means of perfecting humanity, not the self alone. The culture that Arnold endorses in *Culture and Anarchy* has acquired an enormous totalizing power to examine radically dissimilar social alternatives by allowing consciousness to "play freely" over them and to look for ways of integrating their contradictory claims. Sometimes, culture seems to be a simple synthesis of the famous contraries Hebraism and Hellenism, which Arnold identifies, respectively, with doing and thinking, and defines as "strictness of conscience" and "spontaneity of consciousness." Culture, however, tilts toward Hellenism, because that is what the times demand: the current age is too involved in action, in doing, and is preoccupied overmuch with obedience to "machinery" without considering the ends toward which that machinery is deployed. What Arnold means by "machinery" is largely the isolated workings of things in themselves, without a consideration for the larger effect such things might have on society as a whole. Arnold insists that culture allows one to see the larger picture because it is disinterested; disinterest allows the man of culture to look at social issues from all angles and to see them "as they really are." Such disinterestedness means that culture is classless. Culture does not belong to any of the three classes Arnold describes—the "Barbarians" (aristocrats), the "Philistines" (middle class), and the "Populace" (workers)—yet each of these classes may benefit equally from the operation of culture. Culture is also said to be apolitical as well as classless; in essence neither Liberal nor Conservative, culture may be of use to both.

Despite these claims, Arnold's conception of culture is of course completely political, and the politics of his understanding of culture may be demonstrated both in general and in highly particular terms. First, the notion of culture as a totality depends on the state; but the state that Arnold imagines is quite different from the constitutional government that ruled mid-nineteenth-century Britain:

> Our familiar praise of the British Constitution under which we live, is that it is a system of checks,—a system which stops and paralyses any power in interfering with the free action of individuals [so] that the central idea of English life and politics is *the assertion of personal liberty*. Evidently this is so; but evidently, also, as feudalism, which with its ideas and habits of subordination was for many centuries silently behind the British Constitution, dies out, and we are left with nothing but our system of checks, and our notion of its being the great right and happiness of an Englishman to do as far as possible what he likes, we are in danger of drifting towards anarchy. We have not the notion, so familiar on the Continent and to antiquity, of *the State*—the nation in its collective and corporate character, entrusted with stringent powers for the general advantage, and controlling individual wills in the name of an interest wider than that of individuals.   (74–75)

What Arnold describes here as "the State" derives from the contractarian political tradition of Locke and Rousseau, in which "individual wills" are subordinated to the "general advantage." Arnold allows that there is danger of tyranny in a state so constituted, but he also points out that the various classes are already controlled by their own "administrative" systems. The aristocracy submits to a system of authority involving "lord-lieutenancy, deputy-lieutenancy, and the *posse comitatûs.*" The middle class, also, has its own administrative institutions of "vestrymanship and guardianship." The working class was once controlled by "strong feudal habits of subordination and deference," but these habits are "almost entirely dissolved," and England lacks the system of military conscription that, in France, has managed to introduce "the idea of public duty and discipline . . . to the mind of these masses, in other respects so raw and uncultivated" (76). Since the English masses are every bit as "raw and uncultivated" as the French, and since "old feudal habits" are beginning to slip, the working classes clearly lack the sort of internal controls still evident among the aristocrats and the middle class, and so are most in need of the "stringent powers" of the state. Clearly, at an abstract level the working classes or the "Populace" pose the greatest threat of anarchy.

But the threat of anarchy from the ranks of the working class was not an abstract matter for Arnold. *Culture and Anarchy* has labor unrest and political protest as its real and immediate background: it was written largely in response to the Hyde Park Riots of July 1866 that resulted from protests over the defeat of the Reform Bill earlier that year and led, in part, to passage of the Second Reform Act of 1867. The immediate political changes that inform Arnold's book date from the death of Prime Minister Palmerston in 1865. Palmerston's Whig policies had emphasized foreign affairs and kept domestic legislation out of Parliament. But when Gladstone assumed leadership of the Whigs in Prime Minister Russell's liberal government he turned his attention to internal policies. One of his first acts after the death of Palmerston was the introduction of a franchise reform bill, the effect of which would have been to enfranchise the working class by allowing their representation in the House of Commons. The measure galvanized Conservative opposition and encouraged Robert Lowe's rightist revolt in the House of Commons that led, in turn, to the defeat of the Liberals and to the formation of a Conservative government, backed by Disraeli, with Lord Derby as prime minister. The defeat of the Liberals and the Reform Bill in 1866 was met with demonstrations throughout London, including a group of ten thousand supporters of Gladstone assembled in Trafalgar Square at the end of June. This group of reformists conducted itself peacefully and without incident, but three weeks later another group, called the Reform League, attempted a mass meeting in Hyde Park that led to violence. The leaders of the Reform League marched on Hyde Park and demanded that the gates be opened, but the home secretary ordered that they remain closed, whereupon the reformists simply dispersed and reassembled in Trafalgar Square. The unruly crowd they left behind proceeded to break down the railings and pour into the park. Aside from the damage done to the railings and the flower beds little physical harm resulted, and no people were injured. The real damage was symbolic and political. As Dover Wilson puts it, "The Park was at this time regarded by middle-class Londoners as a pleasure garden set aside for themselves and their families to take the air, and the notion of mass meetings being held there filled them with alarm. . . . It is scarcely too much to say that the fall of the Park railings did for England in July 1866 what the fall of the Bastille did for France in July 1789."[4] After the Hyde Park riots a year of political ferment followed before the opportunistic Disraeli, seeing that political reform was inevitable, backed a bill even more radical than the one Gladstone had sponsored. The Second Reform Act of 1867 made the general election of November 1868 "a foregone conclusion; the new House of Commons was found to be predominantly liberal if not radical in colour."[5] Arnold's attitude toward these events was hardly as reactionary as that of the quasi-aristocratic Carlyle, who had warned that passage of the First Reform Bill would be the political equivalent of shooting the rapids at Niagara Falls.[6] *Culture and Anarchy* accepts the new political order, but makes a reasoned plea for some higher, unifying cultural order that will allow classes and parties to put aside their separatist agendas.

But the political background of *Culture and Anarchy* concerns more than the immediate issues raised by the defeat of the First Reform Bill and the passage of the second. Arnold had a strong sense of history that just as strongly urged him to support government of whatever stripe as necessary to culture: "[F]or us the framework of society . . . is sacred; and whoever administers it, and however we may seek to remove them from their tenure of administration, yet, while they administer, we steadily and with undivided heart support them in repressing anarchy and disorder, and without society there can be no human perfection" (203). He claims that this "rule of conduct is hereditary" and alludes to an unpublished letter written by his father "more than forty years ago, when the political and social state of the country was gloomy and troubled, and there were riots in many places" (203). While it is impossible to know precisely what events Arnold has in mind, given the events of 1866–68, he most likely refers to the Reform Act of 1832 and imagines some political parallels between his father's life and his own. If so, his resolute support of government power occurs in the context of reformist agitation. As in 1866, the early failure of the First Reform Bill in 1831 prompted the nation to riot and near revolution. When Wellington announced his indifference to reform, anti-Wellington demonstrators sported the tricolor as "English agitation for reform assumed a revolutionary character which no one could mistake."[7] Public riots at Bristol, Derby, and Nottingham forced William IV to make plans to leave the country for his own safety. Passage of the Reform Bill of 1832 did little to allay labor unrest, however, as the growing strength of the Chartist movement throughout the 1830s suggests. Indeed, in many ways the Chartists anticipated the anarcho-syndicalists at the end of the century. For example, the anarcho-syndicalist strategy of the general strike was anticipated by the work stoppage known as the "National Holiday" called for by a group of Manchester Chartists in August 1839.[8] The point here is that Arnold's anxiety over some vague condition of anarchy involves, however indirectly, an opposition to labor movements not unlike those affiliated with anarchism proper: "The mid-nineteenth century was dominated by the spectre of Chartism which refused all attempts at exorcism. The tearing down of the park railings which is so regularly and famously asserted to be the signs of anarchy which prompted Matthew Arnold to create *Culture and Anarchy* was not an isolated, sudden or impromptu act, but just another example of the groundswell of popular unrest which . . . kept right on through the fabled 'stability' of Queen Victoria's reign."[9] The limitations of culture in protecting this stability are made quite clear when Arnold quotes his respected father's prescription for dealing with rioters: "As for rioting, the old Roman way of dealing with *that* is always the right one; flog the rank and file, and fling the ring-leaders from the Tarpeian Rock!" (203). The quotation was removed from the second edition of 1875, perhaps because the need for such severe methods was obviated when the rioters received their rights, but it is worth noting that Arnold seems unconvinced of the full worth of the reform movements, both those of the 1830s and the 1860s.

The only comment in *Culture and Anarchy* on the Reform Bill of 1832 is quite telling; Arnold focuses solely on its impact on the Oxford movement, which he associates with "sweetness and light," or beauty and intellect, and the high cultural and theological calling of Cardinal Newman: "But what was it, this Liberalism, as Dr. Newman saw it, and as it really broke the Oxford movement? It was the great middle-class Liberalism, which had for the cardinal points of its belief the Reform Bill of 1832, and local self-government, in politics; in the social sphere, free trade, unrestricted competition, and the making of large industrial fortunes; in the religious sphere, the Dissidence of Dissent and the Protestantism of the Protestant religion" (62). Although Arnold here objects to progressive modernity at large, it is no exaggeration to say that he saw the First Reform Bill as being at odds with the High Church culture he learned from Newman at Oxford, so that it might also be said that *Anarchy and Culture* describes an unbridgeable gap between the labor movement and the Oxford movement. Further, culture as Arnold describes it is basically religious in nature, as he readily admits: in "the character of perfection as culture conceives it, . . . it coincides with religion" (48). One of the ironies here, in the opposition of reform and religion, is that Arnold pits one form of anarchy against another. The results of reform pose, for Arnold, the negative threat of anarchy, but at the same time Arnold's cultural corrective to this threat is a form of positive anarchism. Classical anarchism encourages moral self-direction based on the authority of reason. Such enlightened self-direction is practically synonymous with Arnold's "culture." We are told that freedom, in Arnold's view, "is to be subordinated to . . . right reason" (78). The "practical benefit" of culture is "to like what right reason ordains, and to follow her authority." This is "a much wanted principle, a principle of authority, to counteract the tendency to anarchy which seems to be threatening us" (82). Arnold's idea of counteracting anarchy with a principle that most anarchists would espouse is ironic but understandable, given the High Puritan element in the intellectual tradition that Arnold inherited. The tradition of religious dissent has much in common with anarchism, and examples of this fact are easy to come by, from William Godwin's early career as a dissenter to Kropotkin's observation that the Anabaptists were anarchists at heart.[10] While Arnold targets a debased form of Puritanism as one of the causes of the anarchy he sees about him, his reliance on the inner light of culture makes him a member of Milton's party without, perhaps, his knowing it. Although Arnold does not say this, the figure of John Milton surely embodies the ideal cultural synthesis of Hebraism and Hellenism as few men do. Milton, like Arnold, took human perfection as the end of existence, and took his guidance toward that end from the internal light of right reason. But Milton, unlike Arnold, is much less reluctant to follow the logic of right reason to the inevitable conclusion that reliance on internal authority does away with the need for laws altogether.

Milton's *Tetrachordon,* to give one of many possible examples, argues that "[m]en of most renowned virtue have sometimes by transgressing most truly kept the law; and wisest magistrates have permitted and dispensed it; while they looked not peevishly at the letter, but with a greater spirit at the good of mankind, if always not written in the characters of law, yet engraven in the heart of man by a divine impression." While this encomium is from a divorce pamphlet, the general principle that "[n]no man observes law for law's sake, but for the good of them for whom it was made" has broad implications.[11] Among them is the anarchistic idea of moral self-direction, which is, again, what Arnold's culture amounts to. But Arnold is no anarchist, despite the philosophical similarities described here, precisely because of the paradox that this self-directing culture is not directed toward the self; that is, culture does not serve individual ends, but the collective good of society. This, at least, is the explicit program Arnold outlines, but since the collectivity derives from each individual's consciousness of culture, the explicit program of culture is implicitly anarchistic.

Arnold's culture and anarchy, then, are not quite the antinomies they first appear to be. The critique of Nonconformist religion is based on the Puritan principle of right reason; the anxiety over "doing as one likes" is fueled by the liberty to think as one pleases; and the overall opposition to anarchy derives from the inner authority of culture, an idea not unlike the philosophy of anarchism. Anarchy is overtly a threat to culture, but culture itself implicitly includes that which threatens it. Just as the paired concepts Hebraism and Hellenism have no meaning apart from one another, locked into a reciprocal relationship necessary for the balance and integration of both individual conduct and social order, so anarchy and culture are themselves mutually enforcing: "Culture and anarchy, in other words, stain one another because they are interdependent, terms whose crossings-over situate each side of their supposed antinomy and reveal their complicity."[12] One reason for this crossover effect is perhaps a result of Arnold's own crossover from literary to social critic. In "The Function of Criticism" (1865), Arnold allows that "[w]hat is law in one place is not law in another," and "what is binding on one man's conscience is not binding on another's." In social terms, this type of relativism would be the anarchy of doing as one likes, yet here it is simply intellectual freedom. In the same paragraph, however, Arnold goes on to say that, despite this relativism, "the prescriptions of reason are absolute, unchanging, of universal validity." [13] In the social terms of only a few years later, this prescriptive reason is absorbed by culture, but in 1869 the universal validity of reasoned culture is not so overtly inclusive of anarchism, as reason is of intellectual relativism in 1865. Thus, it may be that Arnold's cultural vocabulary simply could not accommodate social tensions so readily as it did the intellectual problems of literary criticism. Perry Meisel's study of Arnold's rhetorical shifts from figurative to critical and then to social language, however, shows a consistent pattern of contradiction, regardless of whether Arnold writes as poet, critic, or ideologue. Meisel makes the point that Arnold's exposure of the problem of anarchy amounts to the creation of it, a cultural challenge that marks the modern age: "But if Arnold defends against anarchy, he also fathers it, although to say so suggests a more exemplary status for Arnold than . . . is usually . . . concede[d]. If we are less concerned today with the reality of either the threat of Arnold's anarchy or the defense of his culture against it, it is largely because we can thank Arnold the prose-poet, masquerading as empiricist, for inventing our official modern crisis rather than for discovering it." [14] What Meisel means by the "modern crisis" is mainly the recognition that any attempt to recover meaning or value only certifies the permanence of the loss, that every replacement of meaning involves displacement, or, as Meisel puts it, "the desire to seek a place outside of the tradition that enables it." [15] In Arnold's case, the notion of a society perfected by culture involves some instinctive reflex against society itself; moreover, if culture is an "internal condition," then it is naturalized to the point that it is no longer culture, or at least no longer the detached, classless, apolitical construct Arnold claims it to be. The paradox can be presented in terms of late romanticism, with Arnold as yet another anxious, belated figure whose cultural ideal is some precultural condition that obviates the need for constitutional law, free trade, labor organization, and all the other realities of nineteenth-century society Arnold wished to meliorate out of existence through the perfective operation of culture. This desire is confirmed by much of Arnold's poetry, which is replete with anxious figures, such as Empedocles in "Empedocles on Etna," who wishes to "fly for refuge to past times" and recover the "soul of unworn youth." [16] But this romantic dream dissipates in the face of history: Arnold's youth, after all, was his father's age, and that earlier age was no refuge, either for Arnold or his father, who saw all the anarchy then that Arnold saw in his own belated present.

Arnold inadvertently announces what later modernists, such as T. S. Eliot, will try to renounce: that anarchy is not outside of culture, but within it. The hope for culture as a totalizing force that can bind society together has been laid to rest by the endlessly proliferating cultural forms that mark the age of modernism and continue to this day. Modernist culture is characterized by nothing so much as fragmentation, both as an aesthetic in itself and a critical judgment upon it. Culture after Arnold resists all synthesizing attempts to master it as a totality shared by society at large, unless, of course, culture is placed in the hands of totalitarians, in which case the cultural problem of "totalization" is rather handily solved by political oppression. As might be expected, Arnold himself has been imagined as a kind of protofascist: "[A]s far as giving the middle class its Culture was concerned, Matthew Arnold was a fascist with his heart in the right place." He did, in fact, make the point in a letter that "the state should see to it" that everyone "who cannot read Greek literature . . . read nothing but Milton and parts of Wordsworth." [17] Things have turned out rather differently, and the difference may be summed up by applying to Matthew Arnold the grand ambiguity of origins and endings that closes *Paradise Lost*, as Adam and Eve make their way out of the garden: "The world was all before them." For Arnold, the presence of anarchy turned the world of culture around; that world henceforth belonged to both the past and the future. Whether he turned backward to tradition or forward to modernity, culture was all before him, but anarchy was not far behind.

2

Arnold's concerns in *Culture and Anarchy* are also registered by the authors of realist fiction. In this tradition, the threat to culture comes not only from a general condition of anarchy, but also from the ideology of anarchism itself. As anarchism develops from benign theory to outright terror, novelists treat it critically but sympathetically at first (Turgenev's *Rudin*, 1860), then with increasing anxiety (Dostoyevsky's *The Possessed*, 1872), then with irony (James's *The Princess Casamassima*, 1886), and finally as the target of satire (Conrad's *The Secret Agent*, 1907) and even comedy (Chesterton's *The Man Who*

Was Thursday, 1908). This progression recapitulates the general social response to anarchism, and it is perhaps significant that the
satiric and comic treatments of anarchist terror appear well after the
terror has ended. Dostoyevsky's novel is also highly satirical, but
unlike Conrad's and Chesterton's, Dostoyevsky's commentary on anarchism is almost contemporary with the events he describes. This
sense of immediacy acknowledges the urgency Dostoyevsky felt about
anarchism, and expresses his desire to grapple with it as a moral
problem for which a solution was desperately needed. As we shall
see, for Dostoyevsky as for Arnold the solution to the moral problem
posed by anarchism was a cultural one. By contrast, Turgenev's novel
places anarchism in the idealistic context in which it made its first
appearance among the intelligentsia of Russia.

The relatively sympathetic treatment accorded to the proto-
anarchistic figure Rudin in Turgenev's novel of the same name is
due to two obvious factors. First, anarchism was still in its formative
theoretical stage in the mid-1850s when the novel was written, and,
second, Turgenev was a friend and countryman of Bakunin, on
whom the character Rudin is modeled. In truth, Rudin cannot be
called an anarchist at all. In the novel, Rudin's estranged friend
Lezhnev terms him "a true busybody politician," while the narrator
says only that "[a]ll Rudin's thoughts seemed to be directed towards
the future." [18] Even though the character's politics are not described
in detail, Rudin's physical appearance, at least, is clearly based on
Bakunin's: Rudin is "tall, slightly round-shouldered, curly-haired,
swarthy, with irregular, but expressive and intelligent features and a
liquid brilliance in his lively dark-blue eyes, with a straight broad
nose and finely chiselled lips" (52). His "broad chest," and especially
his "leonine head of hair" (78), recall attributes of Bakunin's appearance frequently mentioned by those who knew him. [19] In other ways,
however, Turgenev departs from his model in significant respects.
Rudin's rebelliousness is more controlled and tolerant than Bakunin's, and this departure of fiction from fact is matched by other
differences between the novel and the life that account for the variation in temperament. Bakunin traced his revolutionary personality
to the resentment he felt over the strict, authoritarian treatment he
was subjected to as a child; he "attributed his passion for destruction
to the influence of his mother, whose despotic character inspired
him with an insensate hatred of every restriction on liberty." [20] Ru-

din's mother, on the other hand, "was a woman of utmost kindliness and thought the world of him: she lived on oatmeal and used every penny she had on him" (82). In general, the biographies of Rudin and Bakunin are only sporadically parallel: they have in common their student life in Moscow, youthful devotion to German idealism, and, later, a wandering, exilic condition. Rudin's exilic status, however, is more existential than political, largely a matter of not being able to fit in with existing elements in Russian society or to find an appropriate career. Rudin tries to become a professor, as Bakunin did, but he also attempts a career as an agronomist and even a businessman. Although the chronology of the novel is not clear, Rudin's wanderings in Russia occur at approximately the same time as Bakunin's in Europe, when he began his revolutionary life and moved about from Paris to Brussels to Dresden.

The narrative of *Rudin* is confined almost exclusively to the provincial estate of Darya Mikhaylovna Lasunsky, a widow whose household consists of her two young sons, her seventeen-year-old daughter Natalya, and Natalya's aged governess, Mlle. Boncourt. Other principals include the permanent guest Pandalevsky, a foppish musician who toadies up to Darya Mikhaylovna by spying on everyone else, and various neighboring gentry who visit the estate from time to time. The plot of the novel concerns the abortive romance of Rudin and Natalya, who falls in love with his intelligence and eloquence. Rudin's interest in new ideas is challenged by the brutish cynic Pigasov and by the insistently provincial Lezhnev, but Rudin's brilliant conversation makes him the new favorite of Darya Mikhaylovna, who installs him in her estate as a companion for herself and her daughter. This arrangement comes to an abrupt end when Pandalevsky overhears Rudin and Natalya declare their love for each other; the spy subsequently informs Darya Mikhaylovna, who insists that Rudin quit the estate. Rudin then begins the aimless life described above.

While the main plot of the novel is hardly political and only tangentially related to Bakunin's life, Turgenev was quite careful to align the temperament of Rudin with that of his friend. Bakunin had the reputation of being "immensely energetic" and highly emotional, known more for his ability to elaborate upon the ideas of others than to originate his own.[21] Rudin, likewise, is said to be possessed of great enthusiasm (157); he overwhelms people with "his rushing and impassioned dialectic" (67), but however excellent he may be at developing an argument, "the ideas weren't produced in his head: he took them from others" (95). Another feature of Bakunin's personality was that his extravagant interest in ideas weakened his attachments to people. In the novel, the alienated friend Lezhnev is evidently based on Bakunin's friend Vissarion Belinsky, who first met Bakunin as a student of romanticism in Moscow. Lezhnev criticizes Rudin in terms almost as severe as the words Belinsky used to describe Bakunin: "A marvelous man, a deep, primitive leonine nature—this cannot be denied him. But his demands, his childishness, his braggadocio, his unscrupulousness, his disingenuousness —all this makes friendship with him impossible. He loves ideas, not men. He wants to dominate with his personality, not to love." [22] The ideas themselves are sparse in *Rudin,* but they are clearly stamped with the romantic philosophy Bakunin first picked up in Moscow in 1837. The best example of the intellectual tenor of the novel is Rudin's Hegelian explanation of the relationship between egoism and truth:

> Rudin began speaking about egoistical ambition, and he began speaking very effectively. He argued that a man without ambition is a nonentity, that ambition was the lever of Archimedes with which the earth could be moved, but at the same time the only person who deserves the name of man is he who knows how to control his egoistical ambition, as a rider controls a horse, who can sacrifice self-interest to the general good . . .
> "Egoism," he concluded, "is suicide. The egocentric man dries up like a solitary, barren tree; but egoism as an active aspiration to perfection is the source of all that it is great. . . . Yes! A man must destroy the stubborn egoism in his own personality, in order to give it the right to express itself!" (61)

Here, Fichte's admonition to renounce the individual ego for the sake of the absolute sounds through, along with Bakunin's own Hegelian idea of creative destruction.

Although Bakunin himself has been called a type of "the 'superfluous man' made famous by Turgenev," [23] Rudin's ardent ideas prove less superfluous than at first they seem. Even Lezhnev recovers his former admiration for his old friend, whose emotional power enlivens everyone he meets: "We have all become intolerably rational, indifferent, and effete; we have gone to sleep, we have grown cold, and we should be grateful to anyone who rouses us and warms us, if only for a moment! It's time to wake up!" (157). While the statement in isolation may be interpreted to imply spiritual renewal rather than political revolution, the revolutionary meaning grows when it is placed in the context of other statements, including Rudin's cryptic observation that "on an oak—and an oak is a strong tree—the old leaves only begin falling when the young ones have begun to break through" (90). In 1860, Turgenev added a new ending to the novel he had completed four years earlier that forces a reassessment of the political meaning of much of the novel. The original ending has the narrator siding with the reliable but sedentary provincial Lezhnev, and merely taking pity on the rootless and superfluous Rudin: "The long autumn night set in. Happy is he who sits under a roof on such a night, who has a warm nook to go to. . . . And may the good Lord help all homeless wanderers" (180). The new ending needs to be quoted at length:

> In the midday heat of 26 June 1848, in Paris, when the rising of the "national workshops" was already being suppressed, in one of the narrow streets of the Faubourg St. Antoine a battalion of regular army was taking a barricade. Cannon-fire had already smashed it; those of its defenders who remained alive were abandoning it and thinking only of their own safety when suddenly on the top of it, on the broken body of an overturned omnibus, there appeared a tall man in an old frock-coat with a broad red scarf tied around his waist and a straw hat on his grey dishevelled hair. In one hand he held a red flag, in the other a blunt, curved sword, and he was shouting something in a strained, high-pitched voice, scrambling up the barricade and waving both the flag and the sword. A Vincennes sharpshooter took aim and fired. . . . The tall man dropped the flag and fell face forward like a sack, just as if he was falling at someone's feet. . . . The bullet had passed through his heart.
>
> "*Tiens!*" said one of the fleeing *insurgés* to another, "*on vient de tuer le Polonais.*"
>
> "*Bigre!*" the other answered and both of them dashed into the cellar of a house with closed shutters and walls pock-marked by bullets and shell-shot.
>
> The *Polonais* was Dmitry Rudin.   (180–81)

The new conclusion alludes to Bakunin's revolutionary involvement that grew throughout the 1840s and reached a climax in 1849. He was, indeed, present in Paris when revolution broke out in February 1848, and lived with the working-class national guard. He did not fight on the barricades, however; but he did secure a loan of two thousand francs from the rebels to be used "for revolutionary work" and set out for eastern Europe with the intent of fomenting a pan-Slavic rebellion. In this connection, the mistaken identification of Rudin at the end of the novel as a *Polonais* chimes with Bakunin's long-standing interest in Polish affairs. In 1832, as a young artillery officer in Minsk and Grodno he witnessed the aftermath of the anti-czarist insurrection of 1831. In 1847, he delivered his first public speech to a group of fifteen hundred Polish refugees at a ceremony commemorating the 1831 insurrection. Bakunin's pan-Slavic efforts of 1848 came to naught, but he did wind up in Dresden in 1849, where he witnessed the flight of the king of Saxony and five days of provisional, revolutionary government. In Dresden Bakunin *did* fight on the barricades, and was arrested when the Prussian troops retook the city. Unlike most of the insurrectionists, Bakunin escaped execution, but was held for a year in a Saxon jail before being transferred to Austria and then to Russia, where he was imprisoned from 1851 to 1857, then banished to Siberia until the time of his escape in 1861. It was only after his return to Europe (via Japan and America) that his true anarchist phase began.[24]

Turgenev's new conclusion to *Rudin* telescopes three aspects of Bakunin's revolutionary activity into one event: it combines his Paris activity with his Polish sympathies, even as it elides Rudin's death on the barricades with Bakunin's capture and imprisonment. In this light, the ending is quite ambiguous. On the one hand, since the ending was written before Bakunin's escape from Siberia, Turgenev seems to imply that a noble death on the barricades is preferable to political exile. On the other hand, he may have regarded Bakunin's revolutionary potential as so dangerous to society that his death would have been the preferred outcome to his career in 1848. The ending therefore emphasizes the ambivalent status Rudin has throughout the novel: as a force of both renewal and instability, substance and superfluity, the character represents a welcome change who wears out his welcome rather quickly. It is also possible to read the ending as an expression of Turgenev's naturalistic, anti-Hegelian philosophy. Given such a philosophy, the conflicts that the novel chronicles between nature and society, and between ego and altruism, are irreconcilable. In the novel, the belief in a selfless society that is beneficial and good is represented by Rudin's mentor; the egoistic nature of man is represented by the self-centered aristocrat who becomes Rudin's temporary patron, and Rudin is caught between these two forces. The effects of the conflict are played out in the meeting of Rudin and Natalya, where Rudin shows himself to be incapable of the satisfactions of nature and ego that human love would entail. Instead, he submits to an abstract fate and consents to suffer.[25] Turgenev's pessimistic belief that environment and heredity are immutable forces therefore works against the politics of the novel, making Rudin's death at the end of it a meaningless sacrifice that is fully consonant with naturalism. This will not be the only instance when the politics of anarchism proves to be incompatible with a traditional cultural form (as we shall see in Chapter 3), which only makes the contrary point that one day the old forms will not suffice for the artist with anarchistic sympathies.

3

The period of Bakunin's imprisonment and exile (1849–61) corresponds to the period between the turbulent revolutionary era in Europe and the age of peasant unrest in Russia. In *Rudin*, Turgenev charted the route taken by a member of the Russian intelligentsia from romanticism to revolution, which also happens to be the first phase of Bakunin's political development. In *The Possessed*, Dostoyevsky chronicled the collapse of romanticism and revolution into anarchistic nihilism, a movement that also matches an important phase of Bakunin's later career. While some biographers question how well Dostoyevsky knew Bakunin or whether he ever met him at all, and critics disagree over how closely the character Stavrogin in *The Possessed* resembles Bakunin,[26] there is no question that Bakunin is part of the general mélange of idealism, liberalism, socialism, and nihilism that Dostoyevsky satirizes in the novel. Indeed, the general political tenor of the work was evident to Dostoyevsky from the start. As he was preparing to write his novel he expected it to "turn out to be nothing but a pamphlet" that would succeed "in a tendentious rather than an artistic sense."[27] The strongest specific connection between the novel and anarchism concerns Bakunin's fanatical "disciple" Nechaev, who seems, in fact, to have turned the older anarchist into the advocate of the violence for which he is so well known today. When Nechaev conspired with four other revolutionaries to murder a student named Ivanov for no apparent reason, Dostoyevsky took note in a letter of October 1870: "One of the main events in my tale will be Ivanov's murder by Nechaev." [28] One does not have to commit what one critic calls the "gross error" of taking Dostoyevsky's "highly exaggerated and polemical narrative as a precise rendering of social conditions" [29] to say that the Nechaev affair was a decisive influence on the writing of *The Possessed.* The characters Peter Verhovensky and Shatov are not "precise renderings" of their historical counterparts Nechaev and Ivanov, but they are the means whereby history is rendered into cultural form.

Bakunin met Sergei Nechaev in Geneva in 1869. The young student from Moscow was Bakunin's junior by some thirty years, but the older man was immediately taken with Nechaev's revolutionary ardor and they became friends. Together they formed one of the innumerable anarchist associations Bakunin was so fond of establishing (often with only himself numbering the full membership). This one was called the "World Revolutionary Alliance" and Nechaev was "designated as Agent No. 271 of the Russian section." [30] Together they collaborated on seven revolutionary pamphlets, the best-known being the "Revolutionary Catechism." It is now believed that Bakunin only approved this particular pamphlet but did not have a hand in writing any part of it himself. [31] In any case, the bombastic document is unyielding in its promotion of violent revolution:

> The revolutionist despises every sort of doctrinarianism and has renounced the peaceful scientific pursuits, leaving them to future generations. He knows only one science, the science of destruction . . .
>
> The nature of the real revolutionist precludes every bit of sentimentality, romanticism or infatuation and exchange. It precludes even personal hatred and revenge. Revolutionary passion having become a normal phenomenon, it must be combined with cold calculation . . .
>
> . . . Our business is destruction, terrible, complete, universal, and merciless . . .
>
> Let us join with the bold world of bandits—the only genuine revolutionists in Russia. [32]

To Dostoyevsky, this kind of revolutionary ardor amounts to demonic possession—hence the title of the novel with its opening epitaph from the New Testament story of the devils cast into the herd of swine. When Nechaev returned to Russia from Geneva he provided Dostoyevsky with a specific instance of demonic revolutionary possession when he murdered Ivanov. Of equal importance, however, is the general equation of revolutionary fervor with possession, an analogy

Bakunin made himself. In his *Letters to a Frenchman* (1870), Bakunin encouraged revolutionary activity in the unstable period following the Franco-Prussian War by urging his readers to "unbridle that popular anarchy . . . let it loose in all its breadth, so that it may flow like a furious lava, scorching and destroying everything in its path. . . . I know that this is a dangerous and barbarous way, but without it there is no salvation. It is essential that [revolutionaries] should be *possessed by a demon,* and nothing but the anarchy of revolution can fill their bodies with this demon."[33]

In the novel, this type of anarchistic nihilism is opposed by liberalism and idealism, but this does not mean that liberalism and idealism are therefore any less "demonic" than nihilism. Nihilism may be the most extreme form of "possession," but it is only one of the many devils of European ideology that Dostoyevsky sees as an impediment to the establishment of an orthodox Christian but culturally authentic Russian state. In the novel, the liberal idealist Stephan Trofimovich Verhovensky is opposed by his nihilist son Peter Verhovensky, and one of Dostoyevsky's points seems to be that the idealism favored by the father and the generation of Russian intelligentsia that came of age in the 1840s has resulted in the nihilism of the 1870s. The two groups confront each other at a "literary matinee" where Stephan Trofimovich Verhovensky voices his support of culture in terms that recall Matthew Arnold's subtler argument for anarchy as the alternative to culture: "Shakespeare and Raphael are of greater value than the emancipation of the serfs, than nationalism, than socialism, than the younger generation, than chemistry— and perhaps even than mankind itself! And it is this way because they represent the very highest human achievement, an achievement of beauty without which I wouldn't be willing to go on living."[34] The man of culture takes a dim view of social change: "The former serfs are free and they heartily whack at each other with cudgels instead of being flogged by the former serf owners" (507). Here, the intelligentsia and the revolutionaries are at odds; elsewhere, however, the two groups come together. Peter Verhovensky gains support from the gentry for his revolutionary activities not because of shared beliefs but because of fashion. Dostoyevsky satirizes Turgenev's interest in European intellectual fashion when he parodies him in the figure of Governor von Lembke, who becomes involved with the nihilist Peter Verhovensky but fails to understand the implications of that involvement. Dostoyevsky also uses the Governor's wife to make the point that even the gentry can be overtaken by the "devils" of political revolution when he describes Mrs. von Lembke's periodic interest in "violent and eccentric movements" as a form of divine inspiration: "[S]he felt somehow that she was some sort of chosen creature, almost an anointed one, upon whom 'a tongue of flame' had descended" (327).

Dostoyevsky is capable of satirizing both the older generation of Russian intellectuals and the younger group of revolutionaries. Romantic idealism and "utilitarian" nihilism alike are subject to his satire because they are both variants of an alien culture, a pair of European devils Dostoyevsky would have liked to exorcise from Russia. Indeed, Dostoyevsky pointed to the lesson Pushkin learned, after "having assimilated Europeanism through every pore": that Russian culture "could never be truly European and was confronted with the problem of its historical destiny." He even described the Russian people as "separated into two parties"—the Slavophils and Westerners—engaged in "a furious civil war" that is really a war for Russian cultural identity.[35] At the end of his life Dostoyevsky set down some notes for an article titled "Socialism and Christianity" that described a philosophy of history in which the kind of individualism encouraged by anarchism is a symptom of decadence. In the earliest primitive ages, "God is the collective idea of humanity, the masses, *everyone.* When man lives in masses (in the primitive patriarchal communities, about which legends have been left)—then man lives *spontaneously.*" This period is followed by "the transitional period, i.e., further development, i.e., civilization. (Civilization is a transitional period.) In this further development comes a phenomenon, a new fact, which no one can escape; this is the development of personal consciousness and the negation of spontaneous ideas and laws (authoritarian, patriarchal laws of the masses)." The advent of personal consciousness also negates faith in God, a condition that is clearly decadent: "The disintegration of the masses into personalities, or civilization, is a diseased state."[36]

The diseased state of civilization describes the condition of Europe as Dostoyevsky saw it. The cure for this condition was not to be found in politics, but in a return to the human ideal embodied by the example of Christ: "This would lead to the restoration of whatever unity is still realizable on earth; and such new unity . . . would be on a higher level—it would no longer be a unity of instinct, but one achieved through a self-conscious surrender of the will." [37] Interestingly, one of the few models that Dostoyevsky had for this unified society was at least partly anarchistic. A young clergyman and Slavophil named Afanasy Prokofievich Shchapov saw religious schism in the Russian Orthodox Church "as a native form of defiance against the imposition of foreign customs and ideas," that is, as a reaction to those same European influences that so concerned Dostoyevsky. In a work titled *The Land and the Schism*, Shchapov described the sect of the Beguny (Runners or Wanderers), who rejected every form of secular law and wandered throughout Russia in defiance of "all the obligations imposed upon them by the godless state." The Beguny have been called "religious and unself-conscious anarchists." Dostoyevsky came to see this type of religious dissent as "a protest against the domination of Western ideas and values; and he sought in the heretical theology of the sects an insight into the indigenous essence of the Russian folk character." [38] Joseph Frank compares Dostoyevsky himself to another wanderer, the one described by Matthew Arnold in "Stanzas from the Grande Chartreuse": "Wandering between two worlds, one dead, / The other powerless to be born, / With no place to rest [his] head." [39] Like Arnold, Dostoyevsky rejected the politics of his own time because he saw at the end only anarchy, nihilism, and decadence; also like Arnold, the idea of culture he imagined as an alternative to the abyss has much in common with anarchism.

4

Henry James's *The Princess Casamassima* (1886) makes Dostoyevsky's peripheral issues of culture and class central to the novel of anarchism. In *The Possessed*, aristocratic interest in the anarchist underground as a form of politico-social "slumming" is, at best, secondary to the larger philosophical theme that Russian culture must be based in Christian morality. Also, Dostoyevsky's novel presents the nihilistic world of Russian anarchism as a demonic but unified front against order of any kind, political or otherwise: Stavrogin is "demonized" in the special sense implied by the title of the novel and keeps the nihilist "faith" throughout. In James's novel the members of the political underground are not quite so unwavering in their commitment to the cause, and the aristocrats are not the only characters who gravitate toward ideologies outside of the class into which they were born. The Princess Casamassima's curiosity about the lower orders of society is a predictable eccentricity of her class, but Hyacinth Robinson's aristocratic instincts are harder to comprehend. On the surface, at least, the explanation that James offers for his lower-class hero's dual affinity for radical politics and aristocratic culture is the deterministic drive of heredity. As the illegitimate offspring of a proper English aristocrat and a Frenchwoman with a revolutionary lineage, Hyacinth feels his blood pulling him in two very different directions.

"You see I am quite the Naturalist," James wrote to his friend T. S. Perry as he was "collecting notes for a fiction scene" that wound up in *The Princess Casamassima*.[40] Other letters of this period make James's interest in the naturalist school clear, as do references in the novel itself "to certain members of an intensely modern school, advanced and scientific realists," whom Hyacinth means to read.[41] But whether the work is truly typical of the naturalist school is an open question. This question of genre, in turn, complicates the presentation of politics in the novel; that is, the scientific dictates of naturalism run counter to the aims of revolutionary politics. The naturalistic novel usually assumes that the machinery of environment and heredity is sufficiently powerful to cancel out the kind of human intervention in individual and social destiny that politics involves: evolution, not revolution, forms individuals and shapes society. It is also true that naturalist writers, at least those who follow the model of Zola most closely, set their fictional experiments in motion to show just how powerfully oppressive present society is, and there is no mistaking the moral and political intent of such a presentation. In Zola's *Nana*, if the title character's choices for individual development are taken away by the deterministic dictates of the social environment, the implicit message is that the social environment needs to be reformed. The naturalist novel, however, cannot include any concrete efforts toward reformation as part of its narrative as the narrative itself is governed by the deterministic "laws" it describes. The conundrum of the deterministic narrative produced by the socially progressive author has many implications. One is that naturalism, paradoxically, may not be that far removed from the art for art's sake sensibility that can easily be taken as its aesthetic opposite. The two modes seem to be opposed because of the radical differences in social milieu that each involves. No one is likely to imagine Huysmans's Des Esseintes having the characters from Zola's *Germinal* over for dinner after a day at the mines, and no one has to, since Huysmans's break with Zola is a fact of literary history. But this separation of the decadent aesthete from the moralistic naturalist collapses when the political implications of naturalist fiction are held up to the light. The method of naturalism means that Zola's novels are just as hermetic as Huysmans's: his self-contained systems of deterministic laws box the naturalist into a political aporia just as securely as the aesthete's rituals of taste close him off from social reality. In a curious way, then, the quasi-aristocratic James is perfectly suited to author a naturalist novel. Indeed, *The Princess Casamassima* only makes explicit the conservative implications of the deterministic formula whereby environment and heredity combine to limit the possibility of political change, especially that radical variety of change envisaged by anarchism.

The deterministic limitations placed on Hyacinth Robinson are announced early on in the name that James invents for his hero's environment: Lomax Place. The oxymoronic name suggests an intensity of social deprivation—the maximum of lowness—that anticipates the paradoxical social trajectories of the characters. The social origin of practically every character, in fact, is either "high" or "low," but low and high alike imagine social careers that take them in a direction contrary to their origins. Hyacinth's lowness and liberal politics derive from his mother, Florentine Vivier, whose father "had fallen, in the blood-stained streets of Paris, on a barricade, with his gun in his hand" (123). As a young boy, Hyacinth visited his mother in Newgate Prison, but only learned the reason for her imprisonment years later, when he read the *Times*'s account of the episode in the Reading Room of the British Museum. The "report of his mother's trial for the murder of Lord Frederick Purvis" makes Hyacinth assume, as does everyone else, that the murder of the duke is proof of paternity, and that he is, indeed, Lord Frederick's son: "the reflection that he was a bastard involved in a remarkable manner the reflection that he was a gentleman" (122, 123). Hyacinth's dual heritage and double identity is mirrored by his adoptive mother Amanda Pynsent and his surrogate father Anastasius Vetch. Miss Pynsent is "a poor little woman who [takes] lodgers" to supplement the meager income from her sewing shop. She also adores the aristocracy, reads novels about them, pours over Burke's *Peerage,* and has the fantasy of catering to the fashionable world of London society, as her shop sign indicates:

MISS AMANDA PYNSENT.

Modes et Robes

DRESSMAKING IN ALL ITS BRANCHES. COURT-DRESSES,
MANTLES AND FASHIONABLE BONNETS   (24)

Her neighbor Mr. Vetch, on the other hand, has "the nerves, the sensibilities, of a gentleman." We are told that "the shape of his hand was distinctly aristocratic," even though he "play[s] a fiddle at a second-rate theatre for a few shillings a week" (17). His artistic vocation requires that he wear evening dress, a boutonniere, and a monocle, but the aristocratic garb belies his politics—"his blasphemous republican, radical views, and the contemptuous manner in which he expressed himself about the nobility" (17). This pattern of "class oxymoron" is really the figure in the carpet in this novel: the aristocrats follow the downward arc into social deprivation, while those who are truly deprived are urged upward into the cultural space vacated by the slumming blue-bloods.

The Princess Casamassima thinks of herself as somehow outside the class distinctions that inform her every action. When Hyacinth visits the Princess at her fashionable South Street home he is overawed by her splendor and elegance. Sitting on a sofa of "rose-coloured brocade, of which the legs and frame appeared to be of pure gold," his eyes playing over "the innumerable *bibelots* . . . involved in the personality of a woman of high fashion," Hyacinth feels that "their beauty and oddity revealed not only whole provinces of art, but refinements of choice, on the part of their owner" (200). When the Princess appears she makes a point of separating herself from these aristocratic refinements: "I ought to let you know that I have very little respect for distinctions of class—the sort of thing they make so much of in this country" (203–4). Her companion, Madame Grandoni (whose name seems to turn *grand* into a diminutive), remarks on the Princess's interest in "the lower orders, the *basso popolo*": "Oh, she wishes to raise them" (195). How much she raises the lower orders is questionable, but she does make the effort to "lower" herself by giving up her country estate, changing her London address to a working-class neighborhood, trading her English butler for an Italian maid, reading books on "Labour and Capital" (406), and using her estranged husband's money to finance the social revolution. Like Hyacinth, the Princess is of mixed parentage, "American on the mother's side, Italian on the father's" (205), but, unlike Hyacinth, she feels the urge of blood from her "lower" half and is therefore destined for democracy. She meets Hyacinth through her would-be lover Captain Sholto, who later takes the measure of the Princess's politics when he tells Hyacinth: "I was looking for anything that would turn up, that might take her fancy. Don't you understand that I'm always looking? There was a time when I went in immensely for illuminated missals, and another when I collected horrible ghost-stories (she wanted to cultivate a belief in ghosts), all for her. The day I saw she was turning her attention to the rising democracy I began to collect little democrats. That's how I collected you" (305–6). In other words, the Princess Casamassima's interest in politics is, at base, aesthetic. Elsewhere, Madame Grandoni consoles the Prince Casamassima by telling him that his wife's interest in Hyacinth is hardly romantic: "I told you the other day that she is making studies of the people—the lower orders. The young man you saw is a study" (215). The Princess herself tells Hyacinth she wants to know "the *people*" because they are "the most interesting portion of society." The connection of this new interest in the people with her earlier interest in ghost stories is clear: "I can't leave them alone; they press upon me, they haunt me, they fascinate me" (204). Also, Captain Sholto's comment about "little democrats" refers to Hyacinth's small stature, an attribute that makes the man (and his politics) all the more "collectible." At Hyacinth's first visit to the Princess's South Street home, the first thing she says when she makes her entrance betrays the element of connoisseurship in her political ardor: "I have kept you a long time, but it's supposed not, usually, to be a bad place, my salon; there are various things to look at, and perhaps you have noticed them. Over on the side, for instance, there is a rather curious collection of miniatures" (201). Hyacinth has been enlisted as her guide to the political underworld of London—"I expect you to take me into the slums—into very bad places" (210), but it is clear that the experience of visiting these "bad places" is not categorically different from hearing ghost stories, and that the diminutive Hyacinth is one more in her collection of miniatures.

Hyacinth Robinson becomes active in radical politics when he makes the acquaintance of Paul Muniment, a Scotsman whose accent and straightforward manners seem to locate him securely in the working class. At first, Hyacinth imagines that Muniment has recruited him as a "high type" in his "subterranean crusade against the existing order of things" (105). But the existing order eventually works out just fine for Muniment, a chemist's assistant, who later experiences "a rise, at the chemical works," and takes a most unrevolutionary attitude toward the wretched of the earth: "he sometimes emitted a short satiric gleam which showed that his esteem for the poor was small and that if he had no illusions about the people who had got everything into their hands he had as few about those who had egregiously failed to do so" (348). The "subterranean" revolutionary, then, is also a self-made man working his way up the economic ladder. The pattern of class oxymoron is repeated in the person of Muniment's sister Rosy, an "irrepressible invalid" possessed of such "contradictious optimism" that she construes her inability to leave her room as a great social advantage: "I know all about the London season, though I never go out" (166, 167). Rosy's politics are even more "contradictious" than her brother's: "I haven't the least objection to seeing the people improved, but I don't want to see the aristocracy lowered an inch. I like so much to look at it up there" (102). Rosy's lowness is literally elevated, at the height of "seventy-seven stairs," and the aristocracy looks up to her in the person of Lady Aurora, who has turned the advantages of her class to charity work. She climbs the stairs to reach the heights of London lowness, and sit with the optimistic invalid. The paradoxical class-logic is so pervasive in *The Princess Casamassima* that it informs diction and imagery alike. The first "appearance" of Lady Aurora and Rosy —who both bear literary names related to the dawn—is in total darkness. Hyacinth first visits the Muniments' flat at night and finds the place unlighted. The "small bright voice" of Rosy announces "we are sitting in the dark. . . . Lady Aurora is so kind; she's here still" (83).

The multiple reversals set in motion by James's oxymoronic treatment of class drive the plot of the novel to its ironic denouement. The downwardly mobile Princess abandons Hyacinth because, she claims, "he is not like me. . . . He's a tremendous aristocrat" (422). But Hyacinth's aristocracy is not of class but of culture, and he eventually abandons politics for civilization and its discontents: "The monuments and treasures of art, the great palaces and properties, the conquests of learning and taste, the general fabric of civilisation as we know it, based, if you will, upon all the despotisms, the cruelties, the exclusions, the monopolies and the rapacities of the past, but thanks to which, all the same, the world is less impracticable and life more tolerable—our friend Hoffendahl seems to me to hold them too cheap" (353–54). Just as Hyacinth gives up his earlier political calling, Lady Aurora gives up her charity work and returns to society, in part because the Princess has gained the affections of Paul Muniment, for whom she had developed a vaguely matrimonial yearning. Muniment's own removal from the politics he espouses is certified both by his cultivation of the Princess's company and by a certain distrust of his allegiance to the cause on the part of his radical colleagues. The anarchist leader Hoffendahl chooses not to convey the crucial order to Hyacinth instructing him to assassinate a duke through Muniment but through a German comrade, Schinkel. In the end, neither Muniment nor the Princess are "trusted at headquarters" (540) while Hyacinth, somewhat improbably, is. At first he intends to commit the act in the name of the social revolution in which he no longer believes solely out of an aristocratic sense of duty, until an even stronger impulse makes itself felt, namely, "the horror of the public reappearance, on his part, of the imbrued hands of his mother." The fear of repeating in his own life the sins of the mother and thereby reviving the sense of "a personal stain" (544) upon them both drives Hyacinth to turn the gun intended for the duke upon himself.

Hyacinth Robinson's suicide, then, does not follow solely from his inability to reconcile politics and culture. In fact, he is all but resolved to give up both for "a quick flight" somewhere, "for an undefined purpose" with Millicent Henning, the childhood playmate who has grown up into a handsome shopgirl with a generous breast and social ambitions. He has the hope that Millicent, with her "spontaneous, uncultivated mind," might be capable of some "invention" or "inspiration" that could save him: "Mightn't she help him—mightn't she even extricate him?" (546). In this frame of mind he hurries to the shop where she works, only to find Captain Sholto there ahead of him. The two men exchange looks whose meaning "requires perhaps no definite mention" (548), since the mere pres-

ence of Sholto confirms his place in Millicent's affections. Direct
narrative commentary about Hyacinth's subsequent thoughts and
actions ends at this point, but the immediate events leading up to
the suicide imply that the act is motivated as much by disappointed
love as by anything else. In fact, the probable causes for the suicide
are manifold: the fear of reviving public memory of his mother's
shameful act combines with the successive loss of the three people who have done so much to form Hyacinth's cultural, political,
and sexual identity—the Princess, Paul Muniment, and Millicent
Henning.[42]

Such complications are lost on Hoffendahl's associate Schinkel,
who, together with the Princess, finds Hyacinth's body with a bullet
through the heart. He also finds the pistol the suicide has used, picks
it up, and reflects that "it would certainly have served much better
for the Duke" (553). Given Hyacinth Robinson's cultural maturation, the ironic end of *The Princess Casamassima* suggests that, yes, the
pistol should have been used on the Duke, that the growth of culture
is preferable to the perpetuation of the old social order. But had he
fulfilled his anarchist mission, Hyacinth, the child of culture, would
have destroyed himself anyway. One possible conclusion the ironic
ending suggests is that anarchy is culture and not politics: one does
not combat but compensates for the other. Culture, not politics, can
reform society, the master irony being that the old political norms,
the ancient oppressive structures, have produced a liberating culture
that allows individuals to experience anarchistic freedom. Hyacinth,
for example, is never so free as when he roams the streets of Paris
and Venice taking in the monuments of the past. The culture of the
past, in fact, gives Hyacinth what the politics of the future promises.

The elevation of culture over politics in a novel by Henry James
can hardly be called surprising, but the explicit and detailed treatment of politics in this particular novel complicates the predictable
positioning of high culture. The politics described in the novel
clearly pose a threat to culture, but the nature of the threat is not so
clear. Lionel Trilling was the first to make an extended argument for
an authentic representation of anarchism in *The Princess Casamassima,* noting many details of resemblance between the novel and
actual anarchist practice. Trilling observes, for example, that the
revolutionaries in James's novel are not the proletarian factory workers favored by socialists but the tradesmen and artisans preferred by

anarchists: one is a cobbler, another a cabinetmaker, a third is a barber; Hyacinth and Eustace Poupin, a former Communard, are both bookbinders. Members of such vocations were attracted by anarchist politics, and the emphasis on bookbinding is especially interesting, as that was the profession of the German anarchist Johann Most. Trilling argues that the much-traveled Most is the model for the mysterious Hoffendahl, who never appears in the novel but nonetheless remains a compelling political presence.[43] In Germany, Most had been a socialist but was expelled from the Social Democratic Party when he came under the influence of Bakunin's ideas. In 1878 he left Germany for London where he founded *Die Freiheit* (Liberty), an anarchist paper in which propaganda by the deed was openly encouraged.[44] When Czar Alexander II was assassinated in 1881, Most editorialized his approval in *Freiheit* through an article titled "At Last!" in which the deed was termed "heroic" and "Brutus-like." As a result of his endorsement of political assassination Most was arrested and sentenced in late June 1881 to sixteen months in prison.[45] Although the action in James's novel cannot be precisely dated,[46] some of the events evidently occur over the same period as Johann Most's imprisonment. The point of this speculation is that Hoffendahl's identity as Most may be implied by the fact that he never appears: his absence may be an indirect reference to Most's imprisonment. But it seems unlikely that James would have to strain to establish a single, exact historical correspondence for the fictional Hoffendahl. Another critic proposes the German terrorist August Reinsdorf as the model for Hoffendahl, noting that James most likely would have read about Reinsdorf's plot to assassinate the kaiser in the *Times* during December 1884.[47] It is true that these events appeared in the newspapers as James was preparing to write *The Princess Casamassima,* and that Reinsdorf delegated the assassination of the German emperor to his associates, as Hoffendahl orders the murder of the Duke in the novel. Reinsdorf, however, only committed the action to subordinates because he had injured his foot (a reference in James's novel to Hoffendahl's "mutilated hand" [250] may echo this detail) and could not perform the deed himself. Moreover, the attempt was botched when the would-be terrorists Reinsdorf entrusted with the bomb allowed it to become so waterlogged in a rainstorm that it failed to detonate.[48] The whole affair seems rather bungling and amateurish in comparison with the impression of masterly calculation that James suggests through his evocation of the mysterious Hoffendahl. In any case, James would not have been limited to Reinsdorf and Most as models for his German mastermind, since from 1884 on there were quite a few anarchists from Germany living in exile in London: Victor Dave, Josef Peukert, John Neve, Otto Rinke, and others. The purpose of German anarchism in London, however, was primarily the exportation of propaganda back to Germany, not interference in the political life of Great Britain. In addition, the German anarchists generally kept to themselves.[49] Hoffendahl's position as the leader of an international group of English, Scottish, and French anarchists in James's novel is in large degree historically anomalous.

The idea that *The Princess Casamassima* offers "a very accurate account of anarchism," as Trilling has it, is somewhat off the mark. In 1952 George Woodcock reacted to Trilling's claim by asserting that James's version of anarchism "did not in any way represent that movement as it existed in the 1880's or at any other time."[50] Support for this claim comes from the historical record of the anarchist movement, which never relied on the sort of hierarchical system of revolutionary authority, with Hoffendahl at the top, that James devises for the novel. As Woodcock says, "An authoritarian circle of conspiratorial leaders, such as James imagines in *The Princess Casamassima,* was wholly inconsistent with the conception of spontaneous action and also with the general rejection of discipline which is implied in the doctrine and the very name of Anarchism."[51] Woodcock also observes that the political organization of the revolutionaries in the novel resembles that of the Italian Carbonari or the French Blanquists more so than it does the anarchists'. Blanqui, for example, "organized his followers in small, self-contained groups, each of which was in contact only through one representative with the level above."[52] This type of organization is suggested by James's novel, especially when Hyacinth receives the assassination order from Hoffendahl through the intermediary Schinkel. While it is true that the Blanquists might have suggested this cunning model of revolutionary organization to James, the model is also suggested by the Fenians, whose presence James would surely have felt more directly in the early 1880s in London than that of the Blanquists. While anarchist and Fenian terror are in no wise similar in terms of motivation (since the anarchists were ideologically opposed to nationalism), they are

quite similar in their effects. Indeed, Fenians were often called anarchists in both the popular and the socialist press because of their
shared recourse to dynamite.[53] A good example of this type of confusion concerns Johann Most himself. When the Fenians assassinated
Lord Frederick Cavendish in Phoenix Park outside Dublin in May
1882, Most was suspected of involvement in the affair even though
he was in prison at the time. The offices of *Die Freiheit* were raided
and two of Most's printers arrested, so strong was the suspicion of an
anarchist-Fenian alliance.[54] What seems likely, therefore, is that
James took this widespread notion of a conspiratorial underground
and created his own version of it for the novel, combining elements
from Fenianism and Continental anarchism as he saw fit, but without
concerning himself with the historical veracity of the unlikely political amalgam constructed thereby. James's presentation of anarchism
is, in a sense, accurate after all, but the "accuracy" he achieves is
indistinguishable from the popular, journalistic conception of an
anarchist "conspiracy" that appeared in the papers.

   With the exception of the unseen Hoffendahl, the revolutionaries in James's novel are compromised in various ways: Hyacinth by
aestheticism, Paul Muniment by careerism, and the Princess by a
perverse variety of class-engendered idealism. The lesser characters,
likewise, profess extremely curious forms of radicalism that James
delivers to the reader in highly satiric terms. The Communard Poupin, for instance, is a comic character whose politics are presented
with broad strokes of humor, as in this passage: "he believed that the
day was to come when all the nations of the earth would abolish
their frontiers and custom-houses, and embrace on both cheeks, and
cover the globe with boulevards, radiating from Paris, where the
human family would sit, in groups, at little tables, according to affinities, drinking coffee (not tea, *par exemple!*) and listening to the music
of the spheres" (67). The passage is a good indicator of James's
attitude toward politics in the novel, as is the description of the
Frenchman's home, decorated with "little portraits (old-fashioned
prints) of revolutionary heroes" (72). It is not clear whether the
prints derive from the revolution of 1789 or that of 1848, but the
question is less important than the general implication that political
revolution is old-fashioned, antiquated, obsolete—in short, unnecessary. But if the social revolution is populated by the inept and antiquated, then how can it pose a threat to culture? The answer may be

that *both* politics and culture are threatened by capitalist materialism. It is easy to make this argument by citing certain of James's other works, notably *The American Scene,* where the threat to culture comes from a society that is fragmented by the kind of separatist, competitive efforts that capitalism requires. James looks at the American scene and sees an empty, disconnected cityscape where the very buildings, the skyscrapers of New York, offer "the vividest lectures on the subject of individualism." [55] In *The Princess Casamassima,* the only "American" character is the Princess herself, but she pairs off with Paul Muniment, who, at novel's end, is clearly devoting himself more to his own economic advancement than to the advancement of society. Together with the Princess's abandonment of high culture, Paul Muniment's choice of materialism over progressive politics makes the two representative of something very like the sort of Americanism that James regarded as the antithesis of culture.

The threat to culture, then, is not necessarily anarchistic, but it is anarchic. As one critic puts it, "James's cultural conservatism is not simply a relapse into an outdated traditionalism, but a conscious response to the fragmentation and mechanization of modern life." [56] What is missing from modern life is the coherence that culture affords. In this assessment James has much in common with his friend Matthew Arnold; indeed, *The American Scene* has been called a "rewriting" of Arnold's *Culture and Anarchy.*[57] *The Princess Casamassima* likewise rewrites a number of Arnold's anxieties about class and culture, as when the anarchists meeting at their Bloomsbury bar proclaim that the only way to effect the social revolution is "to pull up the Park rails again—just to pluck them straight up" (238). James refers here to the Hyde Park Riots of 1866 that Arnold takes as evidence of anarchy and of a society in need of a corrective culture. James also uses Arnold's vocabulary when he has the Princess refer to herself and Hyacinth as a pair of barbarians set to sweep away the decadent old regime of established politics (270). Although the usage here involves the un-Arnoldian equation of barbarism with some regenerative social force, the Arnoldian meaning is incorporated by way of irony: an aristocrat uses the term to refer to herself, thereby unconsciously echoing Arnold's linkage of "our aristocratic class" with the barbarians.[58] James also has the Princess echo Arnold's admonition in "The Function of Criticism" that the duty of the critic is "to see the object as it really is" when she says of English society that she means "to learn for myself what it really is, before we blow it up" (270). But verbal parallelism is less important than the paradoxical ideology of culture that James and Arnold share. In both writers culture is threatened by the "anarchy" of a type of social modernity that is fragmented, materialistic, and individualistic. At the same time, however, culture itself has those same features insofar as it can only enter human consciousness in highly individual terms that are themselves produced by materialist conditions.

The ideology promoted by James and Arnold formulates culture as a highly coherent and unified tradition, but the actual human experience of that tradition is necessarily fragmented into an infinity of highly individualistic aesthetic responses that compose the consciousness of culture. In *The Princess Casamassima,* on two occasions Hyacinth has the sensation of feeling himself a tiny, atomistic fragment adrift in some larger, impersonal entity. The first comes in the context of the "social revolution" when he regards himself as "a mere particle in the immensity of the people" (151); the second arises when he spends the night at the Princess's country estate amid a profusion of "prints, mezzotints and old engravings," whereupon "it seemed to him more than ever that Mademoiselle Vivier's son was a tiny particle" (258). The passages make the point that the separate sensations of politics and culture are analogous: both are reducible to a highly particulate, individualistic experience not unlike the atomistic experience of anarchism. In fact, James, more so than Arnold, suggests an experience of culture that seems to transpose the politics of anarchism in that he welcomes the cultivation of a private aesthetic, and is far less anxious than Arnold about making culture assume the task of unifying society.[59] The personal, particulate experience of culture that James encourages therefore appears as an aesthetic version of the practice of "doing as one likes" that Arnold construed as anarchy.

5

Joseph Conrad's *The Secret Agent* continues the history of anarchism traced thus far through Turgenev's *Rudin,* Dostoyevsky's *The Possessed,* and James's *The Princess Casamassima,* as idealism and destructive revolution give way to terrorism, or "propaganda by the deed." Conrad's novel, published in 1907, provides a fictional explanation for the explosion at Greenwich Observatory on 15 February

1894. The accidental bombing was caused by one Martial Bourdin, who was severely injured in the blast and died a few days later, but without having revealed his motivation or his political connections, if any. In fact, investigations at the time soon revealed that Bourdin had a number of connections to anarchism. He had been a member of the French section of the anarchist Autonomie Club after his immigration to London; earlier, in Paris, he had associated with a society of tailors (Bourdin was by profession a ladies' tailor) called "L'Aiguille" (The Needle) that was largely anarchist; and, most important for Conrad's purposes, he was the brother-in-law of H. B. Samuels, publisher of the anarchist journal *Commonweal.* This last detail is significant because another London anarchist, David Nicoll, was jealous of Samuels's position at *Commonweal* and used the Greenwich episode to cast doubts on Samuels's loyalty to the cause. In Nicoll's version of events, published as the *Greenwich Mystery* in 1897, Bourdin is portrayed as an obedient simpleton "looking into his [Samuels's] eyes with loving trust," while Samuels is said to be in the pay of the police.[60] Neither assertion about the character of the two men is corroborated elsewhere,[61] but Nicoll's account was taken up by Conrad in his story of the trusting idiot Stevie and the self-serving police spy Verloc. In truth, Bourdin and Samuels can hardly be said to have collaborated at all in bringing about the bombing. Further, there was no reason to believe the observatory itself had been targeted at all: Bourdin may have been delivering the explosives to someone else, or may have been attempting to hide them for later use.[62] The "explanation" that the explosion was some kind of anarchist attack was fabricated at the time by the Conservative press and government. No evidence of any kind was offered to establish the event as an anarchist act, and the assertion that it was may have been a form of political propaganda directed against the Fenians, since "all the bombings in the metropolis in the last decade of the nineteenth century had Fenian nationalist origins."[63] In this connection, even though Conrad used Sir Robert Anderson's *Sidelights on the Home Rule Movement* for background information when he planned the novel,[64] he leaves Irish nationalism out of it and instead elaborates upon the fiction already provided by the government: that the bombing was an anarchist outrage.

According to the "Author's Preface" Conrad published in 1920, the novel was inspired by the "already old story" of the Greenwich bombing and by the "criminal futility" of anarchist terror.[65] In fact, when Conrad conceived the idea for the novel in 1905, propaganda by the deed was also already old, having been rejected by most anarchists as an ineffective weapon against government authority. The active terrorist phase of anarchism began in 1881, when Czar Alexander II was assassinated and the anarchist Congress of London officially endorsed the practice as a propaganda tool. The high tide of terrorist action occurred in the 1890s: in 1892, François Ravachol planted bombs in the homes of the judge and prosecutor who had sentenced a group of May Day protestors the year before; in 1894, Sadi Carnot, the president of France, was stabbed by an Italian anarchist; after this, several other heads of state fell at the hands of anarchist assassins: Premier Castillo of Spain in 1897, Empress Elizabeth of Austria in 1898, King Umberto of Italy in 1900, and President McKinley in 1901. An international antianarchist conference was held in Rome in 1898, but by then propaganda by the deed had almost run its course, with organized anarchists turning toward the general strike as the preferred method of social disruption.[66]

Anarchist bombing was becoming an increasingly remote possibility when Conrad's novel was published, and there is even something slightly anachronistic about the practice in 1894, when the novel is set. The anachronism is explained, however, in that the bombing is not planned by an anarchist group but by a foreign government. The government is unnamed, but it is likely to be that of Russia, since the first secretary of the embassy, Mr. Vladimir, speaks in "guttural Central Asian tones" and has czarist or, at least, royalist sympathies. The purpose of the terrorist act, moreover, is not to encourage the collapse of authority but to goad the public into supporting "a universal repressive legislation" (31, 26). An anarchist act is required to "stimulate the . . . vigilance of the police—and the severity of the magistrates" because the "general leniency of the judicial procedures here [in England], and the utter absence of all repressive measures, are a scandal to Europe" (14–15). The political irony deployed here, therefore, has an autocrat loyalist advocating anarchism for the purpose of "the accentuation of unrest" (15) that will, in turn, require the authorities to enact repressive measures to deal with that unrest. There is also some philosophical irony in Vladimir's notion that the terrorist act is to be directed against "science," which he calls the "sacrosanct fetish of today" (27), because so many anarchists used scientific positivism in support of their political theories. Although the anarchists never made it clear how terrorist acts—including the assassination of political figures—would lead to the stateless society, the rationale for those acts was clearly political, as in the chilling example of Emile Henry, who bombed a Parisian cafe in 1894 (just three days before the Greenwich explosion) and defended the act at his trial by saying, "There are no innocent bourgeois." [67] Vladimir, however, insists that "[a] bomb outrage to have any influence on public opinion now must go beyond the intention of vengeance or terrorism. It must be purely destructive. It must be that, and only that, beyond the faintest suspicion of any other object" (28). While some anarchists might have thought of the division of the world into time zones as an extreme imposition of order by authority, so that an attack on the site of that authority might make sense from an anarchist perspective, this rationale is not entertained in the novel at all. The Greenwich bombing is presented as an anarchist act all right, but the act is so larded with irony that its political meaning is rendered absurd: antistatist scientific anarchism is sponsored by the state in an attack on science. In addition, the attack on Greenwich Observatory must appear pointless, so as to subvert subversion. At the same time, however, the agents of the law are effective mainly because they operate outside of it, in secrecy. Thus, active anarchism is subverted, but covert anarchism is endorsed as the only means of maintaining order in an increasingly fragmented society.

This absurdist quality extends to the description of all the anarchist characters who gather in the shop of Verloc, the secret agent in the service of both Vladimir's embassy and the London police. All the men who form the revolutionary circle about Verloc—Karl Yundt, Alexander Ossipon, and Michaelis—are parody versions of different varieties of nineteenth-century leftist ideology. All three are delegates of the "International Red Committee," but none of them seems worthy of the revolutionary calling they claim. Karl Yundt calls himself a terrorist but, as the narrator informs us, he "had never in his life raised personally as much as his little finger against the social edifice" (43). Instead, he merely dreams of an ideal anarchism that would purge the world of pessimism and other ills, an absolute destructiveness with a purely beneficent effect: "I have always dreamed . . . of a band of men absolute in their resolve to discard all scruples in the choice of means, strong enough to give themselves frankly the name of destroyers, and free from the taint of that resigned pessimism which rots the world. No pity for anything on earth, including themselves, and death enlisted for good and all in the service of humanity—that's what I would have liked to see" (38). Alexander Ossipon is the scientific revolutionary who relies on Cesar Lombroso's racist theories of physiognomy to detect degeneracy, while appearing to be a "degenerate" type himself, at least from the perspective of the narrator, who observes: "The disdainful pout of Comrade Ossipon's thick lips accentuated the negro type of his face" (45). Another irony attaches to Ossipon's dual allegiance to scientism and emotionalism: "The only thing that matters to us is the emotional state of the masses. Without emotion there is no action. . . . I am speaking now to you scientifically" (46). Finally, Michaelis is full of revolutionary energy but is physically inert, traits reflected in his political rhetoric, the point of which is simply that the present social system is inherently flawed and will eventually collapse of its own accord: "[H]e saw already the end of all private property coming along logically, unavoidably, by the mere development of its inherent viciousness" (39). Thus, the proper revolutionary course of action is no action at all, but rather an attitude of patient detachment: "History is made by men, but they do not make it in their heads. The ideas born in their consciousness play an insignificant part in the march of events. History is dominated by the tool and the production—by the force of economic conditions. Capitalism has made socialism, and the laws made by capitalism for the protection of property are responsible for anarchism. No one can tell what form the social organization may take in the future. Then why indulge in prophetic phantasies?" (37). Avrom Fleishman points out that Ossipon's philosophy echoes Marx's dictum that "men make their own history." He adds that "Conrad seems to have ascribed an exaggerated form of Marxism to the anarchists, and then showed its issue in non-Marxist utopian dreams." [68] The larger point to be made is that Conrad exaggerates this and other inconsistencies in revolutionary politics for comic effect. But he also takes the outright reactionary stance that any form of revolutionary sentiment derives from either fanaticism or vanity. The narrator puts forth the view that those "social rebels" who are not fanatics are "accounted

for by vanity, the mother of all noble and vile illusions, the companion of poets, reformers, charlatans, prophets, and incendiaries" (48).

Given this division, most of the political figures in the book are
products of vanity, but one is clearly driven by fanaticism. The character called "The Professor" is also called "the perfect anarchist,"
but despite this designation there is little about him that justifies the
use of the term. He positions himself outside the law by putting
himself beyond its reach: enough explosives are strapped to his body
to blow up himself and everything around him, including any arresting officer foolish enough to try and apprehend him. But by
placing himself outside the law he also positions himself outside
society, and in this regard he is no anarchist. He also espouses a
program of complete destruction without any sort of political program to go along with it, as when he says to Ossipon: "You plan the
future, you lose yourselves in reveries of economical systems derived
from what is; whereas what's wanted is a clean sweep and a clear start
for a new conception of life. That sort of future will take care of itself
if you will only make room for it" (67). The Professor is less an
anarchist than a terrorist without portfolio. Unlike the actual anarchists of the nineteenth century, he has no political model for future
society once the present one is swept away. The overriding irony
involved here concerns the character's anti-individualistic attitude:
"What happens to us as individuals is not of the least consequence"
(66). Over the course of the novel, however, the Professor's power is
revealed to be extremely limited because he can only act as an individual, and individual action alone is not sufficient to affect any but
a small portion of the great mass of humanity. In grappling with the
problem of the Professor's potential terrorism, Chief Inspector Heat
is consoled by the idea that the "teeming millions struggling upon
the planet"—including conventional criminals—are his allies
against the brand of terror represented by the Professor. The Professor is perhaps the least political figure in the novel: he expresses
disdain for all three delegates of the International Red Committee
and allies himself with no one. If he is the perfect anarchist, he is so
only in the sense that he perfects or brings to full completion the
anarchist concept of moral self-determination; the irony of this type
of self-determination, however, is that it is purchased at the price of
self-destruction.

If the Professor is the anarchist whose fanaticism drives him to the farthest verge of politics and makes him virtually apolitical as a result, then Verloc is the anarchist whose vanity allows him to absorb all manner of contradictory politics so that he becomes politically superfluous in the process. In one sense the two characters are contraries: the Professor's obsessive ideological focus is countered by Verloc's relaxed ideological diffusion. But they are curiously similar in that focus and diffusion come to the same thing in the end: both characters are isolated and outside of politics altogether, even though both have delusions of their political importance. Early in the novel Verloc gazes through the park railings at Hyde Park Corner and imagines himself the protector of the well-off Londoners "cantering past harmoniously" within (9). Standing at the site of the July 1866 riots, Verloc here seems as concerned as Matthew Arnold was to stay anarchy and maintain order. Aside from this general conservative concern, however, Verloc's politics are hard to pin down, and multiple ironies attach to his various ideological guises. His career as a bourgeois shopkeeper provides the cover for the royalist role he plays as an agent for a foreign government, while, at the same time, his underground life as an "anarchist" is sufficient subterfuge to make him useful to the British police, who use him to keep an eye on subversive political activity. To call Verloc a double agent, however, would be oversimple: he is required to assume one identity in his relations with Mr. Vladimir at the embassy, another in his meetings with Inspector Heat of the London police, yet another when he works with the revolutionary delegates, and still another with his wife at home. Each role interferes with the other. His marriage to Winnie is against anarchist principles (as Mr. Vladimir points out); his evident royalism and feigned anarchism, each incompatible with the other, are both incompatible with the Liberal British government who gains by his services as a police informer; his profession as a vendor of pornographic publications and other "shady wares" does not harmonize with "his vocation" as "a protector of society" (3); and all of Verloc's roles seem incompatible with his personality, whose main features are dullness and inertia. Although the novel has been called a precursor of the spy novel or espionage thriller, there is nothing thrilling about Verloc's metamorphosis from embassy agent to police spy, or from anarchist advocate to domestic dullard—mainly because there is no metamorphosis at all: Verloc is a consistent nonentity who does not change. Conrad's satirical point here may be that politics simply doesn't matter: one man's anarchist is another man's royalist.

Conrad relies on the method of comic exaggeration to suggest that all of the revolutionary characters in *The Secret Agent* are hypocrites at best or deluded madmen at worst. Yundt the terrorist never challenges the status quo; Ossipon the socialist survives by exploiting "silly girls with savings-bank books" (48); and Michaelis the "Marxist" anarchist lives off the largess of an aristocratic patroness who finds his radical views fashionable. Finally, the Professor and Verloc cancel each other out as radically dissimilar but equally ineffective figures. The sum of all this satire would seem to point favorably toward the society the revolutionary characters oppose, but the stable forces of liberal society come off almost as badly as their radical opponents. The police in particular seem more anarchistic than the anarchists, and just as hypocritical. For example, Chief Inspector Heat can only investigate the Greenwich bombing by operating outside the law, without using any of the official methods available to him. When Heat conducts his investigation he takes "pains to avoid all the police constables" and "maneuver[s] in a way which in a member of the criminal classes would have been stigmatized as slinking" (184). Heat also seems more interested in placing blame on an appropriately suspicious party—in this case, Michaelis—than in actually solving the crime. The Assistant Commissioner who takes over the case does so partly to protect Michaelis from Heat's machinations, since his wife frequents the same social circles as Michaelis's wealthy patroness. Like Heat, the Commissioner can only investigate the crime by behaving "as though he were a member of the criminal classes" (137). Earlier, the Professor asserts that the "terrorist and the policeman both come from the same basket. Revolution, legality —counter moves in the same game; forms of idleness at bottom identical" (64). Conrad's satire is not quite so reductive as this, but the perfect anarchist's political position may not be that far removed from the author's. Indeed, the absence of any clearly defined ideological base for the satire raises a number of questions about Conrad's politics. His treatment of the revolutionaries and of the police collapses them into the same "class" of criminals. In addition, the treatment of the representatives of the Liberal government hardly encourages the view that the author participates in that ideology any more than he participates in anarchism. Sir Ethelred, the home secretary, is under political attack over his bill for the nationalization of fisheries, which Tootles, his assistant, calls a "revolutionary measure" and his critics think is "the beginning of social revolution" (132). Sir Ethelred and the "revolutionary" Tootles are both comic figures, and it is evident that Conrad's ungrounded satire is not satire after all, but a form of irony that reduces every ideology to the same absurd, ineffectual level.

There is no question that *The Secret Agent* makes a critique of anarchism, but it is difficult to locate any political or moral principle that is used to take the measure of anarchism itself. This is both a political problem and an artistic one, since the absence of any sort of ideological ground would seem to obviate critical irony, or at least make it difficult to sustain the irony over the course of the book. The critique would have been easier to manage had Conrad articulated some ideology to counter anarchism, as E. Douglas Fawcett did in an earlier anti-anarchist novel, *Hartmann the Anarchist; Or, The Doom of the Great City*. This futurist novel, published in 1893, is set in the London of 1920, during a period of economic depression after "the Continental Wars," when "a severe reaction had set in against liberalism, and a stronger executive and repressive laws were urgently clamoured for." [69] In this political environment, Mr. Stanley, the narrator, urges a gradual program of socialist reform and advocates evolution over revolution. He is also running for Parliament, and his constitutionalist methods of reform run counter to the aims of the anarchists led by Rudolf Hartmann, who thinks, "like some eighteenth century writer, that man must revert to simpler conditions of life and make a new start" (27). Hartmann also believes that "the present human race [is] 'only fit for fuel' " (26). He devises a lighter-than-air vehicle—or "aëronef" (37)—christened the *Attila*. "Behold the craft that shall wreck civilization and hurl tyrannies into nothingness" (63), one of Hartmann's followers proclaims when it is unveiled to Stanley. The *Attila* proceeds to rain fire on London, blowing up the Houses of Parliament, among other things, until the crew mutinies and Hartmann destroys them and kills himself by dynamiting the aëronef in midair in a spectacular explosion. The moral seems to be that anarchistic destruction destroys itself. Fawcett's novel is truly a simple tale (unlike Conrad's novel, despite the subtitle), but Fawcett has in common with Conrad the view of anarchism as destructive madness fueled by technology: Hartmann has his miraculous metal that weighs less than air and the Professor his near-perfect detonator. But the Professor does not really profess the politics of anarchism, whereas Hartmann does, at least when he urges reversion to "a simpler condition of life." The politics of Hartmann and Stanley, in other words, capture in a crude way the larger ideological conflict between anarchism and socialism that belongs to the political history of the late nineteenth century. One looks in vain for such an ideological conflict in *The Secret Agent,* but finds irony in abundance. Correspondingly, irony is in scant supply in *Hartmann the Anarchist.*

Ideology and irony rarely find their way into the same narrative: very few authors have the skill to assert and dissemble at the same time. A good example of a "political" novel in which irony obviates ideology is G. K. Chesterton's *The Man Who Was Thursday.*[70] The plot of the novel concerns a group of six men, each bearing the name of one of the days of the week, who sit on the supreme anarchist council in London presided over by the mysterious president, Sunday. As the novel proceeds, each of the six is revealed to be a secret agent, and the principal anarchist, Sunday, turns out to be the man who recruited them all to, in effect, spy on each other. The conceit in *The Secret Agent,* whereby revolution and legality become "counter moves in the same game," is taken a step further in Chesterton's novel, and the novel itself seems one step further removed from ideology: the characters in *The Man Who Was Thursday* are policeman disguised as anarchists, but they could just as well be Shriners disguised as Elks for all the political meaning the story generates. In the Chesterton novel, irony is an end in itself, and dissembling is everything. In Conrad's case, for all his dissembling he appears to assert something; if nothing else, he asserts the absurdity of politics, and he does this not only by dissembling himself but also by showing that it is in the nature of politics to dissemble. In *The Secret Agent,* therefore, the most pathetic character is the idiot Stevie, who is also the most honest character and the one who states political truths in the baldest possible terms: "Bad world for poor people" (140). This truism, however, does not qualify as an ideological core on which to base the critique of other ideologies, largely because it is uttered by a person of limited mental abilities. Only an idiot, it seems, would be so bold as to take a consistent political position.

Several conclusions can be drawn from the literary procedure at work in *The Secret Agent*. First, irony may be cognate with Conrad's politics, or rather, the only mode in which those politics can operate. Conrad is usually understood as the conservative son of a revolutionary father who "enjoyed many reactionary and royalist connections," but who eventually came to see all politics as "destructive of the individual life." [71] In a famous formulation, Irving Howe applied to Conrad an axiom based on the son's separation from his father's revolutionary nationalist agenda in Poland: "When the children of revolution revolt, it is against revolution: Conrad as a young man escaped from the world of both his father and those who had persecuted his father." [72] The political position of the landless, seafaring exile is easy to reconcile with the artistic position of the relentless ironist. Indeed, Howe also says of Conrad that his critical distance is so great the writing always communicates the sense of "a man who has *cut himself off*" (95). The sense of ironic removal is so intense, Howe adds, that "one yearns for the relief of direct statement almost as if it were an ethical good" (96). Now while the ethical good of ideology necessarily varies with the ideologue and with particular historical conditions, such relativism does not detract from the quality of direct statement all ideology requires. In Conrad's case, the ironic resistance to direct statement is part of an antipolitical posture that, together with his validation of individualism, is fully consistent with one form of anarchism. In addition to the purely individualist strain of anarchism suggested by Conrad's ironic technique, the terrorist variety of anarchism is also enacted in a certain way through the form of the novel itself. Chapter 4 contains the first report of the explosion in which Stevie is blown to bits, and this chapter is followed by three more dealing mainly with the police investigation of the bombing. Chapter 8 and most of 9 return to the chronology leading up to the explosion that has "already" taken place, even though it is never narrated directly. The anarchist "attack" on the world's clock at Greenwich Observatory seems to have the effect of disrupting the chronology of the novel, as if time itself has been exploded. Here, the ironist and the anarchist operate in concert.

A second conclusion that follows from the relation of irony and anarchism in *The Secret Agent* is that irony itself may be a form of artistic anarchism; that is, irony might be the only literary mode that allows for equivalent levels of dissimulation in the face of incompatible politics. In 1918, Thomas Mann commented on the incompatibility of irony and politics when he defined the ironic mode as a condition of skepticism and self-doubt that makes political commitment problematic: "But 'ironic' politics? The word combination seems all too strange and especially all too frivolous for one ever to find it valid, much less to admit that politics itself is altogether and always of ironical character."[73] Curiously, the phrasing suggests that irony cannot be political, but politics might be ironical; that is, Mann's remark about the impossibility of "ironic politics" might itself be ironic, for surely he knows that the politician, like the ironist, is capable of saying one thing and meaning something else.[74] Indeed, Mann's essay on "Irony and Radicalism" involves some rather elusive, equivocal rhetoric. Written near the end of World War I, the essay is remarkable for the way it elides the contemporary period of aggressive German nationalism into a cosmopolitan ideal of burgherly order that insists upon "spiritual-moral" solutions to "the human question" rather than political ones (434). Mann's elisions and equivocations are especially slippery on the subject of art and ideology. Sometimes, the separation of creative art and radical politics is clear and uncomplicated: "It is basically disloyal to use art's criticism of life for ameliorative propaganda purposes" (424). Elsewhere, however, we are told that art can have "political consequences," but this does not mean it should be defined as "a political instrument," lest the artist misunderstand the nature of "his special and ironic type of leadership" (424–25). Irony is critical, but not political, precisely because it "is always irony towards both sides" (422). This formulation would seem to cover Conrad's case, along with the observation that "[i]rony and conservatism are closely related moods" (430). And Mann, like Conrad, also suggests an alliance between the ironist and the anarchist when he says that the artist is "not only not useful to the state, but even rebellious to it" (423). At one point, in fact, Mann comes off as a kind of burgher Bakunin when, after distancing himself from both radicalism and conservatism, he nonetheless claims that "[i]n cases such as mine, destructive and conserving tendencies meet, and as far as one can speak of effect, it is just this double effect that takes place" (431). The double effect of irony, then, involves a basic removal from political commitment to a *particular* ideological position: the antipolitical artist who wishes to make some critique of, say, both anarchism and socialism has no choice but to settle into the ironic mode.

In this expanded sense, irony may be the "ideology" of modernist culture itself, an issue much larger than the question of Conrad alone. In fact, irony functions as a means of distancing the writer from politics not only in Conrad's fiction, but also in Dostoyevsky's and James's as well. All three of these writers experienced either voluntary or forced exile from their homelands, and it is tempting to see in their physical removal from a particular *polis* a basis for the ironic detachment from politics in their art. Irony and exile are also parallel in the art of quite a few of the better-known modernist figures, notably Ibsen, Joyce, Kafka, and Beckett. Some of these artists had actual ties to anarchism, but even those who did not still participate in the general condition of anarchism by using irony to keep their art outside of politics. In the increasingly political world of the late nineteenth and early twentieth century, irony, not ideology, emerges as the primary method of making the political possible for art, even as politics itself becomes ideologically impossible for the exiled artist.

3

RESPONSES
Culture in the Anarchist Camp

No single author can be used to summarize the positive role of anarchy in culture, as Matthew Arnold was used in the last chapter to argue the negative. The anarchist equivalent of Arnold is nowhere to be found: no aesthetic theorist can serve as the anti-Arnold to make the case for anarchy *and* culture, as Arnold argued for their mutual exclusion. As we have seen, Arnold's argument ultimately subverts itself, as he comes to recommend what is really an enlightened philosophical anarchism against the social "anarchy" of labor unrest and political reform. But the cultural anarchism that shadows Arnold's social anarchy hardly makes *Culture and Anarchy* a pro-anarchist document. The novels of Dostoyevsky, James, and Conrad, no less than Arnold's treatise, also imply that culture might have the anarchic potential to replace the state, but their ironic removal from ideology hardly qualifies as an endorsement of anarchism. Paradoxically, the reaction to anarchy that leads conservative writers away from politics and toward culture as a means of unifying society may be more important to the development of the modernist aesthetic than the positive response to anarchism offered by more progressive writers. The novels by William Godwin, the Rossetti sisters, and Frank Harris discussed in this chapter all show that sympathy with progressive politics is no guarantee of an aesthetic advance. The experience of these writers "in the Anarchist camp," as the Rossetti sisters phrase it, poses anew the problem of anarchy and culture.

Sympathetic accounts of anarchism by English authors at the turn of the century are, to some degree, retarded by the form of the novel itself. The argument is often made that the novel is the cultural form par excellence for the expression of day-to-day experience in the capitalist nation-state, and it very well may be that the ideological influences that have shaped the novel into its traditional realist form make it an inappropriate medium for the cultural expression of anarchism. For example, in *A Girl among the Anarchists* Helen and Olivia Rossetti chronicle their involvement and eventual disillusionment with the anarchist underground in London, but even before they reveal this resolution they give it away through the writerly style of the novel itself. Indeed, the style of *A Girl among the Anarchists* is completely within the tradition of the nineteenth-century novel, and the tradition requires a formal mode of narrative discourse that cannot accommodate the largely oral culture of anarchism. As Paul Avrich and Richard Sonn have shown, whether at Chicago street fairs or in Montmartre cabarets, in the nineteenth century the kind of culture that practicing anarchists preferred was insistently oral in character.[1] Oral culture gets round the problem of illiteracy that many anarchists faced (especially in Spain) and helps to account, for instance, for Emma Goldman's interest in modern drama as an important cultural medium for anarchist ideology. As for the Rossetti sisters, they show their ability to mimic oral culture through their use of working-class dialects, but the vernacular style is used only for comic effect. The conventional nature of their novel actually prevents them from treating anarchist culture with full sympathy, even when their heroine is most sympathetic to anarchism. In the case of Godwin's *Caleb Williams,* the conventions of the Gothic romance at the end of the eighteenth century interfere with anarchist ideology almost as much as irony does in Conrad's *The Secret Agent* at the beginning of the twentieth: in the end, Godwin's enlightened libertarianism is subverted in favor of romantic sentimentalism. Likewise, the conventions of naturalism interfere with anarchism in Frank Harris's *The Bomb* almost as much as they do in Turgenev's *Rudin* or Henry James's *The Princess Casamassima,* even though he writes with considerable sympathy for his anarchist hero. *Caleb Williams, A Girl among the Anarchists,* and *The Bomb* are aesthetically retrograde novels, mainly because they are merely expressive of radical politics: anarchy and culture are kept separate, and the failure to integrate the two is reflected in the writers' reliance on extremely conventional novelistic forms. One of the things that distinguishes modernism from this literature is the modernists' ability to embody politics through aesthetic form itself. An examination of this procedure, whereby politics and poetics are conflated, must wait for a later chapter. For now, the contrary operation in which the poetics of literary form actually run counter to politics must be considered, along with one of the earliest strategies for reconciling them. Percy Bysshe Shelley succeeded in reconciling literary form and ideological content, but only because of an idealistic turn of thought that transformed poetry and politics together into Poetry alone.

1

Shelley's *Defense of Poetry* is one of the few documents that makes an extended, consistent argument for the interrelationship of libertarian politics and artistic expression. The *Defense,* however, is not purely anarchistic, even though Shelley was strongly attracted to the libertarian ideas of William Godwin. Still, the *Defense* deserves mention here for its conflation of culture and politics into Poetry, understood in the special sense as the motive force for enlightened change. Given Shelley's broad redefinition of the term, Poetry involves not only beauty but "social renovation," and in this double sense poetic compositions, however diverse and fragmentary, form the "episodes to that great poem which all poets, like the cooperating thoughts of one great mind, have built up since the beginning of the world."[2] The sociocultural spirit of Poetry is Platonic in origin and Hegelian in operation: as the ideal language of liberty, Poetry can only be created by the poet inspired and linked to the source of that ideal (Shelley refers to the "Ion," Plato's parable of the inspired rhapsode); once inspired, however, the poet transfers his divine goods into the realm of history, where their beneficent effect is manifest over time. As proof of the political good of Poetry, Shelley makes the curious hypothetical argument that had Locke and Rousseau never lived society would have been delayed only "a century or two" in arriving at its present state of enlightenment; "[b]ut it exceeds all imagination to conceive what would have been the moral condition of the world if neither Dante, Petrarch, Boccaccio, Chaucer, Shakespeare, Calderón, Lord Bacon, nor Milton, had ever existed" (*DP,* 292). Poetry, in brief, is completely amalgamated with political reform: "The most unfailing herald, companion, and follower of the awakening of a great people to work a beneficial change in opinion or institution is poetry" (*DP,* 297). Since Poetry is nothing less than "the spirit of the age," inspired poets influence great events in history. But just as the Platonic rhapsode does not fully understand all that he says, so Shelley's political rhapsodes are "the hierophants of an unapprehended inspiration; . . . the trumpets which sing to battle and feel not what they inspire; the influence which is moved not, but moves. Poets are the unacknowledged legislators of the world" (*DP,* 297).

The question now arises whether the politically unconscious politics of Poetry that Shelley describes has anything to do with anarchism. As an admirer and disciple of William Godwin, Shelley's own political sensibility was a bit more activist and involved than might be inferred from the famous conclusion to the *Defense of Poetry* just cited. He was a strong supporter of reformist agitation in England, which support is registered in the ballad titled "The Mask of Anarchy." The poem was written in response to the so-called Peterloo Massacre of 16 August 1819, when a group of drunken soldiers charged a peaceful rally for parliamentary reform held in Saint Peter's Field, Manchester. At least six people were killed and perhaps as many as five hundred injured.[3] In the allegorical poem, "Anarchy" is ironically personified as a composite of the despotic authority of church and state:

> . . . he wore a kingly crown,
> And in his grasp a sceptre shone;
> On his brow this mark I saw—
> "I AM GOD, AND KING, AND LAW!"[4]

Anarchy is challenged by the female allegorical figure of Hope, who is about to be crushed beneath the apocalyptic "white horse" that Anarchy rides upon, when a strange, vaporous "Shape" appears and moves among the oppressed. The amorphous Shape is clearly the spirit of liberty, but as "with step soft as wind" it passes "o'er the heads of men," the spirit also influences others as Poetry does in the *Defense:* "Thoughts sprung up where'er that step did fall" (304). The spirit urges the "Men of England" to revolt against the despotic "anarchy" of God, King, and Law:

> Rise like Lions after slumber
> In unvanquishable number
> Shake your chains to Earth like dew
> Which in sleep had fallen on you—
> Ye are many—they are few.   (305)

While one might argue that this peroration admonishes the populace to shake off the "anarchy" of law for the anarchy of individual liberty, the poem can hardly be taken as evidence of outright political anarchism.

The *Defense of Poetry*, however, alludes to a few specific ideas closely identified with important strains of anarchist ideology, such as "mutual dependence" and the "emancipation of women" (*DP*, 278, 289). The *Defense* also alludes to "the principle of equality," which in Shelley's political thought is quite particular; that is, "the theoretical rule of the mode in which the materials of pleasure and of power produced by the common skill and labour of human beings ought to be distributed among them" (*DP*, 288). This political model is usually termed *equalitarian*, which refers to a social system "in which every person would possess an equal amount of private property." [5] As Shelley puts it in *A Philosophical View of Reform*, "Equality in possessions must be the last result of the utmost refinements of civilization; it is one of the conditions of that system of society towards which with whatever hope of ultimate success, it is our duty to tend" (*PVR*, 253–54). The equalitarian society that Shelley envisaged anticipates the anarcho-communism of Kropotkin, even as his endorsement of the labor theory of value looks forward to Proudhon's economic formulations. Finally, the description of poetic power that closes the *Defense* suggests a basically anarchistic attitude: "But even whilst they [the inspired poets] deny and abjure, they are yet compelled to serve the power which is seated upon the throne of their own soul" (*DP*, 297). Even though the power of Poetry is construed here as a universal force outside of the self, when that power is sited within the poet the self becomes the sovereign, the source of all authority. The idea is as orotund as the rhetoric, and Shelley does not indicate whether nonpoets might also have an analogous experience of self-sovereignty. Poetry makes the individual self the medium for universal truths for the good of society. True anarchism is not quite so selective as Shelley's Poetry, but at least by making Poetry the vehicle of both political ideas and aesthetic ideals, Shelley comes as close as anyone to imagining a society where anarchy and culture are integrated.

2

Shelley's politico-aesthetic construct of Poetry is a highly theoretical formulation that anticipates the modernist tendency to embody ideology in aesthetic form rather than simply express it directly, the poet's own participation in the expressivist aesthetic of romanticism notwithstanding. By contrast, William Godwin's attempt to integrate anarchy and culture does not partake of either the idealistic realm of Shelley's politics or the abstract context of modernist aesthetics. Godwin is at the cusp of rationalism and romanticism, a transitional position that affects the writer's practice as both an ideologue and a novelist, as the author of both the *Enquiry Concerning Political Justice* and *The Adventures of Caleb Williams.* To some extent, the form of the novel and the form of the treatise bleed into one another. *Things as They Are; or, The Adventures of Caleb Williams* started out as a novelistic exploration of the same political issues Godwin had presented earlier in his rationalistic *Enquiry,* but, as we shall see, politics and poetics began to interfere with each other over the course of the novel's composition. The experience of writing the novel, in fact, appears to lie behind Godwin's decision to rewrite parts of the treatise once the novel was completed.

The political backgrounds of *The Adventures of Caleb Williams* are clear from the details surrounding the preface to the novel that Godwin added to it on 12 May 1794, the date Prime Minister Pitt suspended habeas corpus to arrest Thomas Hardy. The man was one of Godwin's radical associates in the London Corresponding Society, "an organization perceived by Government at the time to be fomenting political 'revolution' on French Jacobin lines."[6] Hardy's arrest was followed by that of eleven other radicals, including Godwin's friend Thomas Holcroft, all charged with "constructive treason." In October Godwin published *Cursory Strictures on the charge delivered by Lord Chief Justice Eyre,* a pamphlet criticizing the basis for the arrest that helped to secure the acquittal of the accused.[7] Given this background, Godwin's decision to date the preface 12 May is consistent with his plan to make the novel the register of contemporary political realities. Critics have pointed out a number of points of correspondence between *Caleb Williams* and the politics of the 1790s in England. In general, the novel can be read as a response to Edmund Burke's *Reflections on the Revolution in France* (1790), which has been called "the blueprint for conservative thinking for generations to come": Burke's "passionate but deeply calculated defence of the aristocratic concepts of paternalism, loyalty, chivalry and the hereditary principle—in short what he called the 'mysterious wisdom' behind 'antient opinions' and 'rules of life'—soon called forth angry responses from British dissenting radicals" (xiv). Conservative fears of a revolution in Great Britain led to the royal proclamation against seditious publications in May 1792. Thomas Paine's *Rights of Man* was the primary target of this proclamation, and Paine himself, albeit in absentia, was charged with seditious libel and put on trial in December 1792.[8] The event is noteworthy because Godwin attended the trial and was reportedly "furious" that Paine's attorney had not adequately defended the author's right to publish "such writing and such enquiries" as "ought to be permitted in a free society" (xxi).

The trial of Paine and the charge of libel are immediately relevant to *Caleb Williams* because the plot of the novel devolves upon a number of unjust trials, some of which include libelous accusations leveled against the innocent hero. Caleb Williams is faced with a moral quandary when he discovers that Mr. Falkland, the country squire he serves and admires, has murdered a neighboring squire, one Barnabas Tyrrel. As his name suggests, Tyrrel is a tyrant: he exacts severe reprisals on any tenant of his land who does not do exactly as he demands. When a tenant named Hawkins refuses to place his son in Tyrrel's service, the squire relentlessly persecutes both father and son. His campaign of terror includes flooding Hawkins' farmland and poisoning his livestock. Hawkins seeks legal recourse against these offenses, hoping against hope that "there is some law for poor folk, as well as for rich" (75), but he is helpless against Tyrrel's power to protract and otherwise manipulate the legal process. As narrator, Caleb Williams frequently comments on the ineffectiveness and unjustness of the legal process: "Wealth and despotism easily know how to engage those laws as the coadjutors of their oppression, which were at first intended (witless and miserable precaution!) for the safeguards of the poor" (75). With Hawkins and his son effectively ruined, Tyrrel turns his attention to his homely cousin Emily Melville and begins to dote on her. Tyrrel's story intersects with Falkland's when Emily is trapped in a burning building and Falkland comes to her rescue. Her subsequent praise of the noble Falkland makes Tyrrel jealous, and he exacts a perverse revenge against Falkland by forcing Emily to marry an unfeeling bumpkin. The ever-chivalrous Falkland intercedes and stops the marriage, whereupon Tyrrel becomes incensed and publicly humiliates Falkland, striking him in the process. Soon after this episode, Tyrrel is found murdered, and suspicion falls on Hawkins and his son, both of whom have ample motivation for the crime. But Tyrrel was actually killed by Falkland, who encourages the fiction that the Hawkinses are the murderers and keeps silent when father and son are tried, convicted, and executed. Later, Caleb Williams is on the verge of discovering Falkland's secret and Falkland knows it, so he confesses his crime and subsequent subterfuge to his servant. Williams agrees never to divulge the secret, and the pact forms a terrible bond between the two men. Paradoxically, Falkland's confession is a source of great power over Williams, mainly because the master's reputation is so great that any falsehood he manufactures will outweigh any truth his servant tries to tell. The master's power is put into effect when Williams leaves Falkland's estate, essentially because the conditions of service—including the burden of the secret—have become so oppressive that he cannot bear to remain. When Falkland discovers his servant's escape, he accuses him of theft, and, given Falkland's standing in society and the nature of the law, the accusation alone is taken as proof of the crime. At this point the adventures of Caleb Williams begin in earnest, as he is pursued night and day by the police and, later, by Falkland's agent Gines, who is paid to keep an eye on Williams and is unrelenting in his pursuit of him. The story of Williams's narrow escapes from the authorities and from bounty hunters, his capture, trial, imprisonment, escape, recapture, re-escape, and so on, has won the novel its reputation as an early suspense thriller, but that reputation is somewhat unjust, given Godwin's clear political intentions and didactic purpose.

Godwin's 1794 preface, withdrawn from the original edition but published in the second of 1796, states that the narrative "is intended to answer a purpose more general and more important than immediately appears in the face of it" (3). The purpose is political, but Godwin has shifted the mode of politics from the public sphere that includes Burke's reactionism and Pitt's censorship to the private sphere "of domestic and unrecorded despotism by which man becomes the destroyer of man" (3). The domestic version of a despotism that is normally treated in the larger arena of national politics will be instructive, Godwin says, because the smaller, local treatment will help persuade "the public" what is already "known to philosophers," that "the spirit and character of the government intrudes into every rank of society. But this is a truth highly worthy to be communicated to persons whom books of philosophy and science are never likely to reach" (3). *Caleb Williams,* therefore, is presented as the novelistic equivalent of Godwin's formal treatise on political justice, an equivalency reflected in the novel's many encomiums on the failures and inequities of political and legal authority.

Early in the novel, many of the principles originated by Godwin and that will later be termed anarchistic are put into the mouth of Falkland in his disputes with Tyrrel. Godwin believed that human problems could be resolved through reasonable and sincere conversation: "Conversation accustoms us to hear a variety of sentiments, obliges us to exercise patience and attention, and gives freedom and elasticity to our disquisitions."[9] Falkland is clearly employing the Godwinian principle of conversation when he says to Tyrrel, "I had hoped that, by mutual explanation, we should have come to a better understanding" (33), and he cannot fathom why anyone would "refuse a proposition dictated by reason, and an equal regard for the interest of each" (32). These appeals fall on deaf ears, perhaps implying that the murder of Tyrrel has its cognate in the political necessity of assassination in the case of tyrants who will not listen to reasoned discourse. Falkland's role as a Godwinian man is short-lived, however, and he is soon revealed to be a Whiggish figure along the lines of Edmund Burke: " 'It is very true,' said Mr Falkland, 'that there is a distinction of ranks. I believe that distinction is a good thing, and necessary to the peace of mankind' "(80). Later, the "anarchistic" aspects of Falkland are explained by reference to the conventions of chivalry, which serve in place of systems of law: "I am sure things will never be as they ought, till honour and not law be the dictator of mankind, till vice be taught to shrink before the restless might of inborn dignity, and not before the cold formality of statutes" (182). In keeping with the "domestic" scheme announced in the preface that makes private politics reflect the larger public model, Falkland is a figure of royalty: "He exhibited, upon a contracted scale indeed, but in which the truth of the delineation was faithfully sustained, a copy of what monarchs are, who reckon among the instruments of their power prisons of state" (184). Godwin's revolutionary point could not be clearer: government derives its power from the threat of punishment embodied in law and manifested in incarceration. Here, the novel repeats almost verbatim the argument in Godwin's *Enquiry Concerning Political Justice* that governments are driven to "maintain social order entirely by severity of punishment" unless its subjects respect their "governors and superiors" because of the "sacredness" of the offices they occupy. In a note to this passage Godwin states that the argument for an aristocratic order maintained either through fear or reverence is "the great common place of Mr. Burke's *Reflections on the Revolution in France*" (*Enquiry*, 499). Falkland, then, despite his early practice of Godwinian reason and conversation, is clearly a chivalrous aristocrat whose ideology of "inborn dignity" recalls the politics of the royalist Burke.

If Falkland is the royalist, Caleb Williams is the anarchist, resolving not so much for revolution as for individualist independence from politics altogether: "I thought with unspeakable loathing of those errors in consequence of which every man is fated to be, more or less, the tyrant or the slave. I was astonished at the folly of my species, that they did not rise up as one man, and shake off chains so ignominious, and misery so insupportable. So far as related to myself, I resolved—and this resolution has never been entirely forgotten by me—to hold myself disengaged from this odious scene, and never fill the part of the oppressor or the sufferer" (162). As he was to be for the romantic poets who followed Godwin, Caleb Williams's role model is Milton's Satan, whose stoic rationalization of his expulsion from heaven into hell is given in the famous lines: "The mind is its own place, and in itself / Can make a heav'n of hell, a hell of heav'n." These lines are echoed in Godwin's novel when Williams contemplates his "outcast state" in Newgate prison: "Adamant and steel have a ductility like water to a mind sufficiently bold and contemplative. The mind is master of itself; and is endowed with powers that might enable it to laugh at the tyrant's vigilance" (195). Williams is not always so stoic as he appears here, but it is generally true that he is concerned more with avoiding the law than with changing the system that makes the law possible. In fact, Godwin's critique of the current social structure does not depend so much on what Caleb Williams says and does, as on the dramatic treatment of authority. Both the tyrant Tyrrel and the royalist Falkland are represented as perfectly law-abiding but absolutely ruthless and corrupt. What ultimately destroys the power they possess is the corrupting influence of the power itself, a point Godwin makes through another Miltonic reference. When Caleb Williams meets his pursuer Falkland for the last time for what will be Williams's vindication, Falkland is reduced to a condition of "death-like weakness and decay": "The idea of his misery thrilled through my frame. How weak in comparison of it is the imaginary hell, which the great enemy of mankind is represented as carrying everywhere about with him!" (294–95).

Williams's delight in the misery of Falkland, however, gives way to sympathy in the revised ending that Godwin substituted for the original one four days after completing the novel. The original ending shows a different side of the heroic stoicism evoked earlier in the novel. Evidently on the point of madness, Caleb Williams ends a rambling letter, and the novel, with these words: "True happiness lies in being like a stone—Nobody can complain of me—all day long I do nothing—am a stone—a GRAVE-STONE!—an obelisk to tell you, HERE LIES WHAT WAS ONCE A MAN!" (346). One critic observes that this ending provides "a conclusion to the novel that under-score[s] in a very predictable way the political critique behind the narrative, wringing the maximum emotional anguish from the potentially oppressive use of political power."[10] In other words, *Things as They Are* remain the same; the oppressiveness of Falkland's aristocratic order ends up reducing the powerless Williams to the lowest level of human happiness. In the *Enquiry*, we recall, Godwin had classified humanity according to a scale of happiness, with the laboring classes at the bottom of the scale: the best that can be said of the worker is that "[h]e is happier than a stone"(*Enquiry*, 393). By saying that "[t]rue happiness lies in being like a stone" the fictional character in the novel makes ironic reference to the political intentions of the author of the treatise.

The revised ending, the one that Godwin actually published, is not so easily reconciled with either the treatise or the political critique implicit in the narrative itself. Indeed, the new ending offers the surprising denouement of Caleb Williams, having his rightful day in court at last, suddenly forgiving his persecutor:

"I have told a plain and unadulterated tale. I came hither to curse, but I remain to bless. I came to accuse, but am compelled to applaud. I proclaim to all the world that Mr. Falkland is a man worthy of affection and kindness, and that I am myself the basest and most odious of mankind! Never will I forgive myself the iniquity of this day. The memory will always haunt me, and embitter every hour of my existence. In thus acting I have been a murderer—a cool, deliberate, unfeeling murderer—I have said what my accursed precipitation has obliged me to say. Do with me as you please! I ask no favour. Death would be a kindness, compared to what I feel!" (334)

One commentator has observed that the two endings recapitulate the novel's dual title: the first ending is consistent with the static politics of *Things as They Are,* while the second suggests a more dynamic, psychological turn in *The Adventure of Caleb Williams.* To say further that the new ending, in turn, reconciles the contrasting political and psychological demands of the dual title, so that "at their highest levels of practice, art and philosophy are in harmony," seems questionable.[11] If anything can be reconciled here, it is not the two endings with each other, or the new ending with the politics of the novel up to that point, but the revised ending and the revisions to the *Enquiry* made in 1796 and 1798. Critics have noted that in the second edition of 1796 Godwin began to "retreat from the strident rationalism" of 1793 and to place greater stress on "the role of feeling and sentiment." One explanation for this change is the possible influence of Mary Wollstonecraft,[12] whom Godwin met in 1795. But it also seems evident that the retreat from reason occurred sometime during the writing of *Caleb Williams,* since the novel form itself in the late eighteenth century required Godwin to complement his rational faculties with imaginative invention: the poetics of the literary form, in short, ran counter to Godwin's politics.

   A specific example of the way the sentimental elements in *Caleb Williams* echo through the revisions to the *Enquiry* can be seen in a note that Godwin added to the third edition of 1798. The note is appended to the last chapter of the *Enquiry,* in which Godwin admonishes "the enlightened and accomplished advocates of aristocracy" to join in a new advocacy of equality: "While this sheet is in the press for the third impression, I receive the intelligence of the death of Burke, who was principally in the author's mind when he penned the preceding sentences. In all that is most exalted in talents, I regard him as the inferior of no man that ever adorned the face of the earth; and, in the long record of human genius, I can find for him very few equals" (*Enquiry,* 788). The praise of Godwin's ideological adversary Burke resembles Caleb Williams's praise of his antagonist Falkland: "A nobler spirit lived not among the sons of men. Thy intellectual powers were truly sublime, and thy bosom burned with a godlike ambition" (336). Also, just as Williams's admiration of Falkland reverses the prior politics of the novel, so Godwin in his note to a passage on the need for aristocratic participation in the political principle of equality undercuts his own argument when says that Burke has "very few equals." Finally, Williams argues for the goodness of Falkland by saying that his former master began life "with the purest and most laudable intentions," until he "imbibe[d] the poison of chivalry" (336–37). Likewise, Godwin calls "the aristocracy with whom [Burke] lived unjust to his worth" and says that this same aristocracy "in some degree infected his own mind" (*Enquiry*, 789). Surely Godwin's charitable view of Burke, like Williams's guilt-ridden recognition of the compromised but innate goodness of Falkland, is the product of sentimental reflection rather than rationalistic inquiry.

The drift toward sentiment in the *Enquiry*, then, has some precedent in *Caleb Williams*. The new ending of the novel shows that Godwin came to recognize the psychological relationship of Falkland and his servant Williams as more important than the political relationship. This interpretation makes sense given the number of "sentimental" elements in the novel (such as Godwin's representation of a band of noble robbers), but the sympathy extended to Falkland at the end may also involve the recognition that he as well as Williams has been a victim of the inherent viciousness of authority, since the current social system assigns only two possible roles to all of humanity, that of either tyrant or slave. Falkland, after all, was goaded into his troubles by the tyrant Tyrrel, so he is in a manner innocent of the oppression visited upon Williams, even though he happened to be the agent of that oppression. Caleb Williams thus appears as the positive victim of government, while Falkland is the negative victim whose own false consciousness and erroneous belief in the power available to him lead to his ruin. There is also something profoundly anarchistic in the sympathy Williams feels for Falkland, as the sympathy implicitly acknowledges the absence of any external standards of judgment. Thus, *Caleb Williams* puts feeling in the place of reason as the measure of human justice, thereby complementing the rationalistic *Enquiry* with romantic sentiment. To some extent, at least, it seems evident that the political message Godwin set out to impart through the medium of fiction was affected by the form of the novel itself, and modified in the process.

An illustration of the way the politics of Godwin's novel was shaped by eighteenth-century aesthetic conventions involves his use of the sublime. Ironically, Edmund Burke's *Philosophical Enquiry into the Origin of our Ideas of the Sublime and the Beautiful* of 1754 may have furnished the means whereby Godwin was able to subvert Burke's conservative politics of 1790. The sublime, according to Burke, involves a feeling of awe or astonishment upon the recognition of forces so vast that the human subject cannot comprehend them and feels diminished as a result. Faced with the sublime, man's rational abilities are suspended: "In this case the mind is so entirely filled with its object, that it cannot entertain any other, nor by consequence reason on that object which employs it." [13] Falkland's power inspires this sensation in Williams: "Mr Falkland had always been to my imagination an object of wonder, and that which excites our wonder we scarcely suppose ourselves competent to analyse" (307). Burke's sublime may be evoked through natural or supernatural means: certain forces in nature, such as hurricanes and floods, appear limitless in their power and inspire wonder and awe as a result; similarly, the imagination is capable of overwhelming itself through the evocation of supernatural terrors, such as those manufactured by the authors of Gothic novels. Elements of conventional Gothic fiction are present in *Caleb Williams*, but Godwin has also contributed something new by suggesting that *political* forces may have as much sublime power as natural or supernatural forces. The political sublime appears in the novel in the form of Falkland's power over Williams, which Falkland himself likens to omnipotence: "You little suspect the extent of my power. At this moment you are enclosed with the snares of my vengeance unseen by you, and, at the instant that you flatter yourself you are already beyond their reach, they will close upon you. You might as well think of escaping from the power of the omnipresent God, as from mine!" (150).

Since Godwin has already established that Falkland is a contracted model of the monarch, it is easy to see Falkland's pursuit of the reprobate Williams as an allegory of invasive government, "an engine of State with its extensive, 'all-seeing' spy network, hellbent on destroying the efforts of political radicals to achieve electoral reform" (xxxiii). Indeed, the sense of surveillance evoked as Caleb Williams flees his pursuers, only to discover, again and again, how hopeless is his escape from the all-seeing Falkland, recalls Michel Foucault's descriptions of panoptic power in *Discipline and Punish:* "Did his power reach through all space, and his eye penetrate every concealment?" (249). Godwin uses a religious metaphor from his Calvinist background to describe what is really a political situation: "Whithersoever I removed myself, it was not long before I had occasion to perceive this detested adversary in my rear. No words can enable me to do justice to the sensations which this circumstance produced in me. It was like what has been described of the eye of Omniscience pursuing the guilty sinner" (316). Foucault points to Bentham's panopticon model of the prison as a model, also, of the eighteenth-century state.[14] Godwin, likewise, refers to Bentham when he rejects the Christian notion that the state can be organized on the basis of "fear of future punishment": only a fool would believe in a God of this sort, "a tyrant perpetually controlling us with his lash, with this additional horror, that he is acquainted with all our most secret motions, and sits like Jeremy Bentham, perched on top of his Panopticon, to spy into our weaknesses."[15] The panoptic God or government stands opposite to the anarchist ideal of individualism and moral self-determination. *Caleb Williams* is a novel and not a treatise, but even so it makes a strong political argument by unmasking the raw force of the organized, invasive power of government that is the most extreme alternative to anarchism. It is the same power that, in different ways, will be described later on by Kafka and Foucault.

3

Caleb Williams can hardly be described as a sympathetic account of anarchist politics because the novel appears so early in the history of anarchism. True, the hero of the novel makes the choice to remain outside of government and laws, but only after government and its laws have effectively driven him from society: he does not choose his political position so much as he is forced into it. Oddly enough, more knowing and sympathetic narratives of anarchism appear only at or near the end of anarchism, early in the twentieth century when the ideological strength of the movement has already begun to wane. One such belated narrative is Helen and Olivia

Rossetti's *A Girl among the Anarchists* (1903), a semifictional memoir of the sisters' adolescent involvement in the anarchist underground in London during the 1890s. The Rossetti sisters adopted the pen name Isabel Meredith to collaborate on the story of their early enthusiasm and eventual disillusionment with radical politics. The sisters, together with their brother Arthur, began publication in 1891 of their anarchist newspaper *The Torch: A Revolutionary Journal of International Socialism.* They worked on the journal in the basement of their parents' home until 1894, when the organ was moved to separate offices; two years later, the sisters lost interest in the publication and in anarchist politics. *A Girl among the Anarchists* compresses the sisters' involvement in radical politics from five to two years, concentrating the documentary effect of the book, which is also heightened because the pseudonymous author is also the narrator, making her reminiscences seem all the more authentic. Isabel Meredith is only seventeen years old when she decides to abandon her comfortable Victorian home for life among the anarchists. The tender age of Isabel derives from the fact that Olivia was sixteen when *The Torch* was conceived, while Helen was only thirteen. The narrative can therefore be read as a *Bildungsroman* consolidating the education and growth of the Rossetti sisters into the joint persona of Isabel Meredith.

As a *Bildungsroman,* the novel traces the political coming-of-age of a sheltered Victorian girl who makes a remarkable transition from the comforts of home to the hazards of the street. The Rossetti children decided to establish *The Torch* after reading Kropotkin's "Appeal to the Young," a political pamphlet encouraging anarchist involvement among the younger generation. The pamphlet dates from 1880 and is directed mainly to an audience of "intellectuals"— doctors, scientists, lawyers, engineers, teachers, and artists—who have finished their education and are set to begin their careers. Kropotkin assures the young members of the "well-to-do classes" that when they join their professional abilities to the "cause of the revolution" they will experience "a complete, a noble, a rational existence." The ringing conclusion asserts that once well-to-do and working-class youth unite their will to the revolution "that very moment will justice be done; that very instant the tyrants of the earth shall bite the dust." [16] That such sentiments should have found their way into the advanced Victorian household of William Michael Rossetti (brother of the poet Dante Gabriel) is not surprising. The father of the Rossetti children may have worked as a clerk in the Excise Office, but he was also the author of a series of "Democratic Sonnets" on such topics as the Paris Commune and tyrannicide.[17] The Rossettis' next-door neighbor, David Garnett, gives this account of Kropotkin's meeting with the Rossetti children when he called on William Michael in 1891: "[W]hen Prince Peter Kropotkin first visited Rossetti, he was informed that his presence was requested in the nursery. He bustled off, full of benevolence, and was considerably surprised when a girl of fourteen handed him a printed sheet of paper and said drily: 'Will you sign a statement to say that you agree with the political platform of *The Torch?*' The eminent anarchist was delighted to do so. . . ."[18]

In the novel, Isabel Meredith mentions that her interest in politics was originally stimulated by a reading of Kropotkin's "Appeal to the Young."[19] Also, Kropotkin himself appears in the novel as Count Voratin, an "Anarchist and scientist . . . who had sacrificed wealth and high position and family ties for his principles." Isabel says she "nourished an almost passionate admiration for Voratin as a thinker and a man, and his writings had gone far to influence my Anarchist leanings" (25). The dual influence of both the historical Kropotkin and his fictional counterpart Voratin leads Isabel toward revolutionary politics. She is finally persuaded to join the cause of anarchism when she meets "the famous Nihilist" Nekrovitch and another Russian, Kosinski. Nekrovitch is evidently modeled on the revolutionist S. M. Stepniak, well known in radical London circles over the last fifteen years of the nineteenth century,[20] while Kosinski, somewhat improbably, seems inspired by the legend of Bakunin. Kosinski is said to have escaped from Russian prisons and made his way to America before becoming "actively engaged in the Anarchist propaganda all over Europe" and playing "a leading part in the revolutionary movements of recent years"; he is also "known to be an ascetic and a woman-hater." All of these details recapitulate the biography of Bakunin, so it is certainly appropriate that Kosinski is "also engaged on a life of Bakounine" (26). In any case, the two Russians have a profound impact on Isabel Meredith: Nekrovitch convinces her of "[t]he right to complete liberty of action" and "that morality is relative and personal and can never be imposed from without," while Kosinski persuades her that abstract ideas are nothing without active social involvement: "Kosinski was right. I felt one must go the whole length or altogether refrain from dabbling in such matters" (13, 18, 34). Isabel is soon initiated into the underground world of activist anarchism when she volunteers to do propaganda duty for *The Bomb,* an anarchist publication that has its historical counterpart in *Commonweal* (which had published the Rossetti sisters' articles on Italian affairs).[21]

When Isabel Meredith walks into the squalid office of *The Bomb* she finds herself in the midst of a crisis: a police spy has informed on the anarchists and two of their number have been arrested. The action results from what the newspapers describe as an attempted "anarchist outrage" that has its historical basis in the Greenwich bombing: "[A] loud explosion had aroused the inhabitants of a quiet suburban district, and on reaching the corner of ——— Park whence the report emanated, the police had found, amid a motley débris of trees, bushes, and railings, the charred and shattered remains of a man. These, at the inquest, proved to have belonged to Augustin Myers, an obscure little French Anarchist" (39). The Rossetti sisters' treatment of the Greenwich affair in their novel seems much closer to the historical record than does Conrad's in *The Secret Agent,* at least on certain points. For example, the Rossettis make no attempt, as Conrad does, to contrive an explanation for the explosion but present instead a list of the different possibilities that were bruited about at the time:

> Various conflicting theories were mooted as to the motive which prompted the conduct of the deceased Anarchist, but no confirmation could be obtained to any of these. Some held that Myers was traversing London on his way to some inconspicuous country railway station, whence to take train for the Continent where a wider and more propitious field for Anarchist outrage lay before him. Others opined that he had contemplated committing an outrage in the immediate vicinity of the spot which witnessed his own death; and others, again, that, having manufactured his infernal machine for some nefarious purpose either at home or abroad, he was suddenly seized either with fear or remorse, and had journeyed to this unobserved spot in order to bury it.   (40)

One point of similarity between Conrad's novelistic handling of the bombing and the Rossettis' treatment concerns the notion of a police conspiracy. As we have seen, Conrad mainly follows David Nicoll's biased version of the events, in which Martial Bourdin was said to have been manipulated by his brother-in-law, H. B. Samuels, whom Nicoll also claimed had ties to the police. The Rossettis attribute the action of the bomber Augustin Myers to the "undue influence and power" of his brother Jacob, another anarchist now suspected of disloyalty because he has been seen drinking at a pub "with a well-known detective" (49). The anarchists' suspicion of Jacob Myers is similar to the treatment accorded Samuels by the *Commonweal* group: "Jacob was in fact accused of having egged on his unfortunate brother to his doom in order that he might turn a little money out of the transaction between newspaper reports and police fees" (50). The anarchists agree to sever their association with Jacob Myers, and the description of the meeting at which this decision is made might be based on firsthand experience. At least one of the Rossetti sisters is supposed to have been present at the offices of *Commonweal* when Samuels was expelled.[22]

In the novel, the *mouchard* Myers implicates two other anarchists in the outrage, and Isabel Meredith's first task as a girl among the anarchists is to intercede on their behalf. She is called upon to use her wealth and wit for the defense of the accused, but the effort ends in failure. The narrator then sums up the whirl of activity that marks the first phase of her life as an anarchist:

> The first weeks of my experience in the Anarchist camp had flown by with astounding rapidity. The chapter of my experiences had opened with the expulsion of an alleged spy and *agent provocateur,* and had closed with the sentence of penal servitude passed on two of my new-found comrades. Between these two terminal events I seemed to have lived ages, and so I had, if, as I hold, experience counts for more than mere years. Holloway and Newgate, Slater's Mews and the Middle Temple, barristers and solicitors, judges and juries and detectives; appointments in queer places to meet queer people—all this had passed before me with the rapidity of a landscape viewed from the window of an express train; and now that the chapter had closed, I found that it was but the preface to the real business I had set my shoulders to. (74)

The real business is the resumption of publication of the anarchist journal, relocated and renamed *The Tocsin*. The ramshackle offices of *The Tocsin,* located above a cockney greengrocer's shop, soon become a magnet for an international mixture of anarchists and political hangers-on, mostly Italians. Isabel appears to do most of the work: she learns to set type and operate the printing press, as well as look after a growing number of foreigners who, having no place to stay, take up residence in the office of *The Tocsin*. Isabel also assists in the escape of Matthieu, a famous dynamitard, from an anarchist safe-house once the police discover his whereabouts. The episode involves a great deal of cunning and intrigue, but Isabel's experiences do not often involve this type of adventure. Over the course of the novel her idealistic faith in anarchism is severely tested by such comrades as the compositor Short, whose name suggests that, unlike Isabel, he has not gone "the whole length" for anarchism. Isabel soon infers that although Short does not "care one jot for [the] 'humanity' of which he prated so freely, . . . he found in a certain section of the Socialist and Anarchist party that degree of satisfaction and covetousness which appealed to his degraded soul. Besides which the movement afforded him grand opportunities for living in sloth and sponging on other people" (134). This description squares with that of Geoffrey Byrne, another member of the *Torch* group, who wrote that the printer Tom Cantwell and the sometime editor Ernest Young were simply taking advantage of the Rossetti sisters' wealth and goodwill. Cantwell and Young had gotten to know the sisters earlier because of their role at *Commonweal;* when that publication folded and *The Torch* started up, the two made their rather dubious services available to the Rossettis. Byrne's judgment of Cantwell and Young is very like Isabel Meredith's view of the slothful, sponging Short: "With such a pair of despicable, lying, cowardly humbugs I have nothing in common. How could I? I have never lived out of the movement or sponged on Comrades as Cantwell and Young are doing. I was never kept by two girls (whose youthful inexperience prevented them from seeing through the wiles of a lying scab) for nearly two years . . . and then repaid them by laziness, lying and mischief-making and finally by filth, lice and trouble-making driving them disgusted and heartsick out of the English movement."[23] As Short and other figures whom Isabel had earlier admired or at least tolerated decline into mindless eccentricity or outright madness, her disillusionment with the movement grows. That disillusionment is complete when she witnesses the death of a woman whose husband has been ruined by the influence of Kosinski. On her deathbed, the woman gives a warning to Isabel: "[B]eware, he will ruin you too; he has no heart, no religion; he cares for nothing, for nobody, except his cruel principles" (264). Isabel decides to break with Kosinski, saying, "The dead woman was right" (268), as earlier she had said, "Kosinski was right" when her bourgeois values were challenged. Now, she asserts basic human values in her break with Kosinski: "Why should we ruin our lives? To what idol of our own creation are we sacrificing our happiness? We Anarchists are always talking of the rights of the individual, why are you deliberately sacrificing your personal happiness, and mine?" (268).

Isabel Meredith ultimately rejects anarchism on humanistic grounds, but the rejection is not complete. Immediately after the break with Kosinski, she intends to resume her work at *The Tocsin,* but is prevented from doing so because the police have shut down the publication. As Graham Holderness observes, all along Isabel had separated the banal politics of anarchism from its idealistic principles: "true anarchism is admired both for its purity and for its decisive political will expressed in acts of terrorism," while "politics" is relegated "to the realm of the trivial and the sordid." [24] The sense of sordidness that she has lived through rises to Isabel's consciousness after the break with Kosinski. She has "the uncomfortable consciousness that my hair was disordered and wispy, my hat awry, my skin shiny; and this sub-consciousness of physical unattractiveness heightened the sense of moral degradation" (270). The concern with fashion and appearance that suddenly makes itself felt in the closing chapter recapitulates an issue suggested at the outset by the title of the novel: *A Girl among the Anarchists* implies that anarchists are male by definition, and that a woman risks the loss of certain conventional notions of femininity by moving among them. In this context, Jennifer Shaddock's argument that the novel subverts Victorian norms only to reassert them in the end is valid: "The novel's concluding vision for woman's self-fulfillment and self-determination is astonishingly bleak given its earlier development of a defiantly expansive space for woman's emancipation." [25] Nevertheless, the denouement of the novel is not nearly so bleak as other late Victorian narratives of the New Woman. One of the better-known of these is Grant Allen's *The Woman Who Did* (1895), which tells the story of Hermione Barton, a radically independent New Woman who advocates free love and complete equality between the sexes.

Hermione and her illegitimate daughter have a hard life after her lover dies and her family abandons her, but things get worse for the heroine when her daughter grows up to be moralistic and conventional. The daughter is ashamed of her liberal mother and of her own illegitimacy, both of which stand in the way of matrimony. Faced with these developments, Hermione Barton, like Emma Bovary before her, kills herself by swallowing prussic acid.[26] Allen's *The Woman Who Did* is the more conventional version of the unconventional woman, while *A Girl among the Anarchists* goes much farther into areas of experience traditionally denied to women. Actually, Allen's simultaneously moralistic and sensational novel is the subject of a comic scene in *A Girl among the Anarchists,* as if to make the point that Allen's story is a less authentic account of the New Woman than the Rossettis' narrative. In their novel, *The Woman Who Did* is read by *The Tocsin*'s henpecked proofreader, "a benevolent old gentlemen of obsolete customs" whose wife cannot tolerate her husband's pursuit of " 'advanced' literature' " (143–44). Because of its strong basis in underground political experience, *A Girl among the Anarchists* stands up rather well against Allen's and other narratives of the New Woman that are less grounded in reality. Isabel Meredith's removal from full female emancipation at the end of the novel may disappoint, but the novel is finally satisfying for the rich, documentary treatment of anarchist activity that can be gotten in no other way. The whole of chapter 9, for example, is devoted to "Some Anarchist Personalities" and offers a wide-ranging exposition of anarchism in general, including, among other things, a reasoned defense of Emile Henry's attack on the Café Terminus.

Read as a documentary chronicle of actual participation in the anarchist movement, the novel offers some surprising insights into the relation of anarchy and culture. One of the cultural implications of Isabel's sense that her shiny skin and wispy hair mirror some form of moral degradation is not only that anarchism is "masculine" but also that it is inherently unaesthetic. Curiously, one of the things that attracts Isabel to the anarchists is their unattractiveness, or at least their plain, unadorned, unaesthetic appearance. In fact, Isabel is put off by the dandyism of the socialists, whose concern with appearance suggests that politics, also, is merely a matter of fashion: "I had never understood why Socialism need imply the arraying of oneself in a green curtain or a terra-cotta rug, or the cultivation of flowing locks, blue shirts, and a peculiar cut of clothes" (17). In "An Appeal to the Young," Kropotkin addressed his reader with the understanding "that you are not one of the fops, sad products of a society in decay, who display their well-cut trousers and their monkey faces in the park, and who even at their early age have only an insatiable longing for pleasure at any price." [27] Isabel Meredith is clearly following Kropotkin when she expresses "no desire or ambition to be a mere dilettante Socialist, and as dirt and squalor had to be faced, well, I was ready to face them" (56). The anarchist Kosinski is a long way from the fop Kropotkin warns against and the dilettante Meredith eschews. Indeed, Kosinski's unfashionable appearance shows a "marked indifference to opinion" and an evident cultivation of the politics of dirt and squalor: "He was clad in a thick, heavy, old-fashioned blue overcoat with a velvet collar, which he refused to remove, baggy nondescript trousers, and uncouth-looking boots" (29). "From the first moment Kosinski interested me," Isabel says (29). Other anarchists in the novel are equally indifferent to fashion, no mean observation in view of the highly aesthetic period in which the story is set. In addition, the two most important anarchist characters, Kosinski and Giannoli, express outright hostility to art. Isabel takes Giannoli to the National Gallery and shows him Leonardo's *Virgin of the Rocks*, whereupon the anarchist says: "I hate art. . . . I consider it one of the most noxious influences in the world. It is enervating and deteriorating. Art has always been the slave of religion and superstition, from the ancient Egyptians and Assyrians to our own times" (210). Here, the view of art may derive from Bakunin's atheistic disapproval of religious subject matter, but even this explanation cannot fully account for Kosinski's aversion to art. When Isabel suggests a meeting at a gallery, Kosinski objects in the strongest possible terms. " 'No, please, don't,' answered the Russian in genuine alarm; 'you know how I hate art, Isabel. It goads me to madness. We must think of some other place' " (232). Even though *The Bomb* is said to have been founded by "a great artist," there is precious little interest in art or artists in *A Girl among the Anarchists*. The novel as a documentary record of anarchist activity suggests that the anarchists were removed from aesthetic circles, and that it was the artists who were attracted to anarchism, not the other way around.

4

Frank Harris's novel *The Bomb* is, like the Rossetti sisters' story of Isabel Meredith, a sympathetic, firsthand account of life among the anarchists. Also, like the earlier novel, *The Bomb* was based on historical events, though Harris did not have any personal involvement in those events himself. In 1886, a bomb was thrown into the ranks of the police in the Haymarket area of Chicago when the officers attempted to break up a protest meeting. The bombing was most likely motivated by revenge against the police for firing on a labor demonstration at the McCormick harvester factory two days earlier. Wholesale arrests of anarchists followed the Haymarket bombing.[28] August Spies and Albert Parsons, who both edited anarchist newspapers, were put on trial with six other labor leaders, even though the state had no evidence to link them to the bombing. Most historians agree that "[t]he process was clearly a show trial, since no attempt was made to prove complicity in the bombing: the prosecution sought only to prove that the accused were anarchists and revolutionaries." A guilty verdict was rendered, and four of the eight had been executed by the time subsequent evidence was produced to show that none of the defendants had played any part in the bombing.[29]

The Haymarket bomber was never caught, but Harris creates a culprit in the person of his novel's narrator, one Rudolph Schnaubelt, a German immigrant who becomes involved in the labor movement. In the actual Haymarket affair, an anarchist named Schnaubelt was suspected of having thrown the bomb, but he was never apprehended.[30] When *The Bomb* was published in 1908 it was ridiculed by German anarchists who were familiar with the Haymarket affair; likewise, historians today dismiss the scenario Harris invents to account for the bombing.[31] The novel is presented as Schnaubelt's account of his own political motivation and is written from Schnaubelt's point of view to memorialize the anarchist movement in Chicago and its charismatic leader, another German immigrant named Louis Lingg. An interesting psychological feature of this historical novel concerns the parallelism of Schnaubelt's political relationship with Lingg and his romantic relationship with his girlfriend Elsie. Lingg's political conversion of Schnaubelt doubles Schnaubelt's sexual conquest of Elsie, up to the point where Schnaubelt resolves to throw the bomb. He knows that the act will be the consummation of his political life with Lingg; at the same time the bombing will make normal life with Elsie impossible. The affair with Elsie, therefore, goes unconsummated, as Schnaubelt's sexual desires are displaced in favor of politics. When Schnaubelt and Lingg agree to meet so Lingg can deliver the bomb, the situation is rendered with all the ardor of a romantic tryst. "Come for me," Schnaubelt says to Lingg, "at eight": "and I held out my hands. He took both my hands in his, and involuntarily I bent forward, and we kissed, for the first name, kissed as comrades and lovers." [32] The treatment here of political ardor as a species of homoerotic attraction seems intended to ennoble the otherwise ignoble act of blowing human beings to bits. Such nobility and sublimation, combined with the absolute brutishness of the police, elevates the terrorist act and makes it seem logical and justified, the result not only of Lingg's ideology but of Schnaubelt's love.

The ideology that so inspires Schnaubelt is a curious mixture of socialism and anarchism, with the anarchist element compounded further into a strange blend of terrorism and syndicalism. The combination is historically anomalous, since syndicalism arose partly out of the realization that propaganda by the deed was a political dead end. The anarchist movement in Chicago, as it was in other American cities, was formed almost exclusively of European immigrants who had brought anarchist ideas with them from their native countries. Italian and Russian immigrants in particular imported both the strategy of the general strike and such important labor issues as the eight-hour workday. In general, the German immigrants did not transport anarchist ideas with them from Europe because Germany was never so receptive to anarchist ideas as the Mediterranean and Slavic countries. Once in America, however, many German workers came under the influence of the anarchist Johann Most, who had himself been influenced by Bakunin and advocated propaganda by the deed. When Most came to America in 1883 he insinuated himself into the labor movement that antedated his arrival and tried to make terrorism the complement of the strikes that immigrant laborers were already using for the limited purpose of improving working conditions.[33] Thus the situation created in the Harris novel, in which terrorism and labor agitation are combined, has some historical basis, but the combination is still a far cry from the idea of "syndicalist terrorism" suggested by *The Bomb*. At no time was the dynamitard imagined as an ally of the syndicalist, whose energies were devoted to the general strike as the means of undermining capitalist authority. But Louis Lingg, like Hartmann the anarchist in Fawcett's novel (see Chapter 2), sees new political possibilities in the combination of technology and terror: "Every discovery of science . . . strengthens the individual. In the past he had one man's life in his hand; a single oppressor could always be killed by a single slave. . . . But now the individual has the lives of hundreds in his hand" (153). How the workers will benefit from this techno-anarchism is not clear. The anarchists in *The Bomb* have little to say about the general strike, but they do support a group of foreign workers who strike at a meat-packing plant. This support takes the form of a propaganda campaign urging American-born workers to join the immigrant strikers, mostly Germans and Swedes. Thus, Harris's novel is anarcho-syndicalist in the limited sense that anarchist activity is devoted to labor organization and the improvement of working conditions.

In the novel, anarchism is defined by Louis Lingg as an ideal of self-government: "We want to govern ourselves, and neither govern others nor be governed by them" (189). In its ideal form, Lingg's anarchism would include some kind of administrative apparatus that is indistinguishable from state socialism: "[I]n my view a certain amount of socialism is needed to bring a wider freedom to men, and with completer freedom and stronger individualism I dream of a State industrial army, uniformed and officered, employed in making roads and bridges, capitols and town halls, and people's parks, and all sorts of things for the common weal" (192). The uniforms and officers, not to mention the town halls and capitols, indicates the presence not only of state authority but hierarchies within the state. Lingg's anarchism becomes even more atypical when he says, "[W]e are suffering from too much individualism; the problem is how to limit individualism, how far socialism should come into life" (111). What he means by "individualism" here is laissez-faire capitalism, which would be eliminated by nationalizing those industries currently controlled by the capitalists (railroads, insurance companies, banks, and so on). Paradoxically, in Lingg's formulation the type of "individualist" he describes "has given up his freedom to join with other men in Joint Stock Companies" to "increase his power to plunder the community" (111). On the other hand, the small businessman who does not exchange his freedom for power over others is the proper sort of individualist. Basically, the ideal "anarchism" Lingg describes would combine the small-scale, bottom-up, pre-industrial model of mutualist society that Proudhon had in mind with the large-scale, top-down, industrial model of communism that Marx envisaged. When Schnaubelt hears Lingg's explanation of this all-purpose ideology, in which "a perfect modern state" would "embrace both socialism and individualism" (293), his political conversion is complete: "As he spoke the light dawned on me; this was the truth if ever it was heard from human lips; the exact truth struck in the centre. The individual should be master of all those industries which he could control unaided, and no more. Joint Stock Companies' management was worse even than State management; everyone knew it was more inefficient and more corrupt. All my reading, all my experience, leaped to instant recognition of Lingg's insight, to instant agreement with him. What a man he was!" (112–13). Such enthusiasm over an anarchist-socialist alliance now seems just as anomalous as the amalgamation of terrorism and syndicalism that Harris imagines, contributing further to the hybrid nature of the novel as something between historical fiction and political fantasy.

The strange ideology Harris manufactures in *The Bomb* may be due to the author's attempt to give to his immigrant characters a set of ideas that he thought was appropriately "German." Nineteenth-century labor movements in Germany, with their large industrial unions, welcomed state intervention,[34] so it may be that Lingg's notion of state administration of certain industries is meant to impose a German model on American labor. To some extent the ideology of the fictional Louis Lingg reflects that of his historical counterpart, whose collectivist side emerged in his active support of trade unions, while his autonomist leanings were manifest in his advocacy of propaganda by the deed. Lingg had been converted to the terrorist cause by the German anarchist August Reinsdorf in 1883, and he brought his conviction in the value of dynamite to the Chicago labor scene. In 1886 he urged an audience of workers to take up arms against the capitalists: "We must fight them with as good weapons, even better, than they possess."[35] Still, this perspective was not the dominant view among the German immigrant anarchists in Chicago, so the emphasis on terrorism created by Harris's focus on Lingg distorts the syndicalist ideology of the rank and file. Likewise, Harris distorts the populist, largely oral culture of Chicago anarchism through his presentation of Schnaubelt, whose elevated literary tastes do not include the "Workers' Marseillaise" or the "Hymn of the Proletariat" that were actually sung at anarchist rallies.[36]

Many of the cultural interests of the anarchists in Harris's novel are linked to their German background. Schnaubelt describes himself in youth as a "freethinker" whose mind was opened up by Heinrich Heine. Later, after the bombing, Heine's name is again invoked, along with Goethe's, to lend some rather anachronistic support to Ruskin's assertion, apropos the Paris Commune, that "the capitalists are the guilty thieves of Europe" (273). As this reference suggests, the narrator's Germanic tastes are amalgamated with Harris's anarcho-aesthetic interests, so that Ibsen, Anatole France, and Tolstoy join Ruskin, Heine, and Goethe, along with Carlyle and Balzac, in the anticapitalist camp (273). Lingg himself is compared to Shelley for his sensitivity to "the else unfelt oppressions of mankind" (118). When Lingg and the other anarchists are imprisoned and await execution, an international outcry against the injustice is led by William Morris in England and by William Dean Howells in America (298), a reference to the actual support given to the Haymarket group by a number of prominent writers (including George Bernard Shaw and Oscar Wilde).[37] Aside from the allusions to the socialist Morris and the anarchist Tolstoy, the cultural references in *The Bomb* are not indicative of any clear sensibility that necessarily deserves the name "anarchist"; rather, Ibsen, Ruskin, and the rest are simply the "leaders of modern thought" (293). In his speeches, Louis Lingg endorses only a few very general cultural programs: he is in favor of state aid to artists because "[l]ife must be made richer by making it more complex" (121). Culture in Lingg's "anarchist" utopia has a purpose not unlike that of the Temperance League: "I would have a modern city with laboratories at every street corner, and theatres and art studios and dancing halls, instead of drinking saloons" (190). Harris's vision of an abstemious modern city is actually consistent with the emphasis on health and hygiene advocated by the Spanish anarchist Francisco Ferrer around the time the novel was published, and so is the somewhat anti-intellectual notion that books impede learning: "Our education leans too much on books; books develop memories, not minds" (124). For all its inconsistencies, *The Bomb* actually captures something of the contradictory culture of anarchism as it was developing in the first decade of the twentieth century. That culture was marked, on the one hand, by a group of "modern" writers who either celebrated individualism (Nietzsche, Stirner, Whitman, Heine, Goethe) or exposed a society in need of reform (Balzac, Ibsen, Zola); on the other hand, a countermovement developed that emphasized nature and physical culture over intellectual experience.

The three novels presented in this chapter are all in the anarchist "camp" in more than one sense of the word. For Harris and the Rossetti sisters especially, anarchism seems to have been a kind of temporary cultural encampment, after which they moved on to other things. Also, none of the three novels stands out as great literature, and all have a certain camp quality in the aesthetic sense of "attractive mediocrity."[38] More important, however, Godwin, the Rossettis, and Harris each offer a history of anarchism in miniature. Godwin's *Caleb Williams* represents the early theoretical phase of the movement that developed out of the French Revolution and Rousseau's writings. *A Girl among the Anarchists* moves from theory to the first stage of anarchist practice in the Rossettis' defense of Emile Henry and their sympathetic attitude toward terrorism in general; the novel also captures the sense of disillusionment subsequent to the severe repression of anarchism as a result of propaganda by the deed. In its idealization of violence, *The Bomb* does not completely represent the next phase of anarchism, but Harris's treatment of his hybrid anarchists and their involvement in strikes and other labor issues approximates the move to anarcho-syndicalism. This movement from theory to terrorism to labor activity covers a period of one hundred years, but these same historical stages are repeated in the highly concentrated period of anarchist activity in the city of Paris over a mere quarter-century. This period, in turn, provides the impetus for an important exploration of politics and culture on the part of anarchists and artists alike. The various affinities and antipathies they felt for each other leads at last to the tensions and contradictions between ideology and aesthetics in the early modernist period.

4

AFFINITIES
Anarchism and Cultural Promotion

The idea of politics and culture integrated to the point of inter-changeability is both radical and idealistic. This is especially true of Shelley's conception of Poetry discussed in the previous chapter: that is, the root or *radix* of politics is the cultural ideal of Poetry. This romantic idea, however eccentric, anticipates some of the formulations of the relationship of politics and culture made by later anarchists. At first, the role of art in the anarchist revolution was limited to the documentary task of depicting reality as it is, to the faithful representation of those elements in society whose very ordinariness rendered them invisible to the bourgeois *artiste*. Along these lines Proudhon's *Du Principe de l'art et de sa destination sociale* had urged the artist "to present the interaction between individual and environment" in order to help other individuals understand "the various values of existence." This conception of the artist as a realist observer who helped to educate the masses was modified by Kropotkin, who regarded the artist as the conscience of humanity, an individual whose creative contributions to society had the power to change it.[1] By the end of the century, Jean Grave and Oscar Wilde, among others, imagined an anarchist utopia where everyone would have time to devote to art once the workday had been reduced to only a few hours, or even eliminated altogether. Where Proudhon urged the realist artist to observe society and Kropotkin charged the revolutionist with changing it, Grave imagined his utopian artist as the embodiment of society itself. In *La Société future*, Grave called art the "supreme manifestation of individualism"; cultural production was destined to become the primary activity in anarchist society since "[a]narchism itself represented art."[2] Again, as with Shelley, the political and the cultural are amalgamated into a single construct.

This ideal of politico-cultural integration, however, offers no insight into the kind of culture the anarchists had in mind. Are some types of literature more anarchistic than others? If society evolves to the point where everyone practices art, does that mean the artist ceases to exist? What painters and writers of the past are anarchistic today, and what makes them so? Answers to questions like these are hard to come by. The anarchists themselves do not speak with a single voice on cultural matters, if they speak at all. And when they do speak, what they have to say is not always distinguishable from the utterances of the orthodox. As a novelist, William Godwin hardly stands apart, on aesthetic grounds, from other writers with more traditional politics than his. Likewise, Proudhon's promotion of realism and his interest in Courbet does not mean that either realism or Courbet is necessarily anarchistic. And Bakunin was often ambivalent about the value of art when he was not openly opposed to it. Kropotkin, however, is another matter, as he participates in the general tendency to "politicize" the role of literature and the arts. Only in the late nineteenth century do avant-garde politics and avant-garde culture begin to complement each other, as artists express sympathy for anarchism and anarchists incorporate certain artists into their political programs. Whether anarchy and culture are truly integrated at the turn of the century must remain, for now, an open question. But there is no doubt that affinities existed between anarchists and artists as the nineteenth century wound down, especially in Paris, and the phenomenon has many ramifications for literary art in the age of modernism and beyond.

1

A number of elements combined to make Paris the capital of urban anarchism in the late nineteenth century. Baron Haussmann's transformation of the city during the Second Empire displaced thousands of Parisians, creating an undercurrent of unrest at the same time that the vast boulevards and other changes to the cityscape suggested a new spirit of progressive modernity. The collection of old medieval neighborhoods had been erased and a new metropolis put in its place. Perhaps the loss of the old Paris and the formation of the new produced in the displaced populace that longing for the past, simultaneously accompanied by hope for the future, that is the hallmark of much anarchist thinking. But this is speculation; what is clear, however, is that Haussmann's renovations were widely perceived as an intentional effort to segregate the bourgeoisie from the proletariat, with the shopkeepers and small tradesmen located in the center of the city and the workers quite literally relegated to its margins: "Haussmann's modernity had been built by evicting the working class of Paris from the centre of the city, and putting it down on the hill of Belleville or the plains of La Villette."[3] But it is only partly true that Paris was reshaped into a city with a bourgeois center and a proletarian periphery; to a certain extent Paris was not so much divided as layered, so that the expansive, modern metropolis merely masked the smaller, local life of the old medieval village Paris had been. This assertion is borne out by the nature of the labor force: more than 90 percent of businesses employed fewer than ten workers per establishment. Given the size of the labor force—about six hundred thousand workers in 1870—and its breakdown into small groupings, the proper conditions existed for a reorganization of labor into anarchist collectives, a possibility enhanced by Napoléon III's tolerant attitude toward labor unions.[4] These workers also formed the main audience for journals devoted to anarchism. Most of the subscribers and readers of *La Révolte,* Jean Grave's anarchist newspaper of the 1880s (which had a circulation of 6,000), were workers. The literacy rate was generally high during the Second Empire, Napoléon III having made public education available to all children up to the age of twelve, and there was no shortage of newspapers and journals to satisfy the needs of the working-class audience.[5] Another contributing element to the growth of the anarchist milieu in Paris was Montmartre, which still retained the appearance of a village well into the nineteenth century. In fact, the butte of Montmartre was only annexed into the city in 1859, when it became part of the eighteenth arrondisement. Prior to this, the area had been outside the jurisdiction of Paris, one consequence of which was that no excise tax was charged on the wine that was sold there. The butte of Montmartre was also honeycombed with lime quarries, and the miners who worked them drank the inexpensive *vin de pays* during the week and supported the bars, whose clientele became more fashionable on Sundays and holidays.[6] Around 1860, the network of cheap bars and cabarets, together with the quasi-independent status of Montmartre and its working-class populace, formed a cultural infrastructure that would prove supportive to anarchistic interests in the future. This layering of simple village life and urban bohemianism forms one backdrop of Parisian anarchism, but still more important is the fact of the Paris Commune.

The Paris Commune was by no means a purely anarchist venture; on the contrary, the politics of the Commune cannot be called "pure" in any sense. Nonetheless, of the sixty-four elected representatives who formed the first communal government on 28 March 1871, twenty were followers of Proudhon. In addition, slightly more than half of the original sixty-four came from the class of artisans and small tradesmen so amenable to anarchist philosophy. A recent commentator notes that only two members of this initial group "had any knowledge of Karl Marx" and that "the only generalization which can usefully be drawn from the statistics is that none of them had any significant connection with the heavy mechanized industries which had been burgeoning in the suburbs of Paris throughout the Second Empire (and which would eventually become the focal point of Marxist Communism)."[7] Historians today are generally agreed that the Commune was no proletarian revolution, but neither was it ideologically consistent with all points of anarchism. In a general sense, however, the Commune can be aligned with anarchist principles, as it was formed in the aftermath of the Franco-Prussian War largely upon a rationale of resentment over the statist decrees handed down from Versailles. Even though a republic was declared after Napoléon III's defeat by the Prussians, in the wake of the war the National Assembly immediately instituted a number of conservative policies that most Parisians found unacceptable. Principal among these was the reduction of the number of paid members of the National Guard and the Law of Maturities, which ended the wartime moratorium on repayment of loans and other debts and required immediate repayment, with interest. The financial impact of the debt measure on working-class Parisians was considerable; as for the curtailment of the guard, many Parisian workers, otherwise unemployed, had come to depend on the meager payment of one and a half francs per day they received as National Guardsmen.[8] When Adolph Thiers, the provisional executive of the National Assembly, failed in his efforts in early March 1871 to disband the National Guard in Montmartre (where two of Thiers's generals were killed in the attempt), the Commune was born.[9] Essentially, the city of Paris had seceded from the government of France.

While secession was unprecedented, the Commune itself already had a proud revolutionary history. The municipality of Paris, or the *commune de Paris,* had played an important role in the French Revolution, organizing the sansculottes to pressure the national government from 1789 to 1795, and, in 1792–93, forming the citizens into volunteer armies to defend against foreign invasion.[10] In 1871, many of the Communards elected to the municipal council still held to the Jacobin principles of that earlier revolutionary era and hoped to make the Commune the vehicle of an enlightened dictatorship that would rule the whole of France. The supplementary elections of 16 April lessened the strength of the Jacobin faction and made socialist representatives of various revolutionary stripes a majority.[11] Although Marx defended the Communards in his pamphlet *The Civil War in France,* more or less claiming them as his own, they "were not the factory proletarians that his theory predicted would crush capitalism and introduce socialism."[12] Paul Avrich notes that Proudhon's influence far exceeded that of Marx, an influence "reflected in the title of 'Federals' by which the Communards were known."[13] The number of Proudhonist mutualists among the Communards included the union leader Eugène Varlin and the painter Courbet, while the Bakuninists were represented by Elie Reclus, his brother Elisée, and Louise Michel, whose heroism on the barricades earned her the epithet "the red virgin of the commune."[14] The anarchist tendencies of the Commune may be summarized as follows:

> The Commune was against centralization; its aim was a federation of communes. The Commune was for a people's government in which distinctions between governors and governed would be erased: representatives would receive wages of average workers, be popularly elected, and be subject to immediate recall. The Commune was militantly antireligious: the aim was to free humanity from clerical machination and superstition. And finally, the Commune was for destruction of bourgeois property: cooperative ownership and self-management of production were envisaged.[15]

All of these points argue for some fundamentally anarchistic strain in the constitution of the Commune, which is not quite the same as saying that the Commune was an anarchist revolution.

Just as a wholesale identification of the Commune with anarchism should not be made, at the same time the point needs to be stressed, again, that the nineteenth-century anarchists' traditional rivals cannot claim the Commune, either. The linkage of Commune politics with Marxist ideology needs to be exposed as a mistaken association because of some of the later cultural ramifications that follow from the connection. In truth, Marx at first did not support the establishment of a commune in Paris at all, thinking such action rash and premature given his own long-term, dialectically informed view of the social revolution.[16] As already noted, the anarchist contingent far outnumbered the Marxist in the makeup of the Communal council; moreover, the Commune's manifesto, which promised "the voluntary association of local initiatives," was written by the Proudhonist Pierre Denis, whose "vision of a France split up into a collection of autonomous Communes" is rather different from Marx's vision of the future of society.[17] In *The Civil War in France* Marx takes some pains to argue that the Commune's disposal of the corrupt state of Napoléon III does not imply the abolition of government itself: "While the merely repressive organs of the old governmental power were to be amputated, its legitimate functions were to be wrested from an authority usurping pre-eminence over society itself, and restored to the responsible agents of society." The argument that the Commune intended merely to purge government of its excesses in order to restore its proper administrative authority is one of Marx's understandable fictions, as is the claim that "[t]he Paris Commune was, of course, to serve as a model to all the great industrial centres of France."[18] Marx's post facto appropriation of the Commune for the cause of Communism, combined with the extremely tangential relationship of such important avant-garde writers as Lautréamont and Rimbaud to the events of 1871, have evidently fueled the idea that some allegiance between avant-garde art and Marxist politics grew out of the Commune (an idea widely held by the surrealists, Breton in particular). In fact, avant-gardism is no more a part of the brief history of the Commune than Marxism is. The Commune's Federation of Artists turned Proudhon's friend Courbet into an administrator presiding over meetings for twelve hours a day. As for the other leading artists of the day, including Corot, Millet, Manet, Degas, Daumier, and Renoir, they had all vacated Paris or were otherwise avoiding the Commune.[19] Members of the literary avant-garde, such as Edmond de Goncourt and Gustave Flaubert, were either too reactionary or too cynical to take an interest in the affairs of the Commune. The cynicism, at least, was justified when the Committee of Public Safety began a campaign of censorship, eventually suppressing dissent in the popular press by placing political restrictions on no fewer than twenty-seven newspapers.[20]

Such transgressions of the libertarian spirit, however, are as nothing beside the terrible vengeance wrought by Thiers's troops in the last days of the Commune. In the end, the anarchist tendencies within the Paris Commune and its brutal defeat formed an important cultural memory for many later anarchists in Paris. For the first time, anarchism had a history and a heritage that was more than theoretical. As the "childhood memory" of later anarchists, the story of the Commune fueled their activities. Some justified their terrorist acts as a form of vengeance against the government in retribution for the fallen Communards. This rationale was offered by one Henri Ribeyre, one of the few journalists who dared defend the senseless bombing of the Café Terminus by Emile Henry. Ribeyre linked Henry's motivation to his memory of the Commune, since the bomber's father had indeed been a Communard.[21] A number of anarchists far less dangerous than Emile Henry saw themselves as successors to the Communards, and so did the police. Richard Sonn quotes a police report of 30 April 1894, in which the anonymous informer "Legrand" describes the Montmartre cabaret owner Maxime Lisbonne: "The Concert Lisbonne has always been a socialist-anarchist center. And Lisbonne, while being prudent, preciously tries to conserve his Communard title. His political past is very much in his present fortune, and it is not rare to hear a spectator say: he has been in the Commune, he has been a colonel, he has been deported, etc. This same political past assures him a politico-literary clientele."[22] The informer's insight that political panache may be parlayed into cultural fortune is less reactionary than it seems, given that the truth of his observation has been borne out again and again in the history of politics and culture. Lisbonne's manipulation of his revolutionary persona to attract "a politico-literary clientele" will not be the last time that anarchism is co-opted and used as a cultural commodity. In fact, the cabaret culture of Montmartre is an early example of a certain type of bourgeois interest in leftist politics that turns political activity into an aesthetic experience and vice versa, so that the mere consumption of culture is somehow construed as an actual political act.

2

In the nineteenth century, there is no question that anarchism was consistently underwritten by less-than-revolutionary individuals, a point illustrated, in part, by the subscription lists of anarchist journals. True, Kropotkin and Elisée Reclus subscribed to Jean Grave's *La Révolte,* but so did Edouard Drumont, editor of the anti-Semitic journal *La Libre Parole.* Well-known, socially respectable authors like Anatole France also subscribed, as did the more obscure but equally respectable Mallarmé. Of the painters and artists who read *La Révolte* regularly—including the decadent Octave Mirbeau, the symbolist Paul Adam, and the neo-impressionist Paul Signac—not all could be said to be politically committed (only Signac remained a lifelong leftist).[23] As Jean Pierrot puts it:

> [W]e must not exaggerate the extent of this commitment on the part of a few younger writers to the anarchist cause. . . . [M]ost writers restricted themselves to an expression of interest merely, without offering any concrete support. . . . Moreover, the reasons for this sympathy with anarchism were much more intellectual than political. If some groups of young writers were favorably inclined to the movement, it was above all because they regarded it as providing a political equivalent of the individualism they were advocating in literature. They saw anarchism not as a popular movement but, on the contrary, as an aristocratic one.[24]

At the same time, this notion of anarchism as an artistic fashion should not be exaggerated, either. While it is true that many regarded anarchism not as a political cause but as a cultural commodity, it is also true that the majority of Jean Grave's readers were workers and artisans who can hardly be charged with the sin of political slumming. In this regard, Grave himself is an exemplary anarchist figure, and his career captures many of the contradictory currents within Parisian anarchism.

Born in 1854, Grave was sixteen years old at the time of the Commune. His father fought as a member of the Commune's beleaguered National Guard, and Grave himself was a member of the guard's youth reserve, though he never saw action. Like so many anarchists of the 1880s and 1890s, then, Grave's Communard background made him an ideological Other throughout the Third Republic. He was also trained in his father's trade as a shoemaker, and for a time he worked as a cobbler—precisely the kind of useful, independent vocation favored by anarchists like Proudhon. Grave, however, was mainly influenced by Kropotkin, and the two anarchists' careers were intertwined for some forty years. In 1883, Grave moved to Geneva to edit the newspaper founded by Kropotkin, *Le Révolté* (The Rebel). He brought the bi-monthly publication back to Paris in 1885, began issuing it as a weekly in 1886, and changed its name to *La Révolte* (The Revolution) in 1887. In 1891, several articles appeared in the newspaper commenting on two events related to the May Day demonstrations of that year. The first involved a group of anarchists who exchanged gunfire with the police at the Paris suburb of Clichy; Grave's paper, of course, sided with the anarchists. The second event was more serious, and *La Révolte* condemned the action of government troops at Fourmies in northeastern France, who had put down the labor demonstration and killed ten workers. When Grave refused to divulge the author of the most critical article, "Viande à Mitraille" (Meat to be slaughtered), he was arrested, tried, and sentenced to six months in prison. While in prison Grave worked on a novel and finished the theoretical work for which he is best known, *La Société mourante et l'anarchie*. Grave's theoretical analysis of the dying society and anarchy led to a second prison term in 1894, following the passage of the first of the Three Exceptional Laws or *lois scélérates* enacted by the government in response to the extraordinary wave of anarchist terror from 1892 to 1894: in March 1892, the anarchist-criminal Ravachol blew up the houses of the prosecutor and judge involved in the trial of the Clichy anarchists; in December 1893, Auguste Vaillant threw a bomb into the Chamber of Deputies; in February 1894, Emile Henry threw the bomb at the Café Terminus in the Saint-Lazare station; and in June 1894, the Italian anarchist Santo Caserio assassinated President Carnot in Lyons. Grave was arrested after the Café Terminus explosion and charged under the first of the Exceptional Laws, which made any journalistic encouragement of terrorism a criminal offense. The jury agreed with the charge that Grave's *La Société mourante et l'anarchie* violated the new law, and the man was put in prison for writing a book. Grave was in the first months of his two-year sentence when President Carnot was assassinated and the third of the Exceptional Laws was passed. This latest anti-anarchist legislation made it a crime even to make apologies or excuses for propaganda by the deed. Numerous intellectuals of varying political persuasions, including the socialists, objected to the third Exceptional Law as prohibiting free speech and threatening legitimate criticism of government policies. Nonetheless, the government brought a case against a group that it believed comprised the leading anarchists, and Grave was hauled out of jail and back to the courtroom as perhaps the most prominent figure in the famous Procès de Trente, or Trial of the Thirty.[25]

The Thirty were accused of criminal conspiracy against the government, and the indictment made no distinction between philosophical advocacy of anarchism and actual commission of terrorist acts. The refusal to discriminate between intellectuals and criminals was part of the prosecution's strategy, and accounts for all the defendants' being treated as though cut from the same cloth, regardless of their backgrounds or careers. Of the Thirty, eleven were common criminals, and these criminals—mostly petty thieves, including the notorious Ortiz—were tried along with Grave and other journalists and critics. These included Charles Chatel, former editor of the literary-anarchistic revue L'Endehors, and Félix Fénéon, the prominent art critic who made anonymous contributions to L'Endehors and other anarchist organs, but who held down an administrative job at the War Office.[26] Given the way these defendants comported themselves on the witness stand, it soon became evident that the prosecution's strategy to criminalize anarchism by association had backfired. Fénéon, in particular, came across as anything but a criminal in his clever ripostes to the questions put to him by Judge Dayras, as Joan Halperin reports:

> JUDGE DAYRAS: You were the intimate friend of the German anarchist, Kampffmayer.
> FÉNÉON: The intimacy could not have been very great. I do not know a word of German and he does not speak French. . . .
> JUDGE DAYRAS: It has been established that you surrounded yourself with Cohen and Ortiz.
> FÉNÉON (smiling): One can hardly be surrounded by two persons; you need at least three. (Explosion of laughter.)
> JUDGE DAYRAS: You were seen speaking with them behind a lamp-post!
> FÉNÉON: Can you tell me, Your Honor, where behind a lamp-post is?[27]

Fénéon kept up this manner even when he was faced with the serious charge of being in possession of the types of detonators used by anarchists to set off their bombs. Fénéon claimed that the detonators were found in the street by his late father:

> JUDGE DAYRAS: That is not possible. One does not find detonators in the street!
>
> FÉNÉON: And yet Monsieur Meyer, the examining magistrate, said to me one day: "You should have thrown those detonators out the window!" So you see one can find such objects on the public way. *(Laughter.)*
>
> JUDGE DAYRAS: That is not very likely. Your father would not have kept such things. He was an employee of the Banque de France and it is difficult to see what he could have done with them.
>
> FÉNÉON: I do not actually think he would have used them any more than his son, who was employed at the War Office.[28]

Jean Grave was hardly the equal of Fénéon in this type of verbal gamesmanship. In fact, he had a tendency to stutter in such situations, but he mastered his nervousness and defended himself vigorously, disavowing violence while arguing that his only "crime" was the free expression of political opinions. The jury completely exonerated Grave, Fénéon, and the other journalists and critics, but found Ortiz and the rest of the ten criminals guilty of theft. Thus, the petty criminals went to jail, while the real anarchists walked out of the courtroom, except for Grave, who returned to prison to finish his earlier sentence, the unjustness of which was now apparent.[29]

Although the anarchist group in the Trial of the Thirty had been vindicated, the decisive blow against one type of anarchism had been struck—mainly by the anarchists themselves. After 1894, in France and elsewhere, the era of propaganda by the deed was largely over, as most anarchists concerned themselves with the broader and more socially integrated issues of labor and education reform. The Trial of the Thirty also marked a turning point in anarchist culture, as it was the culmination of the government's campaign to eradicate anarchist expression. The *lois scélérates* resulted in extremely repressive measures taken against the anarchist press: both *La Révolte* and *Père Peinard* were closed down early in 1894. Other journals, such as *La Revue Blanche,* were not affected, mainly because their orientation was not overtly political, even though anarchists contributed to their columns. There is a touch of irony in this situation, especially in the case of Fénéon, who went on to write for *La Revue Blanche* and may have had some actual involvement in anarchist bombings, unlike

either Grave or Pouget.[30] While it is not completely true that anarchist culture was on trial in 1894, a look at the three publications
connected with Grave, Pouget, and Fénéon can provide some useful
insights into that culture, which was, after all, closely linked to social
change in anarchist theory. Most anarchists believed that widespread
social changes could only occur in the context of some kind of count-
erculture that would present an alternative to the prevailing bourgeois
entertainments of the salon, the opera, and the moralistic novel.[31]

In a sense, culture *was* on trial in the Procès de Trente. One
defendant, the Swedish painter Ivan Agueíl, was arrested because of
the pictures he painted: his portraits of his friend Fénéon and of an
actress known for her portrayals in Ibsen's plays were cited as evidence
of the painter's involvement in the alleged anarchist conspiracy. It
makes sense, therefore, to consider the kind of culture associated with
the anarchist organs whose writers and editors were in the dock:
Pouget's *Père Peinard*, Zo d'Axa's *L'Endehors* (whose contributors included Fénéon), and Grave's *La Révolte*. Of the three, *Père Peinard*
might be seen as the one paper that actually justified the state's position that anarchists mingled with criminals. The entire paper was written in the colorful slang of the *argotique* cultural milieu that included
criminals, prostitutes, and déclassé artists.[32] Consequently, *Père Peinard*
promoted the oral culture of the cabarets and streets of Montmartre,
all with a decidedly irreverent slant that was not above occasional cele-
brations of well-known criminals. For example, the paper printed the
blasphemous lyrics to the ballad "Père Duchesne," sung by the terrorist Ravachol on his way to the gallows.[33] The insistently oral quality of
the writing in *Père Peinard* has led one commentator to regret that
Pouget never had access to radio broadcasts, since that medium would
have been better suited to his purposes than print.[34] A particularly fine
example of the argot style makes the point about orality, but it also
illustrates the connection between politics and culture that the paper
encouraged its readers to make themselves:

> Arrivera bien un jour, nom de dieu, où l'art fera partie de la vie
> des bons bougres, tout comme les biftecks et le picolo.
>   Du coup les assiettes, les cuillères, les plats à barbe, les chaises, les
> lits, les armoires tout le fourbi quoi! en y ajoutant les étoffes pour
> frusquer les bonnes bougresses aussi bien que celles à rideaux. . . .
> Tout, tout, cré pétard, aura des colorations mirobolantes et des formes
> galbeuses.

A ce moment, l'artisse ne reluquera pas l'ouvrier, du haut de son
faux-col: les deux n'en feront qu'un.

Mais, pour qu'on en vienne là, faut que la Sociale marche grand
train et qu'on soit en pleine civilisation anarchote.[35]

An English translation by Joan Halperin conveys the sense of argot
involved in such expressions as *nom de dieu* and *des bons bougres,* as
well as in the use of slightly irregular diction, such as *artisse* for *artiste*
and *anarchote* for *anarchique:*

> Day'll come, Goddam, when art will fit into the life of ordinary Joes,
> just like steak and vino. Then, plates, spoons, chairs, beds—the whole
> works, what d'ya think! . . . everything, great guns, will have nifty
> shapes and fabulous colors. When that happens, the *artisse* won't look
> down his nose at the worker: they will be united. But before we get to
> that point, the old Union will have to get up some steam and we gotta
> be slap-dab in the middle of *anarcho* civilization.[36]

This description of art in the coming age of anarchism was evidently
written by Fénéon, who made occasional contributions to *Père Pei-*
nard and promoted the art of Toulouse-Lautrec and other postimpressionists in its pages.

Up to the Trial of the Thirty, however, Fénéon did most of his
writing for Zo d'Axa's *L'Endehors,* described by *Figaro* as an organ for
"anarchist writing and ultra-modern literary criticism."[37] The actual
writers favored by Fénéon in *L'Endehors* and in another journal, *Revue*
anarchiste (later *Revue libertaire*), included Jules Laforgue, Vielé-
Griffin, Gerhart Hauptmann, and other writers of similar symbolist
stamp, along with a group of writers already part of the fin de siècle
anarchist canon: Tolstoy, Ibsen, Nietzsche, Max Stirner, Herbert
Spencer.[38] But Fénéon preferred to take his literature straight, with
no ideology on the side, insisting that all true art was revolutionary
anyway. He had no use for Kropotkin's notion of works of art as
"instruments of the revolution."[39] Fénéon appeared to follow his
editor Zo d'Axa in keeping politics "outside" literature, as the name
of the journal suggests (*L'Endehors* means "the outsider," and Zo
d'Axa always claimed to be apolitical, an "outsider" even to anarchism).[40] This separation of art and ideology is curiously confirmed
by the double life that Fénéon led, as both a functionary in the War
Office and an anonymous contributor to underground papers. The
duplicitous, clandestine nature of *L'Endehors* itself is evidenced by Zo
d'Axa's friendship with Emile Henry, who helped with the prepara-

tion of the journal,[41] and Fénéon's surreptitious acquaintance with Ortiz, the thief convicted in the Trial of the Thirty.[42]

By contrast, no ideological obfuscation attended Jean Grave's straightforward *La Révolte,* which no doubt accounts for the frequency with which Grave was brought up on charges by the police. As the official organ of anarchist ideology, the paper earned Grave his title as "the pope of rue Mouffetard," the Left Bank site of the publication.[43] The voice of anarchist orthodoxy, *La Révolte* was not allied to current developments in the literary avant-garde, as was *L'Endehors,* and it was physically and philosophically remote from the popular culture of Montmartre celebrated by *Père Peinard.* Grave included a four-page "Supplément Littéraire" in *La Révolte* beginning in 1887, but the material it contained was intended to instruct, not divert. Regular features included selections from classical utopian literature, such as Thomas More's *Utopia* and Rabelais's *Gargantua and Pantagruel;* works by contemporary authors sympathetic to the working class, such as those by Tolstoy and Zola; and excerpts of work in the libertarian tradition, such as Thoreau's *On the Duty of Civil Disobedience* or anything by Diderot, one of Grave's particular favorites. The supplement also ran Kropotkin's previously unpublished *Mutual Aid* in installments, and excerpted pieces from Proudhon and Bakunin; more obscure anarchist writers were also represented, such as those associated with the 1848 revolution: Joseph Dejacque, author of the utopian *L'Humanisphère,* and Ernest Coeurderoy, veteran of the revolt against Louis-Napoléon, among others. Grave also published literature by anarchist acquaintances such as Paul Adam, Zo d'Axa, and Octave Mirbeau; he also published the poet Eugène Pottier, who wrote the words to the "International," the working-class anthem. Selections from Grave's novel, *La Grande Famille,* also appeared.[44] This reading list from *La Révolte* is hardly avant-garde, as Sonn notes: "Despite his literary supplement, Grave's *La Révolte* remained the ideological organ, while Pouget spoke for popular, social anarchism, and Zo d'Axa for its literary variant."[45]

But by the end of 1894, all three journals were out of business, and Grave was in a jail cell. He was released under the general amnesty for political prisoners declared under the new president, Félix Faure, in January 1895. By May he had succeeded in raising enough support to publish a new paper, called *Les Temps Nouveaux.* The name itself testifies to Grave's recognition that the times had changed, and that anarchism had entered a new phase. *Les Temps Nouveaux* reflected the new emphasis on anarcho-syndicalism; it also continued to refine the doctrines of anarcho-communism, put forward by its main contributor Kropotkin, now world-famous as the revered "saint" of anarchist politics.[46]

The paper continued in this way until the outbreak of World War I, when publication ceased. Urged on by Kropotkin, Grave supported the efforts of the wartime government of France against the Germans. This expression of nationalist sympathy, albeit in a time of unprecedented crisis, split the ranks of the French anarchists and drew severe criticism from Errico Malatesta.[47] The Italian anarcho-syndicalist accused Grave and other pro-war anarchists of abandoning the basic antigovernment philosophy that is the sine qua non of anarchism, and of undermining internationalist principles of pacifism and complete disarmament. With anarchists taking sides in a war among the nation-states of Europe, anarchism as an international political movement was effectively over. Henceforth, European anarchism would be confined to isolated political pockets, such as Andalusia or Catalonia in Spain, or would be adapted for specific social purposes, such as educational reform. As for the cultural impact of Parisian anarchism, the traditionalism of Grave's *La Révolte* and the ephemerality of Pouget's *Père Peinard* argue, in different ways, that the cultural contributions of *actual* anarchists were extremely limited, with the notable exception of Félix Fénéon. But even Fénéon's advocacy of the new art of the symbolists, the Nabis, and the neo-impressionists seems passive and peripheral in comparison with the more active role taken by, say, the gallery owner Ambroise Vollard, who was a real campaigner for postimpressionist art. In late nineteenth-century Paris, then, anarchy and culture are parallel developments that are not necessarily complementary. The anarchists and artists may go to the same cabarets, drink the same wine, and listen to the same music, but at closing time they go their separate ways, walking side by side only so far before they part.

3

The cultural influence of anarchist politics in France was certainly extensive, but it was also ambiguous. Support of anarchism did not necessarily involve allegiance to avant-garde literature, and promotion of recent artistic developments, literary or otherwise, was hardly limited to those who claimed to be anarchists. While it is true that a number of avant-garde artists and writers in fin de siècle France identified their work with anarchism, the anarchists themselves were capable of distributing their cultural interests over a much broader field than the avant-garde alone. This field included not only the true avant-garde culture of the symbolist journals and salons, but also the popular culture of the Montmartre newspapers and cabarets, not to mention an earlier culture associated with Enlightenment thought (principally the writings of Diderot). The only thing these three cultures have in common is a certain removal from the bourgeois mainstream, a unity imposed not by a similar aesthetic but by a shared ideology. Absent this ideology, much of the culture claimed by anarchists might just as well be claimed by anyone. In short, the anarchist milieu of late nineteenth-century France offers no compelling rationale for the association of a particular type of culture with a particular type of politics: the corrupt argot of *Père Peinard* and the purified poetry of Mallarmé both belong to anarchism, but neither belongs to anarchism alone.

The situation in Spain is rather different, largely because of the activities of the educational reformer Francisco Ferrer. Ferrer's efforts to combine anarchist politics and culture led him to establish the first Escuela Moderna in Barcelona in 1901, which, in turn, provided the model for a large number of Modern Schools that sprang up in Europe and America after his death in 1909. Jean Grave may have been the most important influence on Ferrer, who himself became the most influential anarchist figure to emerge from the Parisian scene. Grave was well aware of the anarchist movement in Spain, which reached a point of crisis in 1883, when large numbers of anarchists were rounded up and imprisoned as members of the notorious but nonexistent Mano Negra. The so-called Black Hand was "invented by Spanish authorities to indicate a nonexistent clandestine anarchist organization, which they used as an excuse to crack down on anarchists."[48] Grave's sympathy for the Spanish anarchists was expressed in the form of a long journalistic campaign urging political progressives everywhere to condemn the government and call for the release of the prisoners.[49] Given Grave's efforts on behalf of the Spaniards, it is not surprising that Ferrer sought him out when he began the period of his Parisian exile in 1885.

Ferrer began his political life as an associate of the radical Republican leader Manuel Ruíz Zorilla when he was working as a conductor on the railway line linking Barcelona to France, where Zorilla was living in exile. Ferrer took advantage of his position with the railroad to serve as Zorilla's courier and to shuttle political refugees from Spain to France. As his involvement in the Republican cause deepened he was forced to join Zorilla in exile in Paris, where he lived from 1885 until his return to Spain in 1901.[50] His years in Paris coincided with the most intense period of anarchist activity, and the already radical Ferrer moved even farther left. He supported himself by teaching Spanish and by publishing a language text, *Espagnol Pratique*. This volume brought Ferrer to the attention of the wealthy heiress Ernestine Meunié, who later gave him a gift of twelve thousand francs that he used to finance the first Escuela Moderna.[51] Ferrer's interest in education was due in part to the influence of Grave, whose *Enseignement bourgeois et enseignement libertaire* he read in 1900 (*MSM*, 4).

The difference between bourgeois and libertarian education was essentially the difference between authoritarian pedagogy that stressed rote memorization of facts and the Rousseauesque tradition that encouraged the development of the child's natural abilities. The libertarian tradition in education had a long history by the time Ferrer became interested in it. The New Harmony community in Indiana and the Temple School in Boston had emphasized radical education in the 1820s and 1830s, as had the Fourierist and other utopian socialist movements of the mid-nineteenth century. Libertarian education also had the support of the Americans Emerson and Thoreau, whom later anarchists claimed as their ideological kin, and the anarchists themselves, from Godwin to Kropotkin, all stressed new models of education in their efforts to abolish government, as all governments relied on traditional schools to produce obedient, conventional, law-abiding citizens. The new educational ideal held up by Ferrer and other libertarian reformers has been described as follows:

> [T]he true function of the teacher was to encourage self learning, to allow each child to develop in his own way, rather than force a predetermined program of study on him. Nor should the teacher smother the pupils under the weight of formal instruction. The emphasis, rather, must be on improvisation and experiment. Rigid programs, curricula, and timetables must be banished from the classroom, and

> instruction given in a manner that will cause the least interference
> with the pupil's freedom. For if a child is not compelled to learn, his
> own curiosity will draw him to the subjects that interest him, and his
> education will be more natural and pleasant, more enduring and
> meaningful.   (*MSM*, 9–10)

With this model of education in mind, and using part of the twelve
thousand francs given him by Mlle. Meunié, Ferrer established the
Escuela Moderna in Barcelona on 8 September 1901, with thirty
pupils distributed among primary, intermediate, and advanced levels
(*MSM*, 20). Boys and girls were put into the same classes, which
by itself established a revolutionary precedent, as the practice of
coeducation was virtually unknown in Spain at the time.[52] As for the
curriculum, the educational emphasis of the school was practical
rather than theoretical; Ferrer wanted his students to have as much
firsthand experience as possible, rather than the "wearisome" practice of getting knowledge through books. He was not opposed to
reading, however, and organized his own publishing house to produce new textbooks and new translations of existing ones. In addition to introductory books on arithmetic, grammar, and natural
science, Ferrer published more advanced works on sociology, anthropology, and religion. Many of these textbooks were overtly ideological in content: *Poverty: Its Cause and Cure* by Léon Martin, *Man and
the Earth* by Elisée Reclus, *Social Classes* by Charles Malato, *Anarchist
Morality* by Kropotkin, and so on (*MSM*, 21, 24). The utopian flavor
of these books is captured by a quotation from *Man and the Earth*
included in a posthumous tribute to Ferrer that terms the volume
"one of the great text-books of the Modern School." In it, Reclus is
so certain that the destiny of mankind is a single *"solidaire* group," a
confraternity of nations, that he is willing to ignore historical reality
in favor of ideological fantasy. All nations, he says, "are in the period
of mutual help, and, even when they collide in bloody shocks, they
do not cease to share the results of the common endeavor. . . .
France and Germany seem like rivals and enemies, it is true, but
[are], at bottom, most intimate friends, since they are toiling strenu-
ously together at the general work which is bound to profit all
men."[53] The quotation also shows that a large portion of Ferrer's
educational agenda was frankly propagandistic; the Escuela Moderna was intended to train individuals in the art of libertarian revolution. As Ferrer put it: "We do not hesitate to say that we want men

who will continue unceasingly to develop; men who are capable of constantly destroying and renewing themselves; men whose intellectual independence is their supreme power, which they will yield to none; men always disposed for things that are better, eager for the triumph of new ideas, anxious to crowd many lives into the life they have." [54]

Since 1901 the Spanish authorities had viewed Ferrer with suspicion but had not interfered with his activities. But when a bomb was thrown at the carriage of Alfonso XIII and his new bride on 31 May 1906, the crackdown began. The bomber failed to assassinate the royal couple but killed 24 people and injured 107 more. His name was Mateo Morral, and he had known Ferrer since 1903 and also worked at his publishing house. Because of this connection, Ferrer was accused of planning the assassination, whereupon he was arrested and the Escuela Moderna shut down for good. Ferrer spent a year in prison before being acquitted at his trial for lack of evidence. Upon his release he temporarily left Spain to promote libertarian education throughout western Europe, especially Belgium. Back in Spain by 1909, Ferrer was part of the demonstrations against Spanish involvement in Morocco organized by the Solidaridad Obrera. The union had called for a general strike as part of the protest, but the demonstrations turned into open insurrection and prompted the government to declare martial law on 27 July. The "Tragic Week" that followed saw wholesale arrests and summary executions. Ferrer was clearly not the "author and chief" of the rebellion as the authorities claimed, even though he had become an advocate of anarcho-syndicalism and promoted the general strike (*MSM*, 27–29, 31). In any case, he was tried and found guilty, and sentenced to die before a firing squad. He was executed on 13 October 1909; his last words, addressed to the soldiers who shot him, were reportedly these: "Aim carefully, my children. It is not your fault. I am innocent. Long live the Modern School." [55]

The death of Ferrer in October 1909 galvanized anarchists everywhere to rededicate themselves to the cause. With the Ferrer affair as its rallying point, the international anarchist movement gained a focus it did not otherwise have. By 1909 anarchism hardly appeared as a viable political alternative. The age of the *attentat* was long since over, and the new strategy of anarcho-syndicalism had not yet succeeded in ushering in the revolution. Despite the interest shown in it by many workers in France, Spain, and Italy, anarcho-syndicalism continued to lose ground to the socialists in attempts to organize workers for political purposes. From late in 1909 to the outbreak of World War I, therefore, anarchism was increasingly isolated from the political life of the West, but at the same time it took on a stronger cultural identity. Although Ferrer himself was not an original thinker in the area of educational reform, and was not particularly attuned to the artistic innovations of his age, the schools and cultural centers that were set up in his name made anarchism a powerful cultural conduit for many artists and writers. The death of Ferrer transformed anarchism from an increasingly inconsequential ideology to a vital cultural magnet for a number of important strains in modern art, more so in America than in Europe. Indeed, the contrast between the Spanish heritage of the Escuela Moderna and the American application of Ferrer's ideas needs some commentary.

Although Ferrer wanted to fuse basic education, anarchist ideology, and cultural activities, the Spanish schools that were set up in his name after his death did not necessarily mean to mix politics and culture. An important fact to keep in mind is that at least half the men and more than 60 percent of the women in turn-of-the-century Spain were illiterate, at least in the southern provinces, so the basic task of teaching people to read and write was paramount.[56] Indeed, the memoirs of several students educated in Spanish schools established by Ferrer disciples show little evidence of widespread political indoctrination, even though the schools were affiliated with the CNT (Confederacíon Nacional de Trabajo), the powerful anarcho-syndicalist organization. A student named Pura Pérez, who attended the Escuela Natura run by Professor Juan Puig Elias in 1933, says she "did not observe any propaganda orientation." Likewise, Diego Camacho, another student at the Escuela Natura, states that he "never heard anarchism spoken of in the school that I attended nor experienced any attempt to bring this movement into the school."[57] The paucity of ideology in the curriculum presented to these students in the 1930s might be attributed to the change in political circumstances since Ferrer first established the anarcho-educational model in 1901, except that most anarchists felt that they were suppressed during the republic even more than during the monarchy.[58] What the students of the Escuela Natura recall of their education (anatomy lessons, nature walks, poetry readings, and so on) is radical only in relation to the extremely rigid model of Catholic education, which stressed discipline and rote memorization. Anarchist ideology, then, did not really mix with basic education, partly because the work of freeing Spaniards from the burden of illiteracy was so great. This same burden affected adult education, which the CNT promoted through the establishment of numerous *ateneos* or "storefront cultural centers" in the working-class barrios of Barcelona. The *ateneos* were also social as well as educational centers, and it is clear that the anarchists who gathered at them were much more political than the children and teachers in the schools. But these adult centers have significant differences from the centers set up by the Ferrer Association in America. For one thing, the organizers of the Ferrer Association did not have the backing of an anarchist organization like the Textile Workers Union of Barcelona, which numbered some seventy thousand members and lent its considerable support to the schools and *ateneos*.[59] Also, the American anarchists were interested in culture in a more highly developed form than were their Spanish comrades, in part because they did not face the problem of illiteracy on such a vast scale. The anarchists at the *ateneos* in Barcelona learned to read and write, while those in New York learned about symbolist drama and modern art (along with English, Spanish, and Esperanto).[60] From the start, then, the anarchist enterprise undertaken in Ferrer's name in America was rather different from developments in Spain.

On the first anniversary of Ferrer's death, the Ferrer Association of New York (founded a few months earlier) held a public meeting and announced plans to establish a day school for children on the model of the Escuela Moderna, as well as a center for adults. With Emma Goldman as the driving ideological force behind it, the Modern School of New York began holding classes for adults on New Year's Day, 1911; the opening of the children's school was delayed until 13 October, the second anniversary of Ferrer's death. The prospectus for the school had been drawn up by Bayard Boyesen, a former English instructor at Columbia University whom Goldman had recruited to direct the educational arm of the Ferrer Association. Boyesen's stated aims for the new school were standard libertarian dogma: the Day School would encourage child-centered, nonauthoritarian integral education. "The personality of the child," Boyesen wrote, "during the sensitive and hazardous years of early youth, must be kept free from the intrusive hands of those who would mould and fashion it according to preconceived models, who would thwart this quality and divert that, in order to fit the child into the ideals of the teacher" (*MSM*, 75). The winter 1912 issue of the school's newsletter confirms the belief in Boyesen's anti-authoritarian principles. A note on "The Question of Discipline" asserts that "[t]he only true discipline is that which springs spontaneously from within—discipline that arises from the necessity of the moment, and not from the compulsion of the argus-eyed teacher."[61] The initial results of applying these ideas to a roomful of children aged four to ten were predictably chaotic. The first teacher lasted only a few weeks, the second a few months. One early "lesson" was given by the school's janitor, who decapitated a cat in front of the students to demonstrate "what life was really like" (*MSM*, 74). Only nine students attended the school at 104 East 12th Street, but they were "wild," according to one of them, and "very badly behaved." This report comes from a student named Révolte, who evidently lived up to his name. The first teacher quit when Révolte's brother threatened to jump out the window of the three-story building (80–81). At least one student quit as well; an anarchist child whose real name was Amour Liber stopped attending and told his father that the methods employed at the school held no interest for him: "They only fight. Nothing else happens."[62]

This complaint was registered during the tenure of the third teacher, Will Durant, better known today as the popularizer of philosophy and history. At twenty-six years of age, Durant at least had the energy to hold his own against the children, who now numbered sixteen at the school's new location on East 107th Street (*MSM*, 96). Durant also had some teaching experience and appears to have had some success instructing his students in reading, arithmetic, geography, and history, with frequent excursions to Central Park and the Museum of Natural History. The children also received training in woodworking at the school's carpentry shop as part of the integral education they were receiving. An account by Durant of "Problems En Route" appears in the Spring 1913 issue of the *Modern School* newsletter. In this report the young teacher describes the work of the first term as "chiefly negative: practically, the best we could accomplish then was to build up day by day in the children a sense of the difference between that beautiful and salutary thing called lib-

erty—the free play of our individual natures—and that unwhole-
some and destructive thing called license—the sacrifice of the liberty
of others for the sake of our own." Durant proceeds to describe
the successes of the second term, including the practice of writing
grammatical errors in correct form one hundred times when *he*
makes them (the children have to write the correct forms of their
errors only twenty times): "What do I teach them? Everything under
the sun, from match-making to French. One of my children is beginning algebra, and rewriting Shakespeare and Charles Lamb; another
is struggling with that regrettable institution called interest; another
is flirting with improper fractions; and the youngest of them is grappling with the mysterious fact that two and two make four." [63]

Durant clearly loved his "natural little anarchists," as he called
them, one in particular. A lively Jewish girl of fourteen named Ida
Kaufmann who lived near the school began to take an interest in it
when she saw how happy the children appeared, playing in Central
Park. She asked to join the school and soon became Durant's star
pupil. He called her "Ariel," although her nickname was "Puck"; he
also called her his " 'Whitman girl,' for surely she personified the
Song of the Body Electric. " One day when all the other children had
gone home, Durant writes, "By some fated accident our bodies
touched, and my whole being was swept electrically with a current of
desire." In Ariel he saw someone whose existence was not bound, as
his had been, by the confines of religion: "she romped and babbled
and laughed and sang with the innocence of a girl who had never
known theology." Durant was a former seminarian whose interest in
sexuality up to this point had been expressed mainly in lectures
about the phallic significance of Christian images, and he was never
so strong a proponent of free love as some of the other libertarians
connected with the Ferrer Association (such as Margaret Sanger). In
fact, it was the fourteen-year-old Ariel who asked *him*, "Do you believe
in free love?" [64] In any event, Durant felt he had to resign his teaching
position, though no one had asked him to do so. Nor was Durant
sufficiently anarchistic to challenge the legal prohibitions against sex
with minors. He married Ariel at City Hall on 31 October 1913; she
was fifteen years old by that time and showed up for the ceremony
on roller skates.[65]

The point these anecdotes are intended to make is simply that
the Modern School actually achieved very little in the way of educa-

tional reform during its stay in New York City. The opinion of the American anarchist Voltairine de Cleyre is telling: "I really think that [people] got swept off their feet by Ferrer's death, and began to holler 'Modern Ed.' without knowing what they were hollering about" (*MSM*, 92). The Ferrer Association's efforts in other areas, however, were much more successful, and the cultural impact more legitimate. The difference between the Day School and the Ferrer Center, which promoted adult education and cultural events, suggests the basic dynamism of anarchism itself, since the children's school looked backward to fundamentally romantic, Rousseauesque ideas, while the center was culturally progressive. The Ferrer Center's many cultural activities included theater productions, poetry readings, public lectures, art classes, and journal publications. The nature of these cultural activities reflects the curious social mixture of the Ferrer Association at large. As Laurence Veysey has pointed out, the Ferrer group in New York City was composed, on the one hand, of mostly Jewish, upwardly mobile immigrants whose libertarian leanings often had some basis in their country of origin, and, on the other, of a fairly well-to-do group of old-stock Americans who saw in the immigrant masses an opportunity to experience radical politics for the first time.[66] The attraction felt by this older group of Americans for the immigrant population is expressed by Carl Zigrosser, who edited the *Modern School* journal from 1917 to 1919 and transformed it from a mere newsletter into one of the finest "little magazines" of the modernist era. In his memoirs of this period, Zigrosser writes:

> My identification with the Ferrer Center . . . was based not only on my sympathy for the underdog but on my quest for new experience. I had lived a relatively sheltered life in pursuit of knowledge, mostly from books. Now I wanted to know people, all kinds of people in every walk of life. I was meeting affluent people, . . . but I felt that there was more to society than its upper segment. I wanted to discover "how the other half lives." I was also fascinated by the idea of New York as a world in miniature. . . . I had a notion of writing an essay on the many foreign enclaves it contained—a kind of voyage around the world in miniature —such as Chinatown, the German section of Yorkville, the Syrian colonies on Washington Street down by the Battery or on Atlantic Avenue in Brooklyn, the Armenians in the East Twenties, the Italians in Greenwich Village and the East Side, small colonies of Spanish, French, and Greeks on the West Side between 14th and 42nd Streets, and the Black

Belt of Harlem. Most picturesque of all was the teeming East Side, the abode of hopes and despairs of many who had emigrated to seek the Promised Land of Freedom.[67]

Not only is Zigrosser attracted to the potential for cosmopolitan and bohemian experience in the immigrant life of New York; he wants to convert that experience into literary form by writing an essay about it. Veysey has noted that a common feature of almost all the nonimmigrant anarchists connected with the Ferrer Association at this time was a pronounced literary ambition. His observation that the involvement of such literary types in the Ferrer Center "may be viewed as a stage in the process of groping toward a mass audience" certainly rings true (consider, for example, the huge readership of Will Durant's books).[68] While Zigrosser's post-Ferrer career was not in literature but in graphic arts, his literary sensibility sounds through when he describes Stewart Kerr, one of his Ferrer Center associates, as "a gentle Scot, who almost seemed to have stepped out of the pages of Henry James's *Princess Casamassima.*"[69] The comparison Zigrosser makes between his Ferrer associate and the fictional anarchist Paul Muniment goes a long way toward explaining the mix of politics and culture that the Modern School promoted.

The literature classes at the Ferrer Center reflected the tastes and interests of those educated, established radicals who were drawn to the bohemian experience of the immigrant Other. The curriculum was a mix of romantic poets and American transcendentalists regarded as precursors of anarchist thought—Blake, Byron, Shelley, Emerson, Whitman, Thoreau—together with a group of European "nihilists": Nietzsche, Ibsen, Shaw (whose increasing distance from anarchism seems to have been less important than the need to have an Irish representative of libertarian ideas). The *Modern School* newsletters of 1913 help to show what the literary evenings at the Ferrer Center must have been like for the curious mix of recent immigrants and old-stock Americans that made up the audience of adult learners. A note in the Spring 1913 newsletter describes the "literary chats" conducted every Monday evening at 8:00 P.M. by Leonard D. Abbot, the first president of the Ferrer Association. Abbot's class, "Radical Literature and Great Libertarians," was said to "bring into our midst such comrades as Walt Whitman, Shelley, Byron, Nietzsche, William Blake, William Morris, Emerson, Maeterlinck."[70] Whitman heads the list of "comrades" in part because his radical individualism was expressed in free verse, a blend of the politically unconventional and the aesthetically innovative. This blend is rarely evident in the pages of the *Modern School* journal itself, however. The Spring 1913 issue also contains much doggerel poetry by the immigrant poet Adolf Wolff, including a poem titled "Walt Whitman" that unfortunately merges the sublime and the bathetic in its description of the poet: "Mountain-like he towers, a Matterhorn / Midst many minor peaks."[71] The issue also includes a translation of a poem by Baudelaire, "The Stranger," done by another immigrant writer, one Félicie Poznanska, who is described as a "pupil and a teacher in the Ferrer School." The description not only blurs the line between teacher and student in typical, anti-authoritarian anarchist fashion; it also shows that the Ferrer Center students were encouraged not just to learn but to use the resources of the center, including the *Modern School* magazine, as a medium for cultural expression. An obscure example of this practice by a famous student is the poem "Travail" by Man Ray:

> The days are dead for me
> And the nights live
> Thru the day I dream
> At night I wake
> And when I wake I die.
>
> I do not count the hours
> Nor watch the sun
> But thru a monotone of time I drift
> My senses numbed
>
> From afar
> Dim music rocks my restless soul to sleep—
> Death's lullaby
> I sleep—I wake—I die.
>
> Give me a draught of life ere I depart,
> Red sparkling life—not over-sweet
> Then let me sleep
> Fatigued.[72]

The quality of the poem may be open to question, but one of the striking things about it is the utter absence of political content. The vaguely symbolist-decadent tone, marked by occasional synesthetic effects ("Dim music"), makes an interesting contrast with the overtly political linkage of literature and libertarian philosophy in Abbot's

Monday evening lectures. Later, under Zigrosser's editorship the *Modern School* magazine published poetry by Hart Crane and Wallace Stevens. While their poetry may have been in a sharper mode of modernism, there always seemed to be a place in anarchist culture for the hazier manifestations of the symbolist aesthetic.

The mixture of libertarian politics and fin de siècle aesthetics also informed the art classes taught at the Ferrer Center by Robert Henri and George Bellows. Although Henri and Bellows represented an earlier tradition of social realism, their classes certainly did not require adherence to a particular style. The relaxed atmosphere of the art classes is captured, again by Zigrosser, in his account of the drawing course he took under Bellows's direction: "I did get a taste of the sheer sensuous pleasure of drawing from the nude, to set down on paper the living breathing forms, and to appraise and control their curves and contours, especially when it was accompanied by lovely music, as was often the case when a young pianist, Hyman Rovinski, played or improvised by the hour."[73] The synesthetic experience of drawing to the rhythm of music has its origins in symbolism, while the practice of working from life is grounded in realism. The different paths taken by Bellows's and Henri's two most successful students, John Sloan and Man Ray, evidence the blend of old and new at the Ferrer Center, since Sloan's Ashcan School is well within the realist tradition, while the modernist orientation of Man Ray grew out of the symbolist aesthetic and led eventually to dada-surrealism. These divergent traditions were able to coexist at the Ferrer Center because anarchism encouraged both social critique and individualist expression. As modernism developed and anarchism receded, however, politics and art became harder to reconcile. The fact that Leon Trotsky took art classes at the Ferrer Center during his brief New York stay in 1917 might be used to argue the contrary, to say that the center provided a common ground for art and ideology. But the Trotsky visit is only incidental to the larger politico-cultural history of the Modern School. In truth, internal tensions existed almost from the beginning, as the reports of the Ferrer Center art exhibit that ran from 28 December 1912 to 3 January 1913 suggest. Alan Wolff's essay on the exhibit from the Spring 1913 issue of the newsletter notes that the art students at the Center "work under the guidance and inspiration of Robert Henri and George Bellows, the sum total of whose teaching amounts to the

command, 'Be thyself.' " He also mentions Cézanne, Matisse, and
Picasso, calling their art "unformed but in the process of formation,
as yet a caricature, a rough sketch, a faint prophecy of the strong,
complex and beautiful being to be." [74] This rather equivocal endorsement of modern art, together with the art teachers' purported encouragement of extreme individualism, is answered in the same issue
of the newsletter by the artist Manuel Komroff when he argues that
"[a]n age of specialization means an age of one-sidedness. Each
thinks himself independent of the other, when in reality they [*sic*]
cannot live without each other." Komroff's essay, titled "Art Transfusion," also argues not only for the interdependence of artists but
also of the arts themselves: "Sculpture, painting and literature are
all trying to be musical, and modern music is weaving designs with
colored shreds of poetry. . . . Each art finds its scope so great that it
may safely include all the remaining arts." [75] In a way, Komroff's brief
for synesthetic art reads like a cultural version of anarcho-
communism, in which individual artists become participants in some
kind of mutualist enterprise, whereas Wolff places art squarely in the
individualist anarchist tradition. Also, Wolff thinks that modern art
is both incomplete and progressive, whereas Komroff imagines it to
be self-contained, in the art for art's sake tradition of the past: "Art
should never try to be anything outside of itself. It should never tell
a story, nor have a moral. It should be itself and nothing more. . . .
Wilde had the right idea when he wrote that art begins where imita-
tion leaves off; and that nature should follow art." [76]

    The double tradition of social realism and fin de siècle avant-
gardism was also manifest in the performances of the Ferrer Center's
Free Theater. The theater began its first season in 1914 at the center,
preceding the better-known Provincetown Players by a couple of
years in producing modern dramas by Maeterlinck, Synge, and others (*MSM*, 142–43). The first production of the Free Theater on 5
September 1914 featured two one-act plays, *Dialogue at the Rising of
the Moon* by the French decadent writer Pierre Louÿs and an original
work by the anonymous playwright "X.X.X." called *Out from the Dark:
A Thieves Comedy*. The latter play was described as "a study of hoboes
and thieves exchanging confidences on a park bench" and seems to
have been designed, in part, to appease the less refined followers of
the Ferrer Center's cultural activities. [77] The pairing of *A Thieves Comedy* with a play by a precious decadent writer speaks again to the

combined immigrant and near-aristocratic membership of the Modern School. Yet another anecdote from Zigrosser's memoirs helps to show why the Free Theater might want to accommodate both street and salon culture in its premier production, as the aesthetic anarchism of the symbolists was not appreciated by everyone at the Ferrer Center. Zigrosser recalls a lecture by Leonard Abbot on Maeterlinck's symbolist drama *Pelléas et Mélisande* that was followed by a discussion that "had been uniform in praising Maeterlinck's sensibility and ability to create and sustain a mood, until the hobo poet, Harry Kemp, got up to speak. He launched such a torrent of invective and burlesque that everybody was shaking with laughter. . . . For him it was all rot, he said, decadent to the last degree." [78] Once again, as with the literature and art classes, the Ferrer Center's theatrical productions tried to muster support for anarchism in both a political and an aesthetic sense, but the ideal of a unified ideology that could include politics, education, and culture became harder to maintain in the face of social reality.

The note about *A Thieves Comedy* quoted above goes on to say that the play's "study" of hoboes and thieves "was evidently inspired by the unemployed demonstrations in New York last spring." [79] This comment, from the newsletter of October 1914, is one of the relatively few references in the *Modern School* magazine to the social tensions that the New York chapter of the Ferrer Association had to deal with in the tumultuous year of 1914. On 4 July of that year a homemade bomb exploded by accident in a residence on Lexington Avenue, killing three anarchists. During the fall of 1914 several actual and rumored bombings contributed to the tensions in the Modern School, not only because of police surveillance but also because of internal disagreements among the Ferrer regulars over the role of violence in the revolution.[80] By the end of 1914, the political, cultural, and educational aims of the Ferrer Association were becoming more independent of one another. Emma Goldman and Alexander Berkman continued to hold forth as the most vocal advocates of anarchist politics in the association itself; the Ferrer Center for adults included political debate and education (mainly language courses and painting classes) but emphasized cultural events; and the Day School for children clearly began to distance itself from politics proper and concentrated on integral education. Harry Kelly, the man most responsible for the day-to-day operations of the Ferrer group, justified the removal of the Day School from New York City to Stelton, New Jersey, by arguing that, while political agitation was "both necessary and desirable," such activity might "have a harmful effect on the children and warp their minds; children require brightness and joy and they can best receive that far, and yet not too far, from the 'madding crowd.'"[81] As the three basic strands of the Ferrer Association began to unravel, the highly focused emphasis on anarchism that had marked its founding days in New York became more diffuse. For example, Zigrosser eventually came to see the purpose of the *Modern School* magazine as radical in a general, not an anarchistic, sense. He wrote that the journal was simply "a medium of expression for creative thinkers and artists. It deals with radical ideas in education, and by education I mean every activity that broadens and enhances life" (*MSM,* 162).

In the end, the relationship of anarchist politics to the culture promoted by the Ferrer Center became increasingly unclear and particularly problematic as artistic trends moved in the direction of modernism. For example, the Ashcan School of Henri, Bellows, and Sloan continued an earlier tradition of political art originated by Courbet and sanctioned by Proudhon, but this tradition is hard to reconcile with the avant-gardism of Man Ray and Max Weber, another Ferrer Center regular. The painters of the Ashcan School were political in the sense that they took as their subjects people on the margins of urban society—peddlers, immigrants, laborers—and made such figures the center of their art. But another group of Ferrer Center artists, led by Man Ray, also frequented Alfred Stieglitz's Fifth Avenue gallery where the latest European art was on view. An anarchist sympathizer himself, Stieglitz had exhibited Matisse in 1908 and was a supporter of both libertarian politics and abstract art (*MSM,* 153). Matisse is a particularly good example to cite in this context, as his painting is largely absent any type of overt political content. How was it possible, then, for such politically innocuous painting to be construed as consistent with anarchism? One answer is that anarchist theory allows absolute freedom to artists to paint as they please, without regard for political content, notwithstanding the fact that most anarchists preferred their art to be transparently propagandistic. Another answer is simply that modernist art, especially in America, is anarchist by association only. That is, people who called themselves anarchists liked it, and they liked it not only because it was new, but also because the bourgeoisie did not. As a result, one minute the lively, documentary realism of the Ashcan School was anarchist art, the next minute the abstract compositions of the fauvists and cubists were. The only aesthetic principle that can accommodate such an extreme shift of taste is radical newness compounded by bourgeois aversion: to be anarchistic, then, culture need only be "advanced."

4

Anarchism as a form of progressive or "advanced" culture was energetically promoted by Benjamin Tucker, editor of the anarchist newspaper *Liberty* in Boston, and, later, in New York City. There, Tucker's anarcho-cultural enterprise was based at his "Unique Book-shop" and publishing house on Sixth Avenue. The establishment was the outlet for reprints of classic anarchist works by Proudhon and Stirner, many of which Tucker translated himself, and for a seemingly unending stream of polemical pamphlets edited or authored by Tucker. The name of the shop is evidently derived from Stirner's book of egoistic philosophy, *Der Einzige und sein Eingentum,* since *der Einzige* can be translated as "the unique one." Tucker's publication of Stirner's book as *The Ego and His Own* in 1907 is important in the history of individualist anarchism. This book and others that Tucker published and promoted had a strong influence on several modernist writers. James Joyce had Tucker's edition of Paul Eltzbacher's *Anarchism* in his library and is reported to have called Tucker "the great political thinker."[82] Another modernist writer to come under the influence of Tucker was Eugene O'Neill. The two met in 1907, and O'Neill frequented the Unique Book-shop on a regular basis, "browsing in all shades of advanced thought, from Tolstoy and Kropotkin to Nietzsche and Shaw, not to mention the works of Tucker himself, which, on O'Neill's own testimony, greatly influenced his 'inner self.' " No doubt it was partly as a result of Tucker's influence that O'Neill later took an interest in the Free Theater productions at the Ferrer Center (*MSM,* 143).

Benjamin Tucker is usually classified as an "individualist anarchist" or an "anarcho-individualist." The terms refer to a conservative shading of anarchism that, following Stirner, values egoism and, following Proudhon, defends the inviolability of the private property that has been earned through individual labor. Although Tucker adapted his politics to changing situations over time, by the first decade of the twentieth century his version of anarchism had settled into the highly libertarian but conservative mold that forms part of the right-wing individualist tradition in America to this date (Tucker, however, maintained liberal views on certain key social issues, such as marriage and the rights of women). Like later avatars of the tradition, Tucker was extremely critical of the authoritarian tendencies of communism.[83] He was particularly eloquent in taking the side of individualist anarchism against state socialism, which he saw as a matter of elevating Proudhon over Marx:

> The vital difference between Proudhon and Marx is to be found in the respective remedies which they proposed. Marx would nationalize the productive and distributive forces; Proudhon would individualize and associate them. Marx would make the laborers political masters; Proudhon would abolish political mastership entirely. Marx would abolish usury by having the State lay violent hands on all industry and business and conduct it on the cost principle; Proudhon would abolish usury by disconnecting the State entirely from industry and business and forming a system of free banks which would furnish credit at cost to every industrious and deserving person and thus place the means of production within the reach of all. Marx believed in compulsory majority rule; Proudhon believed in the voluntary principle. In short, Marx was an *autoritaire*, Proudhon was a champion of Liberty.[84]

Tucker brought the same precise style and ability to formulate clear distinctions to the other political issues that concerned him, mainly mutualist economics and egoistic ethics. His journal *Liberty* from 1888 onward became an organ "for clarifying the fine points of individualist anarchism" and for exploring Tucker's "growing interest in European avant-garde literature and drama."[85]

Tucker's *Unique Catalogue of Advanced Literature* listed "Literature That Makes for Egoism in Philosophy, Anarchism in Politics, Iconoclasm in Art." This catalogue, detailing the stock of books available from the Unique Book-shop, was printed in French, German, and Italian, as well as English. In keeping with the internationalist ambitions of anarchism, Tucker sold original works and translations in those languages. The internationalist theme is conveyed by a 1907 catalogue of Italian books that is bound in covers to make it look like a passport. This catalogue lists about 500 titles, including 30 by Gabriele D'Annunzio, 29 by Zola, 18 by Ibsen, and only 4 by Nietzsche, indicating Tucker's awareness that the German's supposed nihilism was not particularly libertarian.[86] Elsewhere, Tucker had criticized Nietzsche's political limitations: "Nietzsche says splendid things,—often, indeed, Anarchistic things,—but he is no anarchist. . . . He may be utilized profitably, but not prophetably."[87] Tucker's clever wordplay may be one thing that endeared him to Joyce. In any case, the anarchist certainly had a taste for the fin de siècle literature that forms the background of modernism. For example, Tucker published Oscar Wilde's *Ballad of Reading Gaol*, Mirbeau's *Diary of a Chambermaid*, and N. G. Chernyshevsky's *What's To Be Done*, which was advertised as follows: "Written in prison. Suppressed by the Czar. The author over twenty years an exile in Siberia. The book which has most powerfully influenced the youth of Russia in their growth into Nihilism."[88] An idea of just how up-to-date Tucker tried to keep his readers can be gained by a glance at *The Balzac Library*, a small format pamphlet series that reprinted essays on a wide variety of topics from other reviews and journals, many of them European. For example, an article on "The French Novel in the Nineteenth Century," written by Marcel Prevost, that had appeared in the *Revue Bleue* of 14 April 1900, was translated and reprinted as a *Balzac Library* pamphlet only one month later. The essay is a thorough, concise account of the French novel from Balzac to Bourget that generally approves of the French decadent tradition, with its "morose delectation" and "sadness of the restless flesh."[89] Another interesting *Balzac Library* reprint is a translation from the German titled "What Are Dreams?" The anonymous essay originally appeared in the 15 March 1900 issue of *Die Grenzboten* in Leipzig. Tucker's reprint is dated 5 April 1900, and contains what is surely one of the earliest expositions of Freud's ideas in America. The method of the talking cure is described, as well as the idea that dreams signify "a fulfillment of wishes." The essay provides a clear description of Freud's basic insights: "According to Freud, nothing that one has once known is completely forgotten; forgetting is only a temporary pushing into the background, and the place where recollections are stored is not part of the brain, but the soul."[90] The last phrase notwithstanding (the original no doubt would suggest "psyche" rather than "soul" to a later translator), the essay provides an informed and sympathetic summary of some of the key ideas underlying the new science of psychoanalysis.

In his efforts to keep his readers informed of recent intellectual currents, Tucker cast a wide net to cover the cultural developments of his age. The result was a tendency to include nondescript literature in the category of "advanced" work simply because its content was ideologically consistent with anarchism, along with works now recognized for their combination of social insight and innovative technique. In the latter category, Whitman and Ibsen were duly celebrated, even though adjustments had to be made for their ideological shortcomings. Whitman, for instance, is said to be egoistic enough for any anarchist, but "that old prejudice of patriotism" needs excising from *Leaves of Grass* because it "makes him blind to the logic of world citizenship."[91] Similarly, Ibsen is called a great writer who could have been greater if only he had provided solutions to the social problems he pointed out in his plays:

> He gathers together the elements in the problem of life,—the position of women, commercial relations, the obligations of social and family ties, the restraints of religion, and the power of conventional ideas; with magnificent scorn he tells off his indictments against them, holds them up to shame and loathing, and sweeps them off the stage. But he has not solved his problem. It is still there, as puzzling as ever. For he has not even touched the primary element of the whole matter,—the economic question.[92]

What is today called "political correctness" was much in evidence at the turn of the American century, and the use of ideological criteria to determine aesthetic value led Tucker to include much literature in his "advanced" catalogue that now appears of questionable artistic worth. For example, Tucker translated Felix Pyat's *The Rag Picker of Paris* and advertised it as follows:

> A novel unequalled in its combination of dramatic power, picturesque intensity, crisp dialogue, panoramic effect, radical tendency, and bold handling of social questions. Probably the most vivid picture of the misery of poverty, the extravagance of wealth, the sympathy and forbearance of the poor and despised, the cruelty and aggressiveness of the aristocratic and respectable, the blind greed of the middle classes, the hollowness of charity, the cunning and hypocrisy of the priesthood, the tyranny and corruption of authority, the crushing power of privilege, and, finally, of the redeeming beauty of the ideal of liberty and equality that the century had produced.[93]

The last phrase illustrates just how completely aesthetic values have been subsumed by political values, to the point of seeming interchangeable: liberty and equality are beautiful, beauty is free and equal. This tendency to identify radical politics with traditional aesthetic categories such as "beauty," together with Tucker's considerable abilities to clarify and define, led in a direction opposite to the emerging culture of modernism.

Paradoxically, Tucker used his clarifying rhetoric to promote the new, uncertain culture of modernism, but for reasons that were hardly artistic. Once again, advanced politics and advanced literature move in the same direction but on different planes. Additional evidence of this fact is Tucker's promotion of William Godwin's *Caleb Williams,* that aesthetically retrograde novel by the father of anarchism.[94] What is lacking in so much of the radical culture Tucker encouraged is any acknowledgment that technique in addition to content may carry political meaning. In this regard, Tucker follows Jean Grave in advocating works written in a traditional style, although, unlike Grave, he took a greater interest in contemporary literature. But with a few exceptions (notably D'Annunzio), the new authors Tucker promoted wrote literature that was generally unsurprising in spite of its "advanced" status. The practice of putting new wine into old bottles is typical of most of those who took an active role in anarchist politics. Godwin, Proudhon, Bakunin, Kropotkin, Grave, Tucker—none of them entertained the idea that technique might also be revolutionary, or that experimentation could signify political unrest. Peripheral figures such as Félix Fénéon made the connection of anarchism to aesthetics, but the major figures construed culture almost exclusively as content, and had no insights into style or structure. The separation of the artistic avant-garde from the political becomes especially acute as modernism develops. During this crucial early period of the twentieth century, there is no finer example of the problematic interaction of anarchism and culture than the career of Margaret Anderson. A self-professed anarchist who was also a major promoter of modernist culture, Anderson helps us to see how the internal tensions in anarchist ideology drove some anarchists away from the emerging culture of modernism and others toward it. In the case of Anderson, these tensions and contradictions at first produced an uneasy alliance between aesthetic modernism and social modernity, but ultimately led to unbridgeable divisions between them.

5

Margaret Anderson's interest in anarchism can be linked to an earlier adolescent rebellion against a stultifying life of "country clubs and bridge" in her hometown of Columbus, Indiana.[95] In her autobiography *My Thirty Years' War* Anderson describes the experience of going away to college as an "escape from authority" that is couched in cloyingly romantic terms: "I remember only moonlight nights on balconies, violet hunts in the spring, the smell of autumn orchards from class-room windows" (*MTYW*, 7). Such youthful evasions of authority and convention are generally unremarkable, but in Anderson's case the romantic individualism of her college days seems to have informed her life throughout and is a major element in her anarchistic approach to culture. Shortly after her college experience of moonlight and violets Anderson moved to Chicago, where she established the *Little Review,* now regarded as one of the premier avant-garde journals of the modernist period. A few months into the publication of the magazine Anderson heard Emma Goldman speak and experienced a conversion to anarchism. After a lecture by Goldman in May 1914, just as the third issue of the *Little Review* was being readied for press, Anderson managed "to turn anarchist before the presses closed" (*MTYW*, 54). Sure enough, the May issue of the journal features an essay titled "The Challenge of Emma Goldman," in which Anderson quotes Goldman on the abuses of Christianity and government; the limitations that morality imposes on humanity in general and women in particular; and the injustices created by property and wealth.[96] Even before this article appeared, however, the relation of anarchism and other forms of radical politics to the journal's aesthetic agenda had already been made. The very first issue contains an article by Sherwood Anderson titled "The New Note" in which the writer urges the young artists of the day to develop their craft in such a way as "[t]o get near to the social advance for which all moderns hunger."[97] The young poets and novelists who are to be numbered among the progressive moderns are called "the soldiers of the new": "That there are such youths is brother to the fact that there are ardent young cubists and futurists, anarchists, socialists, and feminists" (*MTYW*, 50). In this formulation, the "new spirit" animates the artist and the ideologue alike in the same social advance.

But Margaret Anderson's involvement with anarchism suggests otherwise. While there can be no doubt that in her Chicago and New York periods Anderson thought of herself as an anarchist, the anarchism she professed was hardly like that of the anarchists she admired. Surely no anarchist other than Anderson would have described the relationship of "Art and Anarchism" as she did in the March 1916 issue of the *Little Review:* "An anarchist is a person who realizes the gulf that lies between government and life; an artist is a person who realizes the gulf that lies between life and love. The former knows that he can never get from the government what he really needs for life; the latter knows that he can never get from life the love he really dreams of." [98] The treatment here of art and anarchism alike as separate but similar species of romantic individualism ends up amalgamating anarchy and culture from one perspective and separating them from another. In one sense, Margaret Anderson's aesthetic anarchism can be seen as the logical but improbable development of Matthew Arnold's earlier emphasis on culture as an individually informed means of maintaining public order. Anderson, like Arnold, wants culture to do the work of politics; unlike Arnold, she wants that culture to perform an individualizing rather than a universalizing function. From another perspective, however, Anderson's defense of aesthetic individualism runs counter to the ideology of anarchism, as an exchange between Anderson and the anarchists recorded in *My Thirty Years' War* shows.

A politico-aesthetic dispute arises when the anarchists argue that Oscar Wilde's poem about his prison experience, *The Ballad of Reading Gaol,* is preferable to *Salomé,* Wilde's rather turgid symbolist drama. Alexander Berkman, author of *Prison Memoirs of an Anarchist,* quite understandably takes the side of *Reading Gaol,* and so does Emma Goldman, veteran of several prison stints herself. Anderson prefers *Salomé* and advances the value of art for art's sake, using Imagist poetry to make the argument:

> When I used the black swan in Amy Lowell's "Malmaison" to illustrate a certain way of pointing emotion there was a general uprising. E.G. [Emma Goldman] was a little beside herself.
>
> The working-man hasn't enough leisure to be interested in black swans, she thundered. What's that got to do with the revolution?
>
> But that isn't the argument, I groaned. . . .

> We're talking art, not economics, I pointed out. Anyway it
> makes no difference. Leisure may only give people more time to be
> insensible.
>   If only a few people understand the art you talk about that's the
> proof that it's not for humanity, said Berkman.   (*MTYW*, 126–27)

The disagreement clearly shows that if Anderson can be considered
an anarchist in political terms at all, she is so thoroughly in the
individualist tradition that she could only alienate anarchists such
as Goldman and Berkman, who required association and collective
activity as a means of protest and social change. Elsewhere in her
autobiography Anderson says that she "can't function in 'association' " and expresses "a horror, a fear and a complete lack of
attraction for any group, of any kind, for any purpose" (*MTYW*,
61, 37). While Anderson's relations with Goldman always remained
cordial despite disagreements over the social function of art, she did
not enjoy the same genial relationship with other anarchists who
"were not so fair-minded as Emma Goldman." Leonard Abbot, for
one, believed that Anderson "represented the tragedy of the anarchist movement in America" (*MTYW*, 190).

The "tragedy" Abbot saw in Anderson can also be described
more charitably as a shift from politics to aesthetics, an expression
of anarchism in aesthetic rather than social terms. Anderson herself
agonized over her own inability to convince the anarchists that the
revolution needed to be conducted on the cultural as well as the
social front. In particular, Anderson tried to get the anarchists to see
that art in the service of the revolution was no art at all:

> I have never known people more rabid about art than the anarchists.
> Anything and everything is art for them—that is, anything containing
> an element of revolt. We tried in vain to divorce them from their
> exclusive preoccupation with subject matter. . . . I have never tried to
> explain the *Little Review*'s point of view to anyone—except a few artists
> —without being accused of didacticism, dogmaticism, fanaticism, aes-
> theticism, exoticism, a debauch of art for art's sake. (I never knew what
> was wrong with art for art's sake. Should it be art for money's sake? Is
> there something the matter with art that it dare not exist for itself
> alone?) . . . I have always accepted or rejected manuscripts on one
> basis: art as the person. An artist is an exceptional person. Such a
> person has something exceptional to say. Exceptional matter makes an
> exceptional manner. This is "style." In an old but expressive phrase,
> style is the man.   (*MTYW*, 133–34)

Anderson here provides an extraordinarily clear explanation of aesthetic anarchism that may involve greater philosophical subtlety than
her straightforward language suggests. The closing cliché summa-
rizes an argument that Anderson often made in the *Little Review* at
greater length. The old phrase about style being the man is given
new life when it is understood as Anderson's adaptation of the egoistic philosophy of Max Stirner, whose work Anderson was reading and
discussing around the time she met Goldman (see *MTYW*, 69). In
fact, these two figures—Stirner and Goldman—could not be farther
apart ideologically, and it is easy to demonstrate that, for all her
attraction to Goldman's anarchism, Anderson was really much closer
ideologically to Stirner's egoism.

In *My Thirty Years' War* Anderson presents Goldman as the great
friend of the masses she evidently was, a woman who thought of
anarchism as the active agency for the amelioration of social wrongs:
Anderson records Goldman's remark that "[a]narchism is stronger
than I am. I can't see people suffering without feeling I will die if I
can't help them" (*MTYW*, 84). By contrast, Anderson says of herself
that she has "little need of the humanity of people": "People's humanity is either bad and boring or good and boring. In both cases
one is dragged along the entire gamut of everyday life with them. It
is this—the human drama—that has always been unnecessary to
me" (*MTYW*, 40). Anderson's aloofness can easily be reconciled with
the aesthetic detachment of the modernists she published, but it is
hard to harmonize such elitism with the activist anarchism of Goldman, Berkman, and others. The anarchism Anderson professed owes
a great deal to contemporary conceptions of Nietzsche and to Max
Stirner, whose obscure book, first published in 1844, was rediscovered by the German anarchist John Henry Mackay in 1897. An English translation made by the American intellectual anarchist Steven
Byington (1868–1958) was published as *The Ego and His Own* in 1907.
Anderson would have read this book, as everyone else did at the
time, through the optic of Nietzsche the iconoclast, Nietzsche the
nihilist. Indeed, Stirner's popularity early in the twentieth century
owes a great deal to the parallel "discovery" of Nietzsche. And since
Stirner had been brought to light by a German anarchist and translated by an American one, he entered the canon of anarchist writing
almost immediately. As we have seen, Benjamin Tucker was one of
the earliest and most tireless promoters of Stirner in America (in

fact, he was the publisher of Byington's translation). In Chapter 5, we shall see how easily Stirner's politics could be adapted to modernist aesthetics. For now, it is enough to point out that Stirner converges with anarchism only in the limited sense that both promote the value of individualism. But Stirner diverges from anarchism in that he has no interest in relating the individualism he encourages to any social context whatsoever, except in the negative sense of an individualist separation from society altogether.[99]

Anderson's remarks about her disinterest in humanity are fully consistent with the strain of Nietzschean, Stirneresque "anarchism" that developed in the early years of this century. The essay on Emma Goldman from the May 1914 *Little Review* illustrates this curious construct of anarchism quite well, as Anderson asks of Goldman, "What is she fighting for?" and gives this answer: "For the same things, concretely, that Nietzsche and Max Stirner fought for abstractly." Anderson goes on to summarize the "substance of [Goldman's] gospel" by linking one of Stirner's favorite formulations to Nietzsche's philsophy. In his critique of Christianity, Stirner says that the body is "haunted" by the spirit: "therefore do not wonder if you find in yourself nothing but a spook."[100] Anderson takes this idea, together with Nietzsche's notion of the transvaluation of values, and attributes the mix to Goldman:

> Radical changes in society, releasement from present injustices and miseries, can come about not through *reform* but through *change;* not through a patching up of the old order, but through a tearing down and a rebuilding. This process involves the repudiation of such "spooks" as Christianity, conventional morality, immortality, and all other "myths" that stand as obstacles to progress, freedom, health, truth and beauty. One thus achieves that position beyond good and evil for which Nietzsche pleaded.[101]

The notion of progress presented here depends completely upon a change in intellectual positions rather than a modification of materialist conditions. While it is true that Goldman often cited Nietzsche on the dangers of slave morality and argued that people could free society by freeing their minds, the anarchist never lost sight of actual social and economic realities. Anderson, by contrast, repeatedly emphasizes the need for an internal, psychological transformation as a first step along the road to the anarchist utopia. In an essay with the highly Stirneresque title "To the Innermost," Anderson says that "self-dependence is merely the first of one's intricate obligations to his universe, and self-completion the first step toward that wider consciousness which makes the giving-out of self valuable. . . . [T]hat human being is of most use to other people who has first become of most use to himself." This appeal "To the Innermost" ends with the claim that an "intensity of inner life . . . is the sole compensation one can wrest from a world of mysterious terrors . . . and of ecstasies too dazzling to be shared." [102]

The ardent language conveys a real belief in anarchism as an internal condition, one that does not combat but, instead, compensates for social inequities. The root of this attitude is Stirner's belief that the self is separate from society and that egoistic satisfaction is an end in itself: "Through the heaven of culture man seeks to isolate himself from the world, to break its hostile power." Stirner says this only to dismiss the cultural heaven as no more substantial than the Christian one,[103] a further step along the path to absolute egoism that Anderson obviously was not willing to take herself. In her essay on "Art and Anarchism," however, she comes extremely close to Stirner's anti-Enlightenment aversion to progress and disdain for gradual amelioration of existing conditions:

> Who ever told you that an anarchist wants to change human nature? Who ever told you that an anarchist's ideal could never be attained until human nature had improved? Human nature will never "improve." It doesn't matter much whether you have a good nature or a bad one. It's your thinking that counts. Clean out your minds!
>
> If you believe these things—no, that is not enough: if you live them—you are an anarchist. You can be one right now. You needn't wait for a change in human nature, for the millennium, or for the permission of your family. Just be one! [104]

The kind of egoistic "anarchism" revealed in this passage does not call for social revolution so much as individual transformation, even individual transfiguration. Indeed, Anderson's language is quite evangelical, and some of her invitations to anarchism ("You can be one right now") recall the Christian camp-meeting, as does her habit of terming Goldman's ideology "gospel" truth. The larger point of these observations is that, like evangelical Christianity, Anderson's Stirneresque anarchism requires conversion, an inner change that is an end in itself. Still, in fairness to Anderson it must be noted that the pages of the *Little Review,* especially during the Chicago period, contain frequent appeals for active political involvement in such traditional anarchist areas of action as capital punishment, education, and birth control.[105]

Margaret Anderson's dual emphasis on social issues and individual transformation helps to make the larger point that the ideology of anarchism may take more than one form. As we shall see, in some cases the political ideals of the anarchists were amenable to aesthetic extension by the modernists. But in most cases the aesthetic ideals of the modernists were not amenable at all to the political interests of the anarchists, who needed their art to be fairly straightforward if it was to be used at the service of the revolution. The earlier alliances between artists and anarchists at the end of the nineteenth century do not exactly result in mutual allegiance to the same progressive vision by the beginning of the twentieth. For all the affinities that had existed between anarchists and artists in the past, as the new century took shape the parallel concerns of politics and culture began to separate. The separation is suggested by the dispute between Margaret Anderson and Emma Goldman, who both share the ideology of anarchism but differ sharply over the artistic means of rendering that ideology into cultural form. Thus, in one sense anarchy and culture diverged early in the twentieth century, with politics and art separated into their respective areas of social and aesthetic concerns. In another sense, however, these concerns converged, especially among those artists who found in the individualist tradition of anarchism a political cognate for their aesthetic tendencies. As the politics of anarchism declined and were eclipsed by nationalism and socialism, the heterogenous, fragmented culture that emerged at the same time looked a lot like anarchism. Anarchism succeeded, not as politics, but as aesthetics.

5

AESTHETICS
From Politics to Culture

"**Through** the concept of anarchy, the political and the artistic intermingled, as artists created new styles and sought new subject matter to express their dissatisfaction with industrial society or their desire for a utopian alternative."[1] Most cultural historians would agree with this statement. It implies that progressive politics and the artistic avant-garde shared common assumptions about the form of future society and the nature of artistic expression, with politics and culture moving toward the same general goals. Also, there is no question that anarchists and artists alike at the end of the nineteenth century were in open opposition to bourgeois society. But many artists were also implicitly opposed to the anarchists whose political values they appeared to share because they had little in common with the culture of anarchism put forward by the anarchists themselves. Had the artists and writers of the fin de siècle listened to the likes of Proudhon, Kropotkin, Grave, Tucker, and, later, Goldman, had they continued to work in the didactic mode of social realism the anarchists preferred, modernist art might never have come into existence. In some ways, the failure of anarchism assured the success of modernism; that is, the politics of anarchism was transformed into the culture of modernism by a number of artists who gave aesthetic expression to political principles.

1

The division that emerged in the late nineteenth century between progressive politics and progressive aesthetics reflects the origins and history of the avant-garde. Historiographers have noted that the military term "avant-garde" appears as a cultural metaphor as

early as the sixteenth century, when the French humanist Etienne
Pasquier described one group of poets as "the forerunners of the
other poets."[2] The metaphor acquired political overtones to accom-
pany the cultural meaning in the aftermath of the French Revolution, when Saint-Simon imagined a type of social organization in
which artists would have a leadership role: "[T]hings should move
ahead with the artists in the lead, followed by the scientists, [with]
the industrialists" bringing up the rear "after these two classes."[3]
This general idea of artists in a position of leadership dates from
1820; in 1825, Saint-Simon elaborated upon the idea when he described the "great undertaking of artists" to be nothing less than the
recovery of the Golden Age, a political idea akin to the anarchists'
dual alliance with a romantic past and an enlightened future:

> [T]he men of imagination will open the march: they will take the
> Golden Age from the past and offer it as a gift to future generations;
> they will make society pursue passionately the rise of its well-being, and
> they will do this by . . . making each member of society aware that
> everyone will soon have a share in enjoyments which up to now have
> been the privilege of an extremely small class; they will sing the bless-
> ings of civilization, and for the attainment of their goal they will use all
> the means of the arts, eloquence, poetry, painting, music; in a word,
> they will develop the poetic aspect of the new system.[4]

Matei Calinescu points out the paradox of this formulation: the
artists are in a leadership role, but it is one that follows the didactic
aims of a certain political program determined in advance of the
artistic avant-garde (103). A corollary to this type of proscribed avant-
gardism would be any artistic work that merely points out the inequities of the age, so that the political philosopher may then make use
of the work as a form of social criticism to suggest an alternative
model of society. This type of politico-aesthetic alliance informs, for
example, Benjamin Tucker's promotion of *The Rag Picker of Paris*
(discussed in the previous chapter). In any case, whether the work
projects a progressive vision onto future society or simply makes a
critique of present society, the work itself must be didactic or even
propagandistic, and as such is unlikely to break any new aesthetic
ground. The earlier politicization of the cultural avant-garde did not
necessarily imply that politically progressive art would also involve
aesthetic innovation. At first, the artistic avant-garde was simply an
adjunct to the political avant-garde, an idea that Kropotkin perpetu-

ated when he urged young artists to put their talents to use "at the service of the revolution."[5] That art should be construed as revolutionary *in itself* was a further development of the meaning of avant-garde culture. As a result of these various stages of development, the avant-garde is not a unified politico-aesthetic concept: "The main difference between the political and the artistic avant-gardes of the last one hundred years consists in the latter's insistence on the *independently* revolutionary potential of art, while the former tend to justify the opposite idea, namely, that art should submit itself to the requirements and needs of the political revolutionists" (Calinescu, 104). Given this dichotomy, it is easy to see how socialist-realist art developed in harmony with the political avant-garde, while modernist art achieved a separate "revolution" that was not necessarily political in nature. In fact, modernism is often conceived, with *l'art pour l'art* as its background, as an apolitical avant-garde movement, one that reacted against both conservative and progressive politics.

I suggest a third alternative to this choice between socially progressive modernity and reactionary aesthetic modernism, between politically engaged realist art on the one hand and apolitical purist art on the other, without rehearsing the post facto arguments of postmodernism that inevitably reveal the "real" politics behind the aesthetic purity of the modernists. The argument is simply that much of modernist art is consistent with the politics of anarchism, and that this consistency extends into the form of the work itself. In this respect, modernism appears as the culmination of the further history of the avant-garde, which began to be identified with radical politics around 1845. In that year Gabriel-Désiré Laverdant, a follower of Charles Fourier, published *De la Mission de l'art et du rôle des artistes,* a work that affirmed the joint relationship of the political and the artistic avant-gardes: "Art, the expression of society, manifests, in its highest soaring, the most advanced social tendencies: it is the forerunner and the revealer. Therefore, to know whether art worthily fulfills its proper mission as initiator, whether the artist is truly of the avant-garde, one must know where Humanity is going, know what the destiny of the human race is."[6] While the artistic is still subordinate to the political in Laverdant's futurist formulation, after the revolutions of 1848 the two avant-gardes moved closer together, with anarchist ideology functioning as the basis for their mediation. As

Andreas Huyssen explains, "It is certainly no coincidence that the impact of anarchism on artists and writers reached its peak precisely when the historical avantgarde was in a crucial stage of its formation. The attraction of artists and intellectuals to anarchism at that time can be attributed to two major factors: artists and anarchists alike rejected bourgeois society and its stagnating cultural conservatism, and both anarchists and left-leaning bohemians fought the economic and technological determinism and scientism of Second International Marxism, which they saw as the theoretical and practical mirror image of the bourgeois world."[7] Although not all artists and writers accepted the designation "avant-garde" (Baudelaire, for one, did not),[8] the key point here is that avant-gardism and anarchism were closely connected in the late nineteenth century, as shown by Bakunin's choice of *L'Avant-garde* as the name of the journal of political agitation he founded in Switzerland. Such historical manifestations give weight to Renato Poggioli's claim that "the only omnipresent or recurring ideology within the avant-garde is the least political or the most anti-political of all: libertarianism and anarchism."[9] Also, avant-garde artists were not merely antipolitical in a general sense, as Huyssen notes, but were specifically anti-Marxist, an ideological orientation that forms yet another link between anarchy and culture in the late nineteenth century.

The historical congruence of avant-gardism and anarchism helps to account for the shape that modernism assumed in the early years of the twentieth century. This does not mean that modernist art directs us toward anarchist society the way socialist realism urges the proletarian revolution onward; rather, the politics of anarchism takes aesthetic form with modernism. Ideas particular to anarchism were adapted by poets and novelists in such a way that the outcome of those ideas was aesthetic rather than political. The phenomenon is widespread, but few commentators have noted its implications. Suzanne Clark is one exception when she asserts that Emma Goldman "moved the stage of anarchic action from politics to culture."[10] To this I would add that she had no choice: especially in America where Goldman enjoyed her greatest success as a lecturer and organizer, anarchism was ideologically untenable as a mechanism of political change. That the type of culture that Goldman and other anarchists promoted was often aesthetically retrograde is beside the point. Whether traditional or innovative, the art that the anarchists promoted or that artists with anarchist sympathies produced became an important forum for anarchist politics. By the early twentieth century, propaganda by the deed was a thing of the past, and the new syndicalist strategy faced serious competition from the socialists, whose skill in organizing workers for political ends the anarchists could not equal. Culture, then, was one of the few fields open to anarchist activity. The shift of anarchism from politics to culture was inevitable; moreover, as anarchism settled into the culture of modernism the potential for action was inhibited or obscured by aesthetics. Aesthetic practice became a form of political action. The libertarian lessons of anarchism were taken to heart by artists: they were free from all external authority, including the political avant-garde. For many artists the only way to advance anarchism was through culture, not politics, and then only by means of an aesthetic individualism so radical that it could hardly be recognized as specific to anarchism. The irony is that anarchism encouraged the liberation of culture from the political avant-garde. Calling modernist art apolitical or antipolitical therefore sounds like the Cretin conundrum asserting that "all Cretins are liars": the politics of modernism lies in its aesthetic absorption of anarchism to the point that modernist art can only be political if it does not advertise itself as such.

2

The politico-aesthetic aporia that results from the mixture of moderism and anarchism may provide another explanation for what Theodor Adorno terms "neutralization," which is "the social price art pays for its autonomy." [11] For Adorno, a work of art has a "dual essence": it is at once social fact and autonomous artifact. These two essences, however, are locked into a dialectical relationship that makes the social nature of art and its autonomous status condition one another: art is "social primarily because it stands opposed to society. Now this opposition art can mount only when it has become autonomous. By congealing into an entity unto itself—rather than obeying social norms and thus proving itself to be 'socially useful'— art criticizes society just by being there" (*AT*, 321). But this "critical edge" is dulled as the social conditions under which the work first appeared begin to change: "Works are most critical when they first see the light of day; afterwards they become neutralized" (*AT*, 325). While Adorno clearly sees neutrality as having certain negative implications (when, for example, the "truth content" of art decays as a result of being "buried in the pantheon of cultural exhibits" [*AT*, 325]), neutrality must in some way be not only the social price of art's autonomy but also its proof. Neutrality is the inevitable outcome of autonomy, while autonomy, in turn, results from the paradoxical social function of art that derives from art's resistance to society: "What is social about art is not its political stance, but its immanent dynamic in opposition to society. Its historical posture repulses empirical reality, the fact that art works *qua* things are part of that reality notwithstanding. If any social function can be ascribed to art at all, it is the function to have no function" (*AT*, 322).

Adorno's investigations into the question of autonomy arose in the context of three interrelated conditions: his aesthetic debates with Walter Benjamin (which continued after Benjamin's suicide in 1940); his anxiety over post-Holocaust art (including the issue of whether art after Auschwitz was possible at all); and his analysis of politically committed art (which arose in response to Jean-Paul Sartre's call for *engagement*). Adorno's ideas on aesthetic autonomy are thus freighted with a great deal of personal and intellectual weight that might make them appear remote from the matter under discussion here, namely the infusion of anarchism into modernism. But commentators on Adorno's later work make the point that his arguments about autonomy, especially in *Aesthetic Theory*, are part of a larger "defense of modern art." [12] Another of Adorno's briefs for modernism is the 1962 essay titled "Commitment," which measures the claims of both didactic and engaged art against the modernism of Kafka and Beckett, among others. In this essay, Adorno sets committed art and *l'art pour l'art* into a dialectical relationship whereby "[e]ach of the two alternatives negates itself with the other": "Committed art, necessarily detached as art from reality, cancels the distance between the two. 'Art for art's sake' denies by its absolute claims that ineradicable connection with reality which is the polemical *a priori* of the very attempt to make art autonomous from the real." [13] Modernist art succeeds in mediating the distance between these two poles through "the form of the work itself, whose crystallization becomes an analogy of that other condition which should be. As eminently constructed and produced objects, works of art, even literary ones, point to a practice from which they abstain: the creation of a just life" (*FSR*, 317). At one level, the analogy Adorno makes is fairly simple: the autonomous status of the work of art, including its freedom from all prior claims against it, provides a model for the political status of individuals. A similar analogy informs André Breton's political positioning of surrealism when he asserts that "a unique privilege now and then permits artistic subjectivity to become identical with true objectivity." [14] But Adorno goes beyond the formulation that a work of art is the objective register of subjective political agency when he suggests an actual transfer of politics to aesthetics. That is, aesthetic autonomy is not simply an analogy for political autonomy, but an actual form of political practice: "an emphasis on autonomous works is itself sociopolitical in nature" (*FSR*, 318). Here, as one critic says, "Adorno's thesis drops like a bombshell": [15] "This is not a time for political art, but politics has migrated into autonomous art, and nowhere more so than where it seems to be politically dead" (*FSR*, 318). The relevance of Adorno's theory of neutralization to an earlier transfer of anarchist politics to modernist aesthetics should now be clear. I would argue further that Adorno was able to make modernism the model of a politically charged autonomous art that would be the alternative to the politically engaged art of the 1950s precisely because of that earlier politico-aesthetic "migration" of anarchism into modernism.

Adorno's theories of autonomy and neutralization can of course be read in terms of his original differences with Benjamin in the 1930s, and both the essay on "Commitment" and parts of *Aesthetic Theory* appear now as the end result of Adorno's earlier efforts to restore the "aura" to art whose disappearance Benjamin had charted in "The Work of Art in the Age of Mechanical Reproduction." [16] Indeed, the argument for autonomy seems to supply art with a political aura that is easy to criticize as one more manifestation of idealist ideology. Terry Eagleton's commentary on Adorno's aesthetics, for example, veers into critique when he places the notion of autonomy into the "late capitalist" conditions that presumably produce it. As Eagleton explains, Adorno's aesthetic recognizes that culture is utterly enmeshed with commodity production, "but one effect of this is to release it into a certain ideological autonomy, hence allowing it to speak against the very social order with which it is guiltily complicit." [17] Awareness of this complicity, however, turns autonomy against itself: the aesthetic independence of the work of art is guaranteed by its marginal status as a commodity object. But the reverse is also true, so that no degree of aesthetic purity can completely assure release from the market conditions that make the work appear autonomous in the first place. Adorno's "solution" to this problem of self-negating autonomy is more or less to accept it: "An artistic vacuity which is the product of social conditions, and so part of the problem, can come by some strange logic to figure as a creative solution. The more art suffers this relentless *kenosis* [renunciation], the more powerfully it speaks to its historical epoch; the more it turns its back on social issues, the more politically eloquent it grows" (Eagleton, 349). Eagleton calls this aesthetic "perversely self-defeating" because it is the very independence of art from society that gives it "a critical force which that same autonomy tends to cancel out." This self-canceling paradox is precisely what Adorno terms "neutralization": "The more socially dissociated art becomes, the more scandalously subversive and utterly pointless it is" (349–50). Unless, of course, social dissociation is the subversive point the artist wishes to make, as is the case with anarchist art. Indeed, Adorno's formulation takes on a slightly different coloration if the context shifts to anarchism, because aesthetic individualism and artistic autonomy acquire under anarchism a political legitimacy they would not otherwise have. Imagining modernist art as anarchist in intent leads by a different logic to the same paradox Adorno arrives at, namely, that "the most profoundly political work is one that is entirely silent about politics" (350).

This is the point where the argument for anarchy and culture truly becomes the story of anarchy *in* culture, and it is precisely at this point that the argument needs qualification. That is to say, no definitive proof for the argument that anarchism takes aesthetic form with modernism can be offered. I have argued that it does, not only because fin de siècle avant-garde culture was saturated with anarchistic politics, but also because so many figures associated with modernism had an interest in anarchism as well. The only "evidence" for the ultimate transformation of anarchist politics into modernist aesthetics is the autonomous, heterogeneous, and fragmentary nature of modernist culture itself, which appears to manifest or realize anarchist ideology in artistic form. That is, anarchism and modernism are structurally homologous. The problem with this observation is that the culture of modernism can also be explained in other terms. Rather than a transposition of politics into aesthetics, modernism can be understood, for example, as the aesthetic expression of new psychological insights (the "discovery" of the unconscious), as the artistic response to social crisis (the causes and effects of World War I), or as the cultural register of economic forces (the growth of capitalism and consumer culture). Surely all of these factors played a role in the shape that modernism assumed, and, in fact, all of them complement the argument I advance. The Marxist argument that capitalism, rather than anarchism, provides the explanation for the proliferating forms that modernist culture assumed is, paradoxically, the most complementary of all.

Early in the twentieth century, capitalism is said to have entered a period of "crisis" that has nonetheless become a permanent feature of Western industrial economies. Franco Moretti describes this crisis as the main element in the decline of liberal bourgeois society, in which markets were imagined to be purely self-regulating, ensuring a constant equilibrium of supply and demand. In reality, however, free market conditions, according to the Marxist view, result "in the interruption of the process of circulation of commodities" so that "the two instances of 'buying' and 'selling' separate, and enter into a contradictory relationship.... the consequence is that 'civilized' form of economic crisis—peculiar to capitalist conditions . . .—known as the crisis of overproduction: that is, the seemingly paradoxical condition of the coexistence, on the one hand, of unsold goods, and on the other, of unsatisfied needs."[18] Moretti argues that a "structural homology" exists between "the specific social nature" of the capitalist crisis and "the specific literary structure" of James Joyce's *Ulysses* and other works of canonical modernism. Because of the "inability of the market to assure society's organic functions," culture seeks to compensate for the loss of organic integration with the hope of "restoring a form to society." But the cultural enterprise is doomed from the start. The integrative efforts of culture fail not so much because they mirror the dissociated state of society, but because compensation can only come about, paradoxically, by the removal of culture from society. Thus, art has no choice but to elaborate its own, independent systems: art and culture "will be able to accomplish their task only by postulating a radical autonomy, a formal self-determination that accentuates to the utmost the distance and the heterogeneity of their foundations, which attempt to be organic, from the non-organic reality of everyday social relationships."[19] The explanation repeats, but with greater subtlety, the traditional Marxist arguments of Georg Lukács that "modernism leads not only to the destruction of traditional literary forms, but to the death of literature as such" because of the "subjectivism [of] the experience of the modern bourgeois intellectual."[20] Moretti details the nature of that experience and explains the cultural necessity of the autonomous subjectivism that Lukács condemns. In general, then, the Marxist argument accounts for the proliferating culture of modernism as a manifestation of the ongoing crisis of capitalism. The effects of this crisis were certainly foreseen by William Morris, who mourned the loss of "organic" society and used the term "anarchy" to refer to the free market conditions of laissez-faire capitalism that caused the loss.[21] Calling capitalism "anarchism" in itself does not make the Marxist argument the complement to the anarchist explanation of modernist culture, but it does make the point that the structure assumed by modernist culture has more than one possible homology. Also, in many ways the old Marxist argument that capitalism blurs the lines between cultural and commodity consumption seems much more relevant to theories of postmodernism than of modernism, precisely because modernist artifacts were hardly "consumed" at the time of their production. If anything, the reception accorded all those isolated, misunderstood modernists argues for a cultural positioning that repeats the political positioning of anarchism.

Perhaps the argument for an anarchist infusion of politics into culture can coexist with the Marxist argument: each provides a different type of explanation for the aesthetic shape that modernism assumed, but neither need exclude the other. The Marxist argument is economic, the anarchist political; one concerns unconscious movements in the social infrastructure, the other conscious maneuvers in the cultural superstructure. One virtue of the anarchist explanation is that the argument can be demonstrated in exact terms. Particular examples of the aesthetic absorption of anarchist politics into artistic practice are not hard to come by. A fairly simple instance is Mallarmé's assertion in 1891 that the poet is "on strike against society" (*en grève devant la société*).[22] If Mallarmé's aloofness from his age was an anarcho-aesthetic act analogous to the syndicalists' general strike, the charge of elitism so easily leveled against Mallarmé's opaque, impenetrable poetry takes on a rather different political cast. Another anarcho-aesthetic principle is the idea that art must be included among the basic human needs that all individuals have a right to satisfy. Jean Grave thought that the anarchist revolution would only succeed in transforming society when the possibility of "aesthetic satisfaction" existed for everyone: "For this transformation to endure, it is necessary that the revolution which is accomplished has enough awareness not to brush past the evolution of the individual. The starving do not acquire the possibility of satisfying their physical needs unless they have conditions that can equally satisfy their artistic and intellectual needs."[23] James Joyce, who called himself an anarchist early in his career, developed the concept of "satisfaction" as a major element in the aesthetics he formulated at the same time that he took an interest in radical politics.[24] Many anarchists believed that the social revolution would be achieved only when artistic freedom was assured. Pending that revolution, the artist was justified in going on strike against society, like Mallarmé, or, like Joyce, in seeking aesthetic satisfaction through silence, exile, and cunning.

Joyce and Mallarmé's anarcho-aesthetic solution to the political problems they faced can be traced to the nineteenth-century tradition of egoism, a term that must be understood not as a psychological concept but as a political one. Political egoism was an anarchist strategy before it was an aesthetic one, and the same might be said for other aspects of the modernist agenda that are now perceived as purely aesthetic. In the writings of Max Stirner, for example, egoistic satisfaction is not placed in an aesthetic context, but it is easy to see how the elevation of individual needs over those of the state might be shifted from the realm of politics to the world of art. When Stirner writes about the "criminal code" he says that "punishment . . . must make room for satisfaction, which . . . cannot aim at satisfying right or justice, but at procuring *us* a satisfactory outcome."[25] If the context is shifted from the criminal code to the aesthetic code, some interesting implications result. For one thing, the seemingly apolitical construct of art for art's sake becomes politicized as a form of egoism; for another, the artist becomes a person whose activities must be conducted outside the law (a role that seems to be confirmed by the legal travails of those egoistic modernists Margaret Anderson and James Joyce). Another aesthetic feature of modernist art that has its base in politics is stylistic fragmentation, a technique traditionally regarded as the register of an age in crisis, with the "breakup" of society mirrored in the disintegration of its art. From an anarchist perspective, however, fragmentation does not indicate the dissolution of society but its perfection, the realization of a utopian world divided into independent, autonomous units. The social conditions that allow for political anarchism also allow for aesthetic individualism; while anarchism as a social condition was never fully accomplished, aesthetic individualism was realized in the form of modernism. As the art of satisfaction, egoism, and fragmentation, modernist art is also the aesthetic realization of anarchist politics.

3

The construct of aesthetic individualism in the late nineteenth century developed, in part, out of the anarchist concept of political egoism or self-sovereignty. The egoism of the anarchists recapitulates the aggregate ideology described in Chapter 1, for the egoist is at once a child of both the Enlightenment and romanticism. Both progressive and rebellious, combining the contradictory tendencies of Godwin and Bakunin, the egoist emerges as a kind of rationalistic iconoclast. The aggregate ideology of anarchism held great appeal for those artists at the fin de siècle whose increasing marginalization from society could be taken to certify their "advanced" status in it. The artist seeking a model for enlightened sensibility combined with romantic sensitivity could always look back to Lord Byron as an exemplar of advanced and agonized egoism. Continental Byronism fed into Baudelaire's construction of his own poetic persona, just as American Byronism led eventually to the heroic self fabricated and celebrated by Walt Whitman. What the authors of *Les Fleurs du mal* and *Leaves of Grass* have in common is the adaptation of the romantic sensibility to the progressive, urban scene, which allowed at once for the perpetuation of the past and for the making of modernity. In this context, the cultural logic that leads from Baudelaire to Rimbaud and Lautréamont is inexorable, but only because of the actual anarchist experience of later writers that allowed them to look back to Baudelaire, et al., as politico-aesthetic precursors.

If America has no Rimbaud, that may be because it had no Commune, either, no historical heritage of anarchism to complement the political mystique surrounding Whitman. Indeed, what is lacking in the American tradition of anarchy and culture is some exemplar after Whitman who might serve as a model of politico-aesthetic egoism to later modernist writers. From the anarchists' perspective, Whitman remained one of their culture heroes, despite his insistence on democratic themes. Whitman the poet of liberty was easily assimilated into libertarian politics, and as the author of free verse Whitman was exemplary of the flawed argument that radical politics and radical aesthetics go hand in hand. The same might be said of Nietzsche, whose *Übermensch* was a model for the ethical individualism that anarchism called for, while the German's fragmented, aphoristic style brought a freedom to prose that matched the poetic liberation of Whitman's verse. Both Whitman and Nietzsche were admitted into the canon of anarchist culture, even though their incorporation required some remarkable rhetorical hedging to justify their inclusion. Emma Goldman, for example, overcame ideological objections to Nietzsche's aristocratic inclinations by turning "aristocracy" itself into a mere figure of speech: "Nietzsche was not a social theorist, but a poet and innovator. His aristocracy was neither of birth nor of purse; it was of the spirit. In that respect Nietzsche was an anarchist, and all true anarchists were aristocrats."[26] Likewise, Whitman's expansive individualism could not be fully reconciled to the anarchist model. A paean to Whitman as "The Poet of Nature" in Benjamin Tucker's *Liberty* moderates praise of the poet with the stark truth that "Walt was sometimes mistaken and inconsistent." One of Whitman's "lapses" is said to be his pantheistic tendency to "identify . . . himself so completely with the universe" that "he sometimes forgot he was an egoist."[27] The remark shows that egoism was one of the criteria for inclusion into the cultural model the anarchists had in mind. So long as the artist remained an egoist, his "anarchist" credentials went unchallenged. The emphasis on egoism as a political determinant helps to account for the entrance of Max Stirner into the canon of anarchist culture, even thought Stirner's eccentric philosophy has little in common with anarchism itself.

The relation of Stirner's egoism to aesthetic individualism is subtler than that of Whitman's and Nietzsche's, and harder to establish. Since Whitman was a great poet and Nietzsche was perceived as one, they were both aesthetic in some sense, and both were unquestionably individualistic, even though their individualism did not fully satisfy the requirements of anarchist ideology. Presenting Max

Stirner as a paradigm of aesthetic individualism in an anarchist context is even more problematic, on both the aesthetic and the individualist side of the equation. Stirner's egoism is so complete that it excludes any interest in the problems of society. "What is absolutely lacking" in his philosophy, one commentator notes, "is the ideal of social regeneration common to all anarchists." [28] Further, Stirner was no more concerned with artistic innovation than he was with social regeneration. He has little to say about art, and what he does say indicates his indifference to aesthetic issues: "Our time has its art . . . ; the art may be bad in all conscience; but may one say that we deserved to have a better, and 'could' have it if we only would? We have just as much art as we can have. Our art of today is the *only art possible,* and therefore real, at the time" (291). The attitude toward art expressed here is consistent with Stirner's egoism, which might be described as an absolute commitment to things as they are and to the self as it is, with no thought of changing anything: "Possibility and reality always coincide" (291). Stirner's philosophical egoism is a radical rejection of Hegel's idealism and all other formulations, such as Christianity, that make some future condition preferable to present reality. In fact, for Stirner there is no essential difference between Christian faith in ultimate redemption and Enlightenment belief in the perfectibility of society: "The true man does not lie in the future, an object of longing, but lies, existent and real, in the present. Whatever and whoever I may be, joyous and suffering, a child or an old man, in confidence or doubt, in sleep or in waking, I am it, I am the true man" (289). Stirner's "anarchism" consists mainly in his opposition to the state's interference with the sovereign, autonomous ego: "[W]e two, the state and I, are enemies. I, the egoist, have not at heart the welfare of this 'human society.' I sacrifice nothing to it, I only utilize it; but to be able to utilize it completely I transform it rather into my property and my creature; that is, I annihilate it, and form in its place the *Union of Egoists"* (161). Though later political theorists are right to point out that Stirner is merely on the margins of anarchism, at the turn of the century his position as an anarchist was better established, especially among the individualist anarchists in America and England. One indication of the political status formerly accorded Stirner is his inclusion in the edition of Paul Eltzbacher's influential anthology *Anarchism* (1907) published by Benjamin Tucker, which treats Stirner as the equal of the classical anarchists Godwin, Proudhon, Bakunin, and Kropotkin, as well as Tucker himself.

Stirner's place in the narrative of anarchy and culture was assured in the early 1890s when the German poet John Henry Mackay rediscovered *Der Einzige und sein Eigentum,* published late in 1844 and forgotten until Mackay revived it (Marx's extensive refutation of Stirner in *The German Ideology* was not published until the twentieth century).[29] The near-untranslatable title of the work is known in English as *The Ego and His Own,* which dates back to Steven T. Byington's translation of 1907. The title was suggested by Benjamin Tucker, who published the volume, after Byington and his advisors failed to reach agreement on what to call the book. *L'Unique et sa Propriété,* the title by which the book is known in French, is closer to the German, which can be roughly rendered as *The Unique Individual and Its Property,* or, even more roughly, as *The Unique One and Its Own-ness.* A recent edition of the Byington translation substitutes *Its* for *His* in Tucker's original English title, because Stirner "clearly identifies the egoistic subject as prior to gender."[30] However it was titled, the book was enormously successful in its second incarnation. Within ten years of Mackay's rediscovery, marked by his 1898 biography *Max Stirner: Sein Leben und sein Werk,* the volume was translated into Italian, Russian, and French, in addition to English. All told, Stirner's book appeared in some forty-nine editions between 1900 and 1929.[31]

Partly because of his egoistic nihilism, and partly because of his neologistic, aphoristic style, Stirner's name came to be associated with Nietzsche's, as both writers were appropriated by anarchists and other radical thinkers at the turn of the century. For example, a 1904 article in Tucker's *Liberty* says that Nietzsche "stands near the pinnacle of his generation in the concept of rational ethics. Yet not far from him, either in altitude or distance, stands another commanding figure—Max Stirner."[32] Stirner therefore joined Nietzsche and the Russian nihilists in the iconoclastic camp of anarchist culture. The readers of *Liberty* were also encouraged to think of Stirner's egoism as part of a broader conception of culture that included— in addition to Nietzsche—Ibsen, Whitman, Emerson, Wagner, and Richard Strauss. What "unifies" these figures is simply "the same general impulse of progress" that enables them to take "positions far in advance of their contemporaries,"[33] an impulse, incidentally, that can only be ascribed to Stirner if he is totally misinterpreted. In any case, there is no denying that the anti-aesthetic Stirner had great aesthetic appeal. His book was known to the Danish critic Georg Brandes and to Ibsen as well; in addition, excerpts from a French version of *The Ego and Its Own* appeared in 1900 in the *Revue Blanche,* the most important literary review with anarchist connections.[34] The French conflation of Stirner and Nietzsche is conveyed by a 1913 article by Remy de Gourmont titled "A French view of Nietzsche," in which the critic embraces the "anarchism" of both philosophers:

> We have learnt from Nietzsche to pull down the old metaphysical structure built upon a basis of abstraction. All the ancient corner-stones are crumbled to dust, and the whole house has become a ruin. What is liberty? A mere word. No more morality, then, save aesthetic and social morality: no absolute system of morals but as many separate systems as there are individual intellects. What is truth? Nothing but what appears to be true to us, what suits our logic. As Stirner said, there is my truth —and yours, my brother.[35]

The blurring of the line here between "aesthetic and social morality" has many implications for the migration of anarchism from politics to culture in the prewar modernist period.

The influence of the sort of individualist anarchism Stirner was thought to embody made itself felt in such works as Ibsen's *Peer Gynt,* Gide's *L'Immoraliste,* and other turn-of-the-century works. In these instances, the egoist appears as a fairly simple character type, a personification of the heroic ideal of "anarchistic" behavior that was constantly celebrated by Tucker and other individualists who were also promoters of modern culture. But the purely egoistic character now appears remote from the spirit of modernity that type of "superman" character was said to embody, in part because the overt egoist usually does not convey the rich sense of dialectical play between Enlightenment and romantic values that makes classical anarchism both problematic and attractive. All too often, the "superman" character draws too much on the neoromantic stock of Nietzschean "immorality." The best examples of this type of tired egoism come from the novels of D'Annunzio, as one character after another turns up to "shock the bourgeoisie," each one inevitably "beyond good and evil." This curiously antiquated form of modernity appears repeatedly in the work of two essayists who each made a career of announcing the new: Havelock Ellis and James Huneker. Though Ellis was known mainly as a "sexologist" at the turn of the century, he also wrote a number of introductory essays about leading cultural figures who were also felt to be socially progressive. One collection of these essays is titled *The New Spirit* (1890) and consists of chapters on Diderot, Heine, Whitman, Ibsen, Tolstoy, and Huysmans. The inclusion of Diderot among more recent "new spirits" suggests the probable influence of Jean Grave, who regularly reprinted excerpts from Diderot in the literary supplements to his anarchist paper, *La Révolte*. Indeed, Ellis's introduction to *The New Spirit* shows his sympathy with the political ideal of anarchism: "The old bugbear of 'State interference' (a real danger under so many circumstances) vanishes when a community approaches the point at which the individual himself becomes the State." [36] Ellis also mentions at least three items on the anarchist agenda: the liberation of women, integral education, and universal language (9, 14–15, 25). Typically, Whitman is presented as a model of the new spirit of anarchistic modernity because of his "frank and absolute egoism," as well as his "heroic incarnation of health" (98, 101). As for Ibsen, the playwright is portrayed as another egoist whose art has the purpose of "overthrowing society": "His work throughout is the expression of a great soul crushed by the weight of an antagonistic social environment into utterance that has caused him to be regarded as the most revolutionary of modern writers" (165).

This same equation of modern art with revolutionary egoism is endlessly repeated by James Huneker, the prolific New York critic who was well known during the first two decades of the twentieth century. In *Egoists: A Book of Supermen* (1909), Baudelaire, Flaubert, and Huysmans join Nietzsche, Ibsen, and Max Stirner in Huneker's pantheon of moderns. Huneker connects Stirner's doctrine of absolute egoism to any number of modern literary figures, suggesting, for instance, that Stirner might have taken "mottoes" from Ibsen ("To thyself be sufficient"), Nietzsche ("I am not poor enough to give alms"), and Oscar Wilde ("Charity creates a multitude of sins").[37] The emphasis on Stirner is especially noteworthy. Together with the inclusion of Stirner in Eltzbacher's anthology of anarchist writers, Huneker's strategic placement of the German egoist at the end of a book of "supermen" shows how strong Stirner's reputation was early in the century. The disappearance of Stirner from the modernist canon also suggests that present accounts of that canon need to be revised to include the concept of aesthetic egoism as a political element in modernism.[38] The example of Huneker alone makes the argument for the dual importance of anarchism and aesthetic egoism to the modernist sensibility as it was developing at the time. One of his essays is titled "Anarchs of Art" and makes the rather ponderous case that "anarchy often expresses itself in rebellion against conventional art forms."[39] While Huneker is able to give a concise definition of anarchism as "unfettered self-government" (219), he becomes prolix in his linkage of aesthetic innovation to social revolution. When he tells us that Tchaikovsky "buried more bombs in his work than ever . . . Bakounine with his terrible prose of a nihilist," or that "Wagner might be called the Joseph Proudhon of composers" (217), one gets the sense of a metaphor run amuck. Still, such quotations as these make two important points: the first is that anarchistic, aesthetic egoism was a strong cultural element in the early years of the twentieth century, the second is that even at that time the egoistic sensibility belonged more to the past than the future.

The retrograde quality of the egoism that James Huneker promoted results because of a purely discursive emphasis on the anarchism of modern art that does not do full justice to the political implications of aesthetic form. This does not mean, however, that Huneker's unsubtle but enthusiastic linkage of egoism, anarchism, and modernism was mistaken in any way. On the contrary, this tripartite construction was very much a part of the cultural sensibility at the fin de siècle and beyond, a point that can be made by referencing Max Nordau, who devotes more than a third of his influential book *Degeneration* (published in German in 1892, in French in 1893, and English in 1895) to the topic of modern literature and "ego-mania." The section contains a general exposition of what Nordau, from the perspective of nineteenth-century eugenics, sees as a pathological condition of the ego, followed by detailed discussions of artists from four literary schools—Parnassians, Diabolists, Decadents, and Aesthetes—and two representative figures, Ibsen and Nietzsche, all of whom are said to suffer from egomania (*Ichsucht*).[40] While Nordau does not discuss Max Stirner at any length (most likely because his work was not widely known when Nordau was writing), in his chapter on Nietzsche he does refer to Stirner in a way that establishes the author of *The Ego and Its Own* as an archetype of the "pathology" the writer wishes to expose:

> Nietzsche's "individualism" is an exact reproduction of Max Stirner, a crazy Hegelian, who fifty years ago exaggerated and involuntarily turned into ridicule the critical idealism of his master to the extent of monstrously inflating the importance—even the grossly empirical importance—of the "I"; whom, even in his own day, no one took seriously, and who since then had fallen into well-merited profound oblivion, from which at the present time a few anarchists and philosophical "fops"—for the hysteria of the times has created such beings —seek to disinter him.   (442)

The passage links the phenomenon Nordau describes with anarchism, as does another passage early in the book when, drawing on the theories of his teacher Cesar Lombroso, the author diagnoses the "degeneracy" of the fin de siècle: "In view of Lombroso's researches, it can scarcely be doubted that the writings and acts of revolutionists and anarchists are also attributable to degeneracy. The degenerate is incapable of adapting himself to existing circumstances" (22). Later on we learn that this failure to adapt results from a delusional dependence on the self alone to the exclusion of external reality. The point can be understood through the explanation of the contrary condition of the ego in its healthy, nondegenerate form: "[T]he highest degree of development of the 'I' consists in embodying the self in the 'not-I,' in comprehending the world, in conquering egoism, and in establishing close relations with other beings, things and phenomena" (252).

In Nordau's mind, then, anarchism and egoism are symptomatic of that larger condition of degeneracy revealed in modern literature and philosophy. At first, Nordau's attitude toward the literature he describes seems to preclude the possibility of appreciation. But one of the remarkable things about *Degeneration* is how thorough and insightful much of Nordau's negative criticism is. The chapter on Ibsen, for instance, begins with several pages of summary and commentary that acknowledges Ibsen's strengths as the great poet of ego-mania before the weaknesses are catalogued and classified. The point here is that the unsympathetic scientist makes any number of connections between anarchy and culture that the sympathetic artist might take to heart and act on in a positive, programmatic way. Consider, for example, the following passage about Nietzsche, in which anarchism, egoism, and early modernism are thoroughly conflated:

> Besides anarchists, born with incapacity for adaptation, his "individualism," i.e., his insane ego-mania, for which the external world is nonexistent, was bound to attract those who instinctively feel that at the present day the State encroaches too deeply and too violently on the rights of the individual. . . . These thirsters for freedom believe they have found in Nietzsche the spokesman for their healthy revolt against the State, as the oppressor of independent spirits, and as the crusher of strong characters. They commit the same error which I have already pointed out in the sincere adherents of the Decadents and of Ibsen. . . .   (471)

It is but a short step from this negative conflation of anarchy and culture to their actual integration, provided that the concepts are meliorated and, further, that a crucial adjustment is made that will transform the political egoism of the moderns into the aesthetic individualism of the modernists.

The heroic individualism of Whitman, the ethical individualism of Nietzsche, and so on, are really models of modernity, not modernism; the "superman" was not well suited to the kind of aesthetic individualism that anarchist culture required as that culture moved into the twentieth century. At this point a distinction must be made between aesthetic egoism and individualist aesthetics: the egoist merely creates art to promote the self, while the individualist identifies the self with the art that is created. What I am terming aesthetic individualism here is nonetheless dependent on the concept of political egoism. Margaret Anderson's repetition of the axiom that "the style is the man" is informed by Stirner's egoism, as we have seen. Similarly, Hugo Ball's invention of dada depends a great deal on his involvement with individualist anarchism and on the egoistic formulation whereby "the style of an author should represent his philosophy, without his expressly developing it."[41] This shift from overt expression to aesthetic representation is crucial to the development of modernism: without this maneuver, the politics of a work of art could only be articulated discursively in it, rather than embodied structurally and stylistically by the work itself. Individualism, then is enacted through different aesthetic procedures, rather than simply announced. Paradoxically, the more overt egoists all end up sound-

ing the same, and are all the less individualistic for it. Nietzsche's
Zarathustra is not that different from Whitman's Whitman, and the
feeling of uniformity of expression is only compounded when the
egoism is taken down a notch in the form of, say, a Whitman imi-
tation such as Edward Carpenter's *Towards Democracy* (1883).[42]
Curiously, then, it is the anti-aesthetic Stirner who provides an appropriately anarchistic model of aesthetic individualism, since his brand
of egoism posits the absolute autonomy of the self, a doctrine of ego
for ego's sake that harmonizes completely with *l'art pour l'art*. This
kind of logic is capable of assigning political meaning even to the
hermetic purism of the symbolist poets, who extended the principle
of art for art's sake "as a model for all activities," as Richard Sonn
records:

> Amid the noise of Ravachol's bombs, Pierre Quillard could write,
> "Good literature is an eminent form of propaganda by the deed," not
> by its propaganda but by its very existence. He argued that simply by
> contrasting itself with the sordid reality of society, a beautiful work of
> art constituted an act of revolt. Quillard cited Plato's banishment of
> poets from the Republic as evidence of poets' enduring subversive
> potential. The novels of Zola, by dwelling on contemporary society,
> inevitably affirmed the status quo; by contrast, every Symbolist poem
> was a tiny utopia, an experiment in the absolute.[43]

One writer who devoted much of his career to pointing out such
parallels of political and aesthetic practice was the critic Remy de
Gourmont, whose interest in Stirner has already been noted. Following Mallarmé's analogy of bombs and books, de Gourmont argued
that symbolism "translates literally by the word liberty and, for the
violent ones, by the word Anarchy."[44] The statement goes to the
heart of the matter at issue here, for not only symbolism but modernism itself can be read as a translation of politics into culture.

This formulation seems particularly germane to the modernism
that took shape in the years just prior to World War I. A case in point
is the poetic doctrine of Imagism practiced by Ezra Pound, who is
better known for the fascist politics he cultivated in the 1940s than
for his earlier anarchist tendencies. The Imagist aesthetic places a
high premium on free or open verse forms and on the use of language in a nondiscursive, highly autonomous way. To say that
Pound's Imagist classic "In a Station of the Metro" is "self-contained"
is hardly new, but the phrase captures precisely the principle of

self-containment or self-ownership that Max Stirner's philosophy of egoism encouraged. While Pound's interest in Stirner was probably limited, it is a fact of literary history that the journal where his self-contained poetry appeared was edited by the Stirnerite feminist Dora Marsden, who changed the name of her publication from *The New Freewoman* to *The Egoist* largely because of the influence of Stirner.[45] One version of this history would have the male poets Pound, Eliot, and William Carlos Williams co-opting a feminist journal, purifying it of ideology, and using it as an organ for high modernist literature. Recent research, however, suggests a rather different scenario, one in which Marsden's feminism is expanded to include a broader notion of social reform along libertarian, anarchist lines. In an essay titled "Libertarian Imagism," the critic Robert von Hallberg says that Dora Marsden's "effort to commandeer Imagism into her sense of Individualism, or egoism, was actually opportunistic."[46] The opportunity to broaden the politico-aesthetic base of the journal came in December 1913, when Marsden printed a letter from Ezra Pound, Allan Upward, Richard Aldington, and other contributors to *The New Freewoman* urging that the journal distance itself from suffragism—"an unimportant reform in an obsolete political institution"—and "adopt . . . another title which will mark the character of your paper as an organ of individualists of both sexes, and of the individualist principle in every department of life."[47] The change of name to *The Egoist*, however, did not really involve any change in the basic political philosophy of the journal, which had been subtitled *An Individualist Review* from the outset. Indeed, in the premier issue of *The New Freewoman* Marsden assumed a position not unlike the one her male contributors urged her to take six months later: "it is now clear that the 'woman movement' must find its definition and activity in matters unrelated to voting 'rights.' " Marsden concludes this opening statement of the journal's principles in a thoroughly Stirnerite way: "individual women . . . maintain that their only fitting description is that of Individual: Ends-in-themselves. They are Egoists. They are Autocrats, and government in their autocracy is vested in the Self which holds the reins in the kingdom of varying wants and desires, and which defines the resultant of these different forces as the Satisfaction of Itself. The intensive satisfaction of Self is for the individual the one goal in life."[48]

Marsden's emphasis on egoistic autonomy was so strong that she eventually came to distance herself not only from feminism but from "orthodox" anarchism as well. In an essay titled "The Illusion of Anarchism," Marsden coins the term *archist* to refer to "one who seeks to establish, maintain, and protect by the strongest weapons at his disposal, the law of his own interests." The anarchist, "whose other name is 'Humanitarian,' " is a kind of closet Christian, far too selfless and altruistic for Marsden's political tastes, which tend, again, to Stirner. Her essay on the shortcomings of anarchism contains a remarkable passage on the "opposition to the 'State' " that might have been written by Stirner himself: " 'What I want is *my* state: if I am not able to establish that, it is not my concern *whose* State is established: my business was and still remains the establishing of *my* own. The world should be moulded to my desire if I could so mould it: failing in that, I am not to imagine that there is to be no world at all: others more powerful than I will see to that. If I do make such an error it will fall to me to correct it and pay for it.' Thus the Archist." [49] Thus the egoist. The importance of Stirner to Marsden and her followers is summed up by a blurb from *The Athenaeum* that was used to advertise *The Ego and His Own* in practically every issue of the journal from 1913 to 1915: "It is a book even more relevant to modern thought than to its own age." [50]

The change of name from *The New Freewoman* to *The Egoist*, then, hardly involves any compromise of principles on Marsden's part, and it should not be seen as an accommodation of the aesthetic interests of her male contributors. On the contrary, Marsden welcomed the change because she wanted it herself. As von Hallberg says, "She wanted to have a literary flank to her movement, and Imagism was to be just that, lending cultural breadth to her brand of feminism, and claiming for it too the timelessness and fruitfulness of a philosophy in close touch with the arts." [51] Pound's willingness to represent the literary wing of individualist politics has been traced to the influence of the obscure modernist writer Allan Upward, whose books are said to convey an "urbane, if nonetheless extreme, version of the egoist position." [52] In 1913 Pound wrote a letter to Marsden in which he defined his "philosophical credentials" in generally egoistic terms: "I suppose I'm an individualist." [53] Despite the hesitant tone, the Pound of this period (1913–14) was strongly antistatist and anti-socialist, the very antithesis of his later political incarnation as an admirer of Mussolini. [54] During this prewar period Pound expressed the quasi-anarchist idea that "the special faculties of the individual" justified the artist's inclusion in a "syndicat of intelligence"; he also subscribed to the Stirnerite belief in "no perfectibility except our own."[55] These remarks can be used to argue the point that Pound's poetry bears the imprint of his earlier individualist politics throughout his long artistic career. And even though the later Pound is not, strictly speaking, an Imagist, the politico-aesthetic values that attach to Imagism and to other varieties of early modernism help us to understand how a man who was drawn to a political movement with the mass appeal of fascism continued, nonetheless, to write poetry that very few people were capable of reading. If it is true, as I have argued and as von Hallberg says, "that formal [aesthetic] procedures were understood by poets and readers as implicitly but importantly expressive of political ideas,"[56] then much of early modernism is marked by libertarian politics by way of autonomous form and fragmented style.

The idea that a poem can embody the political ideal of egoism merely by its existence, so that individualist politics is enacted through aesthetic practice, means also that the artist chooses culture as the arena of political action. In the process, the artist exercises individualism by negating it, or rather, by appearing to negate it. The symbolist notion of the artist disappearing into the work of art means that the work does not express individualism so much as embody it. This type of aesthetic individualism involves an identity of life and art that anarchist sympathizers such as Grave and Wilde fully embraced. Indeed, a number of writers conceived of the effacement of their own individuality as a necessary condition of artistic creation. Flaubert, Mallarmé, Pater, Ibsen, Wilde, Joyce, and T. S. Eliot all professed some form of self-effacement, and of these writers, all but Flaubert and Eliot had some connection to egoistic anarchism. In the case of Eliot, however, the disorder of anarchy became the background against which his poetic project was organized. Further, there is some evidence to support the claim that the aesthetic autonomy of Eliot's poetry developed in some degree out of the egoistic autonomy of prewar anarchism.[57] Pater's connection with anarchism is tenuous, but his critique of Matthew Arnold involves a basic defense of the individualist values that Arnold opposed. Also, Pater's impressionism can be understood as a preparatory exercise in egoism, as both an exploration and a validation of the subjective self. Michael Levenson has argued that "the embrace of philosophic egoism in the pre-war years might be seen as simply the deferred conclusion of a few Victorian premises," among them Pater's "willing withdrawal into the 'solitary chamber' of solipsistic perception."[58] The solipsistic impressionism that Pater promoted puts the stress on the first word of "aesthetic individualism," for the good reason that individualism itself is composed of aesthetic impressions, so that the ego is only a coreless collection of everything the mind and senses of the writer have registered. Aesthetic "egoism" in the Paterian sense is rather different from the heavy-handed variety imagined by Ellis and Huneker, since the ego itself is composed of highly particular aesthetic sensations. Aesthetic individualism thus becomes the product of the process whereby, in terms borrowed from Stirner, the artist owns himself so completely that he renders his uniqueness in the form of art. The resulting work is so marked by the artist's personality that it is marked off from other works. This admittedly eccentric formulation is intended to explain the heterogenous field of modernist culture as a form of anarcho-aesthetic practice. The paradox of self-effacement is simply that it allows for greater self-expression, provided expression is understood in abstract terms as the egoistic uniqueness of the creation, the embodiment of ego in the object. The object must therefore differ as much as possible from other objects, in an endless proliferation of artifacts whose originality consists in their refusal to give a clue to their actual origins, whether in the personality of the artist or in the society at large. Aesthetic individualism succeeds most when the culture it produces appears least homogenous, with no universalizing tendencies or stylistic consistency.

4

The transformation of egoism from political principle to aesthetic attitude contributed to the fragmentation of modernist culture in the early twentieth century. Meanwhile, conservative critics in prewar Europe held to the Arnoldian position that culture had entered an age of anarchy, and offered various recommendations and solutions intended to correct this new, disordered cultural condition. A typical critique of modernism was offered by Anthony M. Ludovici, one of Nietzsche's earliest translators, in a lecture series given at University College, London, late in 1910. Ludovici's lecture on "Anarchy in Modern Art" compares "[t]he Art of today" with the Tower of Babel: "those who were at work upon it have abandoned it to its fate, and have scattered apart—all speaking different tongues, and all filled with confusion." [59] The problem is largely due to the "free personality" of the artist, "which he insists upon expressing": "Exaggerated individualism and anarchy are the result" (8). The individualists Ludovici describes suffer from a "democratic disinclination to assume a position of authority," a failure that "contradict[s] the very essence of art" (16). These complaints are registered against the painters and sculptors who today are grouped as impressionists and postimpressionists, including Rodin, Monet, Vuillard, Gauguin, and Whistler. "The best of these artists know, and will even tell you, that there are no canons, that individuality is absolute, and that the aim of all their work is extremely doubtful, if not impossible to determine" (17). *L'art pour l'art* is "absolute nonsense" because art must have meaning and express values (116). Since the "mass of mankind" has "the general desire to obey and to follow," what is needed are "ruler-artists" who will command authority by creating art that will "either determine values or lay stress upon certain values already established" (114–15). This type of artist is actually attracted to anarchy because of the power he has to overcome it, using "Order and Simplicity": "relative disorder is his element, and the arrangement of this disorder is his product. Stimulated by disorder, which he despises, he is driven to his work; spurred by rudeness and ruggedness, his will to power gives birth to culture and refinement. He gives of himself—his business is to make things reflect him" (118). What Ludovici seems to imagine as a corrective to the cultural ills of the early twentieth century is a marriage of Mathew Arnold and Friedrich Nietzsche, that is, an elitist synthesis of taste and power.

The reliance on Nietzsche as the remedy for the problem of anarchy in art is rather ironic, as the very issues of aesthetic fragmentation and individualist autonomy that so trouble Ludovici are attributable, in part, to Nietzsche's influence. At the level of style, Nietzsche's inventive, aphoristic writing anticipates the atomistic style of modernist writers. Nietzsche himself describes this type of style as a sign of decadence. In *The Case of Wagner,* the philosopher points out that an atomistic, fragmented style is the sign of a disintegrating, anarchic society; that is, both style and politics are symptoms of sickness or decay if they are both characterized by atomistic disintegration: "What is the sign of every *literary decadence?* That life no longer dwells in the whole. The word becomes sovereign and leaps out of the sentence, the sentence reaches out and obscures the meaning of the page, the page gains life at the expense of the whole —the whole is no longer a whole. But this is the simile of every style of *decadence:* every time, the anarchy of atoms, disgregation of the will, 'freedom of the individual,' to use moral terms—expanded into a political theory, '*equal* rights for all.' "[60] Given Nietzsche's reactionary, antidemocratic politics, it is easy to turn this analysis of the decadent style against itself and argue that the style, instead, signifies some form of progressive, libertarian politics: an absolute freedom of individual action registered at every level of the style itself. This libertarian context makes possible a political reading of modernism as an aesthetic response to nineteenth-century capitalism, traditional values, moribund morality, and all the other vagaries of "bourgeois society." Critical assessments of the positive value of the type of anarchic "decadence" *qua* modernity that Nietzsche describes are easy enough to make and not hard to find: "A style of decadence is simply a style favorable to the unrestricted manifestation of aesthetic individualism, a style that has done away with traditional authoritarian requirements such as unity, hierarchy, objectivity, etc. Decadence thus understood and modernity coincide in their rejection of the tyranny of tradition" (Calinescu, 171). This formulation ascribes to decadence a political meaning that can easily be reconciled with anarchism if the language is transposed from aesthetic to social terms. Nietzsche, of course, made no such transposition: when he writes of anarchy he means a condition of chaos and decadent disorder, not a harmonious society without laws where all individuals respect the freedom of others. As we have seen, however, by the early twentieth century the anarchists Emma Goldman and Benjamin Tucker claimed Nietzsche as their own. Writers in the conservative tradition as well construed Nietzsche as an anarchist. H. L. Mencken introduced the philosopher to English-speaking audiences in 1913 by telling them that "Nietzsche was an anarchist —in the true meaning of that much-bespattered word."[61] Not all anarchists would, in fact, recognize Mencken's meaning as the true one, since the "ideal anarchy" he has in mind would allow certain individuals to dominate others, "to insure the success of those men who were wisest mentally and strongest physically" (98). Nonetheless, Mencken's repeated arguments against government (e.g., "Knowledge and not government brought us the truth that made us free" [202]), together with his insistence on Nietzsche's "anarchism," helped to form an important association of politics, philosophy, and style in the early modernist period.

A host of ironies attach to these associations. It is ironic that a philosopher who stresses the need for authoritarian politics should be embraced by a group of libertarians, and it is equally ironic that Nietzsche's description of the atomistic style as a sign of decadence should also be taken as the sign of something new. But the atomistic style described by Nietzsche was perhaps the best way for the modernists to make their work seem new, and to evoke responses in readers that would have the *effect* of the modern. While this effect could also be achieved through the naturalistic representation of contemporary society by means of the realist style, a more typically modernist means to the modern involved the abandonment of realist style in favor of a style that was fragmented and discontinuous. The style of literary modernism was not, of course, limited to the atomistic or fragmentary. Indeed, there is no reason why the lucid, straightforward style of, say, Gide in *L'Immoraliste* may not be used to create the aesthetic effect of the modern as well. But the atomistic, fragmented style has come to be virtually synonymous with modernist aesthetics, perhaps because that style extends so completely into the other arts, so that one can see a common aesthetic base in Stravinsky's polyrhythmic music, in Picasso's facet cubism, and in Eisenstein's cinematic montage (which he called "fragments standing in a row").[62] The appeal of the fragment has been described by Roger Shattuck as "a new openness of form in the arts which combines a refusal of traditional orders, deliberate ambivalence of meaning, acceptance of obscurity, comic playfulness, and deep self-irony."[63] Some of these aesthetic values, notably the refusal of traditional orders and the acceptance of comic playfulness, are easily reconciled to the anarchist tradition, and it is not by chance that this is the case. Indeed, the fragmented, atomistic style, so familiar to readers of *The Waste Land* and of *Ulysses*, has a history prior to Eliot and Joyce that is, in part, a political history, and one that some key modernist figures recognized. Hugo Ball, for example, noted the relationship between politics and style in his dada diary of July 1915: "Proudhon, the father of anarchism, seems to have been the first to understand its stylistic consequences. . . . For once it is recognized that the word was the first discipline, this leads to a fluctuating style that avoids substantives and shuns concentration. The separate parts of the sentence, even the individual vocables and sounds, regain their autonomy." [64] Ball had not read Proudhon when he made these observations, and he is mistaken in the assumption that the father of anarchism extrapolated from his politics a theory of style that is similar to Nietzsche's notion of a style of decadence. But Ball's confusion is instructive: it shows how later artists were able to construe a negative description of an anarchic style as a positive prescription for aesthetic anarchism. The first phase of the history whereby an anarchic style comes to be understood as an expression of anarchist politics appears with the observation that the new, postrevolutionary societies of the late nineteenth century were really decadent in some sense, and that a new style was needed to express the condition of decadence. The next phase was the ascription of the decadent condition of society to political anarchy, with the corollary observation that the decadent style of aesthetic individualism might in some way express anarchistic politics. Finally, a further linkage of both decadence and anarchy to modernity results in the identification of the decadent, anarchic style as the appropriate means of representing both the uncertain, dissociated experience of modernity and the egoistic, autonomous response to that experience. In short, the fragmented, atomistic text now associated with modernism was at one time associated with a particular historical situation and with certain political conditions.

The first phase in the gradual amelioration of the fragmented style is evident in Gautier's review of Baudelaire's *Les Fleurs du mal,* in which the critic used the phrase *le style de décadence* to describe the poet's aesthetic evocation of modernity. To Gautier, the phrase was problematic because it might be misunderstood to mean that Baudelaire's style was itself decadent or inferior in relation to some other "healthy" style. But this is not what Gautier means at all. *Le style de décadence* is the style needed to represent the modern, to express the newness that arises at the late stages of empire, when civilization itself is in a state of decay or decadence: "The author of *The Flowers of Evil* loved what is incorrectly called the decadent style, which is simply art that has reached the point of extreme maturity that marks the twilight of aging civilizations. It is an ingenious, complicated, learned style, full of nuances and refinements of meaning, always extending the limits of language, borrowing from every technical vocabulary, taking colors from every palette and notes from every keyboard."[65] The paradox of decadence as Gautier describes it is that the poet must invent a new style to express the experience of modernity, that is, of life in an age of decadence. Old civilizations produce new vices and new desires, and a new language is needed to describe and catalogue them: "It is not easy to write in this style, scorned by pedants, because it expresses new ideas in new forms and uses words never heard before." The classical literary style of French tradition (e.g., Racine) is "not sufficient for an author who is given the hard task of rendering modern ideas and things in their infinite complexity and varied coloring." The model for the style Gautier describes derives from the Roman Decadence, in particular the "speech of the lower empire, already marbled with the greenish streaking of decomposition, and the complex refinements of the Byzantine school, the ultimate form of Greek art fallen into deliquescence" (125). Even though Gautier says the style is "inaccurately" called decadent, the metaphor of decomposition, in which a disintegrating artistic tradition is likened to a decaying body, is a forceful one, and will be extended and elaborated upon by later critics. In particular, the decadent style will come to be seen as representative of a disintegrating society, rather than a decaying artistic tradition. Gautier sees the style, however, as primarily a psychological rather than a social instrument. The poet, for instance, uses the style "to express the most inexpressible thoughts," including "the subtle confidences of neurosis" (125). The psychological import of the decadent style is everything, the social import nothing. In fact, even though Baudelaire had earlier been a supporter of the 1848 revolutions, Gautier tells us that the poet "had an absolute horror of philanthropists, progressivists, utilitarians, humanitarians, utopian thinkers, and all those who mean to make a change in unchanging nature and the inevitable order of society" (126).

The psychological novelist and critic Paul Bourget transformed Gautier's "decadent" metaphor (in which the fragmented style is likened to a decomposing body) into a political metaphor (in which the fragmented style is likened to an anarchic society). In an 1881 article on Baudelaire later reprinted in Bourget's *Essais de psychologie contemporaine* (1883), the critic distinguishes between " 'organic soci-

eties' (in which the energies of the components are *subordinated* to
the goals and demands of the 'total organism') and societies in
decadence, which are characterized by a growing degree of 'anarchy,' by a gradual loosening of the hierarchical relationships among
the various elements in the social structure" (Calinescu, 170). Simply
stated, decadent or anarchic societies are individualistic: "The social
organism becomes decadent as soon as individual life becomes exag-
geratedly important under the influence of acquired well-being and
heredity."[66] Bourget argues that the social movement toward individualism has its aesthetic cognate in stylistic individualism, or, again,
in "le style de décadence." The idea was disseminated to English-
speaking audiences by Havelock Ellis, whose essay on Huysmans in
The New Spirit presents the crucial part of Bourget's formulation: "A
similar law governs the development and decadence of that other
organism which we call language. A style of decadence is one in
which the unity of the book is decomposed to give place to the
independence of the page, in which the page is decomposed to give
place to the independence of the phrase and the phrase to give
place to the independence of the word."[67] Now Bourget is not an
anarchist, and his use of the term *anarchie* is pejorative, but his theory
of decadence provides a conceptual basis for associating the style he
describes with the social ideal of anarchism. The way the various
units of composition in the literary work dissociate from the whole
and assume a separate, autonomous existence is structurally analogous to the decentralized, federated form of society that Proudhon
proposed. While it is unlikely that any anarchist would have read
Bourget and become attracted to aesthetic decadence as a result, it
is entirely possible that artists and writers might have found in Bourget a political context for their aesthetic tendencies. Indeed, soon
after Bourget published his "Théorie de la décadence" in 1881,
"writers who identified themselves as decadents also gave a positive
valuation to anarchy," and anarchism itself was seen as "the perfect
political outlet for their aesthetic tendencies and social noncon-
formism."[68] An example of just such an alignment of decadence
and anarchism is *Le Décadent*, a journal published in the late 1880s
that encouraged both avant-garde aesthetics and radical politics.
Anatole Baju, the editor of the journal, enlisted the support of Paul
Verlaine, the poet of decadence who had also supported the Commune of 1871 and, together with Rimbaud, had associated with

the exiled Communards in London during his stay there.[69] In short, Bourget may not have intended his description of the decadent style to be connected with anarchism, but the connection was made nonetheless.

By the 1890s a number of artists had dual affiliations with both anarchism and decadence in France: the painters Charles Maurin and Toulouse-Lautrec; the novelists Maurice Barrès and Octave Mirbeau; the poets Paul Adam and Stephane Mallarmé.[70] Typically, the connection that these artists made between decadence and anarchism was mainly aesthetic. In England, an added social dimension emerges on the part of those writers who identified themselves with decadence because the homosexual orientation of many of them had no place in the existing order of society. Although the anarchist tradition includes its share of puritanical types—notably Proudhon —it is generally true that most anarchists were quite open to unconventional sexual arrangements. Men and women practiced a form of free love that was usually as monogamous as traditional marriage, but the fact that such relationships existed outside of the state-sanctioned institution of marriage had enormous implications for other types of relationships. In most anarchist circles, homosexual unions were accepted or, at least, not discouraged. Gay men and women who were culturally active and who also claimed allegiance to some form of anarchism include Edward Carpenter, Oscar Wilde, and Havelock Ellis in England, and, later, Margaret Anderson and Jane Heap in America. Of these, Havelock Ellis must be singled out because he did much to disseminate the ideas of Gautier and Bourget to an English-speaking audience, and he did so in a way that fully ameliorated the concept of decadence: "We have to recognize that decadence is an aesthetic and not a moral conception," he says in his essay on Joris-Karl Huysmans in *The New Spirit*, the book that begins with an endorsement of anarchism.[71] The Huysmans essay also makes some interesting arguments that bring anarchism and decadence together, even though the word *anarchism* is never used: "[A]s regards what is called the period of 'corruption' in the evolution of societies, we are apt to overlook the fact that the energy which in more primitive times marked the operations of the community as a whole has now simply been transferred to the individuals themselves, and this aggrandizement of the individual really produces an even greater amount of energy." The passage continues with a linkage of the "age of social decadence" and the "age of individuality," which, combined with the claim that "social 'corruption' and literary 'corruption' tend to go together" (237), leaves no doubt that Ellis means to defend decadence against the charge of enervation, to say that the decadent could be just as energetic and vital as the next man. Further, the coded rhetoric Ellis uses implies a web of relations between the unconventional lifestyle the writer practiced, the decadent literature he enjoyed, and the anarchist politics he encouraged.

The examples of Havelock Ellis and other aesthetes and intellectuals shows that in England no less than in France the artistic response to anarchism was largely positive, mainly because anarchism provided a political context both for a set of highly individualistic aesthetic concerns and for an array of nonconformist, "decadent" lifestyles. But the decadent receptivity to anarchism was not always reciprocated. On the one hand, the anarchist ideologue and the decadent aesthete shared a belief in the inviolability of individual experience, regardless of whether that experience was construed in social or in cultural terms. On the other hand, however, the anarchist joined with the conservative in regarding the decadent as a symptom of a sick society. The decadent in this negative sense is not a refined aesthete whose individual tastes must be admired and respected but, rather, a degenerate who threatens the health of society as a whole. This type of degenerate decadent can have no place in the society of the future unless some wholesale process of regeneration or renewal occurs. In this context, the anarchist becomes an antidecadent agent of renewal, the barbarian who brings an infusion of fresh blood into the dying society.

By the end of the nineteenth century the combination of Enlightenment and romantic values that marks the origins of anarchist thought yield two distinct strains of anarchism, one communistic, the other individualistic. Each of these two strains has a different relationship to decadence. The anarcho-communists, with Kropotkin in the lead, tended toward an ideal of society that was vitalistic and organic. Indeed, Kropotkin's "Darwinian" arguments in favor of an evolution toward mutualism made society itself an outgrowth of a completely natural process. By contrast, the individualist anarchists, typified by Benjamin Tucker, allowed a place for decadence in their ideology, and whenever the decadent aesthete gravitated toward anarchism it was inevitably toward the individualist strain that he tended, as the example of Oscar Wilde shows. One of the paradoxes of this double relationship to decadence is that the anarcho-communists descend from the Enlightenment in their scientific, progressive attitude toward the society of the future, while the society itself seems to participate in the pastoral vision of romanticism. The individualist anarchists, on the other hand, draw on romanticism for their radical notion of human independence, whereas their individualism is somewhat surprisingly suited to an urban scene that has more in common with the Enlightenment than with romanticism. Richard Sonn's summary of the relationship of anarchism and decadence gains in force when the paradoxes that attend the communistic and individualistic strains of the ideology are considered as well: "Anarchism was the ideal political outlet for individualistic, antisocial aesthetes, many of whom had already been labeled decadent. Yet anarchism was a vigorously antidecadent movement that intended to regenerate a corrupt and unnatural social order." [72] The conflict between aesthetic individualism and social regeneration is the basis for much disagreement between artists and anarchists, as the dispute between Margaret Anderson and Emma Goldman recounted at the end of the previous chapter illustrates. From the perspective of most political anarchists, aesthetics comes into play, it seems, only after the revolution has come about. This post facto quality appears, for example, in Jean Grave's remarks, quoted above, about aesthetic satisfaction, where aesthetic considerations form one of the tools to measure the success of the new society. In other words, the critics and aestheticians were more concerned than the ideologues with possible connections between artistic expression and political reality.

5

A concern for the relationship between aesthetic and social issues informs much of the work of Walter Pater, even though the eccentric Pater, cloistered at Oxford, would never be mistaken for a political *engagé*. At first Pater seems about as remote from politics, in any form, as it is possible for a writer to be, and his historical distance from anarchism seems too great to be measured. But Pater encourages a kind of conceptual or even epistemological anarchism in his aesthetic theory, and as such he appears as a necessary transitional figure in the modulation of politics into aesthetics that occurs in modernist culture. The "political" Pater begins to emerge when he is set against the moralistic and authoritarian Arnold. In *Culture and Anarchy*, Arnold repeatedly describes the work of culture as the task of turning "a free and fresh stream of thought" upon whatever problem needs addressing in order "to see things as they really are."[73] This stream of thought derives largely from "the main current of national life flowing around us" (14). The flow of culture is somehow disinterested, even though it participates in national life, thereby allowing one to view issues directly and objectively, without distortion or partisan bias. Pater undermines the objective, stable world of Arnoldian culture, and he does so by using Arnold's own language. The preface to *Studies in the History of the Renaissance* makes direct reference to Arnold's idea of objective vision: " 'To see the object as it really is,' has been justly said to be the aim of all true criticism whatever; and in aesthetic criticism the first step towards seeing one's object as it really is, is to know one's own impression as it really is, to discriminate it, to realize it distinctly."[74] While it is true that here Pater's reference is to Arnold's "The Function of Criticism at the Present Time" and not to *Culture and Anarchy*, the subversion of the Arnoldian idea of objective, dispassionate culture is clear, regardless of where the idea appears. Similarly, where Arnold imagines a purifying "stream of thought," Pater finds instead a "flood of external objects" that thought can only register as "impressions": "unstable, flickering, inconsistent" (59). In *Culture and Anarchy*, Arnold is concerned to use culture as a moral guide to save man from his senses: "To walk staunchly by the best light one has, to be strict and sincere with oneself, not to be of the number of those who say and do not, to be in earnest,—this is the discipline by which alone man is enabled to rescue his life from thraldom to the passing moment and to his bodily senses, to ennoble it, and to make it eternal" (37). Pater echoes Arnold's language again in the famous passage from the conclusion to *The Renaissance* where momentary sensations are praised as the best that life has to give, provided culture, or art, is the source of those sensations: "for art comes to you professing frankly to give nothing but the highest quality to your moments as they pass, and simply for those moments' sake" (62). In brief, Arnold urges the idea that culture has moral value, that it can ennoble and improve individuals for the good of the nation. Pater, on the other hand, uses Arnold's language to suggest that culture is to be valued most for the momentary pleasure it can bring to individual experience. Pater's art actually encourages what Arnold's culture cautions against: thraldom to the passing moment and to the bodily senses. Clearly, Pater's devotion to the moment is a modernist impulse, while Arnold's submission to eternity belongs to the past.

Whereas Arnold urged the artist against modernity, Pater follows Gautier closely in his argument that style must in some way capture the individual artist's experience of the momentary impulses and impressions that make up modern reality. However, for Pater, "imaginative prose," rather than poetry, is "the special art of the modern world." But Pater reasons, as Gautier does, that the modern world is characterized by "the chaotic variety and complexity of its interests." Pater argues that imaginative prose is better suited to capture this chaotic variety and complexity because it is subject to fewer formal restraints than is poetry. A curious proof of this argument is the claim that "the most characteristic verse of the nineteenth century has been lawless verse" (106). Although Pater does not use the word *anarchy,* he comes close: the modern world is "chaotic" and it is most characteristically represented in a style that is called "lawless." Further, his interest in the atomistic particulars of style is clear in his description of the rhythm of prose, which "gives its musical value to every syllable." Pater also follows Gautier in allowing the language of other professions and other experiences that are not strictly literary to become part of the literary tradition. He sees nothing wrong, for instance, with the way "English . . . has been assimilating the phraseology of pictorial art," or "the phraseology of the German metaphysical movement" (109). Gautier's word for this infusion of nonliterary diction into literature is "complexity," and the phrase is "varied coloring" ("les choses modernes dans leur infinie complexité et leur multiple coloration" [125]). Pater echoes Gautier's phrasing in his own fix on the modern world as a place of "chaotic variety and complexity." He also aligns this social and intellectual heterogeneity with stylistic "eclecticism," in which "Racy Saxon monosyllables" are allowed to "intermix" with "long, savoursome, Latin words" (109). All of these stylistic features can be readily assimilated under the rubric of the fragmented, decadent style, whose purpose, as Pater says again and again, is "to possess a full, rich, complex matter to grapple with" (109). Another element of what should really be called aesthetic anarchism is Pater's assertion that imaginative prose cannot render fact, but only an individual writer's "sense of it" (105). Thus, literary art becomes "the representation of such fact as connected with soul, of a specific personality, in its preferences, its volition and power" (106). This is clearly aesthetic individualism, or even aesthetic egoism (in the special Paterian sense described above), which is thoroughly compatible with individualist anarchism.

But Pater is no anarchist, and his influential meditations on the nature of style are not limited to the endorsement of fragmentation, heterogeneity, and complexity. He begins the essay on "Style" by announcing that "all progress of mind consists . . . in the resolution of an obscure and complex object into its component aspects" (103). It is clear, therefore, that Pater's purpose is not merely to articulate the necessity of imaginative prose to convey the impression of modernity, with all its obscurity and complexity, experienced by a "specific personality": rather, the individual artist must do more; he must resolve the complexity, and create "the delightful sense of difficulty overcome" (110). The personality comes into play here in the form of "the necessity of *mind* in style." In brief, Pater thinks of style as atomistic, as "elementary particles of language," and of the individual "mind" *in* the style as living or organic. This mind "foresees the end in the beginning and never loses sight of it, and in every part is conscious of all the rest, till the last sentence does but, with undiminished vigour, unfold and justify the first" (112). Pater's exemplar in this balance of atomistic style with organic design is Flaubert, who knew that any "weakness" in the atomistic unit, whether "word, phrase, or motive," had to result from "an original structure in thought not organically complete" (113). Pater therefore posits a complement to the atomistic fragmentation of the heterogenous style of modernity, which Gautier calls the style of decadence. Pater, in fact, distances himself from decadence insofar as he supplements stylistic disintegration with organic design. The style of modernity may be atomistic, but the structure is integrative. The work of art, then, appears as the dialectical synthesis of the two contrary tendencies of style and structure: atomistic style tends toward fragmentation, but organic design unifies the fragments into the wholeness of art.

Atomism and organicism are not only aesthetic terms; they are also part of the political lexicon of the nineteenth century.[75] We have already seen how heavily loaded *atomism* is as a political term in Nietzsche's vocabulary, signifying the disintegration of society into anarchy, decadence, and democracy— *"equal* rights for all." In a certain sense, an atomistic society was what the anarchists had in mind, if "atomistic" is understood as a term descriptive of the political ideal of individual autonomy. The vision of society as an aggregate collection of autonomous individuals, occupying their separate cells of anarchistic freedom, was countered by conceptions of society that were somehow integrated and "organic." In truth, *organicism* is a favorite metaphor deployed by both reactionaries and progressives, aristocrats and socialists. Indeed, anarchistic "atomism" and socialistic organicism are antithetical terms in the long debate between two rival political camps in the nineteenth century, and the contrary models of atomism and organicism seem to have crossed over, to some degree, from social to aesthetic discourse. For example, the opposition of organic socialism and atomistic anarchism played out in the political sphere in the disputes between Marx and Bakunin has its parallel in the writings of William Morris, where socialism and anarchy—if not anarchism—are radically opposed in the aesthetic sphere. In "Art under Plutocracy," Morris expresses nostalgia for an aesthetic "tradition which once bound artist and public together." At such times, "art was abundant and healthy, all men were more or less artists; that is to say, the instinct for beauty which is inborn in every complete man had such force that the whole body of craftsmen habitually and without conscious effort made beautiful things, and the audience for the authors of intellectual art was nothing short of the whole people" (22). Here, the organic model of an integrated society clearly sounds through. The organic ideal of an abundant, healthy, artistic community can only come about, in Morris's view, through socialist "Association, instead of Competition," which will make possible "Social Order instead of Individualist Anarchy" (83). Now while it is true that what Morris means by anarchy here is laissez-faire capitalism, anarchy by any name is incompatible with the kind of organic community of craftsmen that Morris imagined as the socialist ideal, in which aesthetic individualism has no place. To return to the more specific question of style, Morris has little to say about language. He does note, however, that because the tradition that "once bound artist and public together" is no more, "the artists are obliged to express themselves, as it were, in a language not understanded [sic] of the people." "They have no choice," he says, "save to do their own personal individual work" (22). Morris would prefer a society where artists would not be forced to make such a choice, where artistic expression would be integrated with the organic relations of society at large.

Walter Pater differs from Continental writers who were receptive to the decadent style in that he balances the atomism of that style against organic design. William Morris, in turn, differs from Pater in his wholesale endorsement of organicism, to the point that he would deny aesthetic individualism altogether, if only society would cooperate with his collectivist principles. Morris, then, is fully within the socialist tradition on aesthetic issues, and when this tradition touches on literature the idea of style that results is quite remote from the anarchic style of decadence that Gautier described and Baudelaire embodied. The socialist ideal of culture usually supposes a language that is simple, straightforward, uncomplicated, transparent, natural, healthy, and accessible to all. That is, socialists tend to regard language in populist terms and, in fact, revive the old ideal of a universal language to purify the Babel of modern times. The anarchists were also attracted to the idea of a universal language, and many of them did study Esperanto with the hope that ease of communication among the masses would aid revolution across the linguistic barriers of national lines. But there is an obvious disjunction here between means and ends: if some universal, artificial language could aid the political success of anarchism on an international scale, that same universalizing process might also work against the social—and cultural—ideal of anarchism as a collection of diverse, autonomous communities. This observation has less application to the social ambitions of collectivist anarchists, but surely the prospect of a universal language is not so easily reconciled to the individualist tradition, especially where culture is concerned. In the case of socialism, however, the prospect of a universal language does not pose a threat to the future society: no ideological disjunction arises between politics and culture if all socialists speak the same language. But what would such a language be like? One answer is suggested by Etienne Cabet's *Voyage en Icarie* (1840), where the mid-nineteenth-century communist imagines a socialist utopia called Icaria. This imaginary land was described by a later nineteenth-century writer as "a vast partnership —a great national hive, where each labored according to his abilities and consumed according to his necessities; where crime had vanished with poverty, and idleness with luxurious wealth; where peace

and plenty, liberty and equality, virtue and intelligence, reigned supreme." [76] The language Cabet imagined that the population of such
a society would use may serve as the archetype of the "socialist style"
and a contrast to the anarchic style of "decadent" modernity.

Cabet points out that "the multiplicity and imperfection of languages" is one of the impediments to "the progress of the enlightened ones." The Icarian language offers no such impediments. It is
said to be "perfectly rational, regular and simple"; a language "that
is written as it is spoken, and pronounced as it is written." The
grammatical rules of this language are "very few in number and
without a single exception." As for vocabulary, the words of the
Icarian language are "regularly compounded of only a small number
of roots" whose meaning is "perfectly defined." The language is so
simple that its grammar and dictionary are "contained within one
slim volume," and "anyone can learn it in four or five months." [77]
Even though this description dates from 1840 and bears the mark
of the French classical tradition, the preoccupation with a simple,
accessible language is consistent with utopian socialism in its later
forms, when a universally accessible language is not only imagined,
but actively pursued in practical terms. George Bernard Shaw's interest in Esperanto is an instance of the socialist wish to bind the masses
together through a mutual language. [78] Even though, in theory, the
socialist ideal of an organic community is at least compatible with
the idea of an organic literary structure, in which interconnected
motifs are subject to an overall design, such organicism does not
appear as a major element in socialist aesthetics. Rather, organicism
comes into play only with regard to the artist's relationship to society,
and not with regard to organicist elements in the work itself. Similarly, socialist theories of language emphasize its utilitarian and com-
municative function, not its aesthetic value. While it is true that many
anarchists also took an interest in the construction of a universal
language, these interests were, like those of the socialists, purely
political. The anarchist sensibility splits on the topic of language into
separate political and aesthetic factions, the former universalist, the
latter individualist. This split does not appear in the history of socialist thought, as the socialists do not always make meaningful distinctions between political and aesthetic language.

The incompatibility of socialism with the kind of aesthetic individualism later associated with modernism is perhaps best illustrated

by Oscar Wilde in "The Soul of Man Under Socialism." At first, the title of the essay makes sense, as Wilde sounds the socialist theme of an integrated, organic community. Wilde says he values "Socialism, or Communism, or whatever one chooses to call it" because the conversion of "private property into public wealth" and the substitution of "cooperation for competition will restore society to its proper condition of a healthy organism, and ensure the material well-being of each member of the community." [79] Basically, what Wilde imagines is a society that is on the surface not unlike the socialist community of artisans that William Morris imagined. It makes a difference, however, that Morris's utopia is populated with artisans and Wilde's with artists and aesthetes. Wilde's society is one based not on meaningful work, but on leisure activity. Not unlike Kropotkin and other progressive anarchists, Wilde counts on machines to do the utilitarian work necessary to sustain civilization: "The State is to be a voluntary manufacturer and distributor of necessary commodities. The State is to make what is useful. The individual is to make what is beautiful" (1088). Under such conditions, "the true personality of man . . . will grow naturally and simply, flowerlike, or as a tree grows" (1084). How the socialist utopia of "true, beautiful, healthy individualism" will come into being is not clear, but Wilde does allow that "progress has been made, through disobedience and rebellion" (1081). At different points in Wilde's essay it becomes clear that his socialist utopia and the means to it are obviously at odds. For example, he says that individual disobedience or rebellion is necessary to progress, but, at the same time, "the note of the perfect personality is not rebellion, but peace" (1084). Once installed in its just community of fellow rebels, this personality admits "no laws but its own laws, nor any authority but its own authority" (1085).

What Wilde calls socialism, then, is much closer to anarchism: "Individualism . . . is what through Socialism we are to attain. As a natural result the State must give up all idea of government" (1087).[80] Wilde is even further from socialism in his aesthetic ideology: "The form of government that is most suitable to the artist is no government at all" (1018). Of the various forms of government available, democracy is the most objectionable of all, especially with regard to art: "One who is an Emperor and King may stoop down to pick up a brush for a painter, but when the democracy stoops down it is merely to throw mud" (1099). Wilde's anarchist aristocracy of

art requires the separation of art and the public as a practical necessity: "In England, the arts that have escaped best are the arts in which
the public take no interest" (1091). Where a true socialist would
encourage some form of populist art, Wilde imagines an artistic
populace: "Now art should never try to be popular. The public
should try to make itself artistic" (1090). Wilde's "socialist" ideal of
a society of artists and his antagonism to the public can be reconciled
only if the class of people called "the public" cease to exist. If such
were the case, it is difficult to imagine what the condition of being
an artist would mean for Wilde, since artistic identity is defined
almost exclusively as hatred of the public; a popular artist is an
oxymoron. In order to reach "the uncultivated mind," says Wilde,
"the artist would have to do violence to his temperament, would
have to write not for the artistic joy of writing, but for the amusement
of half-educated people, and so would have to suppress his individualism, forget his culture, annihilate his style, and surrender everything that is valuable in him." Wilde's affinity with aesthetic
anarchism could not be clearer: "Art is individualism, and Individualism is a disturbing and disintegrating force" (1091). Nothing could
be further from the socialist ideal of an organic, integrated society
than Wilde's distanced or dissociated artist, whose "perfect personality" makes impersonality possible: "He stands outside his subject,
and through its medium produces incomparable and artistic effects"
(1093). We have already noted Jean Pierrot's observation that a number of symbolist poets were attracted to anarchism not for political
but for personal reasons, since the individualist ideology under-
scored an artistic practice that was fundamentally elitist: "They saw
anarchism not as a popular movement but, on the contrary, as an
aristocratic one." [81] The formulation holds for Wilde, whose "socialism" turns out to be an aristocratic variant of aesthetic anarchism
that is actually the obverse of socialist politics. Likewise, Wilde's cultural ideology is the complete contrary of the socialist ideal of popular, populist, or communal art.

By 1914, socialists and anarchists were speaking different political languages. The advent of the First World War and the Bolshevik
Revolution would eventually strengthen the political voice of the
socialists and all but silence the anarchists. In 1914 socialists and
anarchists were also speaking in radically dissimilar aesthetic languages, a point that can be made by contrasting two very different

novels published within a few years of one another. The English
publisher Grant Richards brought out Robert Tressel's *The Ragged
Trousered Philanthropists* in 1914, a novel which "describes the work-
man's life of that time, the subjection, deception, and destitution of
the people whose labor helped to create the luxury and glitter of the
Edwardian age." [82] Tressel's book is regarded by critics as perhaps
the highest achievement of socialist literature. Written in a clear,
accessible style, the novel today is out of print and largely unread.
In 1914 Richards also published James Joyce's *Dubliners*, somewhat
reluctantly, but the very next year he rejected as "hopeless" the
manuscript of *A Portrait of the Artist as a Young Man*.[83] It is hard to
imagine two novels more unlike than the one by Tressel that Richards published in 1914 and the one by Joyce he rejected in 1915.
One encourages solidarity and community among like-minded workers, the other celebrates the individualism of the solitary artist. The
first is a model of the clear, organic, socialist style; the other exploits
a variety of styles, including the obscure, atomistic, decadent style
once associated with anarchy but now identified with modernism.
The historical irony must also be noted: in the twentieth century, the
socialist style recedes with the growth of socialism, while the anarchic
style of modernism emerges just as anarchism diminishes. To a certain extent, the modernist style has to be read not only as a reaction
against bourgeois tradition, but also as resistance against, or, at least,
indifference to, socialist reform. The reformation of society and the
reinvention of literary style do not, by any means, go hand in hand.
In the early twentieth century, modernism and modernity are often
in conflict, and more than one modernism emerges out of this conflict. Some species of modernism are informed by radical politics,
some by aristocratic elitism, some by conservative ideology, some by
political ambiguity, and so on. But regardless of the underlying ideology that informs a particular modernism, many of these modernisms
look the same because they are overlaid with anarchism—not political anarchism, but anarchism in aesthetic form.

6

ARTISTS
Anarchism and Cultural Production

By the second decade of the twentieth century, aesthetic anarchism had entered into culture so completely that it made little difference whether individual artists advocated anarchism or not. The case can be made that James Joyce was largely sympathetic to anarchistic thought, whereas T. S. Eliot assuredly was not. Nonetheless, both of these writers worked in the fragmented, discontinuous style so often identified with modernism, a style that developed, in part, out of earlier exchanges between individualist aesthetics and anarchist politics. As a result of such exchanges and interactions, modernism involves a decisive split between avant-garde art and progressive politics, precisely because innovative technique ceases to have political significance. In the nineteenth century, it might have been possible for the politically progressive artist to "shock the bourgeoisie" by making a radical break with the aesthetic conventions bourgeois audiences and readers had come to expect. But when innovation itself becomes the convention the reader expects, or when the audience not only expects but requires surprise, then avant-gardism becomes an aesthetic condition that may be satisfied by an artist of any political stripe whatsoever. In 1922, when Joyce published *Ulysses* and Eliot *The Waste Land,* readers might not have been able to distinguish the political stripes of these writers as readily as we can now. For this reason it is necessary to trace the movement of anarchism into modernism, and to see how artists with varying politics came to camouflage those politics in the same aesthetic dress.

1

From the perspective of twentieth-century modernism, Henrik Ibsen appears as a precursor only: modern in spirit but traditional in technique. Even though his dramaturgy was revolutionary in relation to the theatrical tradition he inherited, it was strictly transparent. Ibsen's technique was not intended to call attention to itself but to produce the naturalistic illusions necessary to allow his presentation of social problems to have their full impact on the audience. Innovative but not experimental, Ibsen's plays now appear the quiet prologue to the more radical creations of Brecht and Beckett, Ionesco and Pirandello. Aside from George Bernard Shaw, who belonged to an older generation, the lone modernist who continued the Ibsenite tradition was Eugene O'Neill, whose reputation appears to be in decline and who hardly seems to merit the label "modernist" at all. By the same token, Ibsen's drama today seems closed off from the modernist era he helped bring into existence and somehow excluded from it. He does have some aesthetic extension into modernism through the work of James Joyce, one of only a few modernist writers who made a careful study of the playwright's artistic, as opposed to dramatic, methods; that is, Joyce took a greater interest in Ibsen's subtle use of image, symbol, and motif than in the social and moral conflicts the plays explored. Nonetheless, Ibsen also influenced Joyce's politics, in that Joyce took Ibsen as the model of the proud, isolated artist self-exiled from an oppressive society. For Joyce, the "political" Ibsen and the "artistic" Ibsen were indistinguishable, and he was not alone in assuming that a political position and an artistic pose were one and the same thing. In terms of anarchy and culture, Ibsen's long career boils down to a decade or so at the end of the nineteenth century, one of the few periods when the political and the artistic avant-gardes came together. The situation is somewhat paradoxical, since few—if any—of Ibsen's plays suggest outright political solutions to the highly ambiguous modern problems they pose. Ibsen's fin de siècle status as an anarchist artist is hard to glean from the "anarchism" in the plays themselves. Their political content was determined mainly by the political context in which they were presented.

Although Ibsen refused to identify himself openly with any political ideology and was not a political activist, he felt a strong affinity for anarchism. "The state must be abolished!" he wrote to Georg Brandes, "In that revolution I will take part. Undermine the idea of the state; make willingness and spiritual kinship the only essentials in the case of a union—and you have the beginning of a liberty that is of some value. The changing of forms of government is mere toying with degrees—a little more or a little less—folly, the whole of it."[1] But this statement is hardly evidence of a commitment to anarchist politics; in fact, the desire to replace government with "spiritual kinship" is more sentimental than ideological. Nonetheless, Ibsen's plays were immediately politicized by his exilic status and by their exclusion from the repertory of Norway's national theater. Even in his adopted Germany, Ibsen was often forced to bowdlerize his own plays, as in the March 1880 production of *A Doll's House*. In the amended version, Helmer forces Nora to look at her sleeping children before she leaves him, whereupon she is overcome by emotion, drops her packed suitcase, and falls to her knees as the curtain falls.[2] The presentation of Ibsen's plays in sanitized form when they were not banned altogether heightened their political meaning and led to alternative approaches to their presentation. The rise of the free theater movement and the introduction of Ibsen into radical political circles are parallel and complementary phenomena.

The most important play in this regard is *Ghosts*, which William Archer called "Ibsen's greatest work . . . [i]n a historical, if not in an aesthetic sense."[3] Published late in 1881, the play was first performed in Chicago in May 1882 by an amateur troupe of Danish and Norwegian immigrants. The professional premier took place in Helsingborg, Sweden, in the summer of 1883. That same year the play was translated into German, and was acted privately there in 1886 and 1887. News of *Ghosts* as a "burning literary and dramatic question in Germany" (as Ibsen put it in a letter to his Danish publisher), combined with an important article on Ibsen as "Un Poète du Nord" in a French review, stimulated Zola's interest in the play in 1887.[4] No doubt Zola found support in *Ghosts* for his own deterministic theories of congenital degeneracy and thought of Ibsen's doomed Osvald as a literary first cousin of the Rougon-Macquarts. Zola encouraged André Antoine, founder of the recently formed Théâtre Libre, to present the first production of *Ghosts* in France. In the meantime, a highly successful performance of *A Doll's House* was staged in June 1889 at the Novelty Theater in London. The following September

Ibsen's identification with the free theater movement began with *Ghosts* as the premier production of the Freie Bühne in Berlin. When news of these productions reached Paris, Zola redoubled his efforts to get Antoine to put on *Ghosts* and promised to help him find a translator for the play. *Les Revenants* was at last produced by the Théâtre Libre on 30 May 1890, with Antoine as Oswald. Antoine was transformed by the experience and immediately resolved to present another play by Ibsen. Three days after the opening of *Les Revenants,* he wrote in his diary that, "despite the incomprehension of the public and the hostile pleasantries of [the drama critic] Sarcey," he would "strike a second blow with another work by Ibsen." [5] The next blow would be *The Wild Duck.*

The Théâtre Libre productions of Ibsen are noteworthy for both aesthetic and political reasons. Critics of the time, accustomed to the patterned clarity of French theater, found Ibsen's "retrospective technique and introspective moods" obscure; one reviewer thought that *Les Revenants* was more like a religious ritual celebrated in a temple than a play performed in a theater.[6] The comment suggests that Antoine's production, despite the thematic resemblance of the play to one of Zola's novels, was somewhat symbolist in its aesthetic orientation. Antoine's decision to produce *Le Canard Sauvage* as the next Ibsen offering of the Théâtre Libre also suggests a symbolist orientation, since *The Wild Duck* relies more on ambiguous symbolism than does, say, *A Doll's House.* In short, Ibsen at the Théâtre Libre appeared to be a way of combining naturalism and symbolism, the dominant aesthetic trends in fin de siècle French culture. In 1893, Lugné-Poë's Théâtre de l'Oeuvre opened with a production of *Rosmersholm* and quickly gained a reputation as an "outpost of Ibsenism" in Paris.[7] Lugné-Poë had stronger alliances with the symbolists than did Antoine, and the contrast of the Ibsen productions at his theater with those at the Théâtre Libre probably made the latter seem more naturalistic than they really were. In any event, symbolism and naturalism were the two centers of gravity that attracted Ibsenite and radical alike, and the resulting mix of aesthetics and politics was played out in the competition between the two theaters. One critic says that the "seeming literary rivalry" of the two companies "was expressed in the way they performed the works of Henrik Ibsen, the Libre playing him as straight social drama and the Oeuvre as a more metaphysical playwright."[8] Although contemporary reviews of

Antoine's Ibsen productions require some tempering of this statement, the larger point to be made is that Ibsen was equally amenable to adaptation by both naturalists and symbolists. For later critics, Ibsen's dual kinship with naturalism and symbolism is evidence of an aesthetic synthesis of those two modes of aesthetic practice. Havelock Ellis, for example, claimed that "among Norwegian poets and novelists various qualities often meet together in striking opposition; wild and fantastic imagination stands beside an exact realism and a loving grasp of nature; a tendency to mysticism and symbol beside a healthy naturalism. We find these characteristics variously combined in Ibsen."[9] This ability to synthesize contrary aesthetic modes is a mark of modernity, or what Ellis calls "the new spirit." The formulation has some force and will be repeated by critics of modernism proper. Edmund Wilson, for example, echoes Ellis's analysis of Ibsen when he explains Joyce's modernism as a synthesis of naturalism and symbolism.[10]

The naturalistic leanings of the Théâtre Libre, not to mention Zola's involvement in it, might lead to the assumption that Antoine's company was more politically *engagé* than Lugné-Poë's highly aesthetic Théâtre de l'Oeuvre. But the opposite appears to be the case, with the symbolists, once again, seeing no contradiction between their obscure aesthetics and their anarchistic politics. Two literary anarchists, Camille Mauclair and Louis Malquin, assisted Lugné-Poë in his theater's first season, which opened with Ibsen's *An Enemy of the People* in November 1893. The performance was preceded by a brief introductory lecture delivered by Laurent Tailhade claiming that "genius, beauty, virtue are antisocial facts of the first order" and that "the superior man is always alone." A young member of the first-night audience enthused over the event in anarchistic rhetoric: "What dynamism and what dynamite! What bombs did we not intend to explode, charged with new explosives, new art . . . bombs that would be fireworks, bouquets of light."[11] A month after the performance, August Vaillant threw an actual bomb into the Chamber of Deputies; he is said to have named Ibsen among those who inspired the act.[12] Whether he had Lugné-Poë's recent production of *Un ennemi du peuple* in mind is not clear, but there is no question of anarchist involvement in the Théâtre de l'Oeuvre. Indeed, this play, more than any other, held a special appeal for the anarchists, especially in the early 1890s. Some of Stockman's dialogue makes him appear as a dynamitard, even though he is speaking metaphorically when he says of his enemies, "I'll smash them into the ground and shatter them! I'll wreck their defenses in the eyes of every fair-minded man! That's what I'll do!" And when the printer Aslaksen counsels moderation, Stockman's would-be publisher Billing responds: "No, no! Don't spare the dynamite!"[13] Felix Fénéon, known now to be an anarchist activist, was a member of the cast of *Un ennemi du peuple*, playing a member of the crowd who shouts down Stockman at the public meeting he has called.[14]

The anarchist appeal of *An Enemy of the People* can also be demonstrated by the reception of Ibsen in Spain. Versions of the plays in the French of Ibsen's official translator Prozor had come to the attention of Spanish critics in 1889. In 1892, Castilian translations of *A Doll's House, Ghosts,* and *Hedda Gabler* were published in the journal *España Moderna*. Interest in Ibsen grew as a result of these translations and the critical attention paid to Ibsen in general, more so in Barcelona than in Madrid.[15] The reasons for Ibsen's tepid reception in Madrid are obvious: that city was the royalist capital whereas Barcelona was the center of separatist politics, whether anarchist or Catalonian in origin. Also, radical politics in Madrid tended more toward socialism than anarchism. Salvador Madariaga, writing in the 1930s, reflected on his own times and looked back on the past when he observed that "Barcelona is anarchist and Madrid socialist. It is safe to say that, when the European labor movement which inspired the First International split, . . . Marx and Bakunin parting in different directions never to meet again, the temperament which underlay their respective doctrines corresponded to the temperaments which underlie Madrid and Barcelona."[16] The Catalans and the anarchists alike looked upon Ibsen as one of their own. Commenting on the success enjoyed by Ibsen's plays in Barcelona, a critic noted the "strange but evident affinity of temperament" between the Norwegian and the people of Barcelona: "Ibsen was an apostle of individualism, and so are all Catalans." Other critics commented on this individualism and compared it to that of the well-known anarchists of the time, finding Ibsen's egoism "more rational" than that of Bakunin, Stirner, Nietzsche, or Spencer.[17] Several of Ibsen's plays were translated into Catalan, including *Ghosts* in 1893. But it was *An Enemy of the People* that, once again, played a dominant role in introducing Ibsen into Spanish culture. The ground was prepared by a former lawyer turned journalist named Juan Maragall, who wrote an article about the play in December 1892; in it, he claimed that Ibsen, "the idol of a certain part of modern youth," should be included among those "poets and philosophers [who] are usually the precursors of great human movements."[18] *Un enemigo del pueblo* was presented four months later in a Castilian version, the first of Ibsen's plays to be performed in Spain. The production was mounted by the Theatre de Noveltats in Barcelona, evidently in a way that emphasized its relevance to contemporary political issues. A reviewer for the paper *L'Avenç* expressed disappointment that the play had been made to serve political ends, noting that Ibsen had been presented as "an agitator for industrial reform, not as a creator of new artistic ideals."[19] The issues raised by the play certainly chimed with the concerns of the Barcelona anarchists, "who might possibly have been led to believe that [Ibsen] had written a manifesto of their philosophy."[20] In addition to such general issues as government corruption and hypocrisy, the rejection of external authority, and the fallibility of majority rule, *Un enemigo del pueblo* touched on some of the specific social problems anarchists sought to remedy. One such issue is the role of government in public health and hygiene, the focus of the play and a concern of the Spanish anarchists in particular. Another particularly Spanish approach to anarchism is suggested by Dr. Stockman's decision at the very end of the play to devote himself to education after his defeat by the benighted majority. In 1911, Havelock Ellis described anarchism in Spain as more "peaceful and humanitarian" than in other countries,[21] and Dr. Stockman clearly appears to be this type of anarchist at the end of the play, despite the inflammatory rhetoric he uses earlier. In his devotion to education, the character Stockman anticipates Francisco Ferrer, who also took the anarchistic but humanitarian approach to social issues later on. Fittingly, Ibsen's English translator William Archer visited Barcelona after Ferrer's death to gather materials for his 1911 biography of the Spaniard, *The Life, Trial, and Death of Francisco Ferrer.*[22]

The popularity of *An Enemy of the People* among anarchist sympathizers is understandable, and this play stands alone among Ibsen's work for that very reason. The appeal of Ibsen's other plays to anarchist sensibilities is harder to explain. *Ghosts,* for example, exposes the hypocrisy of bourgeois society in general and the moral turpitude of one of its institutions in particular through the behavior of Pastor Manders, but the deterministic theme that has the son Osvald paying for the sins of his dissolute father hardly suggests a political solution to the social problems the play details. Emma Goldman's claim that *"Ghosts* has acted like a bomb explosion, shaking the social structure to its very foundations" is hard to credit if those same foundations predestine individuals to a fate that by definition lies outside of politics.[23] *A Doll's House* also announces the deterministic theme through the congenital degeneracy of Dr. Rank, but at least in this play such determinism is countered by the independent action taken by Nora when she leaves her bourgeois husband. Goldman's judgment is that "[w]ith a *Doll's House* Ibsen has paved the way for woman's emancipation."[24] The anarchists' endorsement of free love and the equality of women accounts for the appeal that this play had for them. Also, the moneylender Krogstad's manipulation of Nora and her banker husband's pettiness in money matters chime with the critique of financial institutions that had been a component of anarchist thinking since Proudhon proposed the mutual bank. While *A Doll's House* is at least understandable in an anarchist context, several other Ibsen plays that the anarchists promoted are not. *Rosmersholm* was the play that opened the Théâtre de l'Oeuvre's first season, and while the play is rich in political content, it also reveals the inadequacy of politics altogether. Conservative and liberal politicians alike seek to enlist the support of the highly respected Johannes Rosmer, a former minister turned freethinker, but he rejects both ideologies in favor of an idealistic "democracy" that would "elevate all our countrymen into noblemen [b]y liberating their minds and tempering their wills." Superficially, Rosmer's position resembles that of Dr. Stockman, isolated from both left and right. But Rosmer's isolation is the product of his own self-delusion, which eventually leads to the belief that the double suicide of himself and his friend Rebecca West is an "ennobling" act. The suicide is actually consistent with Rosmer's life, which was merely an evasion of social responsibility all along. Most of the Ibsen plays that drew the attention of the anarchists, *Rosmersholm* included, are either ambiguous or silent on the subject of political commitment; at best, they propose instead ethical solutions to the social problems they explore.

This emphasis on ethical rather than political remedies for social ills comes into play in *The Pillars of Society,* another drama singled out by Emma Goldman as "a tremendous indictment against the social structure that rests on rotten and decayed pillars."[25] Although this play juxtaposes the capitalist values of the shipbuilder Bernick with the near-syndicalist values of the shop foreman and labor leader Aune, the resolution of the play does not involve anything remotely approaching anarchism. On the contrary, the regenerate Bernick is still a capitalist at the end of the play when he confesses certain of his moral lapses. Also, he encourages the townspeople to invest in the scheme to build the railway line that is to serve as a supply link for his shipbuilding enterprise. Earlier, he had intended to conspire with a select group of fellow capitalists in the venture. The new plan will share the wealth with the people, assuming they are willing to take Bernick up on the offer and invest their money. In any event, the ethical turnaround at the end of *The Pillars of Society* involves not the abolition of capitalism but its democratization. The interest in this play shown by Goldman and other anarchists reveals, again, the power of political context to determine political meaning. Goldman's remarks suggest that, once again, only *An Enemy of the People* holds up on its own merits as anarchist in orientation, the play that Goldman sees, with typical overstatement, as "the last funeral rites" of "a decaying and dying social system." Dr. Stockman is called "the regenerated individual, the bold and daring rebel," and the fact that he is "not a practical politician" is a virtue: he owes allegiance to no state or party program.[26] Yet even this play shifts in meaning with the political winds. In 1893, when *Un ennemi du peuple* was first performed by the Théâtre de l'Oeuvre, with Félix Fénéon in the cast, Dr. Stockman's anarchism was simply assumed and thereby assured. In 1898, Fénéon played the same role in a special production of *An Enemy of the People* intended as a protest related to the Dreyfus affair, specifically against the mistreatment Zola was forced to endure after publication of *J'Accuse*. Octave Mirbeau also acted in the production, which was put on by the staff of the anarchistic *Revue Blanche* and featured a revised text that reflected the current political situation and made clear the analogy between Zola and Stockman.[27] The obvious point was that Zola, though alone, was right. The *Revue Blanche* production illustrates how easily the political content of Ibsen's play could be adapted to the prevailing political climate, as the character Stockman, an anarchist in 1893, is transformed into a Dreyfusard in 1898.

Despite Ibsen's concern with social issues, the politics of his plays is not sufficiently consistent to be related to anarchism except on certain isolated points. But this did not stop the anarchists from claiming Ibsen as a fellow egoist, an advanced individual who lived his life apart from political authority. If Ibsen is a case of culture co-opted by anarchism, of the usurpation of the artistic avant-garde by the political, that process has some interesting results. In the 1890s, the political and the artistic avant-gardes took Ibsen as a rallying point and proceeded in concert. By the first decade or so of the twentieth century, however, the aesthetic Ibsen was losing ground to the political Ibsen. Indeed, the language that the political avant-garde used to advance the revolutionary Ibsen was aesthetically retrograde. In her 1914 essay titled "The Modern Drama," Emma Goldman subordinates Ibsen and other dramatists to the "Nietz-schean" process whereby social discontent "affects all phases of human thought and action, and seeks its individual and social expression in the gradual transvaluation of existing values." The "modern drama" is said to be "the strongest and most far-reaching interpreter of our deep-felt dissatisfaction."[28] Goldman's discussion of Ibsen, in fact, offers little insight into anything other than the playwright as social critic, so that there is ultimately no aesthetic distinction made between Ibsen's plays and Goldman's rhetoric, no suggestion that the plays might be anything other than political rhetoric themselves. It was precisely this type of separation of aesthetics from politics that James Joyce sought to rectify, and he took his inspiration from Henrik Ibsen.

2

Joyce's first publication, written when he was eighteen years old, was a review article of Ibsen's final play, *When We Dead Awaken*. The title of the essay, "Ibsen's New Drama," refers not just to Ibsen's most recent play but to a new conception of drama itself. In 1900, when Joyce's article appeared in the *Fortnightly Review*, the doubling of Ibsen into anarchist and artist, naturalist and symbolist, was already a received tradition, which Joyce took stock of in his opening paragraph: "He has been upheld as a religious reformer, a social reformer, a Semitic lover of righteousness, and as a great dramatist. He has been denounced as a meddlesome intruder, a defective artist, an incomprehensible mystic."[29] Against this familiar conception of

Ibsen as either the engaged naturalist ("social reformer") or the rarefied symbolist ("incomprehensible mystic"), Joyce argues for Ibsen as the artist of a special type of drama, one that does not depend "on the action, or on the incidents" or "[e]ven the characters." Instead, Ibsen relies on "the naked drama, either the perception of a great truth, or the opening up of a great question, or a great conflict which is almost independent of the conflicting actors" (*CW*, 63). For the early Joyce, "drama" is an important aesthetic concept, one that is actually opposed to "literature," which is always marked by dependence on conventions of various kinds, whether verse form or the aforementioned action, incident, and character. In Joyce's view, Ibsen is able to write drama because he eschews convention: "Ibsen has chosen the average lives in their uncompromising truth for the groundwork of all his later plays. He has abandoned verse form, and has never sought to embellish his work after the conventional fashion" (*CW*, 63). Joyce developed this idea of drama as a nonconventional, universalist form of art in a lecture given in January 1900 when he was a student at University College. The lecture "Drama and Life" gives fuller expression to the ideas that Joyce only touches on in the Ibsen article:

> Human society is the embodiment of changeless laws which the whimsicalities and circumstances of men and women involve and overwrap. The realm of literature is the realm of these accidental manners and humours—a spacious realm; and the true literary artist concerns himself mainly with them. Drama has to do with the underlying laws first, in all their nakedness and divine severity, and only secondarily with the motley agents who bear them out. When so much is recognized an advance has been made to a more rational and true appreciation of dramatic art. (*CW*, 40)

This lecture and the Ibsen article, along with a 1902 essay on the Irish poet James Clarence Mangan, lay out a set of aesthetic ideas that is hard to reconcile with the politics of anarchism and socialism that attracted Joyce's attention as a young man. He seems clearly to have moved beyond the simple equation of progressive politics and avant-garde art made earlier by the symbolists and later by Emma Goldman. In fact, in his *Fortnightly Review* article Joyce mentions that *When We Dead Awaken* clearly supersedes *An Enemy of the People*, that favorite "anarchist" play. In one sense, of course, the artist and the anarchist are alike in that both are isolated, individualistic, and aloof from bourgeois society. But this is a superficial consideration given Joyce's formulation, which places *all* of human society, bourgeois or otherwise, in a secondary position, subject to the operation of the "changeless laws" that govern it. As Robert Spoo puts it, Joycean "drama" avoids "the empty shows of history by virtue of the 'underlying laws' with which the true artist . . . intimately communes." [30] In some ways, the aesthetics of drama is consistent with that strand of aristocratic anarchism whose social position is defined by the familiar image of the ivory tower. But in actual practice, Joyce's politico-aesthetic position is more accurately captured by the squat image of the Martello tower that opens *Ulysses*. That tower, built by William Pitt as a defense against a possible invasion of revolutionary Frenchmen, is home to Stephen Dedalus, poet and aesthete. The figure may be taken to stand for a larger fact of Joyce's artistic career, namely that his aesthetics is somehow *housed* by politics and history, so that the "accidental manners and humours" of any given day (say, 16 June 1904) are bound up with "the underlying laws" that give rise to history. If the artist is outside history, the work nonetheless winds up within it.

Ibsen the self-exiled artist may be the primary model for the egoist outside of history, but if he were Joyce's only political exemplar then his anarchism would be a precious matter indeed. But Joyce had other politico-aesthetic models more directly connected to historical conditions. In addition to Ibsen, Shelley and Oscar Wilde combined anarchistic principles with artistic practice, and Joyce admired them both. Dominic Manganiello in *Joyce's Politics* points out a number of instances where Joyce echoes Shelley, as when Stephen says in *Stephen Hero,* "The poet is the intense center of the life of his age to which he stands in relation than which none can be more vital." [31] While not so overtly political as Shelley's, Stephen's remark is recognizable as a paraphrase of the idea that "[p]oets are the unacknowledged legislators of the world." Also, when Joyce has Stephen call the artist "a priest of eternal imagination," [32] he echoes Shelley's definition of the poets as "hierophants of unapprehended inspiration." Manganiello also sees Joyce's characterization of Shem the Penman in *Finnegans Wake* as "anarch, egoarch, hiresiarch" as a possible allusion to Shelley's sonnet "Political Greatness," which describes the new, Promethean man ruling "the empire of himself." [33] This type of political individualism is indistinguishable from aesthetic anarchism in Oscar Wilde's essay "The Soul of Man Under Socialism." As we have seen, what Wilde terms "socialism" is quite close to individualist anarchism, and his argument that the artist functions best in a society without government must have appealed to Joyce. Joyce evidently felt a strong attachment to this essay, since he requested permission from Wilde's publisher to translate it into Italian.[34] Though he never followed through with the project, the plan squares with Joyce's interest in the individualist anarchism of Benjamin Tucker. Joyce's interest in anarchist politics in general and in Benjamin Tucker's writings in particular is well established. One source has Joyce stating that Tucker "was the great political thinker,"[35] while Joyce's friend Frank Budgen offers a more restrained view: "An occasional vague reference to the pacific American anarchist, Tucker, was the only indication I ever heard of a political outlook."[36] Manganiello gives evidence to support the claim that "Joyce's reading of anarchist literature was extensive" and says that Joyce's "principal political authority was Benjamin Tucker, chief American exponent of individualist anarchism."[37] Indeed, the anarchist principle of individualism is clearly heard in *Stephen Hero* in the form of "that ineradicable egoism which he was afterwards to call redeemer" (*SH*, 34). It is safe to say that early in Joyce's career the word *ego* was a political rather than a psychological term and that the art he practiced, or intended to practice, would be a form of iconoclasm. The combination of political egoism and artistic iconoclasm is part of a formula for aesthetic anarchism that makes Stephen "the herald of a new order" (*SH*, 42). In taking the anarchist as a partial model for the artist Joyce regarded political and aesthetic liberation as congruent and interdependent, and he looked to Tucker as perhaps the principal exemplar of individualist anarchism.

Joyce may also have looked to Wilde as a politico-aesthetic precursor, mainly because the politics that Wilde advocates in "The Soul of Man Under Socialism" is quite close to Tucker's. Manganiello comments that "Joyce probably realized for the first time in Wilde's tract that his demand for absolute freedom to accomplish his aesthetic aims could be made consistent with the political view of Tucker, who stressed respect for individual liberties."[38] The plan to translate Wilde was made in 1909, after Joyce had returned to Trieste from Rome, where he had taken note of the activities of socialists and syndicalists during an intense period of political activity that included the socialist congress of 1906. The unrealized Wilde project of 1909 seems to belie Joyce's assertion two years earlier that he had lost interest in "socialism and the rest." [39] But the disavowal may also mean that Joyce had not lost interest in politics so much as shifted that interest toward aesthetics. The Wilde essay certainly lends support to the idea that an artist may give expression to anarchism in aesthetic form simply by making an uncompromising commitment to art.

In addition to Ibsen, Wilde, and Tucker, other writers who helped Joyce reconcile anarchism with aesthetics include Joseph Conrad, Mikhail Bakunin, and John Stewart Mill. Jane Ford has examined Joyce's personal copies of books by these authors and noted certain markings in Joyce's hand that show a concern for the general problem of individualist behavior in social context, and, sometimes, a more particular interest in anarchism. In his copy of Mill's *On Liberty,* Joyce marked Mill's introductory remarks on Aristotle's observation "that man is naturally a political animal" and drew a line alongside this statement: "how to make the fitting adjustment between individual independence and social control—is a subject on which nearly everything remains to be done." [40] While Mill is not an anarchist, the problem of individual freedom and "social control" that he singles out is more acute for the anarchist than it is for, say, the liberal or the conservative, so it makes sense for someone with anarchist leanings to bracket the passage, as Joyce did. Another of Joyce's marks in a book by Joseph Conrad shows an interest in matters still more specific to anarchism. Joyce lined this sentence from "The Informer," a story in a Conrad collection titled *A Set of Six:* "The printing of anarchist literature was the only 'activity' she seemed to be aware of there." The sentence describes a well-to-do young girl not unlike one of the Rossetti sisters who is involved in underground politics in London but is ignorant of the full range of anarchist activity, which includes the manufacture of bombs. The story is based on the same slightly skewed information about London anarchism that Conrad got from Ford Maddox Ford and used in *The Secret Agent.* Since Joyce had himself made Ford's acquaintance by the time he was working on *Ulysses,* it is tempting to think that he might have had access to some of the same information about fin de siècle anarchism as Conrad did. [41] In general, however, Joyce took very little interest in the activist, confrontational variety of anarchism alluded to in "The Informer." Although Joyce's copy of Bakunin's *God and the State* is unmarked, the few passages from this book that seem to be echoed in *Ulysses* concern economics, not the violent revolutionary tactics for which Bakunin is more generally known.[42]

Like other writers (including Conrad), Joyce used the black-clad, bomb-throwing anarchist figure for comic effect, as when, in the "Circe" chapter of *Ulysses,* Leopold Bloom is suspected of planning an anarchist outrage. Bloom is stopped by two policemen who accuse him of planting "[a]n infernal machine with a time fuse" on a city street because he is dressed in black. In reality, Bloom wears black because he has been to a funeral, and the "bomb" he has deposited turns out to be a bundle of cold meat he feeds to a stray dog (*U,* 385). Elsewhere in *Ulysses,* anarchism appears in a much more complex light than in this brief comic episode from "Circe." In the "Aeolus" chapter, set in a newspaper office, Stephen Dedalus enters with an older acquaintance, Mr. O'Madden Burke, who, like him, affects a certain casual, bohemian style of dress, including the "loose ties" associated with artists. Their mode of dress prompts another character to comment: "Paris, past and present. . . . You look like communards." Someone else adds, "Like fellows who had blown up the Bastille." These references to earlier periods of revolutionary and anarchist activity are followed by an allusion to a political assassination that took place on 16 June 1904, the date on which *Ulysses* is set (the newsroom setting accounts for the fact that the characters know about it): "Or was it you shot the lord lieutenant of Finland between you? You look as though you had done the deed. General Bobrikoff" (*U,* 111). The reference to "propaganda by the deed" suggests an anarchist context for the act, which in reality was motivated by Finnish nationalism (Nikolai Ivanovich Bobrikoff was a Russian military officer bent on using his dictatorial powers as governor-general to Russianize Finland).[43] Stephen's cryptic response to the joking accusation is, "We were only thinking about it" (*U,* 111). "He only *thinks* about political assassination," Robert Spoo comments, "because he is sworn to destroying religious and political institutions in a bloodless, Blakean coup of the mind and spirit." Spoo adds that "[n]ot long after this mild, unnoticed profession of anarchism, Stephen makes his first genuine attempt to come to terms with Dublin aesthetically and historiographically" by telling the story he calls "The Parable of the Plums," which many critics regard as a artistic breakthrough for the troubled young artist.[44] In other words, there is a causal relationship between the character's pacifist, intellectual anarchism and his capacity for artistic growth.

Later in *Ulysses*, Stephen *"taps his brow"* and says, "But in here it is I must kill the priest and the king" (*U,* 481). By having the character tap his brow Joyce probably alludes to the egoist Max Stirner, so called because of his large forehead (German, *Stirn*).[45] Through most of the novel Stephen has been haunted by Christianity in the form of a ghostly memory of this dead mother, another likely reference to Stirner, who treats Christian beliefs as so many spooks, ghosts, and goblins that the egoist is obligated to exorcise from himself. The ghostly faith is perpetuated, in Stirner's view, by the irrationalist lineage of women: "out of confidence in our grandmothers' honesty we believe in the existence of spirits."[46] In *Ulysses*, Stephen Dedalus is preoccupied on several occasions by a strange riddle about a "fox burying his grandmother" (*U,* 22). The final reference to this riddle occurs in the same episode where Stephen says he must "kill" the priest and king: "Burying his grandmother. Probably he killed her" (*U,* 456). Stephen's need to kill the ghost of Christianity is dramatized by the hallucinatory scene where an apparition of the dead mother rises up against her son and he tries to strike it down (*U,* 475). The scene is only "anarchistic" if it is read through the egoistic tradition of Max Stirner, but such egoism was precisely what Joyce and other modernists understood anarchism to be. These references to intellectual anarchism suggest that Joyce's fictional character in 1904 is at roughly the same stage of political development that Joyce himself was around 1906–7, his most intense period of interest in socialist and anarchist politics. "[A]s this was the formative period for his ideas about history and literature, it should not be surprising that a kind of aesthetic anarchism informs much of his later work."[47] Indeed, there does appear to be a strong link between Joyce's later work and his earlier politics.

Joyce had thought of his art in political terms from the very beginning of his career. Early in 1904 he completed a piece titled "A Portrait of the Artist," an autobiographical sketch that is also a highly political document. In this essay, the young Joyce, not yet twenty-two, positions himself against the prevailing order of society in favor of a gradual transformation presented in organic terms, with the artist as an engendering agent of the transformation: "To those multitudes not as yet in the wombs of humanity but surely engenderable there, he would give the word. Man and woman, out of you comes the nation that is to come, the lightning [lightening?] of your masses in travail; the competitive order is employed against itself, the aristocracies are supplanted; and amid the general paralysis of an insane society, the confederate will issues in action."[48] As Manganiello has pointed out, the organic metaphor is most likely derived from Karl Marx. In his *Critique of the Gotha Programme* (1875), Marx described the communist society of the future "not as it has *developed* in its own foundations, but, on the contrary, just as it *emerges* from capitalist society; which is thus in every respect, economically, morally, and intellectually, still stamped with the birth marks of the old society from whose womb it emerges."[49] The metaphor at work here describes the political gradualism that Marx believed was necessary for the transformation of society, an attitude that runs counter to the hope of sudden upheaval more common to anarchism. Organic metaphors in communism or state socialism, however, are not only applied to the emergence of the new society, but are also used to describe the new society itself. These socialist formulations feed into Joyce's aesthetics and form a counterpoint to the Ibsenite anarchism of his early artistic career. Also, the organicism common to socialist political theory may have carried over to some extent into Joyce's aesthetics and narrative practice. There is no question that much of Joyce's art relies on underlying structures based on organic models of various types (the growth of the individual in *Dubliners,* the parallelism of embryonic, stylistic, and emotional development in *A Portrait of the Artist as a Young Man,* and so on).[50] At the same time, Joyce's style becomes increasingly atomistic, and resembles more and more the so-called decadent style that conservative critics associated with anarchy. This oscillation from the larger satisfaction of organic structure and the momentary pleasures of atomistic style can hardly be attributed solely to Joyce's evident oscillation between socialism and anarchism, but there is no denying that the development of Joyce's art and his interest in turn-of-the-century politics are often parallel.

Joyce's early political fluctuations are hard to chart, but the documentary evidence sustains the idea that Joyce identified his art less with socialism and more with anarchism as his career progressed. The "Portrait" essay of January 1904 dismisses "anarchy"—somehow

linked with "the folk"—as one of those timid heterodoxies, along
with the "blue triangles" of theosophy and the "fish gods" of Celtic
myth, that the artist must revenge himself against in favor of the
gradualist socialism of Marx that sounds at the essay's conclusion.[51]
Later in 1904 his brother Stanislaus recorded in his diary that Joyce's
socialism continued unabated: "Jim boasts . . . of being modern. He
calls himself a socialist but attaches himself to no school of socialism." [52] The next year (May 1905) Joyce defended his "political opinions" in a letter to Stanislaus as "those of a socialistic artist" (*SL*, 61).
In August 1906 Joyce continued to defend his political opinions
against his brother's skepticism in rather strong terms: "You have
often shown opposition to my socialist tendencies. But can you not
see plainly . . . that a deferrment [*sic*] of the emancipation of the
proletariat, a reaction to clericalism or aristocracy or bourgeoisism
would mean a revulsion to tyrannies of all kinds" (*SL*, 94). In October of the same year Joyce wrote that he "was following with interest
the various socialist parties" at the Socialist Congress of Rome. He
took particular interest in the syndicalist Arturo Labriola, who reminded Joyce of Arthur Griffith, founder of Sinn Fein. This interest
may mark the beginning of the modulation to anarchism. Indeed,
both Sinn Fein and syndicalism have affinities with anarchism; at
the very least, Labriola's syndicalism is at some remove from state
socialism, as Joyce's description of Labriola makes clear: "He belongs
or is leader of the sindacalists [*sic*]. . . . They assert that they are the
true socialists because they wish the future social order to proceed
equally from the overthrow of the entire social organisation and
from the automatic emergence of the proletariat in trade-unions
and guilds and the like" (*SL*, 117). This letter prompted still more
criticism from Stanislaus, and Joyce responded this time not by de-
fending his opinions, but by agreeing with the criticism: "Of course
you find my socialism thin. It is so and unsteady and ill-informed."
In the same letter Joyce identifies himself with his anarchistic mentor
Ibsen by stating that "my action, and that of men like Ibsen &c, is a
virtual intellectual strike." Here, the influence of Labriola is expressed by a formulation that makes the artist a member of an aesthetic *syndicat* that refuses all dealings with bourgeois society, unlike
those "blacklegs of literature" Padraic Colum and William Butler
Yeats (*SL*, 125).

Without question, by the end of 1906 Joyce no longer felt the need to call himself a "socialistic artist." In January 1907, in fact, he composes an epiphany in which the artist, albeit ironically, has a new identity: "Scene: draughty little stone-flagged room, chest of drawers to left, on which are the remains of lunch, in the centre, a small table on which are *writing materials* (*He* never forgot them) and a saltcellar: in the background, small-sized bed. A young man with snivelling nose sits at the little table: on the bed sit a madonna and plaintive infant. It is a January day. Title of above: *The Anarchist"* (*SL,* 142). It is clear from the context of the letter that the "young man" is Joyce and that this portrait of the artist as a young anarchist is inspired by the "egoarch" Henrik Ibsen (*"He* never forgot them" refers to Ibsen). This epiphany may account, in part, for the entry in Stanislaus's diary, dated 11 April 1907, in which he says that Joyce had shifted his politico-aesthetic allegiance from socialism to anarchism, "prefer[ing] to say that like Ibsen, he was an anarchist, though not a practical anarchist after what he called the modern style."[53] Around this time, however, Joyce writes to his brother that "[t]he interest I took in socialism and the rest have left me. . . . I have no wish to codify myself as anarchist or socialist or reactionary" (*SL,* 151–52). What is striking about this record of Joyce's interest in politics is how it corresponds to the writing of *Dubliners.* And that interest, particularly the interest in socialism, declines as the book is completed. This is not to say that *Dubliners* is socialist art, but certainly the style of that book, as well as its class interests, are congruent with Joyce's claims to be a "socialistic artist" as he was writing it.[54] After all, the book was published in the same year and by the same publisher as Robert Tressel's *The Ragged Trousered Philanthropists,* a classic work of socialist literature. What is even more arresting, however, is that the time of Joyce's self-codification as a socialist artist ends as the period of his radical literary experimentation begins.

Whether this transformation was a conscious one or not is difficult to say. But Joyce seems to have painted himself into an aesthetic corner by claiming to be a socialist artist on the one hand, and, on the other, by pursuing an aesthetic program and a literary style incompatible with the clarity of expression and the encouragement of community that socialist art generally requires. In the same letter in which Joyce defended his interest in socialism, however "thin," he also said that he would be "content to recognise myself an exile" (*SL,* 125). Raymond Williams has commented on the somewhat poignant position of the exile with socialist sympathies, and on the utter incompatibility of the condition of exile and the politics of socialism:

> The exile, because of his own personal position, cannot finally believe in any social guarantee: to him, because this is the pattern of his own living, almost all association is suspect. He fears it because he does not want to be compromised (this is often his virtue, because he is so quick to see the perfidy which certain compromises involve). Yet he fears it also because he can see no way of confirming, socially, his own individuality; this is, after all, the psychological condition of the self-exile. Thus, in attacking the denial of liberty he is on sure ground; he is wholehearted in rejecting the attempts of society to involve him. When, however, in any positive way, he has to affirm liberty, he is forced to deny its inevitable social basis: all he can fall back on is the notion of an atomistic society, which will leave individuals alone.[55]

Two interrelated points need to be made here. The first is that Joyce's acceptance of exile has a certain logic given his waning interest in socialism. The second point is that the aesthetic of fragmentation that Joyce turned to after *Dubliners* and *Stephen Hero* was also incompatible with the practice of socialist art. But these two points reinforce each other if the context shifts to anarchism. I do not mean to suggest, however, that Joyce's experience of socialism left no mark on his aesthetics at all. On the contrary, Joyce's artistic career gains a certain politico-aesthetic coherence if it is seen as an ongoing process with socialism and anarchism as opposing impulses that condition one another in various ways.

Generally speaking, critics tend to consolidate Joyce's interest in socialism *and* anarchism into a general political attitude limited to the period of aesthetic apprenticeship (1904–7) that produced *Dubliners* and *Stephen Hero*.[56] Despite this consolidation of the two schools of political thought in the early Joyce, one tendency in political discussions of the later Joyce is to dissociate them, and to think of *Ulysses* as socialistic and of *Finnegans Wake* as anarchistic. I refer mainly to an earlier critical tradition of American leftists (Trilling, Wilson, Howe) who admired *Ulysses* "for its sympathy with progressive social ideas,"[57] and to more recent critics who focus on the anarchic politics of style in *Finnegans Wake* (Kristeva, Eagleton, French).[58] I believe that something might be gained by taking this later tendency to discriminate between socialism and anarchism back to the early Joyce. As we have already observed, in the nineteenth century socialism and anarchism were more often than not competing schools of political thought, as the rivalry of Marx and Bakunin illustrates. Benjamin Tucker, whom Joyce admired, informed the readers of *Liberty* that "the man who thinks they are one and the same thing is simply a fool." [59] Thus, it should mean one thing to think of Joyce as a "socialistic artist" (*SL,* 61), as he called himself in 1905, and something else again to think of him as an anarchistic artist. Indeed, if socialism and anarchism are seen as competing political discourses, and those political discourses ramify in some way into Joyce's aesthetics, some fundamental tensions have to result.

A politico-aesthetic issue of great importance to the early Joyce is the question of egoism, of the place of individualism in artistic production. At the turn of the century the communist politics of socialism and the individualist politics of anarchism were clearly opposed. Writers for the socialist organ *Justice* condemned anarchism as among "the worst manifestations of the most extreme form of individualism." [60] Egoism is for the socialist a problematic attitude, but not for the anarchist: Benjamin Tucker, we recall, advertised titles available from his "Unique Book-shop" in New York as "The Literature that Makes for Egoism in Philosophy, Anarchism in Politics, Iconoclasm in Art." [61] As we saw in the previous chapter, the political issue of individualism was also put into the context of art by William Morris and Oscar Wilde, and the contrast of their views could not be more extreme. In "Art under Plutocracy," Morris imagines an organic integration of art and society as an ideal condition, one that involves a radical reduction of aesthetic individualism. He longs for the return of a tradition that "once bound artist and public together." [62] This ideal can only be realized through socialist "Association, instead of Competition," which will make possible "Social Order instead of Individualist Anarchy" (83). Wilde appears to reply directly to Morris in "The Soul of Man Under Socialism" by saying that "[i]ndividualism . . . is what through Socialism we are to attain. As a natural result the State must give up all idea of government." [63] Wilde's "socialism," then, is clearly anarchistic, especially regarding the artist: "The form of government that is most suitable to the artist is no government at all" (1018). Also, nothing could be further from Morris's socialist ideal of the artist integrated into society than Wilde's distanced or dissociated artist, whose "perfect personality" makes impersonality possible: "He stands outside his subject, and through its medium produces incomparable artistic effects" (1093). This contrast of Morris's socialism and Wilde's anarchism appears to point Joyce more in the direction of Wilde. But the contemporaneous composition of *Dubliners* and *Stephen Hero* argues against a uniformly anarchistic attitude on the issue of egoism. The egoism of that antisocial antisocialist James Duffy has no redemptive value in the story "A Painful Case" from *Dubliners*, whereas "that ineradicable egoism" (*SH*, 34) celebrated in *Stephen Hero* does. This double attitude toward egoism is nicely captured on a single page of Stanislaus's diary. In the entry cited above, Stanislaus writes that "Jim boasts . . . of being modern [and] calls himself a socialist." Then, he refers to his brother's "subtle egoism which he calls the modern mind." [64] Perhaps Joyce managed the trick of being a socialistic egoist for a while, but the difficulty of maintaining such a balance shows in the 1907 letter in which he says that "[t]he interest I took in socialism . . . has left me." In that same letter he says he wishes to resume "the expression of myself which I now see I began in *Chamber Music*" (*SL*, 151). The role of socialistic artist assumed by Joyce for the writing of *Dubliners* did not comport well with the desire for self-expression. Perhaps the difference between socialism and anarchism, or the political tension between collectivism and egoism, was recapitulated in Joyce's temperament in the form of aesthetic tension between self-effacement and self-expression.

Another political difference between the two schools of political thought with possible aesthetic ramifications for Joyce involves the socialist idea of gradualism. Again, the coda to the 1904 "A Portrait of the Artist" draws on Marx for the metaphor likening the evolution of society to embryonic development, and certainly the idea of gradual, progressive reform is more of a socialist than an anarchist attitude. This same attitude may have informed some of Joyce's thinking about *Dubliners*. He wrote to Grant Richards that in writing the book he had "taken the first step towards the spiritual liberation of my country" (*SL*, 88), and the idea that liberation is to be achieved in steps or stages is consistent with the gradualist ideal of socialism, an ideal that Joyce articulated even in 1906 when he cited the Marxist tenet that "capitalism is a stage of progress" (*SL*, 125). Or as Bloom puts it in the "Eumaeus" chapter of *Ulysses*, "A revolution must come on the due installments plan" (*U*, 525). Unlike Bloom, Stephen

Dedalus is no gradualist. In *Stephen Hero*, Stephen has the anarchist's characteristic impatience with the long view taken by his rival Mac-Cann, whose socialistic "care of posterity" Stephen rejects: "he could not understand what right the future had to hinder him from any passionate exertions in the present" (*SH*, 52).[65] As "a fiery-hearted revolutionary" (*SH*, 80) who believes that "[a]ll modern political . . . criticism dispenses with presumptive States" (*SH*, 186), Stephen clearly has more in common with the anarchists than the socialists. But since he does not feel the need to "undertake an extensive alteration of society" (*SH*, 146), Stephen's anarchism exists mainly to serve his aesthetic ends. In fact, he imagines himself as a kind of aesthetic dynamitard when he describes the "manifesto" titled "Art and Life" as "the first of my explosives" (*SH*, 81). The notion of *Dubliners* as a socialistic "first step" is not easy to reconcile with the idea of the aesthetic anarchist's first explosion. Taken together, *Dubliners* and *Stephen Hero* suggest an aesthetic tension between tradition and innovation that has its socialist-anarchist cognate in the political tension between gradual reform and accelerated revolution.

The socialist notion of gradual maturation may also have something to do with the artistic schema of *Dubliners,* and even with the general Joycean practice of grounding stylistic transformations in structures based on some principle of organic maturation. But the organic element recedes in Joyce's work, and the recession has prompted some criticism that helps to make the argument that Joyce's ideological removal from socialism was registered in his aesthetic shift toward a more fragmented, modernist style. Fredric Jameson makes the socialist critique of the modernist style when he says of *Ulysses* that "the organic unity of the narrative" fails to "serve as a symbol for the unity of experience" because of "the process of universal fragmentation."[66] The remark illustrates what Raymond Williams has argued at length, namely that " 'organic' is . . . a central term in . . . Marxist thinking," and that in both the Marxist and the conservative traditions, the organic is opposed and threatened by the atomistic.[67]

We have already noted how in the nineteenth century the atomistic text was often taken as a sign of a disintegrating or decadent society. Joyce's parallel interest in anarchism and in the so-called decadent style is also clear. In fact, much if not most of Joyce's writing may be described in terms of the atomistic, fragmented, neologistic style of decadence. Joyce's description of the "style of writing" (*SH,* 27) that Stephen practices in *Stephen Hero* is quite close to the decadent style described by Gautier and decried by Nietzsche as atomistic and anarchic. This "style of writing" mixes vocabularies by combining "the antique and even the obsolete" with a "certain crude originality of expression" (*SH,* 27). Stephen finds words not only in Skeat's etymological dictionary, but also "at haphazard in the shops, on advertisements, in the mouths of the plodding public." The words that Stephen finds are repeated "till they lost all instantaneous meaning for him and became wonderful vocables" (*SH,* 30). This is an extremely atomistic approach to language, and while these "wonderful vocables" are not as yet units of a literary work, when the process of composition is described the work is, again, atomistic in the extreme. When he sits down to write, "He sought in his verses to fix the most elusive of his moods and he put his lines together not word by word but letter by letter" (*SH,* 32). The process of composition as Joyce describes it here sounds like a style manual for *Finnegans Wake.* In other words, the aesthetic that eventually gave rise to the *Wake* seems already to have been formed, in some sense, early in Joyce's career, and the tradition of the decadent or anarchic style seems to have contributed to its formation. I am aware that the combination of atomistic style and organic structure that is so characteristic of Joyce from the *Portrait* on probably has its origins in Walter Pater's essay on "Style." Indeed, Pater thinks of style as atomistic, as "elementary particles of language" and says that the main requirement of literary structure is that it be "organically complete." [68] But Pater's comments actually enforce the larger point: that in the nineteenth century both aesthetic and political discourse were often driven by the same conceptual opposition of organicism and atomism, of integrated and disintegrated structures. Joyce continued in this tradition, for it is evident that his structural organicism is compatible with socialism, and his stylistic atomism with anarchism.

Thus far, in suggesting ways in which socialism and anarchism might be seen to ramify into Joyce's art, I have presented them as largely oppositional, forming a politico-aesthetic balance of sorts. But if Joyce's atomistic, fragmented style is taken as the aesthetic cognate of anarchistic thought, then the balance shifts to anarchism. The balance can be restored somewhat by noting that Joyce's treatment of socialistic characters in his fiction becomes increasingly sympathetic. In both *Stephen Hero* and the *Portrait*, the debates between Stephen and MacCann take on a different tone if they are read not as a conflict involving a misogynist and a feminist, or an artist and a propagandist, but an anarchist and a socialist. As a humorless, tone-deaf, oversober celibate, MacCann is a fairly ridiculous figure in *Stephen Hero*. But Joyce later redrew MacCann to make him a much more sympathetic character. Indeed, in the *Portrait* the socialist activist seems to win the "war of wits" (*P*, 196) with the anarchistic aesthete, who settles for an intellectual standoff: "You are right to go your way. Leave me to go mine" (*P*, 198). By the time of *Ulysses*, MacCann's pacifism, internationalism, and utopian socialism have found their way into the character of the likable Leopold Bloom, perhaps as a result of Joyce's reading of Guglielmo Ferrero, who attributed the rise of socialism not just to Marx but to the Jewish "race" in general.[69]

One area of concern to Joyce where socialism and anarchism do not seem to be in competition is in the matter of sexual politics. Benjamin Tucker describes marriage and divorce as "equal absurdities," and looks forward to the time "when the love relations between . . . independent individuals shall be as varied as are individual inclinations and attractions."[70] Friedrich Engels says that marriage "turns often enough into the crassest prostitution," and that the wife "differs from the ordinary courtesan in that she does not let out her body on piece-work as a wage worker, but sells it once and for all into slavery."[71] Stephen argues against marriage in *Stephen Hero* in similar terms, saying that the woman "must sell it [her body] either as a harlot or as a married woman" (*SH*, 202). Stephen also follows Engels on the subject of the inevitability of adultery. The Protestant marriage vows, Stephen believes, require a man to swear "to do something it is not in his power to do" (*SH*, 202), and Engels speculates that "the Catholic Church abolished divorce . . . because it had convinced itself that there is no more a cure for adultery than there is for death."[72] This anarchist-socialist critique of marriage is, I believe, one of the things behind Joyce's observation in his notes to the play *Exiles* that since *Madame Bovary* "the centre of sympathy appears to have been aesthetically shifted from the lover or fancyman to the husband or cuckold."[73] In fact, Joyce appears to place this aesthetic shift in a political context by saying that it "has been rendered more stable by the gradual growth of a collective practical realism due to changed economic conditions" (150). It may seem strange to turn cuckoldry into a political condition, but the socialistic acceptance of the inevitability of adultery squares with Bloom's feeling of "equanimity" after the event (*U*, 602). Further, Bloom's status as a sympathetic cuckold has an interesting precedent in socialist literature. The hero of William Morris's verse novel *The Pilgrims of Hope* (1885–86) is converted to communism by a radical orator named Arthur, who becomes his best friend. Arthur has an affair with the hero's wife, but the three socialists do not let sexual betrayal interfere with political solidarity. All three set out for Paris to be a part of the Commune of 1871. They fight on the barricades together; the lover and the wife are killed, but the husband survives. In this case, the cuckold is not only a sympathetic figure, he is downright noble. The name of this noble figure is Richard, and he may be a distant, cuckolded cousin to Richard Rowan in *Exiles* and Leopold Bloom in *Ulysses*.

Although socialists and anarchists might have gotten into bed together on the issue of sexual politics, in the nineteenth century they were mainly rivals. This rivalry is homologous with some of the familiar tensions and contradictions in Joyce's aesthetics. The dynamic balance in Joyce's art of self-effacement and self-expression, tradition and innovation, organic structure and atomistic style is consistent with his early interest in socialism and anarchism, but only if socialism and anarchism are recognized as competing political discourses that require some kind of ideological balancing if one is to entertain both. To the extent that Joyce is a socialistic artist, he is a modern, part of that progressive, liberal tradition that American leftists saw personified in Leopold Bloom. To the extent that Joyce is an anarchistic artist, he is a modernist, part of that revolutionary, individualist tradition personified by Stephen Dedalus. At the turn of the century, northern Europe was the domain of socialist thought, while the anarchists were always much more successful in Mediterranean Europe. When Joyce was in Rome in 1906 he took an interest in the syndicalist politics of Arturo Labriola and, shortly thereafter, in the libertarian politics of Luigi Molinari, both near-anarchists.[74] Joyce's dual interest in socialism and anarchism can therefore be viewed vertically, in a sense, as another set of cultural poles, like Shakespeare and Dante, that the aesthetically peripatetic Joyce constantly moved between. Another politico-aesthetic schema is suggested by the sequence of Joyce's three major works. *Dubliners* is the one work most readily accommodated by socialist ideology; *Ulysses*, part naturalistic and part atomistic, can be described as anarcho-socialist, with elements of Joyce's early socialism forming part of the character of Leopold Bloom even as his individualist anarchism goes to form much of Stephen Dedalus. *Finnegans Wake* is perhaps the most complete expression of aesthetic anarchism ever written, but the work also returns Joyce to the questions raised early in his career by "Drama and Life." *Finnegans Wake* offers abundant evidence for the "underlying laws" of human society, only now Joycean drama does not eclipse history with aesthetics; rather, the historical vision and the aesthetic vision are unified. What brings the political and the artistic together is anarchism, as history itself takes the form of the endlessly proliferating atomistic text of *Finnegans Wake*.

3

The interplay of socialism and anarchism in Joyce may be little more than a figure of speech, a trope that helps to explain certain tensions and key oppositions in the work of the writer that might also be explained in other terms. For example, the more traditional explanation of Stephen and Bloom in *Ulysses* is that the two characters represent Joyce's youth and maturity,[75] not his anarchism and socialism. Something is to be gained, however, by considering the aesthetic implications of the competing ideologies Joyce entertained. Ultimately, in Joyce's case politics and aesthetics are not merely homologous, but actually integrated. Joyce's politico-aesthetic direction is from socialism *to* anarchism, and it is not too much to assert that he would not have written *Finnegans Wake* if the drift had been toward socialism instead. In this sense, Joyce illustrates what may be an important but neglected aspect of modernist culture; namely, that it often involves some kind of dialogue with anarchist politics, and that whatever aesthetics emerges from this dialogue is shaped in some way by the engagement with anarchism, even if anarchism is rejected in the end. The closely connected movements of dada and surrealism illustrate the dynamics of this engagement precisely. In this instance, the ultimate politico-aesthetic direction is away from anarchism and toward socialism. The point, however, is not that anarchism "loses" and socialism "wins" in the history of dada-surrealism, but rather that a particular culture emerged from the political interplay between the two ideologies, and that the culture is incomprehensible without the engagement with anarchism that in fact occurred.

One of the clichés of cultural criticism is that dada is a form of "artistic anarchy."[76] The phrase refers to the aesthetic autonomy enjoyed by the many practitioners of dada. Unlike the surrealists who followed them, the dadaists did not subscribe to common goals or employ a prescribed technique. Even the common designation of dada as "anti-art" is not sufficient to unify the diverse cultural practices of Marcel Duchamp, Francis Picabia, Tristan Tzara, Jean Arp, and the rest: "Dada was not identifiable with any one personality, viewpoint or style, nor did it ever acquire a single coherent programme. The focus of emphasis was continually shifting, never more so than during the war years in Switzerland."[77] Indeed, the fact of the Great War is sometimes used to account for the "anarchism" of dada, in two ways. First, the war forced a large number of artists and writers from different countries to seek asylum in such neutral cities as Zurich, Barcelona, and New York (neutral until 1917); as a result of this migration, the concentration of a diverse international population of émigré artists contributed to dada's unfocused, fragmented aesthetic. Second, most artists who left their homelands for neutral cities were not neutral themselves but opposed to the war; as a result, dada is often regarded as a form of artistic protest against the war, which was viewed as the logical product of progress, profits, and rationalism identified with the capitalist nation-state. Both of these formulations need to be examined, as the dynamics of dada is undeniably more complex than either of them; dada is not simply "artistic anarchy," nor is it merely "artistic protest." Despite the anarchistic rhetoric they employed (itself the heritage of an earlier age), very few dadaists had political connections to anarchism. A good example of this assertion concerns Francis Picabia. The wealthy Picabia, married to the daughter of a French senator, was older by a generation than most of the other dadaists and was given to pronouncements like the following: "Every page must explode, whether through seriousness, profundity, turbulence, nausea, the new, the eternal, annihilation, nonsense, enthusiasm for principles, or the way it is printed. Art must be unaesthetic in the extreme, useless and impossible to justify."[78] This manifesto, which combines Mallarmé's aesthetic anarchism with nihilism, comes from Picabia's dada journal *391* in its

Barcelona phase. What is striking about Picabia and the Barcelona dadaists is how insular their activities were; the group evidently had little contact with actual anarchists, and this in a city where anarchism had not modulated into a café fashion, as in Paris, but remained a viable political tradition.

The apolitical anarchism of the Barcelona dadaists is in stark contrast to that of Hugo Ball, who was clearly affiliated with anarchist groups in both Germany and Switzerland. By most accounts Ball was the originator of dada, the founder of the movement who set the Zurich group on its anarcho-cultural course. Although Ball's status as the founder of dada is sometimes questioned, it is doubtful whether analogous activities by Duchamp and others outside of Zurich would have ever been called dada had it not been for Ball's vigorous, though brief, promotion of the movement. But even in the case of Hugo Ball, the simple identifications of dada with aesthetic anarchism and artistic protest do not hold up.

Before moving to Zurich from Berlin in mid-1915, Ball had been involved in expressionist theater in Munich, where he also wrote poetry and other pieces for the radical journals *Die Aktion, Der Sturm,* and *Die Revolution,* the latter founded by Ball and his friend and fellow poet Hans Leybold. The cultural identity of the review was indicated by the slogan printed above its masthead: "Lässt chaotisch sein" (Let us be chaotic). *Die Revolution* encouraged "Dionysian destructivity and the negation of all values, but in contrast to the other journals of the expressionist avant-garde, Ball's writings also emphasized spiritual regeneration." [79] The linkage of negation and regeneration in Ball's prewar works reflects his earlier scholarly interest in Nietzsche. As a student at the University of Munich during the academic year 1909–10, Ball started a thesis with the title *Nietzsche in Basel.* Though the thesis remained unfinished, Nietzsche continued to be the dominant influence on Ball's work for many years. In his expressionist period, he thought of Nietzsche as he did in the thesis, as a *Kulturreformator* whose Dionysian energies would destroy all repressive institutions based on reason and morality and replace them with new systems and institutions based on aesthetic values.[80] Ball's interest in Nietzsche coincided with his involvement in expressionist theater, as both could be seen as a means of revolt against rationality. The same celebration of irrational forces led Ball and other German intellectuals to enthusiastic support of the war, and to think of the great conflict as a kind of Dionysian process that would purge society of rationalistic materialism and usher in a new spiritual-aesthetic world, beyond good and evil. Ball volunteered for service and was disappointed when he was rejected "on obscure medical grounds." In November 1914, he made an unauthorized visit to the Belgian front, not as a soldier but as an observer.[81] Ball was devastated by what he saw: "It is the total mass of machinery and the devil himself that has broken loose now. Ideals are only labels that have been stuck on. Everything has been shaken to its very foundations."[82] Ball returned to Berlin to rethink his Nietzschean belief in the regenerative power of destructive irrationality.

Having seen the results of irrationality when it was harnessed to the technological power of the nation-state, Ball began to study anarchist theoreticians. His initial diary entry after his return from the front records his preoccupation with Kropotkin, Bakunin, and Merezhkovsky (Ball, 10). The experience at the front seems to have brought to the surface some of Ball's earlier intellectual tendencies toward anarchism that had been overwhelmed by his interest in Nietzsche. When he was in Munich before the war Ball had noted the importance of Oscar Wilde's insistence on the anarchistic autonomy of the artist. At that time Ball also came into contact with the German anarchists Otto Gross and Franz Jung. He planned to publish an anthology of their writings along with selections from John Henry Mackay, the man who had rediscovered Stirner in the 1890s. One result of Ball's growing interest in anarchism was the development of the idea that literature had to involve itself more directly in politics. He made this very recommendation in August 1915 when he published an article on "Die junge Literatur in Deutschland" in *Der Revoluzzer,* an anarcho-syndicalist journal based in Zurich (Mann, 55). The *Revoluzzer* group was organized around the Swiss doctor Fritz Brupbacher (1874–1944), who promoted "the utopian ideal of achieving revolution by means of education" (Mann, 58). When Ball first met Brupbacher he was skeptical of the doctor's pacifist, utopian variant of anarchism because of the emphasis he placed on the proletariat to the exclusion of the intellectual or "brainworker" *(Kopfarbeiter).* Ball also expressed disdain for the terrorist strain of anarchism: "I have examined myself carefully. I could never bid chaos welcome, throw bombs, blow up bridges and do away with ideas. I am not an anarchist" (Ball, 18, 19). These remarks were made in June 1915 and they clearly express antagonism toward both pacifist and terrorist anarchism; nonetheless, as Ball's career progressed he returned to anarchist thought again and again.

Of the major anarchists, the one who most attracted Ball was Bakunin, and it is tempting to see in Bakunin's political philosophy a particularly rich source for Ball's aesthetic ideas. John Elderfield observes that the closing axiom from Bakunin's "The Reaction in Germany"—"the passion for destruction is also a creative passion" —"reads like something from a dada tract." [83] Ball read a biography of Bakunin by Max Nettlau late in 1914 (Ball, 12), which may have had something to do with his involvement with Brupbacher in Zurich, as the Swiss doctor had also authored a book on Bakunin, first published in 1913. An aspect of Brupbacher's understanding of Bakunin that must have appealed to Ball is the notion that the anarchist was an "organic" thinker, unlike the more rationalistic and mechanistic Marx. According to Brupbacher, Bakunin thinks like an artist and looks at reality in a more complete way, combining reason and feeling, will and imagination ("Bakunin dachte mit seinem ganzen Organismus; wenn er etwas ansah, so, wie der Künstler die Dinge sieht, Verstand, Gefühl, Willen, Phantasie, alle waren mit bei diesem Sehen").[84] After reading Bakunin and meeting Brupbacher, Ball himself started a book on Bakunin that he worked on for several years, but never published. The dada diary contains many entries that testify to Ball's interest in Bakunin, as well as his reluctance to subscribe to every element of anarchist ideology, such as abolition of the church. (Ball thought of spiritual matters as existing in a sphere apart from both statist and antistatist ideology [see Ball, 123].) One of the most interesting of Ball's comments about anarchism is indirect, and comes when dada is already mostly behind him, in June 1917. Ball is struck by the fact that Lenin resided just up the street from the Cabaret Voltaire, at Spiegelgasse 12, during the most intense period of dada activity: "He must have heard our music and tirades every evening; I do not know if he enjoyed them or profited from them. And when we were opening the gallery in Bahnhofstrasse, the Russians went to Petersburg to launch the revolution. Is dadaism as sign and gesture the opposite of Bolshevism? Does it contrast the completely quixotic, inexpedient, and incomprehensible side of the world with destruction and consummate calculation? It will be interesting to observe what happens here and there" (Ball,

117). Dada is like anarchism in that it is understood to be the opposite of Bolshevism, as anarchism proved to be in Leninist Russia. Also, the notion of dada as "completely quixotic" is a veiled reference to Bakunin, since Brupbacher had identified the anarchist with Don Quixote (see Mann, 57). There seems to be ample evidence, then, that Ball understood dada in relation to anarchist politics in general and to Bakunin's philosophy in particular.

During his dada period in the first half of 1916 Ball seems to have worked out a kind of synthesis of the two forms of anarchism he rejected in the summer of 1915; that is, he turned the outwardly destructive form of anarchism inward so that he became a pacifist "brainworker" laboring to reform society by means of a particularly coruscating type of culture, destroying old forms of art through a new, revolutionary aesthetic. This type of anarchism is suggested by a diary entry dated 12 March 1916, slightly more than a month after the opening of the Cabaret Voltaire: "Adopt symmetries and rhythms instead of principles. Oppose world systems and acts of state by transforming them into a phrase or a brush stroke" (Ball, 56). The concept of oppositional art combines with the notion that there is something "questionable" about "the nature of art itself, its complete anarchy" (Ball, 58), but anarchy, in turn, may be precisely what the times require: "[P]erhaps it is necessary to have resolutely, forcibly produced chaos and thus a complete withdrawal of faith before an entirely new edifice can be built up on a changed basis of belief" (Ball, 60). Ball understood that anarchy and anarchism were not the same thing, but he also understood that anarchism might allow for anarchy as a kind of purgative process, a demonic cleansing of culture not unlike the Nietzschean reformation he had once sought to achieve through expressionism. In his *Intellectual Biography* of Ball, Philip Mann says that the future founder of dada was somewhat ambivalent about anarchism when he arrived in Zurich. But the ideology at least made it possible for him to integrate his earlier interests in irrationalist regeneration with a more recent interest in pacifism and utopian politics. Mann describes three key elements in Ball's understanding of anarchism at the crucial period when he invented dada. First, anarchism was consonant with an irrational worldview that involved vitalism, primitivism, and Dionysianism. Second, anarchism represented individuals as naturally good and capable of living together harmoniously without the need for external authority. Third, like most anarchists of his time, Ball believed that the true route to revolution lay through education (56–58).

These three elements must be kept in mind in any discussion of dada as Ball conceived it when he opened the Cabaret Voltaire on 5 February 1916. Although the dada-soirees that took place there are legendary for the chaos they caused, the evidence indicates that Ball never intended to incite his audiences to outrage, but to educate them in libertarian politics. The name of the cabaret was not ironic, as the later history of dada might lead one to think, but was selected out of respect for Voltaire as the rationalist precursor of revolution. The choice shows that Ball was concerned with tempering the Nietzscheanism that still fueled his ideas, even though he had abandoned his prewar notion of destructive regeneration. In fact, extracts from Voltaire's writings were read aloud on the cabaret's opening night.[85] On the second, Ball read his pacifist poem "Totentanz," which was also performed "unter Assistenz des Revoluzzerchors."[86] The reference to a "revolutionary chorus" means, presumably, that the anarchists affiliated with Brupbacher and the journal *Der Revoluzzer* assisted in the performance. It is clear from these early presentations, as well as from Ball's diary and his letters to his sister, that the Cabaret Voltaire was first conceived as an educational institution with anarcho-cultural aims: "Ball did not want art for art's sake, but art with a political message, and his choice of programme for the cabaret was determined by this view of art" (Mann, 83).

Ball's own explanation of the purpose of his cabaret is simple and direct. Like the anarchist cabarets of an earlier age in Montmartre, Ball's nightclub began to publish its own review in May 1916. In the first number Ball described the original intent of the Cabaret Voltaire: "It [the review] is intended to present to the public the activities and interests of the Cabaret, which has as its sole purpose to draw attention, across the barriers of war and nationalism, to the few independent spirits who live for other ideals."[87] The emphasis on ideals is telling. Unlike Tzara, who came to dominate Zurich dada, Ball continued to hope that some positive political transformation of society would emerge from his anarcho-aesthetic activities. Also, the Cabaret Voltaire's international mixture of artists and writers was meant to encourage a *synthesis* of the arts, not to encourage the formation of a new movement. Ball's lecture on Kandinsky, delivered in April 1917 at the Galerie Dada, casts light on his activities of a year earlier at the cabaret. In this lecture, Ball expresses the sense of cultural fragmentation he feels in terms derived from Nietzsche and from anarchist terror: "God is dead. A world disintegrated. I am dynamite" (Ball, 223). Against this negative anarchism of destruction Ball sets the regenerative, spiritual anarchism of Kandinsky's art: "His remarks on anarchy remind one of statements by Bakunin and Kropotkin. Except that Kandinsky applies the concept of freedom, in a very spiritual way, to aesthetics." Ball goes on to quote Kandinsky's redefinition of anarchy as "regularity and order," an artistic principle directed by an "inner necessity" that "shapes the external, visible form of the work" (Ball, 227). This neo-Hegelian aesthetics of synthesis is given a curious political twist when Ball contrasts Kandinsky's intuitive artistic method with the more rigid formulations of the cubists: "Cubism operates with grammar, Kandinsky with flexible inner necessity." Although Picasso, for one, was drawn to anarchism early in his career, Ball presents the "grammar" of cubism as a severe, inflexible system of laws that is the obverse of anarchism: "It punishes and rewards, has something in common with the Spanish Inquisition and with the German predilection for right angles in matters of principle. . . . It prussianizes and purifies art" (Ball, 230). The "German" nature of cubism suggests that Ball is recapitulating the Marx-Bakunin split in aesthetic terms. Elsewhere in his lecture Ball refers to the "motley quixoticism" (226) of Kandinsky's art, a comment that indirectly recalls Bakunin, whom Ball consistently identified with Don Quixote, just as his political mentor Brupbacher did.[88] In any case, the Kandinsky essay shows that Ball was more intent on marshaling all the arts to the political purpose of social regeneration than in forming yet another school, along the lines of expressionism or futurism. In this respect, Ball lost out to Tzara, who was constantly engaged in *identifying* dada as an autonomous and specifically aesthetic, not a political, movement, even though Tzara's aestheticism was almost always couched in anti-aesthetic terms. Hans Richter records that "Ball and Tzara were the two opposing poles of Dada,"[89] and in large measure the opposition involves the setting of politics against aesthetics. It is rather ironic that the soiree that truly marks the triumph of the Tzara-led aesthetic wing of dada took place on Bastille Day, 14 July 1916. Shortly afterward Ball abandoned dada and left Zurich with his companion Emmy Hennings for the Swiss countryside to recover his physical and intellectual health at the village of Vira-Magadino.

Although Ball was to rejoin the Zurich group early in 1917 to serve as co-director of the Galerie Dada, he was never again the organizing force that he had been during the first half of 1916—nor did he wish to be. By the end of 1917, Ball had left Zurich for Bern, where he began a brief career (all of Ball's careers were brief) as a political journalist writing for the *Freie Zeitung*. Thus it is instructive to think of the 1916 Bastille Day soiree at the Waag Hall in Zurich, together with an important performance at the Cabaret Voltaire on 23 June 1916, as Ball's farewell to dada. The program for the 14 July *Dada-Abend* records Ball's participation in a simultaneous poem by Tzara and a "Negro Song" by Richard Huelsenbeck. He was also part of a "Cubist Dance," along with Tzara, Huelsenbeck, and Hennings. But it was his solo performance reading the sound-poem "Gadji Beri Bimba," advertised as wordless poetry *(Verse ohne Worte)*, that certified Ball's removal from dada.[90] A few weeks earlier Ball had read several of his sound-poems *(Lautgedichte)* at the cabaret wearing a cardboard costume designed by himself and the painter Marcel Janco: "My legs were in a cylinder of shiny blue cardboard, which came up to my hips so that I looked like an obelisk. Over it I wore a huge coat-collar cut out of cardboard, scarlet inside and gold outside. It was fastened at the neck in such a way that I could give the impression of wing-like movement by raising and lowering my elbows." Since Ball's legs were immobilized by the cardboard cylinder, during a blackout he had himself carried on stage where his manuscripts rested on several music stands. Once in place, Ball began to read, "slowly and solemnly":

> gadji beri bimba
> glandridi lauli lonni cadori
> gadjama bim beri galassala laulitalomini
> glandridi glassala tuffm i zimbrabim
> blassa galassasa tuffm i zimbrabim . . .   (Ball, 70)

This poem, whose title is taken from the opening line, has been described as "somber and pessimistic," in contradistinction to the "playful" animal poems, such as "Elefantenkarawane" (Elephant caravan), that Ball also read (Mann, 86). But "Gadji Beri Bimba" continues with an obvious reference to the rhinoceros in "rhinocerossola," and the language of the poem, especially such words as "zimzalla" and "gadjama," seems patterned after KiSwahili or some generalized idea of "African" language.[91] In other words, the so-called pessimistic poem contains elements of the vitalistic primitivism that was yet another manifestation of Ball's fascination with the irrational. At the same time, Ball evidently read *all* of the poems in a slow, serious manner. Hans Richter, who witnessed the performance, described the way Ball "stood his ground" when his audience erupted with a mixture of delight and outrage, facing them "like Savonarola, motionless, fanatical and unmoved."[92]

Richter's comparison of Ball to Savonarola brings home the point that the sound poems are not nonsensical but spiritual in intent. Like Kandinsky and Marinetti, Ball held to the view that the noun-centered languages of Europe reflected the society's materialistic fixation on objects. By inventing a purely phonetic language based solely on vowels and consonants, the fundamental elements of all languages, Ball hoped to recover the innocent, originary "Adamic" language prior to the Fall. Mann describes the experiment as "a kind of last-ditch fight in the artist's battle against decadent society" (87). The same year that Ball recited his sound poems, Walter Benjamin wrote an essay "On Language as Such and the Language of Man" in which similar concerns over the parallel corruption of language and society are expressed. Benjamin argued that the debasement of language caused by propagandists, for example, "could only be opposed by recalling the earliest 'naming' of things, in which language evinced its originary messianic intensity."[93] While it is true that Ball's and Benjamin's concerns over the fallen state of language in a world gone disastrously wrong spring from similar spiritual impulses, Benjamin's ideas suggest a desire for a transparent language in which reality might shine forth in unmediated clarity. In this regard Benjamin is much closer than Ball, theoretically, to the utopian socialists, whose conception of the ideal language always involves simplicity and clarity. This assertion is borne out by Etienne Cabet's imaginary notion of the language of the Icarians, and by the socialists' practical efforts to make Esperanto an international means of communication. Ball's adamic language, on the other hand, is not designed to communicate insights into reality, but to trace the arc of the spirit. Ball's own account of his Cabaret Voltaire performance makes clear the spiritual, and highly personal, element in the sound poems. Ball describes a moment of anxiety when he became concerned that the climax of his performance had already been reached with the "crescendo" of "Elephant Caravan": "But how was I to get to the end? Then I noticed that my voice had no choice but to take on the ancient cadence of priestly lamentation, that style of liturgical singing that wails in all the Catholic churches of East and West." In the process of chanting the "vowel sequences in a church style like a recitative," Ball describes a *mémoire involuntaire* that is close to a religious experience: "For a moment it seemed as if there were a pale, bewildered face in my cubist mask, that half-frightened, half-curious face of a ten-year-old boy, trembling and hanging avidly on the priest's words in the requiems and high masses in his home parish. Then the lights went out, as I had ordered, and bathed in sweat, I was carried down off the stage like a magical bishop" (Ball, 71). Strangely enough, Ball's cardboard costume turns out to be the modernist vestments of a quasi-Catholic priest.

At least one of the six sound poems Ball created can be given a Christian interpretation, thereby confirming Ball's epiphany of himself as a devout Catholic youth. The opening line of "Wolken" is "elomen elomen lefitalominal," evidently intended to recall the last words of Christ on the cross: "Eli, Eli, lama sabach-thani" (Matthew 27:46). Several commentators have made this observation, and one has expanded it into a reading that makes "Wolken" express the same sort of despair over a ravaged, spiritually empty society as does T. S. Eliot's *The Waste Land*.[94] The second stanza of Ball's poem— "elominuscula pluplubash / rallalalaio"—appears to elide the cry of Christ with the lament of the Rhine maidens from *Götterdämmerung*, just as in Eliot's poem, where the Rhine-maiden refrain of "Weialala leia" is used as a motif to mourn an unregenerate society. The larger point to be made here is not simply that Ball and Eliot express a similar theme in similar language, but that both poets were engaged in a dialogue with anarchy that led, in turn, to some totalizing idea. Eliot turned to religion and myth, seeing the latter as "a way of controlling, of ordering, of giving a shape and a significance to the immense panorama of futility and anarchy which is contemporary history."[95] Ball turned to Catholicism, choosing to live a life of voluntary poverty in Ticino. Up to his death in 1927, he was interested mainly in the monastic tradition and courted greater recognition by the church establishment. Thus Ball finally made his flight out of time from anarchy to authority, leaving anarchy and culture to history.

4

Cultural history shows that Ball's break with dada is unique only in the sense that he ceased to be a creative artist. In this regard he was the only one of the dadaists to live up to their "anti-art" slogan, but the shift toward a totalizing worldview was the only move to make after the First World War. The movement toward various theories of totality was partly compensatory, an effort to remake the world in imagination since it had been shattered in fact. In this sense, Ball's Catholicism is not categorically different from Breton's socialism. But surrealism separates from dada along the lines that socialism differs from anarchism, namely in the socialist-surrealist necessity of central authority: "Unlike Dada where every Dadaist was a president, Surrealism [was] dominated by the unique moral and intellectual authority of André Breton." [96] As a "closed group obedient to doctrinaire theories," [97] the surrealists were ideologically remote from anarchism. The fact involves a paradox, since the surrealist precursors Breton singled out stood against a political background more anarchist than socialist. In his 1934 manifesto, Breton expressed the hope that Lautréamont and Rimbaud would be "restored to their correct historical background: the coming and the immediate results of the war of 1870," that is, the "social cataclysm whose final episode was to be the atrocious crushing of the Paris Commune." [98] As we have seen, the Commune makes more political sense in the context of anarchism rather than socialism, but Breton obviously did not share this view. His references to the Communard Courbet, for instance, as a politically engaged artist (and therefore a surrealist precursor of sorts) do not acknowledge the painter's friendship with Proudhon or his anarchist sentiments. This is not to say that Breton was somehow intent on concealing surrealism's possible anarchist connections; rather, given the political atmosphere of the postwar period, anarchism was simply irrelevant. The age demanded something anarchism could not provide: totality and reintegration of life and art. Consequently, the "corporate experience" of surrealism that included "attendance at daily meetings, drawing up collective tracts," and so on, is an aesthetic mirror of socialism and accounts for Breton's "stubborn but unreciprocated courtship of the French Communist Party."[99] In the France of the 1930s, to be a surrealist was also to be a socialist, at least until 1938, when Breton himself recognized the totalitarian nature of Soviet communism and urged the establishment of "an *anarchist* regime of individual liberty" to complement "a *socialist* regime with centralized control."[100] The curious thing about this unlikely amalgam is that it finally acknowledges surrealism's debt to anarchism at the precise historical moment when anarchism fades from the ideological picture of western Europe.

As Breton's belated advocacy of anarchism suggests, the politics of surrealism often involves some rather gratuitous misrepresentations of history. The "correct historical background," as Breton puts it, of the surrealist precursors Rimbaud and Lautréamont is supposed to be the "social cataclysm" that resulted in the formation and defeat of the Commune, even though the Communards were hardly the socialists Breton imagined them to be. The notion that the Commune was some kind of "proletarian revolution" that might serve as a model for later collectivist causes derives from Marx's defense of the Communards in *The Civil War in France,* but any genealogy that treats the communists as the progeny of the Communards is seriously flawed. The linkage of Lautréamont to socialism via the Commune is particularly egregious, since Isidore Ducasse died—from some unknown cause—during the siege of Paris in November 1870. In his 1929 essay on "Surrealism," Walter Benjamin makes the point that Breton belongs to a French tradition that substitutes "a political for a historical view of the past."[101] The substitution makes possible the surrealist practice of collapsing selected historical events into a political construct of generalized "revolution" populated by figures as diverse (and unrelated) as Freud, Marx, and Lautréamont. The historical grounding of these particular figures is less important than their status as surrealist precursors—models, respectively, for personal, political, and artistic liberation. Once the political is substituted for the historical, almost any group of revolutionaries can be allied with any other, at least from the surrealist perspective. From the historical perspective, however, everyone cannot be invited to the same revolution: the French communists of the 1930s rejected Breton for a reason, and the reason was history.

Benjamin in 1929 rightly observed that if the substitution of politics for history is disallowed then the true revolutionary lineage to which surrealism belongs appears as anarchism, not socialism: "Since Bakunin, Europe has lacked a radical concept of freedom. The Surrealists have one" (189). In Benjamin's essay the precursors of surrealism, likewise, are identified with anarchism: "Between 1865 and 1875 a number of great anarchists, without knowing one another, worked on their infernal machines. And the astonishing thing is that independently of one another they set its clock at exactly the same hour, and forty years later in Western Europe the writings of Dostoyevsky, Rimbaud, and Lautréamont exploded at the same time" (187). Benjamin's metaphor that has the works of Rimbaud and Lautréamont "exploding" at the same moment likens the surrealists' discovery and promotion of those writers to the activity of the anarchist dynamitard. The reference to Dostoyevsky as an anarchist precursor requires some explanation, which Benjamin provides: "One might . . . select . . . from Dostoyevsky's entire work the one episode that was actually not published until about 1915, 'Stavrogin's Confession' from *The Possessed*. This chapter, which touches very closely on the third canto of the *Chants de Maldoror,* contains a justification of evil in which certain motifs of Surrealism are more powerfully expressed than by any of its present spokesmen. For Stavrogin is a Surrealist *avant la lettre"* (187). The curious elision here of surrealism and anarchism into "a justification of evil" must be read in the larger context of Benjamin's concern with what he terms "profane illumination": the intoxicating insight that "goodness . . . is God-inspired; whereas evil stems entirely from our spontaneity, and in it we are independent and self-sufficient beings" (188, 187). The logic of this type of "poetic politics" or "metaphysical materialism" (190, 192) leads Benjamin by a remarkably circuitous route to see the surrealists as simultaneously anarchistic and collectivist; in addition, they are said to be the only revolutionaries around who are fully capable of measuring up to the political demands of the *Communist Manifesto* (192). Certainly Benjamin's reading of surrealist politics is an eccentric one, but his essay does make the important point that only anarchist politics is capable of accommodating the diabolic energies of Lautréamont. Indeed, there may be no finer literary exemplar than Lautréamont to illustrate Bakunin's axiom that the passion to destroy is a creative passion.

In one of the few surviving letters by Isidore Ducasse, the author known as Lautréamont describes *Les Chants de Maldoror* as "the po-

etry of revolt" *(cette poésies du révolte)* and mentions the possibility that
a recent lecture series entitled "The Problem of Evil" might "have
left their mark on people's minds." [102] The author's own reading of
Maldoror as the poetry of revolt does not, in itself, make the work an
anarchist entry in the literature of revolution. But the revolt against
goodness that Maldoror pursues does harmonize with anarchist
thought, since, as Benjamin observes, goodness is always codified
into laws whereas evil is not. The maintenance of the good needs
obedience to external authority, while the pursuit of evil requires
only the internal authority that self-sovereignty confers. The pursuit
of evil is therefore consistent with the anarchist model of individualist morality. Classical anarchism rejects external authority and allows
individuals the right of self-sovereignty without, however, sacrificing
good to evil because the individual retains reason as the guide
to human behavior: the Enlightenment paradigm obtains. But in
Maldoror reasonable human behavior is meaningful only as the object
against which evil unleashes its considerable energy.

This type of "anarchism" in *Maldoror* is not categorically different
from the disdain for limits that all romanticism involves, but Lautréamont's metaphysical revolt is also shaded by materialist reflections
on reality. In the following passage, for example, as Maldoror counsels
an innocent child on the irrelevance of the law, metaphysical and
materialist justifications for anarchism cooperate. The child comments that "everyone prefers heaven to earth," and Maldoror replies:

> —Well, not I. For since heaven, as well as earth, has been made
> by God, you may count on encountering up there the very same evils
> as here below. . . . The best thing for you to do is not think of God and,
> since it is refused you, to make your own justice. Were one of your
> playmates to harm you, would you not be happy to kill him?
> —But that's forbidden.
> —Not as forbidden as you believe. It's only a matter of not letting
> oneself be caught. The justice laws purvey is worthless. . . . There is,
> then, only one way of putting a stop to the situation, and that is to get
> rid of the enemy. Which is what I wanted to drive at—so as to make
> you aware of the foundations upon which present society is based.
> Each man must mete out his own justice: if he does not, he is simply
> an imbecile. He who gains victory over his fellow men is the slyest and
> strongest.   (70)

Here the anarchist argument against law begins with Milton and
ends with Darwin. At first, God is the object of a metaphysical cri-

tique that locates the authority of the law in power, which is then ceded to individuals in competition with one another. The survival of the fittest is equated with a competitive, anarchistic version of Darwinism the exact opposite of the cooperative, mutualist anarchism that Kropotkin also extracted out of Darwin.

For all the Darwinian scientism in Lautréamont, however, *Maldoror* is ultimately affiliated more closely with romanticism, and much of the "anarchism" in the book can be understood as an eccentric variation on the high romantic allegory of repression and liberation, much in the manner of William Blake's visionary poetry. In terms of cultural history, Lautréamont and Blake are related more closely to the age of modernism than to their own times, and both writers had a place in the egoistic anarchism of the prewar years and the period immediately following. The English egoists, in fact, were exposed to Lautréamont in 1914, five years before the dadaists discovered him. An essay on Lautréamont in Dora Marsden's *Egoist* calls the book "unique"—a loaded word in a Stirnerite publication—and ends with a quotation from the writer that must have appealed to the anarchist reader: "it is time to react against that which sovereignly shocks and bends us."[103] The rediscovery of Blake occurs first in the context of the mystical symbolism that marks William Butler Yeats's Celtic twilight period, but it was not long before the visionary Blake gave way to the revolutionary Blake. James Joyce, for one, understood the poet in libertarian terms, as a writer who wanted to free the mind of conventional morality and forge the human conscience anew.[104] In this regard Blake and Stirner reinforced each other, making them both precursors of the anarcho-modernist revolution in literature that took place early in the twentieth century. With Blake, the revolutionary moment often occurs when the individual recognizes his own inhibitions as the basis of enslavement to external authority: political oppression is figured as a psychosexual condition grounded in the repression of desire. Power is projected upon authority by the obedient, law-abiding citizens that Blake ironically terms "the redeemed." When the revolutionary "reprobate" appears on the scene and freely exercises his desire, the oppressive/repressive bands of the redeemed either follow his example and become "evil" themselves, or throttle the reprobate with "good" in order to limit desire—or the spirit of liberty—he has aroused.

Blake's spirit of liberty is usually named "Orc," the energetic figure who rebels against the limits imposed by nature (personified by Enitharmon, the mother of Orc), as in the prophetic poem *America*. In this passage, Orc sings his song of liberty and is confronted by the counterrevolutionary spirit of repression and obedience:

> Rise and look out, his chains are loose, his dungeon doors are open.
> And let his wife and children return from the oppressor's scourge;
> They look behind at every step & believe it is a dream.
> Singing: "The Sun has left his blackness, & has found a fresher
> morning
> And the fair Moon rejoices in the clear & cloudless night;
> For empire is no more, and now the Lion & Wolf shall cease."
>
> In thunders ends the voice. Then Albion's Angel wrathful burnt
> Beside the Stone of Night; and like the Eternal Lion's howl
> In famine & war, reply'd: "Art thou not Orc, who serpent-form'd
> Stands at the gate of Enitharmon to devour her children;
> Blasphemous Demon, Antichrist, hater of Dignities;
> Lover of wild rebellion, and transgressor of God's Law;
> Why dost thou come to Angel's eyes in this terrific form?"
>
> The terror answered: "I am Orc, wreath'd round the accursed tree:
> The times are ended; shadows pass, the morning gins to break;
> The fiery joy, that Urizen perverted to ten commands,
> What night he led the starry hosts thro' the wide wilderness:
> That stony law I stamp to dust. . . ." [105]

Here, the equation of human freedom with evil could not be clearer: Orc is called a demon, an antichrist, and, above all, a transgressor of the law. The character accepts the satanic role of serpent in the garden, "wreath'd round the accursed tree," but from his perspective satanic transgression is the healthy, human response to rationalistic repression: Urizen or "your reason" has perverted joy into obedience. The Blakean allegory seems, at first, merely to extrapolate the Miltonic irony whereby Satan establishes himself as the contrary of God: "Evil, be thou my good." What Blake does, however, is to place God in the perverse position of hating humanity and requiring obedience to the laws that sustain that hatred: "Good, be thou my evil" might be the motto of Blake's Urizen.

Comparisons of Maldoror to Orc, however, are bound to falter over these issues of irony and allegory. There is no question that the Blakean allegory ends up endorsing "evil," so long as "evil" is understood in its reversed, ironic sense as the exercise of human freedom. The same high romantic allegory often obtains in Lautréamont, with human "evil" taking the revolutionary role against the repressive laws of the divine "good." Up to a point, the so-called novel that forms the last canto of *Maldoror* illustrates the allegory in operation. The innocent young Englishman named Mervyn is thrilled at the prospect of adventure and permissiveness that Maldoror holds out to him. Reading Maldoror's letter of invitation to a world of forbidden experience, Mervyn feels a sense of spiritual awakening: "Copious tears drop on to the curious words his eyes have devoured and which open a limitless field of new and uncertain horizons to his spirit" (199). With the prospect of something limitless before him (*le champ illimité* [231]), the young man leaves his proper Victorian home (inexplicably located in France), with all its repressive morality and numbing routine, to experience human freedom in the corrupt streets of Paris. But Lautréamont reverses the reversal that figures good as evil and evil as good. Maldoror lures Mervyn into a trap, thrusts the youth into a sack, beats him senseless, and throws the sack onto a butcher's cart, with this instruction: "There's a dog inside this sack. It has the mange. Slaughter it as soon as possible" (213). The denouement of the story has the butcher hearing Mervyn's whimpers from inside the sack, and so the boy escapes with his life and returns to his room. In a conventional novel, one might look for a moral to this story and say that Mervyn would have been better off to have obeyed his father and remained at home with his family in the first place. But the goodness and innocence of Mervyn's home is presented with such cloying sentimentality that Victorian morality hardly appears as a valid alternative to the immorality of Maldoror. Simply stated, in Lautréamont's novel evil is not so good as it is in Blake, nor is good quite so evil as the typical romantic allegory would have it. Lautréamont not only subverts good and evil; he subverts the subversion and transgresses transgression. This does not mean that *Maldoror* proposes a counterrevolutionary return to moral authority; quite the contrary, in fact. Moral categories are emptied of their meaning altogether: good and evil cease to be valid models for human behavior. *Maldoror*, then, appears as a parody of the high romantic allegory whereby the energetic individual transgresses the limits of society, nature, God. By transgressing transgression in this way, Lautréamont suggests a philosophical dynamic that might be called metaphysical anarchism, but as such it is not a type of anarchism that would have been recognized as anarchistic *politics* by Kropotkin, Grave, Reclus, or any other actual anarchist contemporary with Lautréamont.

If *Maldoror* asserts anarchism through a parodic subversion of romanticism, Lautréamont's *Poésies* make a similar assertion through a parallel subversion of classicism. These two works have long been the twin bones of contention in Lautréamont criticism, since each seems somehow inconsistent with the other. The most traditional view of the *Poésies* reads the work as the moralistic retraction of the immoral *Maldoror*. Isidore Ducasse's letter of 12 March 1870 to the banker Darasse, executor of his father's funds in France, is often cited as evidence of the writer's return to reason after the madness of *Maldoror*. Ducasse mentions the financial failure of his first book, and then concludes that "the poetry of doubt . . . has reached such a point of gloomy despair and theoretical nastiness . . . because it's radically false":

> The poetic moans of this century are only hideous sophisms. To sing of boredom, suffering, miseries, melancholias, death, darkness, the sombre, etc., is wanting at all costs to look only at the puerile reverse of things. Lamartine, Hugo, Musset have voluntarily metamorphosed into sissies. These are the Great-Soft-Heads of our epoch. Always sniveling! That is why I have completely changed method, to sing exclusively of *hope, expectation,* CALM, *happiness,* DUTY. And thus I rejoin with the Corneilles and Racines the chain of good sense and composure brusquely interrupted since the poseurs Voltaire and Jean-Jacques Rousseau.   (261)

In this same letter Ducasse goes on to ask whether his father has instructed the banker "to release my money to me" (262), since the writer requires the funds to defray the costs of printing the preface to his new book. Given Ducasse's financial motives, the sense of newfound moral responsibility expressed in the letter must be regarded with suspicion; likewise, his characterization of *Maldoror* as categorically similar to the moody romantic strain of Lamartine and Musset has to be treated with skepticism. If anything, the letter supports the idea that Ducasse is resolved to subject "good sense and composure" to the same subversive, parodic treatment already exercised on the romantic literature of evil in *Maldoror*.

The *Poésies* themselves confirm this reading, for they are not poetry at all, but, rather, prescriptions for a "new" poetry that repeats the tastes and traditions of the past. In a way, the *Poésies* are a manifesto for the impossibility of art, which perhaps accounts for the appeal they had to the anti-art followers of dada. (The *Poésies* were first published in 1919 in the dada journal *Littérature*.) [106] In the *Poésies*, the author of *Maldoror* states flatly: "I want my poetry to be fit reading for a fourteen-year-old girl" (230). Since in the same document Ducasse names any number of "disturbances, anxieties, depravities" that he nonetheless "blush[es] to name" (224, 225), presumably the manifesto for the poetry that is to be fit reading for the fourteen-year-old girl would not be fit for her to read. The first part of the *Poésies* is filled with this type of irony; the second part is equally ironic, though of a different order. *Poésies II* is mainly a list of self-contained, rationalistic axioms whose originality consists in the fact that a number of them are largely plagiarized from other writers, including the aphorism on the topic of plagiarism: "Plagiarism is necessary. Progress implies it. It closely grasps an author's sentence, uses his expressions, deletes a false idea, replaces it with a right one" (240). Alexis Lykiard points out that the maxim is derived from Vauvenargues's observation that "old discoveries belong less to their original inventors than to those who put them to use"; Lykiard, in turn, observes that in the maxim on plagiarism Ducasse "can refer to the precedent (should justification be required) of one of the very predecessors whose maxim he is 'using.' " [107] One of Ducasse's axioms asserts that "[t]hose who would make literary anarchy under the pretext of novelty lapse into error" (232). The argument could be made that literary anarchy is precisely what Ducasse makes in the *Poésies* through the corrosive double irony that negates romanticism by affirming an absurdist, plagiarized version of the classical tradition. Although one should not make too much of the fact, Proudhon's name comes up in a passage from the *Poésies* that argues the possibility, at least, that Ducasse had some sympathy for anarchism proper:

> The mission of poetry is difficult. It does not dabble in political events, in the way a nation is governed, nor allude to periods of history, coups d'état, regicides, court intrigues. It does not tell of battles man fights, by way of exception, with himself and his passions. It discovers the laws that keep political theory going, universal peace, the refutations of Machiavelli, the wrapping paper of which Proudhon's works consist, the psychology of mankind. A poet must be more useful than any

member of his tribe. His work is the code of diplomats, legislators,
teachers of youth.   (237)

The reference to Proudhon has been read as Ducasse's way of signal-
ing some fellowship with the anarchist in that they both shared the
experience of publishing unsalable books: both Proudhon's tomes
and Ducasse's *Maldoror* were pulped and used as wrapping paper.[108]
This sad affinity between apologists for the artistic and the political
avant-gardes connects Ducasse to anarchism in a fragile way, but
other elements in the passage make the link seem less tenuous. By
suggesting that poets provide the code that diplomats and legislators
follow, Ducasse repeats the argument of the anarchistic Shelley, for
whom poets are "the unacknowledged legislators of the world."

Despite these faint echoes of the anarchist tradition, no real
evidence exists for a true historical relation to anarchism in the case
of Ducasse. So little is known about Lautréamont that the man is
mainly a myth, and a contradictory one at that, as the two names of
the author suggest, each name connected to one work that appears
to negate the other. But the author's actual relation to anarchism
is ultimately less important than the myth of the man, who may
nonetheless be the paradoxical prototype of the "political writer"
that Breton wanted to be, precisely because Lautréamont's literary
revolution occurred outside of politics altogether. The revolution
wrought by *Maldoror* and the *Poésies* is exactly that: both works revolve
around the uncertain center of Ducasse-Lautréamont, where good
and evil, reason and imagination, classicism and romanticism, for-
ever subvert each other. The man who wrote the axiom against the
error of literary anarchism also wrote the texts that support the
reality of anarchistic literature.

5

The case of Isidore Ducasse, no less than that of Ibsen, supports
the idea that literary "anarchism" is often a matter of post facto
politics. Ideological contexts quite remote from an individual author's historical milieu are fully capable of assigning a mixture of
political meanings to the work of art. Benjamin's observation about
Breton—that he substituted "a political for a historical view of the
past"—is by no means limited to the pope of surrealism. This is
simply another way of repeating the truism that the politics of any
given work is more a function of audience than artist, that ideology

is as much a matter of context as content. Hence, in a way, Benjamin's own political view of the surrealists as communist revolutionaries repeats Breton's vision of Rimbaud and Lautréamont as Communard socialists. This treatment of the surrealists and their precursors makes little historical sense, as we have seen, but it makes perfect political sense given the context of European socialism in the 1930s. What fails to make political sense in that context is anarchism, even though anarchism makes more historical sense of surrealism than socialism could ever hope to make. This disjunction of politics and history as it concerns the culture of surrealism obtains mainly in the context of leftist activities in France. But if the context shifts to Spain, then history and politics snap into focus, and surrealism suddenly appears the perfectly logical aesthetic product of anarchistic politics.

By 1930, anarchism had been a political force in Spain for more than sixty years, starting in 1868 when Bakunin's International Social-Democratic Alliance sent the Neapolitan Giuseppe Fanelli to Madrid and Barcelona to promote anarchist revolution. Anarchism first took root, however, not in Madrid or Barcelona, but in the southern provinces of Andalusia. The period between Queen Isabella's abdication in 1868 and the Bourbon restoration of 1874 was a remarkably turbulent era in Spanish politics that produced a republic led briefly by Francisco Pi y Margall, whose belief in federalism had been shaped partly as a result of the translations he had made of Proudhon. Loyal to his Catalan origins, Pi y Margall encouraged self-government among the Andalusian cities of Málaga, Seville, and Granada, as well as in the eastern provinces, mainly Barcelona and Valencia. Separated by language and culture from the Castilian capital of Madrid, where monarchic power had been traditionally housed, the Andalusian and Catalonian Spaniards adapted well to the anarcho-federalist model. After the monarchy was restored, however, anarchist sympathizers had no choice but to move from the model of Proudhon to the methods of Bakunin, who encouraged direct action in the form of the general strike. Such activities came to a halt when the 1878 assassination attempt against Alfonso XII by Juan Olivia Moncasi, a Catalan and disciple of Fanelli, introduced a period of severe political repression that drove the revolutionary movement underground. Anarchists emerged into the open when the liberals resumed power in 1889, a period that also allowed the

Marxists to organize the socialist party. From this point, the history of anarchism during the last decade of the nineteenth century is quite similar to developments in France over the same period: a flurry of bombings and assassinations, followed by strict authoritarian measures to restore law and order. The anarchist response, in turn, was a new focus on educational reform and labor organization: Francisco Ferrer's Escuela Moderna opened in 1901, while the Conferación Nacional de Trabajo (CNT) began to organize the workers into *sindicados,* somewhat belatedly, in 1910. But Spanish anarchism takes on a different character from the French with the outbreak of World War I. In France, even Jean Grave supported the state in the war with Germany, and this nationalistic departure from anarchist principles has much to do with the demise of anarchism in France. In neutral Spain, the advent of the war did not occasion the need for compromise, and the anarcho-syndicalist movement continued to grow, with Barcelona becoming the main center of anarchist activity. Only with the eradication of all forms of leftist politics by Franco's fascist regime at the end of the Spanish civil war did anarchism pass from Spanish history.[109]

This brief exposition of Spanish anarchism has been furnished solely to introduce the problematic politics of Luis Buñuel's cinematic art. Surely the Spanish director must be recognized as one of the most consistently political artists of the twentieth century (his conventional Mexican films notwithstanding), even though his politics is rather elusive. Assessments of Buñuel that emphasize the contradictory nature of his art are quite common: one critic calls him "realist and surrealist, Marxist and anarchist, anti-cleric and mystical, Freudian and post-Freudian."[110] What stands out in this description most is the characterization of Buñuel's politics as both "Marxist and anarchist," a seemingly impossible amalgam, especially in a native Spaniard who came of age during the high tide of Spanish anarchism in the 1920s. During this period, Buñuel says, he and his friends at the Residencia de Estudiantes in Madrid were "very involved" with the CNT and the anarchists: "At that time, people like me who were interested in the social-political aspect of the period couldn't help being drawn to anarchism." He also terms himself, somewhat apologetically, avant-garde ("excuse the word"). His cultural interests during his formative student days focused on Ultraism, the Hispanic avant-garde movement whose best-known representative today is

Jorge Luis Borges but whose membership also included several men who were both Ultraists and anarchists (Buñuel names Pedro Garfias and Angel Samblancat).[111] In his autobiography, Buñuel mentions his "intellectual (and emotional) attraction to anarchy" even as he describes himself as "a Communist sympathizer."[112] He also describes himself as "active in the surrealist group" up until 1932, which brings us to the crux of the politico-aesthetic problem. Buñuel would seem to be one of the few surrealists who felt a real affinity for anarchism, but, like the other surrealists, he was also attracted to the rival ideology of communism (*L'Age d'Or* was once screened under an alternative title taken from *The Communist Manifesto* [*OD*, 24]). This dual interest in two completely incompatible recipes for revolution (Buñuel himself observes that the Spanish anarchists hated the communists more than they did the fascists)[113] comes through in a quotation from Engels that Buñuel used whenever he was asked to explain the politics of his art:

> I will let Friedrich Engels speak for me. He defines the function of the novelist (and here read film maker) thus: "The novelist will have acquitted himself honorably of his task when, by means of an accurate portrait of authentic social relations, he will have destroyed the conventional view of the nature of those relations, shattered the optimism of the bourgeois world, and forced the reader to question the permanency of the prevailing order, and this even if the author does not offer us any solutions, even if he does not clearly take sides."[114]

The interesting thing about this quote from one of the fathers of socialism is its anarchistic tone. The emphasis placed on artistic practice as a way of "destroying" and "shattering" bourgeois complacency recalls Bakunin's notion of destructive passion as a creative impulse. Also, the closing encomium not to "take sides" seems more consistent with anarchist than with socialist politics. Elsewhere, Buñuel seems more explicit in his endorsement of aesthetic anarchism, as when he described his "moral code" to an interviewer as follows: "Morality—middle-class morality, that is—is for me immoral. One must fight it. It is a morality founded on our most unjust social institutions—religion, fatherland, family culture—everything that people call the pillars of society."[115] It is hard to tell if Buñuel intends a reference to the anarchistic Ibsen in that last phrase, but there is no mistaking the general anarchistic tenor of the remark. Buñuel, then, would seem to be a different sort of surrealist than the type normally required by the socialist Breton.

Of the Spanish surrealists active in Paris, Luis Buñuel stands apart as an independent artistic force. Indeed, Buñuel seems to have come to the surrealists fully formed, and to have developed an aesthetic similar to theirs based on a separate set of cultural sources, including the etchings of Goya and other native Spanish art. Although the politics of Buñuel's films is usually discussed in Marxist terms, that context is relevant mainly to his later work, beginning with *Los Olvidados* in 1950. The earlier surrealist films for which Buñuel is best known, however, are not easily assimilated into any model of socialist art. *Un Chien Andalou* is a classic surrealist work, involving the kind of reciprocation between dream and reality that is consistent with the early Freudian focus of surrealism. As is well known, the germ of the film involves two rather different dream images supplied by Buñuel and Salvador Dalí, who collaborated on the scenario. The raw material of the film was Buñuel's dream about an eyeball slashed with a razor, and Dalí's nightmare about ants emerging from a stigmata-like wound in the palm of his hand (*OD*, 15). Buñuel's image has an impact analogous to a terrorist act: it is violent and unexpected. In several of his later films, including the final one, *That Obscure Object of Desire*, Buñuel incorporates random acts of terror as part of the general social milieu surrounding the main action. *Un Chien Andalou* also suggests the aesthetic anarchism of the symbolists and dadaists. Indeed, Buñuel hoped that the film would have the effect of a bomb thrown in the theater, as his remarks of 1930 suggest: "This film has no intention of attracting or pleasing the spectator; indeed, on the contrary, it attacks him, to the degree that he belongs to a society with which surrealism is at war." [116] Buñuel has also said that he filled his pockets with stones before he screened the film, planning to hurl them at the audience when it was over (*OD*, 19). Though Buñuel volunteered very little information about the title that he had used once before in 1927 for a collection of unpublished poems (*El perro andaluz*), a reference to Andalusian anarchism is at least possible. [117] Though *Un Chien Andalou* is mainly psychological in orientation, political nuances are conveyed in the film by the way adherence to social conventions reinforces the repression of sexual desire. Individual liberation is indirectly linked to the liberation of society as a whole. Given this theme, there is some irony attached to the casting of the Catalan anarchist Jaime Miratvilles as one of the priests dragged across the floor as part of the cultural burden of the film's sexually repressed hero.[118]

Buñuel's second film is much stronger in its social commentary and has a sharper political edge. *L'Age d'Or* expresses anarchist attitudes in its adversarial treatment of the church, the aristocracy, and high culture—a kind of three-headed monster with clay feet that lords it over the ironically named "golden age." The church is subverted almost from the outset of the film, with the image of the bishops' skeletons ranged about on the rocks, still draped in their clerical garments as their liturgical chatter fills the soundtrack. An even stronger anti-Catholic statement is made through the remarkable montage showing a woman straining dreamily on a toilet, followed by flushing sounds and images of an undulating cloacal sea, which, in turn, provides the "mortar" that serves to cement the city of Imperial Rome together. The film also makes equally strong statements about class divisions in the scene where a pair of peasants go unnoticed as they drive their cart through an opulent drawing room where a preconcert crowd of aristocrats has gathered. Another unnoticed event is the death of a maidservant, whose screams are ignored as she is burned alive. The satire of clericalism and class combine with the lampoon of high culture in the famous scene where two would-be lovers bang heads, fall out of chairs, and otherwise bungle their way through a romantic rendezvous in a classical garden. They are observed by a priest who looks on quickly but disapprovingly from a distant footbridge. If the film can be said to have a climax, surely it comes when the woman ignores her lover's kiss for the attractions of the marble toe on the foot of the statue beside her. The lush music of the love-death theme from *Tristan und Isolde* swells up as she glides down to kiss and suck the toe of the impassive statue. When the woman transfers her affections from the statue to the Wagnerian maestro, her frustrated lover responds by returning to the château and, to the musical accompaniment of a militaristic march, furiously storms about the bedroom, seizing unlikely objects and hurling them out the window: an unmistakably phallic plow is thrown out, following by a burning tree, a priest (who survives the fall), a stuffed giraffe, and handfuls of feathers. The film ends by reconstructing a scene from the marquis de Sade's *100 Days of Sodom,* only now the leader of the sadistic band of libertines is Jesus Christ. The sexual and spiritual logic of the scene also informs the final image of the film, a cross pinned with clumps of hair, suggesting a form of redemption more erotic than religious. While none of the images in the film can be termed purely anarchistic, it is still true that this particular work stands apart from that of the socialist surrealists because of its overt political references. *L'Age d'Or* is at least consistent with anarchism in its criticism of class structure and church authority, not to mention the wildly independent behavior of the male lead, played by Gaston Modot. After all, at one point he causes a mass revolt that forces his superior to shoot himself, who then falls with a thump and lands on the ceiling.

Un Chien Andalou, which takes the Oedipal conflict as one of its Freudian themes, was financed by Buñuel's mother. The production costs of the anti-aristocratic *L'Age d'Or* were borne by the vicomte de Noailles. The third film, *Las Hurdes,* was made in 1932 on a budget of 20,000 pesetas donated to Buñuel by a working-class anarchist friend named Ramón Acín, who had won the sum in a lottery. An artist and drawing teacher, Acín had earlier collaborated with Puig Elias of the anarchist Escuela Natura in Barcelona (see Chapter 4) on the publication of *Floreal,* a children's review.[119] According to Buñuel, Acín and his wife were executed by the fascists in 1936 (*OD*, 31). If in the first two films Buñuel was biting the hand that funded him, the third suggests true cinematic reciprocation that acknowledges a degree of ideological sympathy with the anarchist backer. The film can hardly be called anarchist propaganda, but the class of people Buñuel documents in it is precisely the *Lumpenproletariat* group ignored by the socialists. The title *Las Hurdes* refers to an isolated, mountainous region in central Spain where the peasants are so backward they have never learned how to make bread, hence the English title of the film, *Land Without Bread.* The Hurdanos survive mainly on potatoes and wild berries; the only meat is pork, but that is only eaten once a year by the "wealthy" families. Bad diet and worse hygiene make the people prone to all manner of disease, so death and premature aging are common. Buñuel lets his camera make the point that the Hurdanos have come to accept their horrible existence as perfectly normal. A particularly powerful sequence shows a filthy stream of water running through the middle of a village. Both a sewer and a source of drinking water, the stream serves many purposes: dogs drink from it, pigs wallow in it, people wash in it. A child of six or so cups water in her hands and offers it to an infant to drink; the baby arches its back and turns away again and again. Then Buñuel cuts to a young boy who bends down voluntarily to drink from the same stream, almost greedily. The montage of contrasting scenes argues that only revolution can reverse the chain of social conditioning in Las Hurdes. The film also reminds the viewer pointedly that the only material comforts in the area are confined to a few churches and monasteries, where the children go to school and a few learn to write quotations by rote from a primer. This type of backward education was precisely what Francisco Ferrer meant to rectify when he started the Escuela Moderna. Buñuel catches one Hurdano scholar writing a slogan on a blackboard for the other children to imitate: "Respect the property of others." It is not hard to imagine the unspoken corrective provided by Proudhon: "Property is theft."

One of the curious things about this documentary film is the way Buñuel captures images that are quite close to those in his two surrealist films. He once called the later film the "twin" of the other two (*OD*, 34). Examples of this "twinning" effect include a scene of a burro being stung to death by a swarm of bees, which recalls the death of the rat stung by the scorpion at the beginning of *L'Age d'Or*, as well as the dead mules atop the pianos in *Un Chien Andalou*. Buñuel also uses a close-up of the dead animal's staring eye surrounded by insects that seems to reference the eye at the beginning of *Un Chien Andalou*. *Las Hurdes* also reports on the malaria problem in the region by giving an entomology lesson on the anopheles mosquito, recalling the cinematic entomology of *Un Chien Andalou* when the camera focuses on the death's-head moth. Another example concerns a remarkable sequence of a goat's falling to its death from the loose rocks of a mountain ridge somewhere in Las Hurdes. The fall was obviously staged, since Buñuel films it from two different angles (in one shot the puff of smoke from the pistol used to kill the goat is visible), as he does the falling objects shoved out the window at the end of *L'Age d'Or*. In fact, the plummeting goat somehow reminds the viewer of the stuffed giraffe in the earlier film falling from the window, down a cliff face, and into the sea. The use of images in *Las Hurdes* that appear to repeat those of the earlier films has the double effect of making the documentary footage seem surreal, and vice versa. More important, *Las Hurdes* invests the images of the earlier films with some retrospective political meaning. Surely those peasants who are so invisible to the aristocrats of *L'Age d'Or* could have come from Las Hurdes, and the later film helps us to understand what it means to ignore such people. The political resonance of *Las Hurdes* is enforced by the report that the fascists ordered Buñuel's arrest for making a film "defamatory to Spain," and by the grant awarded to Buñuel by the Republicans in 1936 that allowed him to add a soundtrack to the film (*OD*, 33, 35).

Buñuel's *Las Hurdes* makes a political statement consistent with anarchism, and in so doing the film may cast a certain retrospective political light on the earlier surrealist films. But those earlier films are clearly more concerned with freeing images from convention than with liberating the masses from oppression. The idea that technique itself requires liberation from various artistic constraints, orthodoxies, or conventions is itself a conventional idea, albeit a fairly recent one, that has developed mainly as a result of the long tradition of avant-gardism over the twentieth century. The conventionalization of avant-gardism cannot but neutralize the political meaning of innovative technique. Looking back on Buñuel's early films today and comparing *Un Chien andalou* or *L'Age d'Or* with *Las Hurdes*, one tends to see the more conventional film as the most political. "[W]hile the first two are films of revolt, *Las Hurdes* explains the reason for the revolt" (*OD*, 35), one critic says, a comment that suggests, on the one hand, that avant-garde technique can be expressive of social discontent, and, on the other, that aesthetic innovation and radical politics are separate categories. After his early surrealist films, Buñuel was careful to keep his technique from overshadowing both social and psychological commentary, and his break with the surrealists occurred largely because of the tendency he saw in some of them to make "the total separation of life and art" (*OD*, 36). As Buñuel averred, "Surrealism was not an aesthetic, just another avant-garde movement; it was something to which I committed myself in a spiritual and moral way" (37). The collaboration with Dalí on *L'Age d'Or* ended early on, Buñuel says, because Dalí "wanted to follow a very aesthetic line," whereas Buñuel preferred a more openly anti-aesthetic approach consistent with the social criticism the film advanced. The opening scorpion sequence, taken from stock footage, appealed to Buñuel because it was "bad photography, but that's why I liked it. I wanted to do anything except please" (21, 23). The Buñuel-Dalí split has much in common with the Ball-Tzara breakup that redefined dada as more aesthetic than political. The final usurpation of politics by aesthetics in the case of dada can be observed in the film *Entr'acte* (1924), directed by René Clair and based on a scenario by the well-to-do Picabia. The film caught Buñuel's interest at first, but it was one of the overly avant-garde works he singled out later on as the antithesis of the type of surrealism he wanted to practice. Indeed, the separation of political and artistic avant-gardism becomes obvious when *Las Hurdes* is compared to the dadaist *Entr'acte*. With its quick cuts and montages, superimpositions, unusual camera angles (a ballerina dancing on a pane of glass filmed from below), slow motion, fast motion, and so on, combined with absurdist dada images (a hearse hung with ham and sausages pulled by a camel through an amusement park), *Entr'acte* may be cinematic anarchism, but *Las Hurdes* is closer to anarchistic cinema.

The contrast between the documentary *Las Hurdes* and the avant-garde *Entr'acte* makes the point yet again that progressive politics and advanced aesthetics rarely proceed in concert, even when they are informed by similar ideologies. In Buñuel's case, the relation of advanced art and advanced politics is further complicated by the two contradictory ideologies he entertained. Indeed, Buñuel appears to have done just that: entertained ideology without making outright political commitments. He never joined the Communist Party, for example, and he was never a member of the CNT or any other anarchist organization. True to the admonition from Engels he was fond of quoting, Buñuel did not "take sides," and the strategy appears to have paid off, paradoxically, in a type of cinema that is deeply political. Buñuel's political disrespect for bourgeois society takes artistic form largely because he maintains a respectful distance from politics. The finest political artists, it seems, have little to do with politics at all. I suggested this paradox at the outset of this study of anarchy and culture by way of Breton's image of the wall separating social renovation from psychological transformation. This image, however, does not adequately convey the paradox whereby social progress and artistic innovation move forward together, but with neither necessarily exercising any strong or lasting influence on the other. A more complete image of political and aesthetic dissociation is suggested in Joyce's *Ulysses,* when the bourgeois socialist Leopold Bloom finally meets up with the aesthetic anarchist Stephen Dedalus, and the two walk together side by side. Joyce sets Stephen and Bloom on "parallel courses," thereby assuring that those courses will never cross. The parallel perambulations of these two sympathetic but contrary characters is an apt analogue for the peregrinations of politics and culture. The two are often seen together, and occasionally they do appear to move along the same path. But even though politics and culture, like Bloom and Stephen, sometimes travel in the same direction, they ultimately head for different destinations.

AFTERWORD

The argument for anarchy and culture ultimately becomes an argument for anarchy *in* culture, for the idea of culture today includes all the variety, multiplicity, and freedom of human expression that anarchism encouraged in the past. Paradoxically, the present state of culture is often decried by conservative politicians, even though such culture is consistent with the political model they endorse: leftist multiculturalism and rightist neofederalism are ideologically incompatible but theoretically reinforcing. The paradox has something in common with the politico-aesthetic phenomenon of the nineteenth century whereby some of the most conservative critics endorsed the anarchic potential of culture, even as they put forth the old ideal of culture as a totalizing force capable of unifying the diverse elements of society. As we have seen, Matthew Arnold assumes that a unifying culture can compensate for the losses sustained by humanity as a result of history, but the culture he promotes ends up as both the product and the province of individual consciousness. Likewise, through the persona of his aesthetic everyman Hyacinth Robinson, Henry James suggests that the despotisms of the past have paid off in the culture of the present, a position that also implies a relationship between political controls and artistic enjoyments that does not favor the totalizing apparatus of the nation-state. As for Dostoyevsky, the writer may not be completely ironic in having the character Stepan Verhovensky make the case that culture is not only more meaningful than history, but than humanity as well: such a view of culture is every bit as nihilistic as the "anarchism" that is the object of Dostoyevsky's satire. Arnold, James, and Dostoyevsky are all alike in that they turn away from politics as a remedy for social

259

disruption and turn toward culture. Such a move cannot but have the effect of politicizing culture, if both culture and politics are seen as competing remedies for the ills of society. Culture thus politicized as an antipolitical alternative to politics has much in common with anarchism, always an ideology construed as somehow outside the petty machinations of politics. Strangely, in this regard the anarchist Proudhon and the moralist Arnold occupy the same ground: anarchism no less than culture is said to operate at some considerable distance from politics.

At about the same time that such mandarins of culture as Matthew Arnold and Henry James kept up the rear-guard conversation between morality and aesthetics, the artistic and the political avant-gardes began their somewhat confused dialogue as well. Out of this period emerged two very different forms of cultural discourse. One assumed an identity of the artistic voice with the political, so that there was ultimately no difference between a play by Ibsen and an essay by Emma Goldman, as both were dedicated to the same end: the reformation of society. As we have seen, in his promotion of "advanced" literature, Benjamin Tucker used political and aesthetic language interchangeably: equality was beautiful, and the pursuit of beauty was every anarchist's libertarian prerogative. In this regard, to some degree Tucker reverses Arnold: he substitutes politics for culture, where Arnold tried to make culture do the work of politics. Indeed, the alternative to the type of retrograde aesthetics announced by the progressive Tucker has more to do with the Arnoldian strategy. If the first form of cultural discourse to emerge from the late nineteenth century makes the political and artistic voices speak with the same progressive accent, the second silences the political voice with aesthetic obscurity. Curiously, this form of cultural discourse repeats Arnold's substitution of culture for politics, but it does so by adopting the individualist ideology Arnold publicly condemned. In this substitution, the symbolist poem becomes a political act, an intense expression of individualism that was all the more complete for being obscure. Ibsen was a modern because his plays implied the need for social renovation, but Mallarmé was a modernist because his poetry showed the value of artistic innovation. Both forms of cultural discourse were anarchistic, but only the second, experimental form survived the decline of anarchism by migrating into modernism.

The infusion of anarchistic principles into artistic practice is something that quite literally occurred early in the twentieth century, prior to World War I. At that time individualist anarchism was particularly strong, especially among Anglo-American artists and writers, and it is chiefly among such modernists as James Joyce, Ezra Pound, Margaret Anderson, and Dora Marsden that one can detect the layering of aesthetics and politics. The politico-aesthetic project of many early modernists occurs in the context of the egoism provided by Max Stirner (and by Benjamin Tucker's promotion of Stirner), especially when the idea of egoism is understood as a principle of both social and artistic autonomy. After World War I, when most of the now-classic texts of modernism began to appear, individualist anarchism ceased to have political meaning. As other ideologies, mainly fascism and communism, began to emerge, the only way anarchism managed to survive as a mass movement was in the form of syndicalism, but even in this form anarchism was limited to only a few areas of southern Europe, mainly Spain. The period from the end of the First World War to the end of the Second can be seen as a time when politics and modernist culture were separated, often forcibly, as in the notorious example in Germany when the National Socialists relegated expressionism to the realm of "degenerate art." Yet it may also be true that during this same period modernist art willingly separated itself from politics, largely because there is something inherently unaesthetic about the kind of culture encouraged by mass movements in any form, whether fascist, communist, or even anarcho-syndicalist. Indeed, an aversion to the masses appears to be an element in the formation of the modernist aesthetic. According to Gustave Le Bon, who announced the science of crowd psychology in 1895 with his *Psychologie des foules*, the person who participates in any mass activity risks a loss of culture: "Isolated, he may be a cultivated individual; in a crowd he is a barbarian—that is, a creature acting by instinct."[1] On this topic, Robert Nye collects evidence to show that symbolist and decadents in the 1890s "saw modern collectivities as a threat to individual autonomy," and that Gabriele D'Annunzio, for one, was "so unnerved at the aspect of the new masses" that for him *l'art pour l'art* functioned both as an aesthetic theory and as a political ideology.[2] D'Annunzio's later attraction to mass politics only confirms this assertion: the move involved a repudiation of his earlier aesthetics that amounted to a betrayal of art, a point emphasized by that "nonpolitical" modernist Thomas Mann.[3] The younger D'Annunzio's anxiety over the masses and the horror of crowds experienced by other fin de siècle artists chimes nicely with the validation of autonomy that the early modernists found in Stirner; at the same time, the emergence of mass politics between the world wars leaves no place except culture for modernist autonomy to operate. True, some modernists were drawn to the authoritarian politics of the period, but their endorsement of such politics is not necessarily reflected in their artistic practice, precisely because of that crucial period when anarchism and aesthetics intermingled during the early days of modernism. Not everyone would agree with this assessment, but at the very least it seems that what Walter Benjamin said of the mass politics of fascism and communism might be said of the individualist ideology of anarchism as well: that it has the power either to aestheticize politics or to politicize art.[4]

But the stateless state of modernist culture is anarchistic only in a broad, conceptual sense that is remote from anarchism as a social movement and a historical force. André Breton's belated desire for an anarchist "regime" helps to make this point, as the regime he imagined—when he imagined it—could not possibly have existed as a historical reality. In some ways, however, this ahistorical, conceptual "anarchism" may be more important to the cultural development of the west in the second half of the twentieth century than the periodic political manifestations of the movement. While there is no denying the significance of such postwar, anarchist-inspired movements as the New Left, the Situationist International, and the anarcho-ecology promoted by Murray Bookchin, anarchism today appears less compelling as a social program than as a cultural condition. In fact, Bookchin himself has recognized that the co-opting of anarchism by culture and the emergence of what he calls "lifestyle anarchism" poses a real threat to the survival of anarchism as a social strategy. He is surely right to observe that many latter-day anarchists practice a form of cultural "rebellion" that poses no threat whatsoever to the survival of the modern capitalist state. As we have seen, anarchism and capitalism have certain structural features in common, and the well-known commodification of culture in late capitalist society provides a perfect context for an antipolitical ideology of anarchism that sets aesthetic satisfaction ahead of social reformation.

This new bourgeois anarchism harmonizes with capitalism because both ideologies assume a certain "stateless" condition as the basis for their highly individualistic practices. Even though the very definition of "bourgeois society" relies on the cooperation of capital and the state, as capitalism developed, the relationship between market and government changed in ways that allowed for a more anarchic environment for both commodity and cultural production. In the crucial early period of capitalist expansion from 1880 to 1920, David Gross says, "Capital more and more leaned on the state to help open up and protect new areas of investment and to reduce economic imbalances created by the market system, while the state leaned on capital for loans and credit to finance its various undertakings." One result of this coupling of political and economic concerns is the disintegration of tradition and the proliferation of newness during the modernist period. Also, while government regulation of certain key industries (such as the banking system) was then and is now necessary to the proper functioning of the modern nation-state, the state came to remove itself from the market so that capital could function in a free, anarchic way in the production of goods and services. Such lawlessness might pose a threat to the state if it were allowed to operate outside the realm of the market, but within that realm it is a positive good, "for only by nurturing practically every kind of undifferentiated yearning and desire—and then transmuting them into an urge to consume—can the economy stay on an upward course."[5] The point here is that the economic system of the capitalist market is something like the evil twin of the political system of anarchist society, at least insofar as both of these "stateless" systems are seen to encourage freedom, autonomy, and aesthetic satisfaction. In the case of the capitalist system, of course, the sense of individualism comes at a certain cost. But more and more people in modern consumer culture seem perfectly willing to ignore the differences between the personal and the commercial in order to acquire the autonomy they need. Any number of radically individualistic identities are available for purchase today, a fact that can be confirmed by visiting the magazine section of any large bookstore, or by leafing through the liberal arts offerings in the catalogues of major universities.

Given the anarchic nature of the market system, it is not surprising that anarchism itself has entered the commercial sphere. If it is true, as Greil Marcus has argued, that a strain of anarchy and culture runs from dada and surrealism to Situationism, from the blues and rock n' roll to punk, an apotheosis of sorts was reached late in 1976 when Johnny Rotten of the Sex Pistols rhymed "anarchist" and "antichrist" in the song "Anarchy in the U.K." The nature of this apotheosis is not so much the recrudescence of the Bakuninist union of creation and destruction, but, rather, the realization that politics and culture can combine to form a highly profitable commercial venture. Marcus finds it "transcendently odd" that a set of leftist political concerns would, as he puts it, *"make the charts,"* but given the structural concord of capitalism and anarchism the Sex Pistols' success is not that surprising.[6] The way Malcolm Maclaren, the group's manager, parlayed his own interest in the anarchist tendencies of the Situationists into a commercial enterprise recalls the way the anarchist cabaret owner Maxime Lisbonne exploited his Commune experience to attract "a politico-literary clientele" in Montmartre a century earlier.[7] But Maclaren's and Lisbonne's exploitation of political sensibilities for commercial purposes surely differs in regard to the market that each entrepreneur sought to satisfy. In Lisbonne's day commercial consumption was not driven by the kind of market available to Maclaren, in which technology and advertising combine to blur the lines between wants and needs, reality and representation, culture and commodity.

The later condition is usually termed postmodern, as in Fredric Jameson's seminal description that sees "aesthetic production today . . . integrated into commodity production generally."[8] To this observation we can add that politics is likewise susceptible to capitalist packaging. Indeed, *anarchism* would seem to be the missing term in Jameson's construct of postmodernism when he notes that "the explosion of modern literature into a host of distinct private styles and mannerisms has been followed by a linguistic fragmentation of social life itself." Likewise, a concept of anarchism seems to underlie the observation that "the stupendous proliferation of social codes today into professional and disciplinary jargons (but also into the badges of affirmation of ethnic, gender, race, religious, and class-factional adhesion)" is sufficient demonstration of "the problem of micropolitics" (17). Jameson describes aesthetic fragmentation and social proliferation as important indicators of the new "cultural dominant" known as postmodernism. But in many ways this recent condition reflects the earlier situation whereby anarchy and culture intermingled during an important phase of the modernist period, with the significant difference that technology and capitalism were not then the enormous cultural conduits they are today. Despite this difference, there is still a basic commonality between modernism and postmodernism that argues for an alliance of the later cultural condition to the earlier one based on a shared relationship to anarchism, whether literal or conceptual.

From the social perspective, the migration of politics into culture has some serious consequences for the anarchist tradition. The ideology of the aesthetic that Terry Eagleton describes as a benign form of state control over bourgeois society has, strangely, begun to penetrate radical politics, so that now rebellion may be conducted on the aesthetic front alone. In this book I have argued that individualist anarchism assumed aesthetic form with modernism early in the twentieth century: a set of political concerns was transformed into artistic expression. Now at century's end a reversal of that earlier modernist process seems to have occurred, with aesthetic experience substituting for social action. The veteran anarchist Murray Bookchin (born in 1921) has recently observed that contemporary anarchists have ceased to be social revolutionaries because of an excessive investment in individualist aesthetics. The title of Bookchin's pamphlet cuts to the heart of the problem: *Social Anarchism or Lifestyle Anarchism: An Unbridgeable Chasm* (1995). According to Bookchin, the anarchist tradition has reached a point of crisis because of the dominance of anarcho-individualism in the Anglo-American world. As we have seen, ideological individualism emphasizes autonomy over collectivity, a move that for activist anarchists like Bookchin amounts to a fundamental betrayal of the revolutionary heritage of Bakunin and Kropotkin. In fact, the autonomy sought by the individualist anarchist is meaningless without the larger condition of social freedom that collectivist anarchists actively pursue: "While *autonomy* is associated with the presumably self-sovereign individual, *freedom* dialectically interweaves the individual with the collective. . . . When applied to the individual, *freedom* thus preserves a social or collective interpretation of that individual's origins and development as a self. In 'freedom,' individual selfhood does not stand opposed to or apart from the collective but is significantly formed—and in a rational society, would be realized—by his or her social existence. Freedom thus does not subsume the individual's liberty but denotes its actualization."[9] The collectivist model of anarchism that Bookchin describes here clearly belongs to the heritage of the Enlightenment, while the autonomists have more in common with the ideological counterstrain of romanticism. Paul Goodman, a contemporary anarchist in the individualist tradition, states that "the chief principle of anarchism is not freedom but autonomy," and this view, Bookchin says, "is worthy of an aesthete but not of a social revolutionary" (12).

Aesthetic autonomy is taken to some length by Peter Lambon Wilson, the self-styled "Hakim Bey" who is the author of *T.A.Z.: The Temporary Autonomous Zone, Ontological Anarchy, Poetic Terrorism* (1991), a kind of bible of the "lifestyle anarchism" Bookchin sees as a serious threat to social anarchism. Bookchin points out that the "politics" of Wilson's ontological anarchism is indistinguishable from New Age mysticism, as this example shows: "There is no becoming, no revolution, no struggle, no path; already you're the monarch of your own skin—your inviolable freedom waits to be completed only by the love of other monarchs: a politics of dream, urgent as the blueness of sky."[10] This egoistic credo derives partly from the anti-Enlightenment philosophy of Max Stirner, although Wilson must resort to some remarkable rhetorical maneuvering in order to get around Stirner's antagonistic attitude toward mysticism. Stirner, we are told, "quite correctly despised what he knew as 'mysticism,' " defined as the "piestic sentimentality" of a deliquescent form of Christianity. Presumably, had he not been born at the wrong time Stirner would have accepted "true" mysticism in such forms as "the hidden illuminist tradition in Western alchemy, revolutionary heresy & occult activism" (*TAZ*, 68). From all of this it is clear that the "temporary autonomous zone" of "ontological anarchy" is simply a state of mind that does not concern itself with the political reality of the state itself: "Our brand of anti-authoritarianism . . . favors states of consciousness, emotion & aesthetics over all petrified ideologies & dogma" (*TAZ*, 67). Small wonder, then, that Bookchin reacts to this "egocentric anarchism, with its postmodernist withdrawal into individualist 'autonomy,' " by saying that it "threatens to render the very word *anarchism* politically and socially harmless" (26). Margaret Anderson's Stirnerite anarchism, we recall, prompted one of her more socially oriented comrades to say that she "represented the tragedy of the anarchist movement in America."[11] Similarly, Book-

chin regards Hakim Bey's anarcho-mysticism not so much as a tragedy but as a travesty of the anarchist tradition. What the modernist
and the postmodernist treatments of anarchism have in common is
a certain aesthetic, postrevolutionary attitude, by which is meant not
that the revolution has come about, but, rather, that the autonomous
ego makes revolution unnecessary.

Whether the postmodernist reversal of aesthetics into politics
that forms the basis of Hakim Bey's "anti-ideological" ideology will
have any lasting cultural ramifications remains to be seen. In many
ways the postmodernist phenomenon mirrors the modernist reversal
of politics into aesthetics, and together the two developments argue,
again, that "anarchism" has become a permanent feature of capitalist culture. For those who continue to hold on to the diminishing
hope that anarchism might one day arrive as a social reality, the
presence of anarchy in culture must surely disappoint. For them,
the shift of anarchism into aesthetics must appear not as a transformation of politics but as a displacement: surely society is where
anarchism belongs, not in some autonomous "zone" of egoistic
aesthetics. More than one hundred years ago Matthew Arnold hoped
that culture might counter the social practice of "doing as one likes,"
and William Morris, likewise, regretted the social currents that gave
the artists of his age no choice but to do "their own personal individual work." For Arnold and Morris, looking at the world from opposite ends of an ideological spectrum, the loss of a collective culture
and a shared aesthetic was a sign of anarchy. For better or worse, in
today's postmodern, postrevolutionary society, anarchy itself is a sign
of culture.

NOTES

Introduction

1. "[T]he anguished tone of Breton's writings as he struggled with his relation to the French Communist Party speaks eloquently to the pressure it once exerted, both in France of the time and on him." Margaret Cohen, *Profane Illumination: Walter Benjamin and the Paris of the Surrealist Revolution* (Berkeley and Los Angeles: University of California Press, 1993), 2.

2. André Breton, "Political Position of Today's Art," in *Manifestoes of Surrealism*, trans. Richard Seaver and Helen R. Lane (Ann Arbor: University of Michigan Press, 1969), 213. Further references to this edition are cited parenthetically in the text.

3. The *New York Times* reported in October 1995 that 137 officeholders at all levels of government elected as Democrats had switched to the Republican Party since the presidential election of 1992. See "Democrats Fleeing to G.O.P. Remake Political Landscape," 7 October 1995, sect. A, pp. 1, 8.

4. "For the man who spent weeks with Trotsky in Mexico writing 'For an Independent Revolutionary Art,' just months before the exiled Soviet's assassination, both esthetic and political questions were clearly matters of life and death." Leslie Camhi, "Extended Boundaries," *Art in America* (February 1992): 43. Quoted in Cohen, *Profane Illumination*, 2 n. 4.

5. See Clint Burnham, *The Jamesonian Unconscious: The Aesthetics of Marxist Theory* (Durham: Duke University Press, 1995). Among the books published by Jameson after the fall of the Berlin Wall are *Late Marxism: Adorno; or, The Persistence of the Dialectic* (London: Verso, 1990); *Signatures of the Visible* (New York: Routledge, 1990); *Postmodernism; or, The Cultural Logic of Late Capitalism* (Durham: Duke University Press, 1991); *The Geopolitical Aesthetic: Cinema and Space in the World System* (Bloomington: Indiana University Press, 1992); and *The Seeds of Time* (New York: Columbia University Press, 1994).

6. André Breton and Leon Trotsky, "Manifesto: Towards a Free Revolutionary Art," in *Theories of Modern Art: A Source Book by Artists and Critics*, ed. Herschel B. Chipp (Berkeley and Los Angeles: University of California Press, 1968), 485.

7. Irving Howe, *Politics and the Novel* (Cleveland: Meridian, 1957), 84.

8. See Fredric Jameson, *The Political Unconscious: Narrative as a Socially Symbolic Act* (Ithaca: Cornell University Press, 1981), and *Postmodernism; or, The Cultural Logic of Late Capitalism;* Donald Drew Egbert, *Social Radicalism in the Arts, Western Europe: A Cultural History from the French Revolution to 1968* (New York: Knopf, 1970); Renee Winegarten, *Writers and Revolution: The Fatal Lure of Action* (New York: New Viewpoints, 1974); Eugenia W. Herbert, *The Artist and Social Reform: France and Belgium, 1885–1898* (New Haven: Yale University Press, 1961); Richard D. Sonn, *Anarchism and Cultural Politics in Fin de Siècle France* (Lincoln: University of Nebraska Press, 1989); and Joan Ungersma Halperin, *Félix Fénéon: Aesthete and Anarchist in Fin-de-Siècle Paris* (New Haven: Yale University Press, 1988).

9. I am borrowing the language of James Joyce in chapter 2 of *Ulysses*. When the Ulsterman Deasy says to Stephen Dedalus, "We are a generous people but we must also be just," Stephen replies: "I fear those big words which make us so unhappy." *Ulysses*, ed. Hans Walter Gabler (New York: Random House, 1986), 26.

10. Raymond Williams, *Keywords: A Vocabulary of Culture and Society*, rev. ed. (New York: Oxford University Press, 1983), 91.

11. Further evidence of the aesthetic turn taken by Marxist theory is supplied by Cohen: "The recent critical popularity enjoyed by Benjamin confirms that the pressures of post-Marxism have helped bring the conjuncture of Benjamin's and Breton's Gothic Marxisms [Cohen's term for Marxist accommodations of the irrational] into view. In the time it has taken me to frame this book, I have been hard-pressed to keep up with the proliferation of work attempting to appropriate Gothic Marxist aspects of Benjamin's musings for cultural theory across the disciplines." *Profane Illumination*, 11.

Chapter 1: Definitions

1. Quoted in Paul Eltzbacher, *Anarchism*, trans. Steven T. Byington (New York: Benjamin R. Tucker, 1908), 183. I use Eltzbacher as a source for quotations because his book was one of the most accessible (in both senses) compilations of anarchist writings available early in the twentieth century. The book met with the approval of Peter Kropotkin, who recommended it to the readers of the eleventh edition of the *Encyclopaedia Britannica* (1910–11) in his article on "Anarchism": "The best work on Anarchism, and in fact the only one written with a full knowledge of the Anarchist literature, and quite fairly, is by a German Judge, Dr. Paul Eltzbacher, *Der Anarchismus*" (1:919). Eltzbacher was not, in fact, a sympathetic critic of anarchism, but his expositions of Godwin, Proudhon, Stirner, Bakunin, Kropotkin, Tucker, and Tolstoy are quite straightforward. The book was published in Berlin in 1900 and was soon translated into Spanish (1901), French (1902), Russian (1903), and Dutch (1903). Benjamin Tucker brought out Byington's English translation in 1908. This translation was reprinted in 1960, when the Libertarian Book Club published it under the imprint of Chip's Bookshop, New York. An editor's preface to this edition includes useful information about Eltzbacher, Byington, and Tucker, along with a publication

history of the book (see editor's preface to *Anarchism: Exponents of the Anarchist Philosophy*, ed. James J. Martin [New York: Chip's Bookshop, 1960], vii–xix). Unfortunately the text of this reprint is corrupt at certain key points (notably the section on Proudhon), so I have relied instead on Tucker's original 1908 edition. Further references to this edition are cited parenthetically in the text as *Anarchism*.

2. Gerald F. Gaus and John W. Chapman, "Anarchism and Political Philosophy: An Introduction," in *Anarchism: Nomos XIX*, ed. J. Roland Pennock and John W. Chapman (New York: New York University Press, 1978), xviii.

3. Raymond Williams, "Anarchism," in *Keywords: A Vocabulary of Culture and Society*, rev. ed. (New York: Oxford University Press, 1983), 37.

4. Richard D. Sonn, *Anarchism* (New York: Twayne, 1992), 3.

5. Friedrich Engels, "The Catchword: 'Abolition of the State' and the German 'Friends of Anarchy,' " in *Marx, Engels, Lenin: Anarchism and Anarcho-Syndicalism* (Moscow: Progress Publishers, 1972), 29.

6. Karl Marx and Friedrich Engels, "Fictional Splits in the International," in *Marx, Engels, Lenin: Anarchism and Anarcho-Syndicalism*, 73.

7. Charles Taylor, *Hegel* (Cambridge: Cambridge University Press, 1975), 542.

8. Jean-Jacques Rousseau, *The Social Contract and Discourse on the Origin of Inequality*, ed. Lester G. Crocker (New York: Washington Square Press, 1967), 109. Further references to this edition are cited parenthetically in the text as *Contract* or *Discourse*.

9. George Crowder, *Classical Anarchism: The Political Thought of Godwin, Proudhon, Bakunin, and Kropotkin* (Oxford: Clarendon Press, 1991), 64.

10. William Godwin, *Enquiry Concerning Political Justice and Its Influence on Modern Morals and Happiness* (New York: Penguin, 1985), 298. Further references to this edition are cited parenthetically in the text as *Enquiry*.

11. Crowder, *Classical Anarchism*, 47.

12. Ibid., 45.

13. Sonn, *Anarchism*, 17.

14. Alan Ritter, *Anarchism: A Theoretical Analysis* (Cambridge: Cambridge University Press, 1980), 42.

15. Crowder, *Classical Anarchism*, 43.

16. K. Steven Vincent, *Pierre-Joseph Proudhon and the Rise of French Republican Socialism* (New York: Oxford University Press, 1984), 69, 254 n. 210.

17. Crowder, *Classical Anarchism*, 17.

18. Quoted by Aaron Noland, "Proudhon and Rousseau," *Journal of the History of Ideas* 28 (1967): 42.

19. Quoted by Crowder, *Classical Anarchism*, 97.

20. Noland, "Proudhon and Rousseau," 49.

21. Vincent, *Proudhon*, 64.

22. Crowder, *Classical Anarchism*, 85.

23. Vincent, *Proudhon*, 64, 253 n. 173.

24. Crowder, *Classical Anarchism*, 84.

25. Quoted by Noland, "Proudhon and Rousseau," 50.

26. Ibid.

27. Noland, "Proudhon and Rousseau," uses the term "anarcho-socialist" (37); Crowder, *Classical Anarchism,* says "Proudhon's work is best understood within the socialist tradition" (76).

28. Crowder, *Classical Anarchism,* 26.

29. Quoted by Brian Morris, *Bakunin: The Philosophy of Freedom* (Montreal: Black Rose, 1993), 7. Further references to this work are cited parenthetically in the text as Morris, *Bakunin.*

30. Sonn, *Anarchism,* 19.

31. Michale Bakunin, "The Reaction in Germany," *Bakunin on Anarchy: Selected Works by the Activist Founder of World Anarchism,* ed. Sam Dolgoff (New York: Knopf, 1972), 57.

32. Sonn, *Anarchism,* 34.

33. Ibid., 38.

34. Peter Kropotkin, *Fugitive Writings,* ed. George Woodcock (Montreal: Black Rose, 1993), 77. Further references to this work are cited parenthetically in the text as *Fugitive Writings.*

35. See Crowder, *Classical Anarchism,* 119–20: "It is not . . . certain that Bakunin and Kropotkin ever read Rousseau at all. Their explicit comments touch on the doctrines of the *Second Discourse, Emile,* and *The Social Contract,* but their understanding of these texts is so superficial that it may be no more than second hand." Crowder also argues that both Bakunin and Kropotkin got their Rousseau secondhand through Proudhon (120).

36. Paul Avrich, *Anarchist Portraits* (Princeton: Princeton University Press, 1988), 8. See also Sonn, *Anarchism,* 30.

37. Michael Bakunin, *Statism and Anarchy* (Cambridge: Cambridge University Press, 1990), 129, 144. Bakunin says Heine's poem " 'The Weaver' . . . predicted an imminent and merciless social revolution" (144).

38. Quoted by James Henry Rubin, *Realism and Social Vision in Courbet and Proudhon* (Princeton: Princeton University Press, 1980), 50–51. Further references to this work are cited parenthetically in the text as Rubin, *Realism.*

39. Quoted by Linda Nochlin, ed., *Realism and Tradition in Art, 1848–1900: Sources and Documents* (Englewood Cliffs, N.J.: Prentice Hall, 1966), 50.

40. Donald Drew Egbert, *Social Radicalism and the Arts, Western Europe: A Cultural History from the French Revolution to 1968* (New York: Knopf, 1970), 219.

41. John Elderfield, introduction to Hugo Ball, *Flight Out of Time: A Dada Diary* (Berkeley and Los Angeles: University of California Press, 1996), xxxviii.

42. Egbert, *Social Radicalism and the Arts,* 215.

43. Mikhail Bakunin, "All-Round Education," in *The Basic Bakunin: Writings, 1869–1871,* trans. Robert M. Cutler (Buffalo: Prometheus Books, 1992), 112.

44. Guy Debord, "The Situationists and the New Forms of Action in Politics and Art," in *Situationist International Anthology,* trans. Ken Knabb (Berkeley: Bureau of Public Secrets, 1981), 318.

45. E. H. Carr, *Michael Bakunin* (New York: Vintage, 1961), 201.

46. Peter Kropotkin, "An Appeal to the Young," in *The Essential Kropotkin,* ed. Emile Capouya and Keitha Tompkins (New York: Liveright, 1975), 10–26.

Chapter 2: Reactions

1. Matthew Arnold, *Culture and Anarchy,* ed. J. Dover Wilson (Cambridge: Cambridge University Press, 1935), 82. Further references to this edition are cited parenthetically in the text.

2. Quoted by David J. DeLaura, "Matthew Arnold and Culture: The History and the Prehistory," in *Matthew Arnold in His Time and Ours: Centenary Essays,* ed. Clinton Machann and Forrest D. Burt (Charlottesville: University Press of Virginia, 1988), 3–4.

3. DeLaura, "Matthew Arnold and Culture," 7.

4. C. Dover Wilson, editor's introduction to *Culture and Anarchy,* xxvi. The historical account of the reform movement is also taken from Wilson's introduction.

5. Ibid., xxx.

6. See ibid., xxiv.

7. Elie Halevy, *History of the English People in the Nineteenth Century,* trans. E. I. Watkin, 6 vols. (New York: Barnes and Noble, 1961), 3:16. Quoted by Robert Giddings, introduction to *Matthew Arnold: Between Two Worlds* (London: Vision, 1986), 17.

8. See Giddings, *Matthew Arnold,* 18.

9. Ibid., 19.

10. Peter Kropotkin, *Fugitive Writings* (Montreal: Black Rose, 1993), 106. For a discussion of the Anabaptists as anarchist precursors, see James Joll, *The Anarchists* (Boston: Little Brown, 1964), 22–27.

11. John Milton, *Prose Writings,* rev. ed. (London: Dent, 1958), 333.

12. Perry Meisel, *The Myth of the Modern: A Study in British Literature and Criticism after 1850* (New Haven: Yale University Press, 1987), 51.

13. Quoted by Meisel, *Myth of the Modern,* 48.

14. Ibid., 39.

15. Ibid., 4.

16. Matthew Arnold, *The Oxford Poetic Library: Mathew Arnold,* ed. Miriam Allott (Oxford: Oxford University Press, 1995), 82.

17. Giddings, *Matthew Arnold,* 21.

18. Ivan Turgenev, *Rudin,* trans. Richard Freeborn (New York: Viking Penguin, 1975), 97, 63. Further references to this edition are cited parenthetically in the text.

19. See Joll, *The Anarchists,* 84–85, 89.

20. Ibid., 84.

21. Ibid., 86, 89.

22. Ibid., 85.

23. Richard D. Sonn, *Anarchism* (New York: Twayne, 1992), 28.

24. Brian Morris, *Bakunin: The Philosophy of Freedom* (Montreal: Black Rose, 1993), 15–16, 6, 14–15, 18.

25. James B. Woodward, *Metaphysical Conflict: A Study of the Major Novels of Ivan Turgenev* (Munich: Otto Sagner, 1990), 6–7.

26. Joseph Frank, *Dostoyevsky: The Stir of Liberation, 1860–1865* (Princeton: Princeton University Press, 1986), 192.

27. Quoted by Gordon Livermore, "The Shaping Dialectic of Dostoyevsky's *Devils*," in *Dostoyevsky: New Perspectives*, ed. Robert Louis Jackson (Englewood Cliffs, N.J.: Prentice-Hall, 1984), 184.

28. Quoted by Marc Slonim, afterword to *The Possessed* (New York: Signet, 1962), 697.

29. Ibid.

30. Morris, *Bakunin*, 43–44.

31. Paul Thomas, *Karl Marx and the Anarchists* (London: Routledge and Kegan Paul, 1980), 290.

32. Quoted by Morris, *Bakunin*, 44.

33. Quoted by Thomas, *Karl Marx*, 289–90.

34. Fyodor Dostoyevsky, *The Possessed* (New York: Signet, 1962), 504. Further references to this edition are cited parenthetically in the text.

35. Frank, *Dostoyevsky*, 101.

36. Quoted by Frank, *Dostoyevsky*, 372.

37. Ibid., 374.

38. Ibid., 136; Frank also notes that Dostoyevsky read *To the Young Generation*, by Mikhailov, Shelgunov, and possibly Chernyshevsky and most likely agreed with the "new principle" the leaflet advanced, one that included independently administered communes that obviated the need for a state apparatus (138).

39. Ibid., 101.

40. Henry James, *Letters*, ed. Leon Edel (Cambridge: Harvard University Press, 1980), 3:61. Letter dated 12 December 1884.

41. Henry James, *Novels, 1886–1890: "The Princess Casamassima," "The Reverberator," "The Tragic Muse"* (New York: Library of America), 221. Further references to the novels in this edition are cited parenthetically in the text.

42. The novel is more involved than the set of relations suggested here, especially as regards Hyacinth's sexuality. There is no question that the character finds Millicent Henning appealing, but this overt heterosexual attraction is matched by Hyacinth's barely repressed homoerotic interest in Paul Muniment. Further, the homosocial nature of the politics in the novel suggests an interweaving of political and sexual identity in Hyacinth's character, since the admiration he feels for Paul is grounded as much in homoerotic as in ideological kinship. For a discussion of this aspect of the novel, see Wendy Graham, "Henry James's Subterranean Blues: A Rereading of *The Princess Casamassima*," *Modern Fiction Studies* 40, no. 1 (Spring 1994): 51–84.

43. Lionel Trilling, *The Liberal Imagination: Essays on Literature and Society* (New York: Viking, 1950), 71, 73–74.

44. Joll, *The Anarchists*, 139.

45. Ernest Alfred Vizetelly, *The Anarchists* (New York: John Lane, 1911; repr. New York: Klaus, 1972), 68, 69.

46. An allusion to a story by Octave Feuillet in *Revue des Deux Mondes* that appeared in April 1881 suggests the period 1879–82, according to Patricia Crick (see note 175 to the Penguin edition of *The Princess Casamassima* [New York: Viking Penguin, 1986], 603). The reference to the Feuillet story appears on page 265 of the Library of America edition.

47. Derek Brewer, introduction to *The Princess Casamassima* (New York: Viking Penguin, 1986), 28.

48. Joll, *The Anarchists*, 140.

49. Andrew R. Carlson, *Anarchism in Germany* (Metuchen, N.J.: Scarecrow, 1972), 1:321, 205.

50. George Woodcock, "Henry James and the Conspirators," *Sewanee Review* 60 (1952): 223.

51. Ibid., 225.

52. Ibid., 224.

53. For example, one J. L. Joynes in an article titled "Dynamite and Despair" that appeared in William Morris's socialist organ *Justice* on 7 June 1884 (vol. 1, no. 21) reacted to "the recent explosions" attributed to "the Irish-American Fenian Party" as an expression of "irresponsible anarchy—as being the worst manifestations of the most extreme form of individualism" (4). The equation of anarchism and Fenianism that regularly appeared in the pages of *Justice* prompted this anonymous response by "an English Anarchist" later in the year, evidently intended to reassure socialists that anarchists are not wantonly destructive or categorically opposed to social organization: "We are drawn together by our social instincts, and moulded into such harmony as we have at present attained, by the perpetual action and reaction of the influence we exert over each other, and by our inherited and acquired habits, sympathies, and beliefs. The Revolution, in breaking up the stereotyped forms into which some of these social instincts and beliefs have crystallized, can, in no sense, destroy the social instincts themselves. . . . [S]elf-interest, intelligently followed, tends to promote the general economic well-being of the community." "Anarchism," *Justice*, 1, no. 43 (8 November 1884): 1.

54. Joll, *The Anarchists*, 139–40.

55. Henry James, *The American Scene*, ed. Leon Edel (Bloomington: Indiana University Press, 1968), 141.

56. Dietmar Schloss, "Culture and Criticism in Matthew Arnold and Henry James," *Amerikastudien: American Studies (Amst)* 36 (1991): 79.

57. Dietmar Otto Schloss, "Culture and Criticism in Henry James" (Ph.D. diss., Northwestern University, 1986), abstract in *Dissertation Abstracts International* 47 (1987): 3052A.

58. Arnold, *Culture and Anarchy*, 102.

59. Douglas W. Sterner, "Priests of Culture: A Study of Matthew Arnold and Henry James" (Ph.D. diss., Rutgers University, 1989), abstract in *Dissertation Abstracts International* 50 (1990): 2217A.

60. Hermia Oliver, *The International Anarchist Movement in Late Victorian London* (London: Croom and Helm, 1983), 102, 106–7.

61. Oliver notes that Samuels remained on good terms with Bourdin's

brother and that he is not known to have received any payment from the police. His finances did not improve after the explosion, which argues against a police payoff. See Oliver, *International Anarchist Movement in London*, 107.

62. Graham Holderness, "Anarchism and Fiction," in *The Rise of Socialist Fiction, 1880–1914*, ed. H. Gustav Klaus (New York: St. Martin's, 1987), 129.

63. Ibid., 129.

64. Frederick R. Karl, introduction to *The Secret Agent: A Simple Tale* (New York: Signet, 1983), 5.

65. Joseph Conrad, author's Preface to *The Secret Agent: A Simple Tale* (New York: Knopf, 1961), xxix. Further references to this edition of *The Secret Agent* are cited parenthetically in the text.

66. Sonn, *Anarchism*, 50–51.

67. Ibid., 52.

68. Avrom Fleishman, *Conrad's Politics: Community and Anarchy in the Fiction of Joseph Conrad* (Baltimore: Johns Hopkins University Press, 1967), 209–10.

69. E. Douglas Fawcett, *Hartmann the Anarchist; Or, The Doom of the Great City* (London: Edward Arnold, 1893), 5. Further references to this work are cited parenthetically in the text.

70. G. K. Chesterton, *The Man Who Was Thursday* (New York: Penguin, 1986).

71. Frederick R. Karl, introduction to *The Secret Agent*, 8, 9.

72. Irving Howe, *Politics and the Novel* (Cleveland: Meridian, 1957), 78. Further references to this work are cited parenthetically in the text.

73. Thomas Mann, *Reflections of a Nonpolitical Man*, trans. Walter D. Morris (New York: Ungar, 1983), 426. Further references to this edition are cited parenthetically in the text.

74. Daniel W. Conway and John E. Seery, introduction to *The Politics of Irony* (New York: St. Martin's, 1992), 2: "It may be the case that Mann both does and does not mean what he says about irony. He may *also* be claiming, via insinuation, that 'politics is altogether and always of ironical character.' We might think of Mann as simultaneously and paradoxically embracing parallel truths, namely that irony is both subversive in character *and* intimately linked to politics."

Chapter 3: Responses

1. See Paul Avrich, *The Haymarket Tragedy* (Princeton: Princeton University Press, 1984), and Richard Sonn, *Anarchism and Cultural Politics in Fin de Siècle France* (Lincoln: University of Nebraska Press, 1989).

2. Percy Bysshe Shelley, *A Defense of Poetry*, in *Shelley's Prose; or, The Trumpet of a Prophecy*, ed. David Lee Clark (New York: New Amsterdam, 1988), 287. Further references to *A Defense of Poetry* in this edition are cited parenthetically in the text as *DP*. References to Shelley's *A Philosophical View of Reform* in this edition are cited parenthetically with the abbreviation *PVR*.

3. Donald H. Reiman and Sharon B. Powers, eds., *Shelley's Poetry and Prose* (New York: Norton, 1977), 301 n. 1.

4. Percy Bysshe Shelley, "The Mask of Anarchy," in *Shelley's Poetry and Prose,* 302. Further references to the poem in this edition are cited parenthetically in the text.

5. Kenneth Neill Cameron, "The Social Philosophy of Shelley," in *Shelley's Poetry and Prose,* 514.

6. Maurice Hindle, introduction to William Godwin, *Things as They Are; or, The Adventures of Caleb Williams* (New York: Penguin, 1988), xi. Further references to Hindle's introduction are cited parenthetically in the text using roman numerals; references to Godwin's novel are cited parenthetically using arabic numerals.

7. Marilyn Butler, "Godwin, Burke, and *Caleb Williams,*" *Essays in Criticism* 32 (1982): 238.

8. Ibid., 237.

9. William Godwin, *Enquiry Concerning Political Justice and Its Influence on Modern Morals and Happiness* (New York: Penguin, 1985), 289. Further references to this edition are cited parenthetically in the text as *Enquiry.*

10. Gary Handwerk, "Of Caleb's Guilt and Godwin's Truth: Ideology and Ethics in *Caleb Williams,*" *ELH* 60 (1993): 944.

11. Kenneth W. Graham, "The Two Endings of *Caleb Williams:* Politics and Aesthetics in a Revolutionary Novel," *Studies on Voltaire and the Eighteenth Century* 265 (1989): 1238.

12. Isaac Kramnich, "A Note on the Text," in Godwin, *Enquiry,* 57–58.

13. Edmund Burke, *A Philosophical Enquiry into the Origin of Our Ideas of the Sublime and Beautiful,* in *Criticism and Aesthetics, 1660–1800,* ed. Oliver F. Sigworth (San Francisco: Rinehart, 1971), 320.

14. Michel Foucault, *Discipline and Punish: The Birth of the Prison,* trans. Alan Sheridan (New York: Vintage, 1979), 207: "The panopticon schema, without disappearing as such or losing any of its properties, was destined to spread throughout the social body; its vocation was to become a generalized function."

15. William Godwin, unpublished paper cited by Hindle, introduction to *Caleb Williams,* xxxii.

16. Peter Kropotkin, "An Appeal to the Young," in *The Essential Kropotkin,* ed. Emile Capouya and Keitha Tompkins (New York: Liveright, 1975), 23, 25.

17. Hermia Oliver, *The International Anarchist Movement in Late Victorian London* (London: Croom and Helm, 1983), 120–21.

18. David Garnet, *The Golden Echo,* 3 vols. (London: Chatto & Windus, 1953), 1:12.

19. Isabel Meredith, *A Girl among the Anarchists* (Lincoln: University of Nebraska Press, 1992), 13. Further references to this edition are cited parenthetically in the text.

20. For a discussion of Stepniak and other Russian radicals, see James W. Hulse, *Revolutionists in London: A Study of Five Unorthodox Socialists* (Oxford: Clarendon Press, 1970).

21. John Quail, *The Slow Burning Fuse* (London: Paladin, 1978), 196.

22. Ibid.

23. Quoted in ibid., 204.

24. Graham Holderness, "Anarchism and Fiction," in *The Rise of Socialist Fiction, 1880–1914*, ed. H. Gustav Klaus (New York: St. Martin's, 1987), 142.

25. Jennifer Shaddock, introduction to *A Girl Among the Anarchists*, xiv.

26. See Grant Allen, *The Woman Who Did* (New York: Oxford University Press, 1995).

27. Kropotkin, "An Appeal to the Young," in *The Essential Kropotkin*, 10.

28. For a concise account of the events surrounding the Haymarket bombing, see James Joll, *The Anarchists* (Boston: Little, Brown, 1964), 142–44.

29. Holderness, "Anarchism and Fiction," 145.

30. Joll, *The Anarchists*, 143.

31. Avrich, *Haymarket Tragedy*, 439.

32. Frank Harris, *The Bomb* (New York: Mitchell Kennerley, 1909), 211–12. Further references to this edition are cited parenthetically in the text.

33. Joll, *The Anarchists*, 139, 141.

34. Albert S. Lindemann, *A History of European Socialism* (New Haven: Yale University Press, 1983), 164.

35. Avrich, *Haymarket Tragedy*, 158, 159.

36. Ibid., 137.

37. Joll, *The Anarchists*, 143.

38. Susan Sontag has made the point that camp "is beautiful *because* it is awful." *Against Interpretation* (New York: Dell, 1969), 293.

Chapter 4: Affinities

1. Louis Patsouras, *Jean Grave and French Anarchism* (Dubuque, Iowa: Kendall/Hunt, 1978), 78.

2. Ibid.

3. T. J. Clark, *The Painting of Modern Life: Paris in the Art of Manet and His Followers* (Princeton: Princeton University Press, 1984), 23.

4. Patsouras, *Jean Grave*, 1, 5 n. 4, 2.

5. Ibid., 23–24, 2.

6. Richard D. Sonn, *Anarchism and Cultural Politics in Fin de Siècle France* (Lincoln: University of Nebraska Press, 1989), 59–60.

7. Rupert Christiansen, *Paris Babylon: The Story of the Paris Commune* (New York: Viking, 1995), 298.

8. Albert S. Lindemann, *A History of European Socialism* (New Haven: Yale University Press, 1983), 126. I have also relied on Lindemann for my basic account of the Paris Commune.

9. Richard Sonn, *Anarchism and Cultural Politics*, 51. Patsouras, *Jean Grave*, 3–4.

10. Lindemann, *A History of European Socialism*, 125.

11. Patsouras, *Jean Grave*, 4.

12. Lindemann, *A History of European Socialism*, 125.

13. Paul Avrich, *Anarchist Portraits* (Princeton: Princeton University Press, 1988), 232.

14. Patsouras, *Jean Grave*, 4. Sonn, *Anarchism and Cultural Politics*, 122.

15. Patsouras, *Jean Grave*, 4.

16. Avrich, *Anarchist Portraits*, 230.

17. Christiansen, *Paris Babylon*, 321.

18. Karl Marx, *The Civil War in France*, in *The Marx-Engels Reader*, ed. Robert C. Tucker, 2d ed. (New York: Norton, 1978), 633, 632.

19. Christiansen, *Paris Babylon*, 317.

20. Avrich, *Anarchist Portraits*, 234.

21. Sonn, *Anarchism and Cultural Politics*, 251, 13.

22. Ibid., 68.

23. Patsouras, *Jean Grave*, 23.

24. Jean Pierrot, *The Decadent Imagination: 1880–1900*, trans. Derek Coltman (Chicago: University of Chicago Press, 1981), 253.

25. Patsouras, *Jean Grave*, 1, 5, 21–23, 31–35.

26. Ibid., 35.

27. Joan Ungersma Halperin, *Félix Fénéon: Aesthete and Anarchist in Fin-de-Siècle Paris* (New Haven: Yale University Press, 1989), 289–90.

28. Ibid., 290.

29. Patsouras, *Jean Grave*, 37–38.

30. Halperin, *Félix Fénéon*, 276.

31. Patsouras, *Jean Grave*, 67.

32. Sonn, *Anarchism and Cultural Politics*, 16.

33. Ibid., 247.

34. Ibid., 140.

35. Félix Fénéon, *Oeuvres plus que complètes*, 2 vols., ed. Joan U. Halperin (Geneva: Librairie Droz, 1970) 1:226. Text originally published in *Le Père Peinard* of 9 April 1893.

36. Quoted by Halperin, *Félix Fénéon*, 259.

37. Halperin, *Félix Fénéon*, 245.

38. Ibid., 262, 243, 265.

39. Ibid., 242.

40. Sonn, *Anarchism and Cultural Politics*, 16.

41. Ibid., 244.

42. Halperin, *Félix Fénéon*, 253.

43. Sonn, *Anarchism and Cultural Politics*, 15.

44. Patsouras, *Jean Grave*, 24–25.

45. Sonn, *Anarchism and Cultural Politics*, 17.

46. Patsouras, *Jean Grave*, 38, 41, 43.

47. Ibid., 87–88.

48. Ibid., 44.

49. Ibid.

50. Paul Avrich, *The Modern School Movement: Anarchism and Education in the United States* (Princeton: Princeton University Press, 1980), 4. Further references to this work are cited parenthetically in the text as *MSM*.

51. G. Normandy and E. Lesueur, "Ferrer's Early Life," trans. Helen Tufts Bailie, in *Francisco Ferrer: His Life, Work, and Martyrdom*, ed. Leonard Abbot (New

York: Ferrer Association, [1910]), 12. G. Normandy and E. Lesueur, "Ferrer and Mademoiselle Meunier," trans. Helen Tufts Bailie, in *Francisco Ferrer: His Life, Work, and Martyrdom*, 16.

52. Martha Ackelsberg, "Education, Preparation and the Spanish Revolution," in *The Modern School Movement: Historical and Personal Notes on the Ferrer Schools in Spain* (Croton-on-Hudson, N.Y.: Friends of the Modern School, 1990), 31.

53. Quoted in "Elisée Reclus 'Man and the Earth'—One of the Great Text-Books of the Modern School," in *Francisco Ferrer: His Life, Work, and Martyrdom*, 39.

54. Francisco Ferrer, *The Origins and Ideals of the Modern School* (London, 1913), 52. Quoted by Avrich, *Modern School Movement*, 23.

55. "Twelve Hours of Agony—How Ferrer Died," *Francisco Ferrer: His Life, Work, and Martyrdom*, 52. This melodramatic account actually presents Ferrer's very last words as follows: " 'Long live the Modern—' The word 'School' was lost in the crack of the rifles."

56. Ackelsberg, "Education, Preparation and the Spanish Revolution," in *The Modern School Movement: Historical and Personal Notes*, 30. Another writer says that "there were 9,000,000 illiterates in Spain in 1898 out of a total population of 17,000,000 residents." See Diego Camacho, "My Experience in the 'Nature School': A Living Memory of Rational Pedagogy," trans. Abe Bluestein, in *The Modern School Movement: Historical and Personal Notes*, 19.

57. Pura Perez, "Recollections," in *The Modern School Movement: Historical and Personal Notes*, 8. Camacho, "My Experience in 'The Nature School,' " in *The Modern School Movement: Historical and Personal Notes*, 28.

58. Camacho, "My Experience in the 'Nature School,' " in *The Modern School Movement: Historical and Personal Notes*, 27.

59. Ackelsberg, "Education, Preparation and the Spanish Revolution," in *The Modern School Movement: Historical and Personal Notes*, 33. Camacho, "My Experience in the 'Nature School,' " in *The Modern School Movement: Historical and Personal Notes*, 20.

60. The *Modern School* newsletters of 1912 and 1913 also list courses for adults in French; Literature and English Composition; Anatomy and Physiology; Life Classes in Art; Music Appreciation; Radical Literature and Great Libertarians; as well as lecture series on such topics as "Art and the Sex Impulse" by Emma Goldman and the "History of Philosophy" by Will Durant. The courses for adults at the Ferrer Center in New York clearly presuppose a high level of literacy and some degree of cultural sophistication.

61. Bruce Calvert, *Modern School* 1, no. 3 (Winter 1912): 10.

62. Benzion Liber, *A Doctor's Apprenticeship: Autobiographical Sketches* (New York: Rational Living, 1956), 482.

63. Will Durant, "Problems En Route," *Modern School* 1, no. 4 (Spring 1913): 4, 5.

64. Will Durant, *Transition: A Sentimental Story of One Mind and One Era* (New York: Simon and Schuster, 1927), 199, 241–42, 247, 241, 245.

65. Will and Ariel Durant, *A Dual Autobiography* (New York: Simon and Schuster, 1977), 54. To the story of the marriage told by Will in *Transition*

(266–71), Ariel adds: "I had no clear conception of the responsibilities I had undertaken. Gaily I proposed, almost in sight of City Hall, to teach my husband how to roller-skate. He tried, floundered from one side to another, fell on his rear, and gave it up as much harder than Plato. We spent our wedding night in my mother's apartment, having as yet no rooms of our own. Everything went well until Will took me into his bed and asked for his marital rights. I was not quite prepared for this, and raised objections, until my mother, hearing my protests, came to us and assured me, 'It's all right, my child; don't be afraid.' I could never resist my mother."

66. Laurence Veysey, *The Communal Experience: Anarchist and Mystical Counter-Cultures in America* (New York: Harper and Row, 1973), 85–86.

67. Carl Zigrosser, *My Own Shall Come to Me: A Personal Memoir and Picture Chronicle* (Philadelphia: Casa Laura, 1971), 77–78.

68. Veysey, *The Communal Experience*, 102.

69. Zigrosser, *My Own Shall Come to Me*, 73.

70. A[dolf] W[olff], "Activities at the Center," *Modern School* 1, no. 4 (Spring 1913): 19.

71. Adolf Wolff, "Walt Whitman," *Modern School* 1, no. 4 (Spring 1913): 7.

72. Man Ray, "Travail," *Modern School* 1, no. 5 (Autumn 1913): 20–21.

73. Zigrosser, *My Own Shall Come to Me*, 72.

74. Alan Wolff, "The Art Exhibit," *Modern School,* 1, no. 4 (Spring 1913): 11.

75. Manuel Komroff, "Art Transfusion," *Modern School,* 1, no. 4 (Spring 1913): 13.

76. Komroff, "Art Transfusion," 13, 14.

77. M[oritz] Jagendorf, "Announcement," *Modern School* 1, no. 10 (1 October 1914): 11. The December issue of the *Modern School* magazine identified Jagendorf himself as the mysterious "X.X.X."

78. Zigrosser, *My Own Shall Come to Me*, 70.

79. Jagendorf, "Announcement," 11.

80. Veysey, *The Communal Experience*, 104–5.

81. Ibid., 94, 107.

82. Dominic Manganeillo, *Joyce's Politics* (London: Routledge and Kegan Paul, 1980), 74.

83. Frank H. Brooks, "Introduction: Putting Liberty in Context," in *The Individualist Anarchists: An Anthology to Liberty (1881–1908)* (New Brunswick, N.J.: Transaction Publishers, 1994), 6.

84. Benjamin Tucker, "Karl Marx as Friend and Foe," *Liberty,* 14 April 1883, p. 2; cited by Brooks, *The Individualist Anarchists*, 97–98.

85. Brooks, *The Individualist Anarchists*, 7.

86. *Benj. R. Tucker's Unique Catalogue of Advanced Literature*, Italian ed., Benjamin Tucker Papers, Rare Books and Manuscripts Division, The New York Public Library, Astor, Lenox and Tilden Foundations.

87. Quoted by Brooks, *The Individualist Anarchists*, 224.

88. Ibid., 238.

89. Marcel Prevost, "The French Novel in the Nineteenth Century," *Balzac*

Library, 14 May 1900, p. 7. Benjamin Tucker Papers, Rare Books and Manuscripts Division, The New York Public Library, Astor, Lenox and Tilden Foundations.

90. "What Are Dreams?" *Balzac Library,* 5 April 1900, 5, 9, 13. Benjamin Tucker Papers, Rare Books and Manuscripts Division, The New York Public Library, Astor, Lenox and Tilden Foundations.

91. Quoted by Brooks, *The Individualist Anarchists,* 232.

92. Ibid., 233.

93. Ibid., 238.

94. A full-page advertisement for Godwin's *Caleb Williams* appears in the back of Tucker's edition of Eltzbacher's *Anarchism,* followed by four pages advertising the works of Proudhon; two for Stirner and "works relating" to Stirner; one page each for the works of Bakunin and Kropotkin; two for Tolstoy; one for a biography of Josiah Warren, "the first American anarchist"; one for George Bernard Shaw's *The Sanity of Art,* his response to Max Nordau's *Degeneration;* and one page advertising "a brace of anarchist classics," one by Herbert Spencer *(The Right to Ignore the State)* and the other by Henry David Thoreau *(On the Duty of Civil Disobedience).* In addition, seven pages are given over to advertisements for Tucker's own books and to various books and items available from the Unique Book-shop. Of particular interest is the advertisement for "Anarchist stickers"—"aggressive, concise Anarchistic assertions and arguments, in sheets, gummed and perforated, to be planted everywhere as broadcast seed for thought." Among the sample slogans: "Considering what a nuisance the Government is, the man who says we cannot get rid of it must be called a confirmed pessimist" and "With the monstrous laws that are accumulating on the statute-books, one may safely say that the man who is not a confirmed criminal is scarcely fit to live among decent people."

95. Margaret Anderson, *My Thirty Years' War* (New York: Covici, Friede, 1930), 9. Further references to this work are cited parenthetically in the text as *MTYW.*

96. Margaret C. Anderson, "The Challenge of Emma Goldman," *Little Review* 1, no. 3 (May 1914): 5–9.

97. Sherwood Anderson, "The New Note," in *The Little Review Anthology,* ed. Margaret Anderson (New York: Hermitage House, 1953), 14.

98. Margaret C. Anderson, "Art and Anarchism," *Little Review* 3, no. 1 (March 1916): 3.

99. See discussion of Stirner's "anarchism" in Chapter 5.

100. Max Stirner, *The Ego and Its Own* (Cambridge: Cambridge University Press, 1995), 36.

101. Anderson, "The Challenge of Emma Goldman," 6.

102. Margaret C. Anderson, "To the Innermost," *Little Review* 1, no. 7 (October 1914): 2–3, 5.

103. Stirner, *The Ego and Its Own,* 65.

104. Anderson, "Art and Anarchism," 6.

105. See, for example, Anderson's comments against capital punishment in her editorial about the execution of Joe Hillstrom in Utah in 1915 ("Toward Revolution," *Little Review* 2, no. 9 [December 1915]: 5); Dr. Rudolf von Liebich's

argument for libertarian education in Chicago ("A Ferrer School in Chicago," *Little Review* 1, no. 8 [November 1914]: 54–55); and an anonymous article devoted to Margaret Sanger's efforts on behalf of the cause of birth control ("Propaganda," *Little Review* 3, no. 1 [March 1916]: 25–26).

Chapter 5: Aesthetics

1. Shearer West, *Fin de Siècle: Art and Society in an Age of Uncertainty* (Woodstock, N.Y.: Overlook, 1993), 33.

2. Matei Calinescu, *Five Faces of Modernity: Modernism, Avant-Garde, Decadence, Kitsch, Postmodernism* (Durham: Duke University Press, 1987), 98. Further references are cited parenthetically in the text.

3. Quoted by Calinescu, *Five Faces of Modernity*, 102.

4. Quoted in ibid., 102–3.

5. Peter Kropotkin, "An Appeal to the Young," in *The Essential Kropotkin*, ed. Emile Capouya and Keitha Tompkins (New York: Liveright, 1975), 23.

6. Quoted by Renato Poggioli, *The Theory of the Avant-garde*, trans. Gerald Fitzgerald (Cambridge: Belknap Press of Harvard University Press, 1968), 9.

7. Andreas Huyssen, *After the Great Divide: Modernism, Mass Culture, Postmodernism* (Bloomington: Indiana University Press, 1986), 5.

8. Poggioli, *Theory of the Avant-garde*, 10. Poggioli says that Baudelaire "mocks the phrase" *avant-garde* because it shows "the predilection of the French for military metaphors."

9. Ibid., 9, 97.

10. Suzanne Clark, *Sentimental Modernism* (Bloomington: Indiana University Press, 1991), 43.

11. Theodor Adorno, *Aesthetic Theory*, trans. C. Lenhardt (London: Routledge and Kegan Paul, 1984), 325. Further references to this edition are cited parenthetically in the text as *AT*.

12. See Richard Wolin, "The De-aestheticization of Art: On Adorno's *Aesthetische Theorie*," *Telos* 41 (Fall 1979): 105–27. Wolin describes Adorno's work as "a monumental effort to vindicate modernism, to authenticate its 'right to exist' from a historico-political point of view" (106). See also Thomas Huhn, "Adorno's Aesthetics of Illusion," *Journal of Aesthetics and Art Criticism* 44 (Winter 1985): 181–89, where *Aesthetic Theory* is called "a weighty defense of modern art" (181).

13. Theodor W. Adorno, "Commitment," in *The Essential Frankfurt School Reader*, ed. Andrew Arato and Eike Gebhardt (New York: Continuum, 1982), 301. Further references to the essay in this edition are cited parenthetically in the text as *FSR*.

14. André Breton, *Manifestoes of Surrealism* (Ann Arbor: University of Michigan Press, 1969), 221.

15. Lambert Zuidervaart, *Adorno's Aesthetic Theory: The Redemption of Illusion* (Cambridge: MIT Press, 1991), 36.

16. Walter Benjamin, "The Work of Art in the Age of Mechanical Reproduction," *Illuminations*, trans. Harry Zohn (New York: Schocken, 1969), 217–51.

17. Terry Eagleton, *The Ideology of the Aesthetic* (Oxford: Blackwell, 1990), 349. Further references cited parenthetically in the text.

18. Lucio Colletti and Claudeo Napoleoni, *Il Futuro del capitalismo: crollo o sviluppo?* (Rome: Bari-Rome, 1970), 153–54; quoted by Franco Moretti, *Signs Taken for Wonders: Essays in the Sociology of Literary Form*, trans. Susan Fischer, et al. (London: Verso, 1983), 184.

19. Moretti, *Signs Taken for Wonders*, 190, 191.

20. Quoted by George Lichtheim, *Georg Lukács* (New York: Viking, 1970), 109, 108. The quotations are taken from Lukács, *The Meaning of Contemporary Realism* (London: Merlin, 1963).

21. William Morris, *Art and Society: Lectures and Essays*, ed. Gary Zabel (Boston: George's Hill, 1993), 83. Further references to this edition are cited parenthetically in the text.

22. Quoted by Calinescu, *Five Faces of Modernity*, 108.

23. Quoted by West, *Fin de Siècle*, 36.

24. The concept of "aesthetic satisfaction" occurs in *Stephen Hero* (the early draft of *A Portrait of the Artist as a Young Man*) with some frequency, as when Stephen argues that what Aquinas means by "the beautiful is that which satisfies the esthetic appetite." *Stephen Hero*, ed. Theodore Spencer (New York: New Directions, 1963), 95.

25. Max Stirner, *The Ego and Its Own*, ed. David Leopold (Cambridge: Cambridge University Press, 1995), 214. Further references to this edition are cited parenthetically in the text.

26. Quoted by James Joll, *The Anarchists* (Boston: Little, Brown, 1964), 170–71.

27. Quoted by Frank H. Brooks, *The Individualist Anarchists: An Anthology to Liberty (1881–1908)* (New Brunswick: Transaction Publishers, 1994), 230.

28. Richard Sonn, *Anarchism* (New York: Twayne, 1992), 21.

29. Sonn, *Anarchism*, 20–21.

30. David Leopold, a note on the translation, *The Ego and Its Own*, xxxix-xl.

31. Michael H. Levenson, *A Genealogy of Modernism: A Study of English Literary Doctrine 1908–1922* (Cambridge: Cambridge University Press, 1984), 65–66.

32. Quoted by Brooks, *The Individualist Anarchists*, 236.

33. Ibid.

34. Joll, *The Anarchists*, 171.

35. Remy de Gourmont, "A French View of Nietzsche," *New Age* 13, no. 2 (10 July 1913): 301. Quoted in Levenson, *Genealogy of Modernism*, 67.

36. Havelock Ellis, *The New Spirit* (Washington, D.C.: National Home Library, 1935), 16. Further references to this edition are cited parenthetically in the text.

37. James Huneker, *Egoists: A Book of Supermen* (New York: Scribner, 1920), 367.

38. Michael Levenson's *Genealogy of Modernism* is noteworthy for the inclusion of a discussion of Stirner in relation to individualist aesthetics in the prewar modernist period. See chapter 5, "Egoists and Imagists," 63–79.

39. James Huneker, *Overtones: A Book of Temperaments* (New York: Scribner,

1922), 219. Further references to this edition are cited parenthetically in the text.

40. Max Nordau, *Degeneration*, 2d ed. (New York: Appleton, 1912), 243. Further references to this edition are cited parenthetically in the text. Nordau is careful to distinguish his term for the pathological ego-state he discusses, *Ichsucht*, from *Selbstssucht*, by pointing out the distinction in French between *egotisme* and *egoisme*, "that is, selfishness." "Egoism [i.e., *Selbstsucht* or *egoisme*] is a lack of amiability, a defect in education, perhaps a fault of character, a proof of insufficiently developed morality, but it is not a disease. The egoist is quite able to look after himself in life, and hold his place in society. . . . The egomaniac, on the contrary, is an invalid who does not see things as they are, does not understand the world, and cannot take up a right attitude towards it" (243).

41. Hugo Ball, *Flight Out of Time: A Dada Diary*, trans. Ann Raimes (Berkeley and Los Angeles: University of California Press, 1996), 23.

42. In a 1922 introduction to *Towards Democracy* (New York: Mitchell Kennerly, 1922), Charles Vale asks, "How much did Edward Carpenter owe to Walt Whitman? The question is almost inevitable, and Carpenter himself has tried to answer it. He compares Whitman's influence with that of the sun or the moon —too deeply rooted and ramifying too complexly to be traced and tabulated" (iii-iv). In a brief introductory note to this edition, Carpenter himself addressed the issue of egotism: "And now with regard to the 'I' which occurs so freely in this book. In this and in other such cases the author is naturally liable to a charge of egotism—and I personally do not feel disposed to combat any such charge that may be made" (xxi-xxxii). This refusal to defend against egotism, however, is based in mysticism, not politics, as these lines from *Towards Democracy* make clear: "I arise out of the dewy night and shake my wings. . . . Deep as the universe is my life—and I know it; nothing can dislodge the knowledge of it; nothing can destroy, nothing can harm me" (4).

43. Richard D. Sonn, *Anarchism and Cultural Politics in Fin de Siècle France* (Lincoln: University of Nebraska Press, 1989), 215.

44. Ibid., 221, 218.

45. Robert von Hallberg, "Libertarian Imagism," *Modernism/Modernity* 2, no. 2 (April 1995): 66. See also Bruce Clark, *Dora Marsden and Early Modernism: Gender, Individualism, Science* (Ann Arbor: University of Michigan Press, 1996), 1–46.

46. Von Hallberg, "Libertarian Imagism," *Modernism/Modernity*, 67.

47. Quoted by Dora Marsden, "Views and Comments," *New Freewoman* 1, no. 13 (15 December 1913): 244.

48. Dora Marsden, "Views and Comments," *New Freewoman* 1, no. 1 (15 June 1913): 5.

49. Dora Marsden, "The Illusion of Anarchism," *The Egoist* 1, no. 18 (15 September 1914): 341, 343.

50. The advertisement appears on the last page of *The Egoist* of 15 December 1915. The ad also includes a quote from the *Morning Post* that shows how completely Stirner's egoism was identified with anarchism: "It [*The Ego and His Own*] must always rank as the most uncompromising attempt to vindicate the all

engrossing egoism that is the intellectual basis of anarchism properly so called."
Also advertised are Paul Eltzbacher's *Anarchism* and Benjamin Tucker's *State
Socialism and Anarchism: How Far They Agree and wherein They Differ.* Tucker was a
frequent contributor to *The New Freewoman* and *The Egoist.*

51. Von Hallberg, "Libertarian Imagism," *Modernism/Modernity,* 67.

52. Levenson, *Genealogy of Modernism,* 72.

53. Pound to Dora Marsden, July 1913; quoted in Jane Lidderdale and
Mary Nicholson, *Dear Miss Weaver* (New York: Viking, 1970), 68.

54. Von Hallberg, "Libertarian Imagism," *Modernism/Modernity,* 77.

55. Levenson, *Genealogy of Modernism,* 73, 76.

56. Von Halberg, "Libertarian Imagism," *Modernism/Modernity,* 64.

57. "It is wonderfully ironic that 'Tradition and the Individual Talent,' the
ur-manifesto of hegemonic modernism, was first published in the last two numbers of the *Egoist,* alongside Dora Marsden's egoistic apocalypse, her concluding
chapters to the *Science of Signs.* The effect of Eliot's doctrine, however, was to
reify and displace early modernism's egoism of existential autonomy as the
aesthetic autonomy ostensibly possessed by the autotelic text." Clark, *Dora Marsden and Early Modernism,* 7.

58. Levenson, *Genealogy of Modernism,* 67.

59. Anthony M. Ludovici, *Nietzsche and Art* (1911; repr., New York: Haskell
House, 1971), 7. Further references are cited parenthetically in the text.

60. Friedrich Nietzsche, *The Birth of Tragedy and The Case of Wagner,* trans.
Walter Kaufmann (New York: Vintage, 1967), 170.

61. H. L. Mencken, *Friedrich Nietzsche* (New Brunswick, N.J.: Transaction
Publishers, 1993), 99. Further references to this edition are cited parenthetically
in the text.

62. Quoted by Roger Shattuck, *The Innocent Eye: On Modern Literature and
the Arts* (New York: Washington Square Press, 1986), 46.

63. Shattuck, *The Innocent Eye,* 46.

64. Ball, *Flight Out of Time,* 22.

65. Théophile Gautier, *Charles Baudelaire* in *Baudelaire par Gautier,* ed.
Claude-Marie Senninger (Paris: Klincksieck, 1986), 124. Further references to
this edition are cited parenthetically in the text in translation.

66. Quoted by Calinescu, *Five Faces of Modernity,* 170.

67. Havelock Ellis, *The New Spirit* (Washington, D.C.: National Home Library, 1935), 240.

68. Sonn, *Anarchism and Cultural Politics,* 294, 295.

69. Renee Weingarten, *Writers and Revolution: The Fatal Lure of Action* (New
York: New Viewpoints, 1974), 220.

70. For an extended discussion of anarchism and decadence, see Sonn,
Anarchism and Cultural Politics, "Conclusion: Anarchy or Decadence?" (290–
301), and Winegarten, *Writers and Revolution,* chap. 14, "Literary Decadence and
Revolutionary Anarchism" (213–28).

71. Ellis, *The New Spirit,* 246. The reference to an anarchistic form of society
is made in the introduction to his book and is quoted earlier in this chapter in

the discussion of egoism. Further references to this edition are cited parenthetically in the text.

72. Sonn, *Anarchism and Cultural Politics*, 297.

73. Matthew Arnold, *Culture and Anarchy*, ed. J. Dover Wilson (Cambridge: Cambridge University Press, 1935), 10, 131. Further references to this edition are cited parenthetically in the text.

74. Walter Pater, *Selected Writings of Walter Pater*, ed. Harold Bloom (New York: Columbia University Press, 1974), 17. Further references to this edition are cited parenthetically in the text.

75. See Raymond Williams, *Culture and Society* (New York: Columbia University Press, 1983), 140, 240, 263–64.

76. Albert Shaw, *Icaria: A Chapter in the History of Communism* (New York: Putnam, 1884; rep., Philadelphia: Porcupine, 1972), 13.

77. Etienne Cabet, *Voyage en Icarie*, 5th ed. (Paris, 1848; repr. Clifton, N.J.: Augustus M. Kelley, 1973), 2: "—Quel est cet ouvrage? dit-il en le prenant pour l'examiner. Quel beau papier! quelle manifique impression! Quoi, c'est une *grammaire!*—Oui, une grammaire et un dictionnaire, lui répon-dis-je; et réjouis-sez-vous! Vous vous plaignez souvent de l'obstacle qu'apportent au progrès des lumières la multiplicité et l'imperfection des langues: eh bien, voici une *langue* parfaitement rationnelle, régulière et simple, qui s'écrit comme elle se parle, et se prononce comme elle s'écrit; dont les règles sont en très-petit nombre, et sans aucune exception; dont tous les mots, régulièrement composés d'un petit nombre de *racines* seulement, ont une signification parfaitment définie, dont la grammaire et le dictionnaire sont tellement simples qu'ils sont contenus dans ce mince volume, et dont l'étude est si facile qu'un homme quelconque peut l'apprendre en quatre ou cinq mois."

78. While the political logic of a universal language was most appealing to the socialist mind, the anarchists also pursued Esperanto as part of a more general effort to render the revolution an international event. The young anarchists of the Modern School in New York, for example, studied Esperanto, "[l]earning to write and sing as well as read it, they corresponded with children in other countries and were taken to Esperanto conventions." Paul Avrich, *The Modern School Movement: Anarchism and Education in the United States* (Princeton: Princeton University Press, 1980), 108.

79. Oscar Wilde, *Complete Works of Oscar Wilde* (New York: Harper and Row, 1989), 1080. Further references to this edition are cited parenthetically in the text.

80. In the 16 May 1891 number of *Liberty*, Benjamin Tucker notes the absurdity of Wilde's contention: "Every day I meet some new man who tells me that Anarchy is the ultimate, but that is to be reached through State Socialism." He also quotes a socialist sympathizer named Powderly to drive home the point: "Oscar Wilde declares that Socialism will lead to individualism. That is like saying that the way from St. Louis to New York is through San Francisco, or that the sure way to whitewash a wall is to paint it black. The man who says that Socialism will fail and then the people will try individualism—*i.e.*, Anarchy—

may be mistaken; the man who thinks they are one and the same is simply a fool." Benjamin R. Tucker, *Instead of a Book by a Man Too Busy to Write One: A Fragmentary Exposition of Philosophical Anarchism* (New York: Benjamin Tucker, 1893; repr., New York: Arno, 1972), 379.

81. Jean Pierrot, *The Decadent Imagination, 1880–1900,* trans. Derek Coltman (Chicago: University of Chicago Press, 1981), 253.

82. Allan Sillitoe, introduction to Robert Tressell, *The Ragged Trousered Philanthropists* (New York: Monthly Review Press, 1962), 1. Sillitoe explains the title of this novel, which is about "a group of painters and decorators, and their families," by noting that the main character, Owen, "tries with marvelous patience and tenacity to enlighten his workmates, to tell them how socialism could level out riches and give them not only a little more to live on, but also real hope of alleviating their inequalities for good. They won't listen, so he calls them philanthropists, benefactors in ragged trousers who willingly hand over the results of their labor to the employers and the rich. . . . This theme is the soul of the novel" (1).

83. Richard Ellmann, *James Joyce,* rev. ed. (New York: Oxford University Press, 1982), 383–84.

Chapter 6: Artists

1. Henrik Ibsen, *The Correspondence of Henrik Ibsen,* trans. Mary Morison (1905; repr., New York: Haskell House, 1970), 208–9. Letter dated 17 February 1871.

2. Peter Watts, introduction to *A Doll's House and Other Plays* (New York: Viking Penguin, 1965), 18.

3. Quoted by Halfdan Gregersen, *Ibsen and Spain: A Study in Comparative Drama* (Cambridge: Harvard University Press, 1936), 16.

4. The performance history of *Ghosts* is taken from Gregersen, *Ibsen and Spain,* 16–19.

5. Quoted by Gregersen, *Ibsen and Spain,* 25: "Je me préoccupe tout de suite après le retentissement, décidément considérable, des *Revenants,* malgré l'incomprehension du public et des plaisanteries hostiles de Sarcey, de frapper un second coup avec une autre oeuvre d'Ibsen."

6. Gregersen, *Ibsen and Spain,* 24.

7. Joan Ungersma Halperin, *Félix Fénéon: Aesthete and Anarchist in Fin-de-Siècle Paris* (New Haven: Yale University Press, 1988), 293.

8. Richard D. Sonn, *Anarchism and Cultural Politics in Fin de Siècle France* (Lincoln: University of Nebraska Press, 1989), 75.

9. Havelock Ellis, *The New Spirit* (Washington, D.C.: National Home Library, 1935), 130.

10. Edmund Wilson, *Axel's Castle: A Study in the Imaginative Literature of 1870–1930* (New York: Scribner, 1931), 24.

11. Sonn, *Anarchism and Cultural Politics,* 75–76.

12. Ibid., 76.

13. Henrik Ibsen, *An Enemy of the People*, in *Ibsen: Four Major Plays*, trans. Rolf Fjelde (New York: Signet, 1970), 163.

14. Halperin, *Félix Fénéon*, 263.

15. Gregersen, *Ibsen and Spain*, 51–52.

16. Salvador Madariaga, *Spain* (New York: Scribner, 1930), 205; quoted by Gregersen, *Ibsen and Spain*, 54 n. 2.

17. Gregersen, *Ibsen and Spain*, 56–57.

18. Ibid., 53.

19. Ibid., 54.

20. Ibid.

21. Quoted in ibid., 56.

22. Paul Avrich, *The Modern School Movement: Anarchism and Education in the United States* (Princeton: Princeton University Press, 1980), 45.

23. Emma Goldman, *Anarchism and Other Essays* (New York: Dover, 1969), 256.

24. Ibid., 255.

25. Ibid., 253.

26. Ibid., 257, 259.

27. Halperin, *Félix Fénéon*, 319–20.

28. Goldman, *Anarchism*, 241.

29. James Joyce, *The Critical Writings of James Joyce*, ed. Ellsworth Mason and Richard Ellmann (New York: Viking, 1959), 48. Further references to this edition are cited parenthetically in the text with the abbreviation *CW*.

30. Robert Spoo, *Joyce and the Language of History: Dedalus's Nightmare* (New York: Oxford University Press, 1994), 152.

31. James Joyce, *Stephen Hero*, ed. Theodore Spencer (New York: New Directions, 1963), 85. Further references to this edition are cited parenthetically in the text with the abbreviation *SH*.

32. James Joyce, *A Portrait of the Artist as a Young Man* (New York: Viking, 1964), 221. Further references to this edition are cited parenthetically in the text with the abbreviation *P*.

33. Dominic Manganiello, *Joyce's Politics* (London: Routledge and Kegan Paul, 1980), 221.

34. Richard Ellmann, *James Joyce*, rev. ed. (New York: Oxford University Press, 1982), 274.

35. Manganiello cites this remark and gives the following source: "Jacob Schwartz at a meeting of the James Joyce Society recorded by *Folkways Records*, 1960 (Gotham Book Mart)." See *Joyce's Politics*, 74 and 239 n. 15.

36. Frank Budgen, *James Joyce and the Making of "Ulysses"* (Oxford: Oxford University Press, 1989), 192.

37. Manganiello, *Joyce's Politics*, 72, 74.

38. Ibid., 222.

39. James Joyce, *Selected Letters of James Joyce*, ed. Richard Ellmann (New York: Viking, 1975), 151–52. Further references to this edition are cited parenthetically in the text with the abbreviation *SL*.

290 Notes to Pages 214–220

40. Jane Ford, "James Joyce's Trieste Library: Some Notes on Its Use," in *Joyce at Texas: Essays on the James Joyce Materials at the Humanities Research Center,* ed. Dave Oliphant and Thomas Zigal (Austin: Humanities Research Center, 1983), 156.

41. Ibid., 150–51.

42. Ibid., 155. Ford quotes this sentence from the first page of Joyce's copy of *God and the State* (London: Freedom Press, 1910)—"Yes, the whole history of humanity, intellectual and moral, political and social, is but a reflection of its economic history"—and urges comparison with this passage from the "Eumaeus" chapter of *Ulysses:* "All those wretched quarrels, in his [Bloom's] humble opinion, . . . erroneously supposed to be about a punctilio of honor and the flag, were very largely a question of the money question which was at the back of everything greed and jealousy, people never knowing when to stop." James Joyce, *Ulysses,* ed. Hans Walter Gabler (New York: Random House, 1986), 526. Further references to this edition are cited parenthetically in the text with the abbreviation *U.*

43. Don Gifford with Robert J. Seidman, *"Ulysses" Annotated: Notes for James Joyce's "Ulysses,"* rev. ed. (Berkeley and Los Angeles: University of California Press, 1988), 140.

44. Robert Spoo, *James Joyce and the Language of History,* 20.

45. "Born as Johann Caspar Schmidt on 25 October 1806 in Bayreuth, . . . 'Stirner' was a childhood nickname (referring to his large forehead, exaggerated by the way in which he parted his hair) that he subsequently adopted as a literary pseudonym and then as his preferred name." David Leopold, introduction to *The Ego and Its Own* (Cambridge: Cambridge University Press, 1995), xii.

46. Max Stirner, *The Ego and Its Own,* 35.

47. Spoo, *James Joyce and the Language of History,* 20.

48. James Joyce, "A Portrait of the Artist," in *"A Portrait of the Artist as a Young Man": Text, Criticism, and Notes,* ed. Chester G. Anderson (New York: Viking Penguin, 1977), 265–66.

49. Quoted by Manganiello, *Joyce's Politics,* 70.

50. For a discussion of this element of Joyce, see chapter 5, "Organic Narrative," of my *James Joyce and the Art of Mediation* (Ann Arbor: University of Michigan Press, 1996).

51. Joyce, "A Portrait of the Artist," 262.

52. Stanislaus Joyce, *The Complete Dublin Diary,* ed. George H. Healey (Ithaca: Cornell University Press, 1971), 54.

53. Richard Ellmann, *James Joyce,* 239.

54. For a discussion of *Dubliners* and socialism, see Paul Delany, "Joyce: Political Development and the Aesthetic of *Dubliners,*" in *The Artist and Political Vision,* ed. Benjamin R. Barber and Michael J. Gargas McGrath (New Brunswick N.J.: Transaction, 1982), 221–31.

55. Raymond Williams, *Culture and Society: 1780–1950* (New York: Columbia University Press, 1983), 291.

56. In *Joyce's Politics,* Manganiello presents Joyce's early politics as a mélange of socialism and anarchism (71, 88). In a later article, however, Manganiello

places greater emphasis on Joyce's interest in anarchism: see "The Politics of the Unpolitical in Joyce's Fictions," *James Joyce Quarterly* 29 (1992): 241–58.

57. Lionel Trilling, "James Joyce in His Letters," *Commentary* 45 (February 1968); repr. in *James Joyce: A Collection of Critical Essays*, ed. William M. Chace (Englewood Cliffs, N.J.: Prentice Hall, 1974), 158. Cited by Jeffrey Segall, "Between Marxism and Modernism, or How to be a Revolutionist and Still Love *Ulysses*," *James Joyce Quarterly* 25 (1988): 421. Segall observes that Edmund Wilson and Irving Howe join Trilling in their approval of the progressive politics of *Ulysses*.

58. A recent example of this emphasis comes from Marilyn French's introduction to a new edition of *The Book as World:* "A structure in which nothing dominates is anarchical: *Finnegans Wake* is an anarchic text. Nothing governs, not even a single language with the worldview implicit in it. Anarchy . . . has often been used to denote lawlessness or chaos, but it denotes a structure in which no element dominates any other." *The Book as World: James Joyce's "Ulysses"* (New York: Paragon House, 1993), xx. Both Ellmann and Herbert Gorman, Joyce's first biographer, present a modulation in Joyce's politics from socialism to anarchism. On this point, the biographers are in agreement with those critics of Joyce who emphasize the politics of style and the revolution of language. Ellmann refers to an entry in a portion of Stanislaus's diary as yet unpublished, dated 11 April 1907, in which Stanislaus records that Joyce shifted his politico-artistic allegiance from socialism to anarchism, "prefer[ing] to say that like Ibsen, he was an anarchist, though not a practical anarchist after what he called the modern style" (*James Joyce*, 239, 768 n. 71). This paraphrase of Stanislaus's diary is consistent with Joyce's letter postmarked 10 January 1907 containing the sardonic epiphany of the anarchist (*SL*, 142). Gorman refers to the "anarchistic conception of the unfettered mind" and says that Joyce's "intellectual anarchy . . . had little or nothing to do with Karl Marx." He also claims that "it would be absurd to insist that [Joyce] was a Marxian or that he acquiesced in any degree to the principle that individual freedom should be subordinated to the interests of the community." See Herbert Gorman, *James Joyce* (New York: Farrar and Reinhart, 1939), 193.

59. Benjamin R. Tucker, *Instead of a Book by a Man Too Busy to Write One: A Fragmentary Exposition of Philosophical Anarchism* (New York: Benjamin Tucker, 1893; repr., New York: Arno Press, 1972), 379.

60. J. L. Joynes, "Dynamite and Despair," *Justice: The Organ of the Social Democracy* 21, no. 1 (7 June 1884): 4.

61. Cover advertisement for *Benj. R. Tucker's Unique Catalogue of Advanced Literature* (New York: Benjamin Tucker, 1907). Benjamin Tucker Collection, New York Public Library.

62. William Morris, *Art and Society: Lectures and Essays by William Morris*, ed. Gary Zabel (Boston: George's Hill, 1990), 22. Further references to this collection are cited parenthetically in the text.

63. Oscar Wilde, *Complete Works of Oscar Wilde* (New York: Harper and Row, 1989), 1087. Further references to this edition are cited parenthetically in the text.

292 Notes to Pages 222–231

64. Stanislaus Joyce, *The Complete Dublin Diary*, 54.

65. On the topic of gradualism, Manganiello notes in *Joyce's Politics* that Joyce was drawn to the syndicalist Labriola, who reminded him "somewhat of Griffith," whose Sinn Fein movement and antiparliamentarianism chimed with the anarchist wish for immediate revolution. Indeed, the English socialist press had long referred to the Fenians as anarchists. "Joyce's choice of [the syndicalist] Labriola" over the more conventional socialist Ferri "indicated his impatience with gradualism" (66).

66. Fredric Jameson, *"Ulysses* in History," in *James Joyce and Modern Literature*, ed. W. J. McCormack and Alistair Stead (London: Routledge, 1982), 131.

67. Williams, *Culture and Society*, 140, 240.

68. Walter Pater, *Selected Writings of Walter Pater*, ed. Harold Bloom (New York: Columbia University Press, 1974), 112, 113.

69. See Giorgio Melchiori, "The Genesis of *Ulysses,"* in *Joyce in Rome: The Genesis of "Ulysses,"* ed. Giorgio Melchiori (Rome: Bulzoni Editore, 1984), 44–45.

70. Tucker, *Instead of a Book*, 15.

71. Friedrich Engels, *The Origin of the Family, Private Property, and the State*, cited in *Literature and Art by Karl Marx and Frederick Engels: Selections from their Writings* (New York: International Publishers, 1947), 71.

72. Ibid., 70.

73. James Joyce, *Exiles: A Play in Three Acts* (New York: Penguin, 1977), 150. Further references to his edition are cited parenthetically in the text.

74. See Dominic Manganiello, "Anarch, Heresiarch, Egoarch," in Melchiori, *Joyce in Rome*, 101–2.

75. Ellmann, *James Joyce*, 359.

76. Herschel B. Chipp, *Theories of Modern Art: A Source Book by Artists and Critics* (Berkely and Los Angeles: University of California Press, 1968), 368.

77. Robert Short, "Dada and Surrealism," in *Modernism: A Guide to European Literature, 1890–1930*, ed. Malcolm Bradbury and James McFarlane (New York: Penguin, 1991), 294.

78. Quoted by Hans Richter, *Dada: Art and Anti-Art* (New York: Oxford University Press, 1965), 74, 76.

79. Anson Rabinbach, introduction to Hugo Ball, *Critique of the German Intelligentsia*, trans. Brian L. Harris (New York: Columbia University Press, 1993), xi.

80. Philip Mann, *Hugo Ball: An Intellectual Biography* (London: Institute of Germanic Studies, 1987), 15–16. Further references to this work are cited parenthetically in the text.

81. Rabinbach, introduction to *Critique*, xi-xii.

82. Hugo Ball, *Flight Out of Time: A Dada Diary*, trans. Ann Raimes (Berkeley and Los Angeles: University of California Press, 1996), 10–11. Further references to this work, and to Ball's "Kandinsky" lecture appended to it, are cited parenthetically in the text.

83. John Elderfield, introduction to *Flight Out of Time*, xxxvii.

84. Fritz Brupbacher, *Marx und Bakunin* (Munich, 1913), 87. Quoted by Mann, *Hugo Ball*, 57.

85. Ball does not mention readings from Voltaire in his diary, but the *Neue Zürcher Zeitung* for 9 February 1916 reported that extracts from the philosopher's writings were read on the cabaret's opening night. See Mann, *Hugo Ball*, 83.

86. For the German text, see Hugo Ball, *Die Flucht aus der Zeit* (Zürich: Limmat, 1992), 80.

87. Quoted by Richter, *Dada*, 14–15. "Es soll die Aktivität und die Interessen des Cabarets bezeichnene, dessen ganze Absicht darauf gerichtet ist, über den Krieg und die Vaterländer hinweg an die wenigen Unabhüngigen zu erinnern, die anderen Idealen leben."

88. Philip Mann, *Hugo Ball*, states that Bakunin was "associated in Ball's mind with Quixote," partly because Fritz Brupbacher's biography of Bakunin portrayed him in that way. The identification was made because Bakunin rebelled against "all scientific and manmade systems," just as Don Quixote refused to accept reality as it was. In his diary, Ball also links Don Quixote with the spontaneous spirit of dada (141, 57).

89. Richter, *Dada*, 44.

90. For the reproduction of the program for the 14 July 1916 dada-soiree, see Ball, *Flight Out of Time*, 74.

91. The poem is cited by Richter, *Dada*, 42, in the following form, which contains the "African" words "rhinocerossola," "zimzalla," and "gadjama":

gadji beri bimba glandridi laula lonni cadori
gadjama gramma berida bimbala glandri galassassa laulitalomini
gadji beri bin blassa glassala laula lonni cadorsu sassala bim
Gadjama tuffm i zimzalla bibban gligia wowolimai bin beri ban
o katalominal rhinocerossola hopsamen laulitalomini hooo gadjama
rhinocerossola hopsamen
bluku terullala blaulala looooo. . . .

92. Ibid., 42.

93. Rabinbach, introduction to *Critique*, xiv.

94. See Mann, *Hugo Ball*, 90, for a discussion of this aspect of the poem, even though comparisons to *The Waste Land* are not made directly.

95. T. S. Eliot, *"Ulysses*, Order and Myth," in *James Joyce: The Critical Heritage*, 2 vols., ed. Robert H. Deming (London: Routledge and Kegan Paul, 1970), 1:270.

96. Short, "Dada and Surrealism," 306.

97. Chipp, *Theories of Modern Art*, 369.

98. Quoted in ibid., 410.

99. Short, "Dada and Surrealism," 305.

100. André Breton and Leon Trotsky, "Manifesto: Towards a Free Revolutionary Art," in Chipp, *Theories of Modern Art*, 485.

101. Walter Benjamin, *Reflections: Essays, Aphorisms, Autobiographical Writ-*

ings, trans. Edmund Jephcott (New York: Harcourt Brace Jovanovich, 1978), 182. Subsequent references to this edition are cited parenthetically in the text.

102. Lautréamont, *"Maldoror" and the Complete Works of the Comte de Lautréamont*, trans. Alexis Lykiard (Cambridge: Exact Change, 1994), 259. Letter to Auguste Poulet-Malassis dated 27 October [1869]. For the French text, see *Œuvres complètes*, ed. Pierre-Olivier Walzer (Paris: Gallimard, 1970), 297. Since this letter is addressed to the publisher who will act as distributor of the novel, the remark about the problem of evil makes the point that a possible audience for such a topic exists. Subsequent references to Lautréamont's work in Lykiard's translation are cited parenthetically in the text; references to the original French are cited in brackets.

103. Remy de Gourmont, "Lautréamont," trans. Richard Aldington, *The Egoist* 1, no. 16 (15 August 1914): 308, 309.

104. Spoo, *James Joyce and the Language of History*, 20.

105. William Blake, *America: A Prophecy*, in *The Complete Poetry and Prose of William Blake*, rev. ed., ed. David V. Erdman (Garden City, N.Y.: Anchor, 1982), 53–54. Spelling and punctuation normalized.

106. Lykiard, introduction to *Maldoror*, 24.

107. Ibid., 313 n. 78.

108. Ibid., 309–10 n. 56.

109. This sketch of Spanish anarchism has been compiled from James Joll, *The Anarchists* (Boston: Little, Brown, 1964), 101–2, 224–74, and Richard D. Sonn, *Anarchism* (New York: Twayne, 1992), 69–98. See also Temma Kaplan, *Anarchists of Andalusia, 1868–1903* (Princeton: Princeton University Press, 1977).

110. Joan Mellen, preface to *The World of Luis Buñuel: Essays in Criticism* (New York: Oxford University Press, 1978), viii.

111. José de la Colina and Tomás Pérez Turrent, *Objects of Desire: Conversations with Luis Buñuel*, trans. Paul Lenti (New York: Marsilio, 1992), 7, 9. Further references to this work are cited parenthetically in the text with the abbreviation *OD*.

112. Luis Buñuel, *My Last Sigh*, trans. Abigail Israel (New York: Vintage, 1984), 154, 138.

113. Ibid., 155.

114. Luis Buñuel, "Poetry and Cinema," in *The World of Luis Buñuel*, ed. Joan Mellen, 110.

115. Quoted by Donald Richie, "The Moral Code of Luis Buñuel," in *The World of Luis Buñuel*, ed. Joan Mellen, 111.

116. Luis Buñuel, "Notes on the Making of *Un Chien Andalou*," in *The World of Luis Buñuel*, ed. Joan Mellon, 152.

117. Buñuel insisted that the title was not arbitrary (ibid.) and denied the explanation offered by Francisco Aranda, who says that the future filmmaker "applied the name 'perros andaluces' in the Residencia to Andalusian Modernist poets who were insensible to the revolutionary poetry of social content praised by Buñuel long before anyone else in Spain." See *Luis Buñuel: A Critical Biography*, trans. David Robinson (New York: Da Capo, 1976), 46 n. In an inter-

view Buñuel said of Aranda's interpretation, "That's not it at all. People find whatever allusions they want when they're determined to find references to themselves." He is referring here to Federico García Lorca, a native of Andalusia who, according to Buñuel, is supposed to have said: " 'Buñuel has made a tiny pile of shit called *Un chien andalou,* and the Andalusian dog is me.' But that wasn't it. *Un chien andalou* was the title of a book of poems I wrote" (*OD,* 14). It must be noted that Buñuel does not explain why he called his book of poetry *El perro andaluz* in the first place. Since Buñuel was notorious in interviews for his reluctance to ascribe conscious intent to many of his artistic choices, his evasiveness on the topic of his film's title suggests that Aranda may be on to something. My own suggestion that the reference to Andalusia may also be a reference to anarchism is purely speculative, and is not intended as an explanation.

118. Aranda, *Luis Buñuel: A Critical Biography,* 60. The other priest is Salvador Dalí.

119. Diego Camacho, "My Experience in the 'Nature School': A Living Memory of Rational Pedagogy," trans. Abe Bluestein, *The Modern School Movement: Historical and Personal Notes on the Ferrer Schools in Spain* (Croton-on-Hudson, N.Y.: Friends of the Modern School, 1990), 25.

Afterword

1. Quoted by Robert Nye, "Savage Crowds, Modernism, and Modern Politics," in *Prehistories of the Future: The Primitivist Project and the Culture of Modernism* (Stanford: Stanford University Press, 1995), 48.

2. Nye, "Savage Crowds," 49.

3. Thomas Mann, *Reflections of a Nonpolitical Man,* trans. Walter D. Morris (New York: Ungar, 1983), 426. Mann's criticism of D'Annunzio's enthusiastic support of World War I is scathing: "D'Annunzio, the aper of Wagner, the ambitious word-reveler whose talent 'rings all the bells,' and to whom Latin character and nationalism form just a means of effect and enthusiasm, the irresponsible adventurer who wanted his ecstasy and his great hour, his 'historical moment,' his marriage with the people, and nothing more—one took him seriously, one took the artist seriously as a politician, in a fateful hour for the country! The artist as panegyrist of war."

4. Walter Benjamin, "The Work of Art in the Age of Mechanical Reproduction," in *Illuminations,* trans. Harry Zohn (New York: Schocken, 1969), 242. Benjamin's argument that fascism has the power to aestheticize politics refers, in part, to the manipulation of such forms of "mechanical reproduction" as film to work its will on the masses to make the experience of mass politics an aesthetic sensation: "[Mankind's] self-alienation has reached such a degree that it can experience its own destruction as an aesthetic pleasure of the first order. This is the situation of politics which Fascism is rendering aesthetic. Communism responds by politicizing art."

5. David Gross, *The Past in Ruins: Tradition and the Critique of Modernity* (Amherst: University of Massachusetts Press, 1992), 42, 53.

6. Greil Marcus, *Lipstick Traces: A Secret History of the Twentieth Century* (Cambridge: Harvard University Press, 1989), 18–19.

7. Richard D. Sonn, *Anarchism and Cultural Politics in Fin de Siècle France* (Lincoln: University of Nebraska Press, 1989), 68.

8. Fredric Jameson, *Postmodernism; or, The Cultural Logic of Late Capitalism* (Durham: Duke University Press, 1991), 4. Further references to this edition are cited parenthetically in the text.

9. Murray Bookchin, *Social Anarchism or Lifestyle Anarchism: An Unbridgeable Chasm* (Edinburgh: AK Press, 1995), 12–13. Further references to this edition are cited parenthetically in the text.

10. Hakim Bey, *T.A.Z.: The Temporary Autonomous Zone, Ontological Anarchy, Poetic Terrorism* (New York: Autonomedia, 1991), 4. Further references to this edition are cited parenthetically in the text as *TAZ*.

11. Margaret Anderson, *My Thirty Years' War* (New York: Covici, Friede, 1930), 190. See also my discussion at the end of Chapter 4.

INDEX

Abbot, Leonard D., 140, 141, 153

Acín, Ramón, 253

Adam, Paul, 123, 129, 189

Adorno, Theodor, 162–65

Adventures of Caleb Williams, The (Godwin), 34, 88, 92–101, 115, 150

Aesthetics, 34–40, 88–89, 91–92, 100, 142, 143, 145–46, 149–50, 153, 157, 161–69, 170, 175, 177, 181–82, 185, 188, 188–90, 191, 193, 200, 201, 205, 211, 214, 220, 224, 227, 233–34, 255–56, 266–67

Age d'Or, L' (Buñuel), 250, 252–53, 254, 255

Agueíl, Ivan, 127

Aldington, Richard, 179

Alexander II, 70, 76

Alfonso XII, 248

Alfonso XIII, 134

Allen, Grant, 107–8; *Woman Who Did, The*, 107–8

America: A Prophecy (Blake), 243

American Scene, The (James), 73

Anarchism, 3–10, 11–15, 16, 49–50, 52–53, 58, 61, 62, 70–72, 75, 76–77, 78–79, 82–83, 84–86, 88, 91, 94–95, 96, 101, 103, 111, 115, 118, 119, 120, 122, 130, 147, 154, 184, 190, 198, 199, 200, 203, 205, 213, 215, 219, 220–27, 230, 231, 232–33, 234, 238, 239, 240, 241, 242, 244–45, 248–49, 250, 256, 260, 262, 263, 267; and avant-gardism, 160–62; and Mikhail Bakunin, 27–29; and decadence, 190–91; defined, 5, 11–12, 13–15; and egoism, 154–56, 169, 170, 177, 179–80, 216; and Enlightenment, 13–14, 15, 21, 26–27; and Fenianism, 71–72, 75; and William Godwin, 19–21; and Peter Kropotkin, 29–32; and modernism, 5, 7, 8, 9, 33, 52, 86, 87, 135, 142, 143, 145–46, 148, 150, 157, 158, 160–62, 163, 164–69, 173, 177, 178, 200–201, 260, 261; and Paris Commune, 120–22; and postmodernism, 264–67; and Pierre-Joseph Proudhon, 21–26; and religious dissent, 49–50, 62; and romanticism, 13–15, 21, 26–28; and Jean-Jacques Rousseau, 15, 18; and syndicalism, 112, 115, 135, 249; and terrorism (propaganda by the deed), 76–77, 111, 113, 115, 124, 215, 234

Anderson, Margaret, 150, 151–57, 168, 177, 189, 191, 261, 266

Anderson, Sir Robert, 75

Anderson, Sherwood, 151

Antoine, André, 203, 204, 205

"Appeal to the Young, An" (Kropotkin), 40, 103

Archer, William, 203, 207

Arnold, Matthew, 6, 41, 42–52, 53, 60, 62, 73–74, 80, 87, 152, 181, 183, 192–93, 259, 260, 267; *Culture and Anarchy*, 6, 42–52, 73, 87, 192; "Empedocles on Etna," 52; "Function of Criticism, The," 50, 73, 192; "Stanzas from the Grande Chartreuse," 62

Arp, Jean, 228

Art for art's sake, 63, 143, 152, 153, 163, 168, 233

Atomism, 194–96, 217, 220, 223–24

Avant-gardism, 2, 117, 121, 131, 143, 150,
    158–62, 188, 201, 202, 210, 229, 249,
    255, 256, 260

Baju, Anatole, 188
Bakunin, Mikhail, 6, 8, 14, 27–29, 31, 32,
    33, 34, 39–40, 53–60, 70, 85, 103, 109,
    111, 117, 129, 150, 161, 169, 172, 175,
    195, 206, 214, 215, 221, 230, 231, 232,
    234, 240, 248, 250, 264, 265
Ball, Hugo, 177, 185–86, 229–38, 256
Balzac, Honoré de, 114, 115, 148
Barrès, Maurice, 189
Baudelaire, Charles, 141, 161, 169, 174,
    186–87, 196
Beckett, Samuel, 86, 163, 202
Beethoven, Ludwig van, 39
Bellows, George, 142, 145
Benjamin, Walter, 163, 164, 236, 239–40,
    241, 247, 248, 262
Bentham, Jeremy, 101
Berkman, Alexander, 144, 152–53
Blake, William, 14, 140, 215, 242–43, 244;
    America: A Prophecy, 243
Blanc, Louis, 23
Blanqui, Jérôme-Adolphe, 23
Blanqui, Louis Auguste, 71
Bobrikoff, Nikolai Ivanovich, 215
Bohemianism, 1, 119, 140
Bomb, The (Harris), 88, 110–15
Bookchin, Murray, 262, 265–67
Borges, Jorge Luis, 250
Bourdin, Martial, 75, 104
Bourget, Paul, 148, 187–89
Boyesen, Bayard, 136, 137
Brandes, Georg, 173, 203
Brecht, Bertolt, 202
Breton, André, 1–4, 121, 164, 238–40,
    247, 251, 256, 262
Brupbacher, Fritz, 230, 231, 232, 233,
    234
Bruyas, Alfred, 38
Budgen, Frank, 213
Buñuel, Luis, 6, 249–58; *Age d'Or, L',* 250,
    252–53, 254, 255; *Chien Andalou, Un,*
    251–52, 253, 254, 255; *Hurdes, Las,* 253–
    55, 256; *Olvidados, Los,* 251; *That Obscure
    Object of Desire,* 251
Burke, Edmund, 92–93, 94, 95, 96, 98–99,
    100
Byington, Steven T., 154, 172

Byrne, Geoffrey, 106
Byron, Lord, 140, 169

Cabet, Etienne, 196–97, 236
Camacho, Diego, 135
Cánovas del Castillo, Premier Antonio,
    76
Cantwell, Tom, 106
Capitalism, 23, 39, 73, 166–67, 195, 262–
    64, 265, 267
Carlyle, Thomas, 47, 114
Carnot, President Sadi, 76, 124
Carpenter, Edward, 178, 189
Caserio, Santo, 124
Cavendish, Lord Frederick, 72
Cézanne, Paul, 143
Chamber Music (Joyce), 222
Chants de Maldoror, Les (Lautréamont),
    240–42, 243–45, 247
Chartism, 48
Chateaubriand, François René, vicomte
    de, 14
Chatel, Charles, 125
Chernyshevsky, N. G., 148
Chesterton, C. K., 52, 53, 83; *Man Who Was
    Thursday, The,* 52, 53, 83
Chien Andalou, Un (Buñuel), 251–52, 253,
    254, 255
Clair, René, 256; *Entr'acte,* 256
Claudel, Paul, 1
Coeurderoy, Ernest, 129
Colum, Padraic, 218
Communism, 23, 121, 147, 239, 250, 256,
    261, 262
Conrad, Joseph, 41, 52, 53, 74–86, 87, 88,
    104, 214; *Secret Agent, The,* 41, 52, 53,
    74–84, 88, 104, 214
Conservatism, 5, 9–10, 12, 13, 82, 85, 92–
    93, 184, 190, 223, 259
Corot, Camille, 121
Courbet, Gustave, 2, 38–39, 120, 145,
    238
Crane, Hart, 142
Culture and Anarchy (Arnold), 6, 42–52, 73,
    87, 192

Dada, 3, 40, 227–35, 238, 246, 251, 264
Dalí, Salvador, 251, 255–56
D'Annunzio, Gabriele, 147, 150, 173, 261–
    62
Dante Alighieri, 226

Darwin, Charles, 29, 32, 241–42
Daudet, Léon, 1
Daumier, Honoré, 121
Dave, Victor, 71
David, Jacques-Louis, 2
Debord, Guy, 40
Decadence, 148, 183–84, 186–91, 193, 194, 196, 223–24
de Cleyre, Voltairine, 139
Defense of Poetry, A (Shelley), 89–91, 116
Degas, Edgar, 121
Dejacque, Joseph, 129
Denis, Pierre, 121
Derby, Lord, 46
Diderot, Denis, 129, 131, 174
Discourse on the Origin of Inequality (Second Discourse) (Rousseau), 15, 17–18, 19, 20, 22, 24, 32
Disraeli, Benjamin, 46, 47
Doll's House, A (Ibsen), 203, 204, 206, 208
Dostoyevsky, Fyodor, 6, 41, 52, 53, 58–62, 74, 86, 87, 240, 259; *Possessed, The,* 6, 41, 52, 53, 58–61, 74, 240
Dreyfus affair, 209
Drumont, Edouard, 123
Dubliners (Joyce), 200, 219, 220, 222, 223, 227
Duchamp, Marcel, 228
Durant, Ariel, 138
Durant, Will, 137–38, 140

Eagleton, Terry, 3, 164–65, 220, 265
Ego and Its Own, The (Stirner), 146, 154
Egoism, 146, 147, 154–56, 168, 169, 170–77, 179–82, 194, 206, 213, 216, 221, 242, 262, 266, 267
Einzige und sein Eingentum, Der. See *Ego and Its Own, The*
Eisenstein, Sergey Mikhaylovich, 185
Elias, Juan Puig, 135, 253
Eliot, T. S., 52, 179, 181, 185, 201, 237
Elizabeth, Empress of Austria, 76
Ellis, Havelock, 173–74, 182, 188, 189–90, 205, 207
Eltzbacher, Paul, 146, 171, 174
Emerson, Ralph Waldo, 132, 140, 172
"Empedocles on Etna" (Arnold), 52
Enemy of the People, An (Ibsen), 205–7, 209, 211
Engels, Friedrich, 14–15, 33, 225, 250, 256

Enlightenment, 13–14, 15, 21, 26–27, 29, 32, 33, 37, 38, 131, 169, 171, 190–91, 241, 266
Enquiry Concerning Political Justice (Godwin), 19–21, 34, 35–37, 92, 96, 97, 98–99
Entr'acte (Clair), 256
Escuela Moderna (Barcelona), 131, 132, 133–34, 135, 249, 254
Exiles, 225, 226
Expressionism, 229, 232, 234, 261

Fanelli, Giuseppe, 248
Fascism, 178, 181, 249, 250, 255, 261, 262
Faure, President Félix, 129
Fawcett, E. Douglas, 82–83, 112; *Hartmann the Anarchist; Or, The Doom of the Great City,* 82–83
Fénéon, Félix, 125–26, 127, 128, 129, 150, 206, 209
Fenianism, 34, 43, 71–72, 75
Ferrer, Francisco, 41, 114, 131–35, 136, 207, 249, 254
Ferrero, Guglielmo, 225
Feuerbach, Ludwig, 27
Fichte, Johann Gottlieb, 27, 28, 55
Finnegans Wake (Joyce), 212, 224, 227
Flaubert, Gustave, 122, 174, 181, 194
Ford, Ford Maddox, 214
Foucault, Michel, 101
Fourier, Charles, 160
France, Anatole, 114, 123
Franco, Francisco, 249
French, Marilyn, 220
Freud, Sigmund, 148, 239, 249, 251, 253
"Function of Criticism, The" (Arnold), 50, 73, 192
Futurism, 234

Garfias, Pedro, 250
Gauguin, Paul, 183
Gautier, Théophile, 186–87, 189, 193, 194, 196, 224
Ghosts (Ibsen), 203–4, 206, 207–8
Gide, André, 173, 185
Gingrich, Newt, 9, 10
Girl among the Anarchists, A (Meredith), 88, 102–9, 110, 115
Gladstone, William Ewart, 46, 47
Godwin, William, 6, 14, 19–21, 26, 27, 34–37, 39, 49, 87, 88, 89, 90, 92–101, 115,

Godwin, William (*continued*)
  117, 132, 150, 169, 172; *Adventures of Caleb Williams, The,* 34, 88, 92–101, 115, 150; *Enquiry Concerning Political Justice,* 19–21, 34, 35–37, 92, 96, 97, 98–99
Goethe, Johann Wolfgang von, 26, 44, 114, 115
Goldman, Emma, 41, 88, 136, 144, 151, 152–53, 154, 155, 156, 157, 158, 161, 170, 184, 191, 208, 209, 210, 211, 260
Goncourt, Edmond de, 122
Goodman, Paul, 266
Gourmont, Remy de, 173, 178
Goya, Francisco, 251
Grave, Jean, 116, 123–27, 129–30, 131, 132, 150, 158, 168, 174, 181, 191, 245, 249
Griffith, Arthur, 218
Gross, Otto, 230

Hakim Bey (Peter Lambon Wilson), 266–68
Harris, Frank, 6, 87, 88, 110–15; *Bomb, The,* 88, 110–15
Hartmann the Anarchist; Or, The Doom of the Great City (Fawcett), 82–83
Hauptmann, Gerhart, 128
Haussmann, Baron Georges-Eugène, 117, 118
Haymarket bombing, 110
Heap, Jane, 189
Hedda Gabler (Ibsen), 206
Hegel, Georg Wilhelm Friedrich, 27, 28, 29, 32, 89, 171
Heine, Heinrich, 34, 114, 115, 174
Hennings, Emmy, 234, 235
Henri, Robert, 142, 145
Henry, Emile, 77, 108, 115, 122, 124, 128
Holcroft, Thomas, 92
Howe, Irving, 5, 84, 220
Howells, William Dean, 114
Huelsenbeck, Richard, 235
Huneker, James, 173, 174–75, 182
Hurdes, Las (Buñuel), 253–55, 256
Huxley, Thomas Henry, 29–30
Huysmans, Joris-Karl, 64, 174, 188, 189

Ibsen, Henrik, 6, 41, 86, 114, 115, 128, 140, 147, 149, 172, 173, 175, 176, 177, 181, 202–10, 211, 212, 214, 217, 218, 219, 247, 250, 260; *Doll's House, A,* 203, 204, 206, 208; *Enemy of the People, An,* 205–7, 209, 211; *Ghosts,* 203–4, 206, 207–8; *Hedda Gabler,* 206; *Pillars of Society, The,* 208–9; *Romersholm,* 204, 208; *When We Dead Awaken,* 210, 211; *Wild Duck, The,* 204
Imagism, 178–79, 181, 190
Ionesco, Eugène, 202

James, Henry, 41, 52, 62–74, 86, 87, 88, 140, 259, 260; *American Scene, The,* 73; *Princess Cassamassima, The,* 41, 52, 62–74, 88, 140
Jameson, Fredric, 3, 7, 223, 264
Janco, Marcel, 235
Joyce, James, 6, 86, 146, 166, 168, 181, 185, 200, 201, 202, 205, 210–27, 242, 257, 261; *Chamber Music,* 222; *Dubliners,* 200, 219, 220, 222, 223, 227; *Exiles,* 225, 226; *Finnegans Wake,* 212, 224, 227; *Portrait of the Artist as a Young Man, A,* 200, 224, 225; *Stephen Hero,* 213, 220, 222, 223, 224, 225; *Ulysses,* 166, 185, 201, 212, 215, 216, 220, 225, 226, 227, 257
Jung, Franz, 230

Kafka, Franz, 86, 101, 163
Kandinsky, Wassily, 233–34, 236
Kant, Immanuel, 27
Kelly, Harry, 144
Kemp, Harry, 144
Kerr, Stewart, 140
Komroff, Manuel, 143
Kristeva, Julia, 220
Kropotkin, Peter, 6, 8, 14, 27, 28, 29–32, 34, 40, 49, 91, 102, 103, 109, 116, 117, 123, 124, 128, 129, 130, 132, 133, 146, 150, 158, 159, 172, 190, 198, 230, 234, 242, 245, 265; "Appeal to the Young, An," 40, 103

Labriola, Arturo, 218, 226
Laforgue, Jules, 128
Lamartine, Alphonse de, 245
Lautréamont, Comte de (Isidore Ducasse), 40, 121, 169, 238, 239, 240–42, 243–47, 248; *Chants de Maldoror, Les,* 240–42, 243–45, 247; *Poésies,* 245–47
Laverdant, Gabriel-Désiré, 160
Le Bon, Gustave, 261

Lenin (Vladimir Ilyich Ulyanov), 9, 231
Leybold, Hans, 229
Liber, Amour, 137
Liberalism, 12, 13, 48–49
Lingg, Louis, 110, 113
Lisbonne, Maxime, 122, 264
Locke, John, 45, 89
Lombroso, Cesar, 78, 176
Louÿs, Pierre, 143
Lowe, Robert, 46
Lowell, Amy, 152
Ludovici, Anthony M., 182–83
Lugné-Poë, Aurélian-Marie, 204, 205
Lukács, Georg, 167

Mackay, John Henry, 154, 172, 230
Maclaren, Malcolm, 264
Madariaga, Salvador, 206
Maeterlinck, Maurice, 140, 143, 144
Malatesta, Errico, 130
Malato, Charles, 133
Mallarmé, Stéphane, 123, 131, 167, 168,
    178, 181, 189, 228, 260
Malquin, Louis, 205
Malraux, André, 2
Mangan, James Clarence, 211
Mann, Thomas, 85, 262
Man Ray, 141, 142, 144
Man Who Was Thursday, The (Chesterton),
    52, 53, 83
Maragall, Juan, 207
Marinetti, F. T., 236
Marsden, Dora, 179–80, 242, 261
Martin, Leon, 133
Marx, Karl, 9, 14–15, 25, 27, 32, 33, 78,
    113, 119, 120, 147, 172, 195, 206, 212,
    217, 218, 221, 222, 231, 239
Marxism, 2, 3, 7, 9, 10, 14, 27, 78, 121,
    147, 161, 166–67, 223, 249, 251
"Mask of Anarchy, The" (Shelley), 90–91
Matisse, Henri, 143, 145
Mauclair, Camille, 205
Maurin, Charles, 189
Mayakovsky, Vladimir Vladimirovich, 2, 3
McKinley, President William, 76
Mencken, H. L., 184–85
Meredith, Isabel. *See* Rossetti sisters
Merezhkovsky, Dmitri, 230
Meunié, Ernestine, 132, 133
Michel, Louise, 120
Mill, John Stewart, 214

Millet, Jean-François, 121
Milton, John, 49, 50, 52, 96, 97, 241, 243
Miratvilles, Jaime, 252
Mirbeau, Octave, 123, 129, 148, 189, 209
Modernism, 5, 7, 8, 33, 52, 86, 87, 135,
    142, 143, 145–46, 148, 150, 157, 158,
    160–62, 163, 164–69, 173, 175, 177, 178,
    181–82, 183, 184–86, 191, 193, 197,
    200–201, 202, 205, 223, 226, 227, 242,
    260, 261–62, 265
Modern School (New York), 136–46
Modot, Gaston, 253
Molinari, Luigi, 226
Moncasi, Juan Olivia, 248
Monet, Claude, 183
More, Thomas, 129
Morral, Mateo, 134
Morris, William, 114, 140, 167, 195–96,
    198, 221–22, 226, 267
Most, Johann, 70, 72, 111
Musset, Alfred de, 245
Mussolini, Benito, 180

Napoléon III, 118, 119, 121, 129
Naturalism, 31–32, 58, 63–64, 204–5, 210,
    211
Nechaev, Sergei, 58–59
Nettlau, Max, 231
Neve, John, 71
New Left, 262
Newman, John Henry, Cardinal, 48
Nicoll, David, 75, 104, 105
Nietzsche, Friedrich Wilhelm, 115, 128,
    140, 146, 147–48, 154, 155, 170, 172,
    173, 174, 175, 176, 177, 178, 182–85,
    194, 206, 210, 224, 229, 230, 232, 233,
    234
Nieuwerkerke, Comte Alfred-Emilien de,
    38
Nihilism, 58, 60, 62, 148, 172, 228
Noailles, Vicomte de, 253
Nordau, Max, 175–77

Olvidados, Los (Buñuel), 251
O'Neill, Eugene, 146, 202
Organicism, 194–96, 197, 198, 217, 223,
    224, 231

Paine, Thomas, 20, 93
Palmerston, Viscount (Henry John
    Temple), 46

Paris Commune, 2, 103, 114, 119–22, 123,
    169, 188, 215, 226, 238, 239
Parsons, Albert, 110
Pasquier, Etienne, 159
Pater, Walter, 181–82, 191–94, 196, 224
Pérez, Pura, 135
Peukert, Josef, 71
Philosophical View of Reform, A (Shelley), 91
Picabia, Francis, 228, 229, 256
Picasso, Pablo, 1, 143, 185, 234
Pillars of Society, The (Ibsen), 208–9
Pirandello, Luigi, 202
Pitt, William, 92, 94, 212
Pi y Margall, Francisco, 248
Plato, 23, 89, 178
Poésies (Lautréamont), 245–47
Portrait of the Artist as a Young Man, A
    (Joyce), 200, 224, 225
Possessed, The (Dostoyevsky), 6, 41, 52, 53,
    58–61, 74, 240
Postmodernism, 9, 10, 160, 264–67
Pottier, Eugène, 129
Pouget, Emile, 127, 129, 130
Pound, Ezra, 178–79, 180–81, 261
Poussin, Nicolas, 2
Poznanska, Félicie, 141
Prevost, Marcel, 148
Princess Cassamassima, The (James), 41, 52,
    62–74, 88, 140
Proudhon, Pierre-Joseph, 6, 13, 21–26, 28,
    34, 35, 37–39, 91, 113, 116, 117, 120,
    124, 129, 145, 146, 147, 150, 158, 172,
    175, 185–86, 188, 189, 208, 238, 246,
    248, 254, 260
Puskin, Aleksandr Sergeyevich, 61
Pyat, Felix, 149

Quillard, Pierre, 178

Rabelais, François, 129
Racine, Jean, 187
Ravachol, François, 76, 124, 127, 178
Reclus, Elie, 120
Reclus, Elisée, 120, 123, 133, 245
Reinsdorf, August, 70, 113
Renoir, Pierre-Auguste, 121
Ribeyre, Henri, 122
Richards, Grant, 200
Richter, Hans, 234, 236
Rimbaud, Arthur, 2, 121, 169, 188, 238,
    239, 240, 248

Rinke, Otto, 71
Rodin, Auguste, 183
Romanticism, 13–15, 21, 26–28, 29, 33, 36,
    55, 92, 169, 190–91, 241, 242, 244, 245,
    246, 247, 266
Romersholm (Ibsen), 204, 208
Rossetti, Arthur, 102
Rossetti, Dante Gabriel, 103
Rossetti sisters (Helen and Olivia), 6, 87,
    88, 101–9, 110, 115, 214; *Girl among the
    Anarchists, A,* 88, 102–9, 110, 115
Rossetti, William Michael, 102–3
Rotten, Johnny (John Lydon), 264
Rousseau, Jean-Jacques, 15–18, 19, 20–21,
    22, 23, 24, 25, 26, 32, 33, 45, 89;
    Discourse on the Origin of Inequality (*Second
    Discourse*), 15, 17–18, 19, 20, 22, 24, 32;
    Social Contract, The, 15–17, 19, 21
Rovinski, Hyman, 142
Rudin (Turgenev), 52, 53–58, 74, 88
Ruskin, John, 114
Russell, Lord John, 46

Sade, Marquis de, 253
Saint-Simon, Claude-Henri de, 159
Samblancat, Angel, 250
Samuels, H. B., 75, 105
Sanger, Margaret, 138
Sartre, Jean-Paul, 163
Schnaubelt, Rudolph, 110
Secret Agent, The (Conrad), 41, 52, 53, 74–
    84, 88, 104, 214
Shakespeare, William, 60, 226
Shaw, George Bernard, 114, 140, 146, 197,
    202
Shchapov, Afanasy Prokofievich, 62
Shelley, Percy Bysshe, 7, 89–91, 114, 116,
    117, 140, 212, 247; *Defense of Poetry, A,*
    89–91, 116; "Mask of Anarchy, The,"
    90–91; *Philosophical View of Reform, A,* 91
Signac, Paul, 123
Sinnett, Jane, 44
Situationism, 40, 262, 264
Sloan, John, 142, 145
Social Contract, The (Rousseau), 15–17, 19,
    21
Socialism, 12, 13, 15, 25, 33, 34, 83, 112–
    13, 195, 197, 198, 199, 200, 206, 213–14,
    217, 218–19, 220–27, 238–39, 248
"Soul of Man Under Socialism, The"
    (Wilde), 198–99, 213, 221–22

Spencer, Herbert, 128, 206
Spies, August, 110
Stalin, Joseph, 4
"Stanzas from the Grande Chartreuse"
   (Arnold), 62
Stephen Hero (Joyce), 213, 220, 222, 223,
   224, 225
Stepniak, S. M., 103
Stevens, Wallace, 142
Stieglitz, Alfred, 145
Stirner, Max (Johann Kaspar Schmidt), 14,
   115, 128, 146, 154–56, 168, 170–74, 175,
   176, 177, 178, 179–80, 206, 216, 230,
   242, 261, 262, 266; *Ego and Its Own, The,*
   146, 154
Strauss, Richard, 172
Stravinsky, Igor, 185
Surrealism, 1, 3, 164, 227, 228, 238–40,
   247, 248, 250, 251, 253, 254, 255, 256,
   264
Symbolism, 142, 178, 181, 204–5, 210, 211,
   251, 260
Synge, John Millington, 143

Tailhade, Laurent, 205
Tchaikovsky, Pyotr Ilich, 175
That Obscure Object of Desire (Buñuel), 251
Thiers, Adolph, 119, 120, 122
Thoreau, Henry David, 129, 131, 140
Tocqueville, Alexis de, 15
Tolstoy, Count Lev Nikolayevich, 114, 128,
   129, 146, 174
Toulouse-Lautrec, Henri de, 189
Tressel, Robert (Robert Noonan), 200,
   219
Trilling, Lionel, 69–70, 71, 220
Trotsky, Leon, 4, 142
Tucker, Benjamin R., 8, 11, 13, 41, 146–50,
   154, 158, 159, 170, 171, 172, 184, 190,
   213, 214, 221, 225, 260, 261
Turgenev, Ivan Sergeyevich, 52, 53–58, 60,
   74, 88; *Rudin,* 52, 53–58, 74, 88
Tzara, Tristan, 228, 233, 234, 235, 256

Ultraism, 249–50
Ulysses (Joyce), 166, 185, 201, 212, 215,
   216, 220, 225, 226, 227, 257

Umberto I, 76
Upward, Allan, 179, 180
Utilitarianism, 12, 13

Vaillant, Auguste, 124, 205
Varlin, Eugène, 120
Vauvenargues, Marquis de, 246
Verlaine, Paul, 188–89
Victoria, Queen, 48
Vielé-Griffin, Francis, 128
Vollard, Abroise, 130
Voltaire, 233
Vuillard, Edouard, 183

Wagner, Richard, 39, 172, 175
Weber, Max, 145
Weitling, Wilhelm, 28
Wellington, Duke of (Arthur Wellesley), 47
When We Dead Awaken (Ibsen), 210, 211
Whistler, James Abbot McNeill, 183
Whitman, Walt, 115, 140, 141, 149, 169,
   170, 172, 174, 177, 178
Wieland, Christoph Martin, 14
Wild Duck, The (Ibsen), 204
Wilde, Oscar, 114, 116, 148, 174, 181, 189,
   191, 198–99, 212, 213, 214, 221–22, 230;
   "Soul of Man Under Socialism, The,"
   198–99, 213, 221–22
William IV, 48
Williams, Raymond, 8, 13, 219–20, 223
Williams, William Carlos, 179
Wilson, Edmund, 205, 220
Wolff, Adolf, 141
Wolff, Alan, 142–43
Wollstonecraft, Mary, 98
Woman Who Did, The (Allen), 107–8
Woodcock, George, 71
Wordsworth, William, 52

Young, Ernest, 106
Yeats, William Butler, 218, 242

Zigrosser, Carl, 139–40, 142, 144, 145
Zo d'Axa (Charles Galland), 127, 128, 129
Zola, Emile, 31, 63, 115, 129, 147, 178,
   203, 204, 205, 209
Zorilla, Manuel Ruíz, 132